Valuing Peak Experience Everyday Lives

Valuing Peak Experience in Everyday Lives takes Abraham Maslow's concept of peak experience and compares how people have encountered transcendent peak experiences and related phenomena, such as flow and peak performance, in their everyday lives. By examining existing research and sharing people's actual encounters in different contexts, such as music, education, sport, creative arts, and nature, the importance and value of peak experiences and self-transcendence in our lives can be better understood and fostered.

The book explores the challenges, benefits, and opportunities presented by understanding peak experience in contemporary contexts. Drawing on research from positive and transpersonal psychology, each of the 12 chapters reports on a work or leisure context where peak experiences have been generated and studied. The chapters are introduced by drawing on relevant theory and research, and then expanded via accounts, vignettes, and examples from people immersed in those activities or contexts to provide a blend of case stories and theoretical foundations.

The book is valuable reading for professional practitioners such as psychologists, educators, coaches, psychotherapists, and those interested in personal development. Also, it will be relevant for students of transpersonal and positive psychology, as well as humanism and human development, interested in understanding transcendent peak experiences and related concepts, such as flow.

Kay A M Weijers is a former professional flautist, advertising sales executive, business owner, and sales trainer. Her life's learnings and experiences have taken her into the field of executive coaching, coaching supervision, and imposter syndrome master coaching. She holds a doctorate in coaching and mentoring from Oxford Brookes University.

Elaine R J Cox is an honorary research fellow with Oxford Brookes University Business School. She holds a PhD in educational research from Lancaster University and is an experienced researcher, author, and editor. In addition to writing books and articles, she is also the founding editor of the *International Journal of Evidence Based Coaching and Mentoring*.

Valuing Peak Experience in Everyday Lives

Insights from Positive and Transpersonal Psychology

Kay A M Weijers and Elaine R J Cox

Routledge
Taylor & Francis Group
LONDON AND NEW YORK

Designed cover image: Getty images @ bjdlzx

First published 2025
by Routledge
4 Park Square, Milton Park, Abingdon, Oxon OX14 4RN

and by Routledge
605 Third Avenue, New York, NY 10158

Routledge is an imprint of the Taylor & Francis Group, an informa business

© 2025 Kay A M Weijers and Elaine R J Cox

The right of Kay A M Weijers and Elaine R J Cox to be identified as authors of this work has been asserted in accordance with sections 77 and 78 of the Copyright, Designs and Patents Act 1988.

All rights reserved. No part of this book may be reprinted or reproduced or utilised in any form or by any electronic, mechanical, or other means, now known or hereafter invented, including photocopying and recording, or in any information storage or retrieval system, without permission in writing from the publishers.

Trademark notice: Product or corporate names may be trademarks or registered trademarks, and are used only for identification and explanation without intent to infringe.

British Library Cataloguing-in-Publication Data
A catalogue record for this book is available from the British Library

ISBN: 978-1-032-83409-2 (hbk)
ISBN: 978-1-032-83222-7 (pbk)
ISBN: 978-1-003-50921-9 (ebk)

DOI: 10.4324/9781003509219

Typeset in Times New Roman
by Apex CoVantage, LLC

Contents

Preface vii
Acknowledgements ix

Introduction 1

1 Peak Experience in Spirituality and Religion 20

2 Peak Experiences in Writing and Reading 43

3 Peak Experiences and Music 66

4 Peak Experiences in the Creative Arts 91

5 Peak Experiences in Education and Learning 114

6 Peak Experiences in Nature and Wilderness 135

7 Peak Experiences in Competitive Sport 156

8 Peak Experience in Therapy 178

9 Peak Experiences in Executive and Life Coaching 201

10 Peak Experience in Extreme Sport and High-Risk Leisure 222

11 Peak Experiences in the Workplace 245

12 Peak Experiences in Relationships, Love, and Sex 266

Conclusion and Insights 289

Glossary and Further Reading *314*
Index *318*

Preface

We wanted to begin this book by sharing our own peak experiences with our readers.

At some point in everyone's life there will be encounters with the transpersonal that have the potential to impact the way we see or approach life. These are ours.

Kay's first peak experience was during her fourth year at music college, playing first flute in an orchestral rehearsal. She watched the conductor, Rudolf Schwarz closely, following his lead:

> Our eyes locked during the timeless passage of the solo which seemed to go on forever, yet hung, suspended in the air yet supported by the orchestra. It was as though I had been transported into another world, a world of transcendence and stillness. We finished playing the piece and the conductor put down his baton and said, "young lady, you have an exceptional talent." The experience of that moment has never left me. It was a peak moment.

That experience for Kay was not so much a peak experience but a peak performance tangled with flow and the unexpected feedback she received from the conductor. The feedback is not dissimilar to what one of our research participants, Graham, experienced from his orchestral colleagues when he opened the *Rite of Spring* with the bassoon solo and the feedback they gave him several weeks later. The experience of feedback from a peak performance is one of the findings in Kay's doctoral study (Weijers, 2021).

Another experience of a peak came when Kay was playing the second movement of Beethoven's *Pastoral Symphony*, a unison solo with the first oboist:

> We played the solo and a quiet energy prevailed, an ethereal quality, time standing still yet connected to an energy that tingled. There was a frisson in the air. We looked at one another in total silence, somehow afraid to speak but then almost simultaneously said, "what happened there?" I can re-live that peak moment, retrieving and visualising the same feelings, thoughts and colours I experienced before.

Kay confirms, she was probably playing at her best: the music just flowed, and yet the memory is distinct and visceral. It was definitely a peak, but I cannot definitely say whether I had a peak experience having performed at my best or a peak performance whilst in flow with other musicians.

One of **Elaine's** first peak experiences was also musical in nature. She was rehearsing with her ladies' barbershop choir when the group of eight achieved an extraordinary "in tune" moment:

> For an amateur group this was quite rare, and an experience that made us all look around at each other, in an uplifting moment of harmony, recognition and togetherness.

Another more profound peak experience was in the context of nature. She was driving along a country lane early one spring afternoon, appreciating the greenness of the countryside and the emergence of the fresh, new leaves when suddenly she felt what she could describe only as a "total oneness with everything."

> I not only felt connected to everything, the fields, grass, trees, sky, atmosphere, but I had disappeared into it. It was a blissful feeling of everything being one, perfect and unflawed. I stopped the car to allow the experience more "space" but it was gone. Since then, I have sought to get that experience back, but despite the core conditions often being right, the experience has never been repeated in the same way.

Elaine's experience illustrates Maslow's observation of one of the features of the peak experience: "the whole universe is perceived as an integrated unified whole" (Maslow, 1970, p. 59). It also echoes Taylor's (2018, p. 42) experience of an "awakening," which he describes as

> a shift in my perception as if someone had pressed a switch. Everything around me became intensely real. The fields and the bushes and trees and the clouds seemed to be powerfully there, as if an extra dimension had been added to them. They seemed more vivid, more intricate and beautiful. I also felt somehow connected with my surroundings. As I looked up at the sky, I felt somehow that space that fills it was the same space filling my own being. What was inside me, as my own consciousness, was also "out there." And also, inside me, there was a glow of intense well-being.

We have both been influenced throughout our lives by our peak experiences and the knowledge that self-transcendence is a possibility. As a result, our peak experiences have fuelled our interest in Maslow's concept and consequently shaped this book.

References

Maslow, A. H. (1970). New introduction: Religions, values, and peak-experiences. *Journal of Transpersonal Psychology*, *2*(2), 83–90.
Taylor, S. M. (2018). An awakening. *The Psychologist*, *31*, 42–47. ISSN 0952-8229.
Weijers, K. (2021). *Peak moments: The experience of coaches*. Doctoral Thesis, Oxford Brookes University.

Acknowledgements

The authors wish to thank each of their participants for contributing their peak experience stories and vignettes for this book. Without their willingness to share their often intimate and private thoughts with us, we could not have created this volume.

We also owe a debt to Abraham Maslow, who we have now come to know as an inspirational and familiar friend.

Introduction

Leontiev (2008, p. 451) has argued that Maslow was a pragmatic idealist whose ideas have not yet been fully assimilated by psychological science and so still contain rich potentials waiting to "disclose themselves to a new generation of scholars." He sees Maslow as a visionary, "despite his rather evident mistakes" and recognises how he was unafraid of going the ways less travelled. Leontiev also considers Maslow to be one of the main reasons that humanistic psychology has been so successful in its mission to change the underlying views of human personality. He claims Maslow's ideas remain relevant to our world today and that his greatest project for us may yet lie ahead (Leontiev, 2008). Similarly, Yalom (1980) declared Maslow is destined to be rediscovered many times before the richness of his thought is fully assimilated.

Our aim in this book is to build on Abraham Maslow's (1964) concept of peak experience by comparing how people have encountered peak experiences in different everyday contexts and exploring with them the positive impact of such experiences on their lives. We hope that by examining Maslow's concept, reviewing relevant research in the positive and transpersonal psychology fields, and then sharing people's actual encounters, the importance of peak experience to aspects of well-being and relationships can be appreciated, understood, and fostered.

In this preliminary chapter, after briefly summarising the early influences on peak experience, we introduce Maslow's seminal work on the topic and its connection with his theories of motivation and self-actualisation. We then look at various definitions of peak experience and pinpoint several related concepts. This discussion will help delimit the terms used in the book and identify and distinguish similar terminology. Once the clarification is complete, we describe how, in 12 specific contexts or areas of work or leisure activity, peak experiences are seen as important to the practice, capability, and happiness of people working or performing in those areas.

According to Hanfling (1992, p. 159), the word "experience" can be used in a very broad sense to cover almost every aspect of conscious living and in a "quite narrow sense to refer to a particular and perhaps very brief incident or episode." Further, as argued by Straś-Romanowska and Kapała (2010, p. 104), the term "experience" can be viewed as having three essential meanings:

1) as the perception of sensory events and their mental processing,
2) as everything that is subject to direct consciousness, and

DOI: 10.4324/9781003509219-1

3) as the movement of consciousness, which results in grasping something mentally and gaining insight.

The expression "peak experience" however, is generally attributed to Maslow (1959, 1962). In his early research into transpersonal experience, Maslow noted how individuals had reported having something like mystic experiences: "moments of great awe, moments of the most intense happiness or even rupture, ecstasy or bliss." He explained how these moments were of "pure, positive happiness when all doubts, all fears, all inhibitions, all tensions, all weaknesses, were left behind" and involved moments of insight and discovery (1962, pp. 9–11). In the course of his study, he realised these experiences were natural, rather than supernatural, and so abandoned the name "mystic" experience and started calling them peak experiences.

Maslow was possibly the first psychologist to recognise the potential for studying psychologically healthy individuals. In his book, *Motivation and Personality* (1954), he incorporated a chapter titled "Toward a Positive Psychology," setting out a future research agenda similar to that of Seligman (2002, 2018). In the second edition of the 1954 text, recognising the progress that had been made, Maslow omitted that chapter on the premise that "the humanistic psychologies, the new transcendent psychology, the existential, the Rogerian, the experiential, the holistic, the value-seeking psychologies, are all thriving and available" (1970a, p. xxiii).

Maslow defined peak experience as "the great joy, the ecstasy, the visions of another world, or another level of living" (1968, p. 170), adding that a peak experience is a brief emotional experience when time stands still, enabling moments of highest happiness and fulfilment.

His investigations also led to the idea that specific settings and activities act as triggers for peak experience: these include solitude, prayer and spiritual connection, meditation, deep relaxation, physical accomplishment, and being in nature. Thus, Maslow observed that the peak experience can happen in a variety of contexts:

> [F]rom moments of love and sex, from the great esthetic moments (particularly of music), from the bursts of creativeness and the creative furore [sic] (the great inspiration), from great moments of insight and discovery, from women giving natural birth to babies – or just from loving them, from moments of fusion with nature, from certain athletic experiences, etc.
>
> (Maslow, 1962, p. 10)

It should also be stressed that every experience is shaped by the environment or context in which it takes place. Every participant in a peak experience therefore brings with them contextual understandings, beliefs, and perceptions that influence the experience. Context has been described as influenced by "cultures and subcultures, organisational mores, socio-economic conditions, the physical environments of home and work, historical and generational effects, social and peer associations, political and religious beliefs" (Cox, 2003, p. 9). This indicates the importance of bringing together and discussing peak experiences in their contextual milieu.

To examine the influence of context on peak experiences, we intend to explore whether they are actually experienced differently in different contexts. We look at how they occur in a range of everyday settings, the potential influence of context on the peak experience itself, and how this may affect the interpretation and definition of what we might call "peakness."

In 1991, Davis, Lockwood, and Wright reported on research where they had asked 246 people whether they have had a peak experience and the reasons why they may or may not have told other people about it. Over three-quarters of them reported that, despite having at least one peak experience, they told only a few other people. The main reasons they gave for not sharing their peak experiences widely were that a) they sensed it to be a special and intimate personal experience that they did not want to discuss; b) they felt it could be devalued or "put down," and c) they could not adequately describe it (Davis et al., 1991, p. 3). This difficulty in sharing is based on the idea that a close examination of our experience makes it necessary for us to bring what is tacit to the surface and "requires us to make a raid on our own inarticulateness" (Street, 1991, p. 3).

The inability to describe peak experience in words is something we have encountered when speaking both to colleagues and to potential participants for this book. Some people have also reported that sharing their peak experiences with us would be difficult for them, as they would bring up too many memories that might be painful to revisit. Although studies suggest people tend not to share their peak experiences, we consider they are still important to try to explore.

As well as extending Maslow's theories, there is much evidence to suggest peak experiences impact well-being. As Davis et al. (1991) related, a significant number of people have experienced intense, positive, and long-lasting effects as a result of the peak experience phenomenon even though they chose to not report them. Indeed, these authors concluded that peak experiences are "the best, happiest, most wonderful moments of one's life" and highlighted some of the key characteristics as

> an almost overwhelming sense of pleasure, euphoria, or joy, a deep sense of peacefulness or tranquillity, feeling in tune, in harmony, or at one with the universe, a sense of wonder or awe, altered perceptions of time and/or space, such as expansion, a feeling of deeper knowing or profound understanding, a deep feeling of love (for yourself, another, or all people), a greater awareness of beauty or appreciation, a sense that it would be difficult or impossible to describe adequately in words.
>
> (Davis et al., 1991, p. 88)

Whitehead and Bates (2016) argue that well-being is closely connected to what people identify as true happiness in life. They explain how eudaimonic well-being, rather than the arguably more transient, hedonistic type of well-being, "incorporates themes such as personal growth, meaning, purpose, and achieving one's full potential" (2016, p. 1579). As such it "presents a more sustained sense of well-being characterised by a constant push towards self-realization." Indeed, Maslow

(1943) believed that both happiness and living a good life are synonymous with fulfilling the particular needs and goals that contribute to individual well-being.

We continue this introduction by outlining early work on peak experience and Maslow's particular contribution. We then look at the related concepts.

Early Influences on Peak Experience

William James's research on people's experiences in the religious context focused on positive change and transformation and culminated in the publication of *The Varieties of Religious Experience* in 1902. In that volume, James assembled a number of personal narratives about what he saw as a special type of consciousness, concluding that

> [i]t is as if there were in the human consciousness a sense of reality, a feeling of objective presence, a perception of what we may call "something there," more deep and more general than any of the special and particular "senses" by which the current psychology supposes existent realities to be originally revealed.
> (1902/1928, p. 82)

This early work then paved the way for more research into other extraordinary experiences.

Of particular interest to our current project are John Dewey's thoroughgoing explorations of experience. Dewey used the term "experience" in three different ways, as identified by Dennis and Powers (1974):

> First, much as it is used in general conversation to describe just those everyday, routine interactions between organism and environment; second to refer to those interactions that have meaning and a thoughtful, purpose quality, and third as an experience in particular, one which bears those marks of being an operation distinguished by a single pervasive quality, reaching the stage of fulfilment or consummation.
> (1974, p. 52)

Dewey's definition of experience has been explained by Latham (2007, p. 253) as involving the "undivided continuous transaction between human beings and their environment." It is not static but involves both the past and the future, and it is always historically situated. In addition to this contextual principle, Dewey noted how everyday experience is happening to us all the time but that just occasionally there are "segments of this experience which are heightened, marked by a sense of wholeness, unity, and fulfilment" (Latham, 2007, p. 253).

Maslow's Theories and His Concept of Peak Experience

Maslow was an early leader in humanistic movement. His work on peak experiences evolved from his studies of human nature and motivation (1943, 1959). As one of the founders of the transpersonal branch of psychology, Maslow's main interest was in researching optimal human functioning and the behaviour and characteristics of healthy and self-actualising people. In this regard, as noted by Kapusta (2018), he established his work on a revised understanding of Freudian psychology, considering Freud's one big mistake to be "that he thought of the unconscious merely as undesirable evil" (Kapusta, 2018, p. 317). Humanistic psychology, by contrast, emphasises the whole person and individual uniqueness, as well as insisting that people have free will and will be motivated to achieve their full potential, to self-actualise, and to transcend. Maslow and other psychologists understood that "unconsciousness carries in it also the roots of creativeness, of joy, of happiness, of goodness" (Maslow, 1968, p. 163).

Theory of Motivation

Maslow is most well-known for his theory of motivation. He argued that it is only after basic needs are met that people can begin to think about "higher" needs such as love and ultimately focus on what he called "self-actualisation" (Norwood, 2009) – peak experiences being seen as an integral part of the attainment of full "humanness."

In his theory of motivation, Maslow (1959) suggested that human behaviour was not controlled by innate psychological drives but by the interaction of a range of different needs, both psychological and physical. He set out five levels of needs with what he saw as the most fundamental at the bottom of what he called an integrated hierarchy. At this level were the physiological needs, such as food, water, and warmth, which take priority and have to be met sufficiently before the next level of "less potent" needs can be addressed. Physiological needs were then followed by safety needs, including security, and another level that included love and belonginess. Esteem needs and the feeling of accomplishment came next, followed by self-actualisation at the very top of the hierarchy. Self-actualisation was seen as the achievement of full human potential, particularly through creativity. However, Maslow (1943, p. 388) was at pains to explain that people can be "partially satisfied in all their basic needs and partially unsatisfied in all their basic needs at the same time," hence his insistence on the term "integrated hierarchy."

Maslow (1943, 1954) further classified the five different needs into two categories: i) the first four levels that he referred to as basic or deficiency needs (sometimes D-needs) and ii) the self-actualisation level that he called the being needs or "B-needs" for short.

Theory of Self-Actualisation

Maslow perceived the self-actualising tendency to be a universal part of human nature, necessary for our healthy growth, development, and being. He described it as "the apex of personal growth, in which we become freed from basic needs and deficiency motivation" (Maslow & Hoffman, 1996, p. 206). Furthermore, when deficiency needs are met for many people in a society, it paves the way for the whole society to be motivated by their self-actualising or B-needs. Indeed, Maslow stipulated that "the self in self-actualisation must not have too individualistic a flavor" (1954, p. 201).

In earlier work, Maslow (1943, p. 382) had described how self-actualisation refers to a person's desire for self-fulfilment but that the form those desires take varies from one person to another:

> In one individual it may take the form of the desire to be an ideal mother, in another it may be expressed athletically, and in still another it may be expressed in painting pictures or in inventions.
> (Maslow, 1943, pp. 382–383)

During his research he also discovered that self-actualising people often reported having transcendental moments of joy in their day-to-day lives. These moments are signalled by what he came to call "peak experiences." He went on to define peak experiences as a particular state of self-transcendence achieved through or following self-actualisation. During peak experiences, he claimed, there occurs "cognition of Being," which he sometimes called "B-cognition" or "B-values," where "the experience of the object tends to be seen as a whole, as a complete unit, detached from relations, from possible usefulness, from expediency, and from purpose" (1974, p. 85).

In his later thinking about how peak experiences seemed to be part of everyday life for many people, Maslow (1969b) explained how the motivation for transcendence appeared to transcend the level of self-actualisation in his hierarchy. He found that while some healthy people were self-actualised and had peak experiences (referred to as "peakers"), others did not ("non-peakers"). Peakers seemed to achieve self-transcendence whilst tolerating deficiency needs. They were not so concerned with material values but sought more intrinsic values and insights. Non-peakers, it seemed, were more concerned with immediate needs rather than contemplation. This suggested to Maslow that transcendence was not an extension of the needs hierarchy. He thus claimed that peak experiences could come to anyone at any time in their life, explaining how for self-actualising people the peak episodes just seem to come "far more frequently, and intensely and perfectly than in average people" (Maslow, 1959, p. 69).

In describing the characteristics of self-actualised people, Maslow came to realise that earlier, he had conflated the characteristics of self-transcendent people and self-actualised people. He began to realise that self-transcendence is actually more defined by peak experience than is self-actualisation. Self-actualisers, he argued, do have peak experiences, but they should be seen as a means of becoming more than just a "self" (i.e., as a means to self-transcendence).

> As he [that is, the person in the peak experiences] gets to be more purely and singly himself he is more able to fuse with the world, with what was formerly not-self, for example, the lovers come closer to forming a unit rather than two people, the I-Thou monism becomes more possible, the creator becomes one with his work being created, the mother feels one with her child.
> (Maslow, 1999, p. 117)

Consequently, for Maslow, self-actualisation appeared to be a transitional goal. For example, in the concluding remarks to his paper on "Peak Experiences as Acute Identity-Experiences," he argues it is "a rite of passage, a step along the path to the transcendence of identity." He then went on to observe that "this is like saying its function is to erase itself" (1999, p. 125).

Self-Transcendence

Self-transcendence, as a concept, refers to "the very highest and most inclusive or holistic levels of human consciousness, behaving and relating, as ends rather than means, to oneself, to significant others, to human beings in general, to other species, to nature, and to the cosmos" (Maslow, 1969a, p. 66). In essence, self-transcended people, Maslow argued, will find meaning in their lives by engagement with something greater than themselves, whether that is through something creative or something public-spirited such as helping others. This shift in cognition he recognised as self-transcendence, and it is here that he focused his research up until his death in June 1970.

Also, it appeared to Maslow that peak experiences were the forerunners of a more permanent self-transcendent state that he termed the "plateau experience" or "plateau-living" (Maslow, 1969a, 1970b). The plateau experience Maslow claimed was longer-lasting and occurred more frequently than a peak experience but still involved self-transcendence. He reasoned that once we have "got over being surprised and startled" by peak experiences we may "live calmly and serenely among the platonic essences, or among the B-values" (1969a, p. 62).

So, echoing Dewey's observation that there are heightened experiences distinguished by feelings of unity and fulfilment, Maslow saw the peak experience as an end in itself: a "self-validating, self-justifying moment which carries its own intrinsic value with it" (1974, p. 89). As already mentioned, he frequently insisted that all healthy people have peak experiences and that they are not necessarily "mystical" experiences but a normal part of everyday life (Maslow & Hoffman, 1996, p. xi).

Concept of Peak Experience

The common features of the peak experience were described by Maslow as unique, transcendental, out-of-time experiences whereby a person experiences reality more vividly, more transparently, and more absolutely (1959, pp. 43–55). The characteristics he included were:

- Objects seen "as a whole, as a complete unit, detached from relations, from possible usefulness, from expediency and from purpose. It is seen as if it were all there was in the universe, as if it were all of Being."
- There is "disorientation in time and space."
- It feels like a "self-validating, self-justifying moment which carries its own intrinsic value with it."
- Perceptions are "relatively ego-transcending, self-forgetful, egoless."

8 *Valuing Peak Experience in Everyday Lives*

- The emotional reaction in the experience has "a flavour of wonder, of awe and humility before the experience there is also a touch of fear (although pleasant fear) of being overwhelmed."

He went on to clarify the peak experience by highlighting the feeling of "transcendental unity" that accompanies it: "It is seen as if it were all there was in the universe, as if it was all of Being, synonymous with the universe" (Maslow, 1974, p. 85). He recorded how the experiences of unity were essential to the nature of peak experiences. Wholeness was high on his list of descriptors too, and he took pains to explain the association with wholeness as "unity; integration tendency to one-ness; interconnectedness; simplicity; organization; structure; dichotomy transcendence; order" (Maslow, 1999, p. 93). Maslow considered that, in transcending dichotomies or polarities, we are open to broader, more accepting perceptions of ourselves and the world around us.

Maslow was also concerned with peak experiences as acute identity-experiences where people are "closest to their real selves" (Maslow, 2011, pp. 97–106). People with access to self-transcendent states of being, he claimed, attend more to the world and make efforts altruistically to improve it. Maslow reported a number of the key states and feelings of peak experiences in *Toward A Psychology of Being* (Maslow, 1968, 2013, pp. 98–107). These can be summarised as:

- Feeling more integrated and unified
- A sense of oneness and connectedness with the environment
- A feeling of being at the peak of our powers, fully functioning
- Feelings of effortlessness and being at one's best
- A feeling of being self-determined and autonomous
- Freedom from inhibitions, fears, or doubts
- Having more spontaneity, playfulness
- Being more creative and impromptu. Ideas come naturally
- A feeling of timelessness
- Independence from basic or deficiency needs such as safety
- A sense of connectedness and empathy with others
- A sense of completion and fulfilment

During his lifetime, Maslow continued to pay attention to the topic of peak experience, and two additional observations are germane to the research undertaken for this book:

1) People may undergo peak experiences in very commonplace circumstances: while waiting for a bus on a sunlit street, listening to a romantic song on the radio, or preparing dinner for the family, suggesting that it is not necessary to be a religious mystic or practitioner to undergo an unforgettable epiphany in daily living. In 1970, Maslow proposed that the great lesson from the mystics is that "the sacred is in the ordinary, that it is to be found in one's daily life, in one's neighbors, friends, and family, in one's backyard" (Maslow, 1970b, p. x).

2) The more emotionally healthy people are, the greater the prospect that peak experiences will arise from ordinary, day-to-day events. For example, Maslow found that highly creative people seemed to have more frequent peaks comprising moments of joy and fulfilment than their apparently less inventive colleagues.

In later works, Maslow described peak experience as "the great joy, the ecstasy, the visions of another world, or another level of living" (1971, p. 176), adding that a peak experience is an emotional experience when time stands still, enabling moments of highest happiness and fulfilment. In these experiences, individuals also appeared to become self-forgetful, unselfish, and ego transcending (Maslow, 1964).

Following Maslow's publications in the 1960s and 1970s there was growing interest in his work, an interest that has not waned. In fact, research into his theories has now found a natural home in the transpersonal and positive psychology fields as well as having applications in strength-based counselling (Hoffman & Ortiz, 2009, p. 469).

Grof (2016) suggests that transpersonal experiences, such as a peak experience, may be defined as involving "an expansion or extension of consciousness beyond the usual ego boundaries and beyond the limitations of time and/or space" (2016, pp. 155–157). These are classified in more detail as:

1) Experiential extensions *within* the framework of objective reality, including temporal expansions of consciousness, spatial expansions of consciousness, and spatial constructions of consciousness
2) Experiential extensions *beyond* the framework of objective reality, including spiritistic and mediumistic experiences, experiences of encounters with supra-human spiritual entities and consciousness of the universal mind

Definitions of Related Concepts: Peak Experience, Peak Performance, and Flow Compared

Despite much interest in the hierarchy of motivational needs and the higher level of being that seems to result from self-actualisation, there is limited empirical or case study research. Maslow died before he could finish his work in this area, and so there are elements of uncertainty around his theory. Ho et al. (2012, p. 248) pointed out that the diffuse nature of self-actualisation makes it "difficult to operationalize in scientific research," and so empirical evidence to support its universality still needs to be established. Similarly, Noltemeyer et al. (2012) confirmed that, despite its often-uncritical acceptance as a theory, the supporting research base was weak. More recently, there has been an interest in measuring self-actualisation prompted by Kaufman's (2018) attempt to develop a Characteristics of Self-Actualization Scale (CSAS).

Perhaps, because of the uncertainty around Maslow's theory, there is much interest in related concepts. Several authors have identified how peak experiences are just one of a variety of self-transcendent experiences. They confirm that features of self-transcendent experience can be found in a range of common psychological constructs and generally support Maslow's argument that they promote well-being and prosocial behaviours. In this section, we explain the two most closely related theories, flow and peak performance, to sharpen the focus of peak experience as the subject of our attention in this book.

Distinguishing Flow

Senecal (2021, p. 296) has noted that both Maslow and Mihalyi Csikszentmihalyi view peak and flow experiences as deeply enriching, emotionally nourishing, and ultimately providing "a sense of meaning and fulfilment in our lives." Indeed, the concept of flow was extended by Csikszentmihalyi in 1990 after interviewing artists, musicians, music teachers, athletes, farmers, assembly line workers, rock climbers, and surgeons to examine the nature and conditions of enjoyment. He was struck by how persistently tasks were carried out by a wide cross section of people with total disregard for fatigue, hunger, discomfort, or time, and how interest was rapidly lost once the task had been completed.

Many authors view flow and peak experience as closely related concepts. For example, Adams and Beauchamp (2019, p. 74) compare Csikszentmihalyi's portrayal of flow as involving "a sense of discovery, a creative feeling of transporting the person into a new reality," with Maslow's (1964, p. 77) observation that during peak experiences "several kinds of attention-change can lead to new knowledge." However, each concept can be experienced as an end in itself or, as Csikszentmihalyi explains, "it is the pursuit that counts not the attainment" (1997, p. 122).

Additionally, unlike peak experiences, the conditions that foster flow are concerned with control. Csikszentmihalyi (1990) claimed that, in flow, we are in control of our psychic energy, and everything we do adds order to consciousness. Flow happens within sequences of activities that require skill, often requiring highly disciplined mental activity or strenuous physical exercise. Rather than the momentary oneness that is ascribed to a peak experience (Marotto et al., 2007), flow is a sustained experience, described by Csikszentmihalyi (1990, p. 3) as a sense of exhilaration, "a deep sense of enjoyment that is long cherished and that becomes a landmark in memory for what life should be like."

Although Csikszentmihalyi's (1990, pp. 3–4) explanation of flow sounds similar to the impact of a peak experience, he distinguishes between the two, describing Maslow's peak experience as "just a spontaneous sense of well-being" (Csikszentmihalyi, 1990, p. 49). Other commentators have described flow as an uplifting event, involving a sense of mastery and control or a sense of invincibility. Privette (1983, p. 1362), for example, defines it as enjoyment of "an intrinsically rewarding, or autotelic, experience." As such, flow-like states are considered to be similar to hypnotic states (Grove & Lewis, 1996), where there is dissociation from one's surroundings, total absorption in the present, and perceptual distortions such as altered perceptions of time. A peak experience, on the other hand, does not necessarily involve action or total absorption in the present. As Marotto et al. (2007, p. 389) explained, a peak experience is a "brief and transient moment of bliss, rapture, ecstasy, great happiness, or joy as well as the temporary disorientation of time and space." By contrast, flow, as its name suggests, involves a longer period of engagement than a peak experience, being a sustained period of complete absorption in a task centred on clear and proximate goals, feedback, and balance of challenge and skill (Csikszentmihalyi, 1990). This temporal distinction suggests peak experience is a separate concept from flow, as the former is more momentary and ephemeral, supporting Wilber's claim that peak experiences are usually "one-time hits" (1998, p. 181).

Another dissimilarity between peak experience and flow is identified by Schouten et al. (2007), who propose that peak experience seems to originate from outside individuals, taking them to heightened emotions whereby they feel intimately connected to some larger phenomenon, such as nature, humankind, or the infinite, which in turn "can generate lasting shifts in beliefs and attitudes including subjective self-transformation" (2007, p. 357). This echoes Csikszentmihalyi's (1997) recognition that, although they may be positively charged, flow states are not necessarily identified by the experience of specific emotions but, rather, by their level of absorption. Thus, flow can be described as an experiential state where there is total connection during a performance situation. Based on these cumulative arguments, we therefore maintain that flow is quite different from what we understand by a peak experience.

Distinguishing Peak Performance

In 1983, Privette, heavily influenced by the work of Maslow, presented a useful analysis of peak experience, peak performance, and flow. In a meta-analysis, she identified the commonalities and differences of these three "constructs," distinguishing them initially as "peak experience (intense joy), peak performance (superior functioning), and flow (intrinsically rewarding experience)" (1983, p. 1361). She classified both peak experience and peak performance as models of optimal human experiencing, whereas she suggests flow is not always at a high level but "shares many qualities with both constructs."

Privette's resulting typologies defined peak experience as involving a high level of joy which is spontaneous and creates unity, fusion, and playfulness. Peak performance was not playful but gave a strong sense of self, fulfilment, fascination, and freedom, while flow she defined as combining fusion with the world, fun, playfulness, enjoyment, and perhaps even ecstasy.

Through her subsequent studies, Privette (2001) further argued that the inner processes of peak performance were, in fact, quite unlike the processes involved in flow or peak experience: in flow, as in peak experience, the self was transcended, whereas in peak performance, full, clear focus on both object and the self were pivotal.

Peak performance can be defined as any endeavour that involves "more efficient, creative, productive, or in some way better than ordinary behavior" (Privette, 1983, pp. 323–324). Privette moreover claimed that clear focus was vital to peak performance: "ordinary focus is fuzzy and may be compared to a photograph snapped with improperly adjusted lens in which figure and ground blur" (Privette,

1981, p. 64). The object of clear focus, she clarifies, may be "anything the person to which the person can be deeply committed or that truly fascinates" (1981, p. 64). Privette explains that peak performance is recognised as an episode of superior human functioning rather than a consistent approach to an activity. Similarly, in Csikszentmihalyi's (1990) original research, it was found half of the peak performance reports involved work-related activities.

Again, some authors have highlighted the similarities between peak performance and peak experience. Marotto et al., for example, maintained that peak performance builds upon and is intimately related to Maslow's notion of peak experience and that, by definition, "all peak performances are peak experiences" (2007, pp. 389–390). Maslow himself had previously suggested that peak experience can result from peak performance (Maslow, 1971), implying a reciprocal relationship between them.

However, Privette and Bundrick (1991) have differentiated succinctly between peak experience and peak performance, upholding that they are parallel self-actualising concepts, compatible in their approach to the study of "positive aspects of human life" (1991, p. 170), but still distinct. The term peak performance can thus be used to define the upper limits of individual *functioning*, whereas peak experience defines the upper limits of *emotions* such as happiness, joy, and ecstasy.

We would argue that it can be misleading for the literature, especially the popular and electronic literature, to conflate peak experience with experiences of flow or peak performance. As discussed, being in flow or giving a peak performance does generate very similar feelings – feelings of well-being, connectedness, and joy – but there are distinct differences that we have begun to identify in this introduction. If people experiencing flow, for example, consider that to be the highest human experience, then they are missing out on the revelation that comes from having a genuine peak experience – an experience defined by its momentariness, etherealness, and sense of unity. The challenge of this book is to explore the nature of peak experience, clarify its definition, and consolidate its position as the ultimate experience a human being can have.

To further differentiate peak performance and flow for the purposes of this book, we share here the experience of Chris, one of the participants in our study. Chris had a peak experience whilst watching a total eclipse of the sun and was able to distinguish the encounter as a relatively brief, externally stimulated, self-transcendent state, giving a feeling of euphoria and a glimpse of oneness with everything. It did not involve the use of skill, endeavour, and awareness of self that accompanies peak performance or the sustained internal energy and concentration that comes from being in flow. Such moments of seemingly spiritual and cerebral transcendence can be viewed as life-affirming peak states that point to what Wilson (2009, p. 3) calls the fundamentally "intentional" nature of consciousness. Wilson contended that rather than being just a subjective illusion, the peak experiences are our connections with the reality of meanings that are present in the world but that are normally hidden from our understanding. Thus, through peak experiences, it is argued we may connect to a fuller world, gaining a "bird's eye view," glimpsing truth that justifies optimism.

Methodology

To explore people's encounters with peak experience in the context of their everyday lives and their ordinary work and leisure activities, we recruited participants who were active in at least one of 12 chosen contexts. We also sought a range of experiences within that context. For example, for the Creative Arts chapter we interviewed professional artists, a hairdresser, and two people involved mainly in craft activities.

We begin each chapter in this book by explaining "local" definitions (i.e., definitions that relate to that context) and reviewing previous research literature for the context under consideration. Then, emphasising the importance of acknowledging the value of individual reflections and perceptions, we adopt a constructivist approach to the inclusion of contributions from participants experienced in each context. Constructivists argue that people have very different experiences because of the distinctions in their languages, backgrounds, and cultures. Our belief in following this approach is that the experiences of our participants do not reveal an ultimate reality, but rather they are the psychological and social constructions that uncover how peak experiences were understood for them.

To maintain confidentiality, each participant was asked whether they wanted to use their real name or a pseudonym. Most chose to use their real names. Also, we made the assumption that our participants were self-actualising, based on the fact that they were all mature, professional people who had self-identified as having peak experiences. However, as identified by Davis et al. (1991), some people still needed time to reflect to bring their peak experiences to the fore. Once they had recalled one peak experience they were then better able to recall others, suggesting a Baader-Meinhof effect may be at play: that is, when they uncovered one peak experience, this triggered them to subconsciously look for more, often without actively thinking about it.

Maslow shared how in his investigations of peak experiences he found almost all people have peak experiences (1968, p. 164). He also shared the kinds of questions that might be asked. We therefore adopted these as the core questions in our interviews, as well as adding questions about the particular context:

- What was the single, most joyous, happiest, most blissful moment of your whole life?
- How did you feel different about yourself at that time?
- How did the world look different?
- What did you feel like?
- What were your impulses?
- How did you change if you did?

The Chapters

Each of the 12 substantive chapters reports on a work or leisure context where peak experiences are encountered. The chapters are introduced by drawing on relevant theory and research and then expanded via vignettes and examples from people

14 *Valuing Peak Experience in Everyday Lives*

immersed in those activities or contexts. Each chapter in the book thus benefits from exemplars and case stories, but at the same time attention is paid to scholarly accuracy and the importance of theoretical foundations.

Chapter 1. Peak Experiences in Spirituality and Religion

In our first chapter, we examine religious and spiritual literatures to gain an understanding of religion and spirituality as contexts for peak experiences. We begin by recognising the essentialist/perennialist and constructivist/contextualist debates prevalent in the literature and make a link to the work of William James. Then, acknowledging the constructivist and contextualist underpinning in Maslow's work, we examine where his idea of peak experience fits according to a range of researchers and commentators. To facilitate our exploration of spiritual and transcendent peak experiences, we then include relevant participant peak experiences.

Chapter 2. Peak Experiences in Writing and Reading

Here we examine peak experiences associated with writing and reading works of literature. Early on, we identify the related concept of "literary epiphany," the term used to refer to attempts by authors to share their own or their protagonist's peak experiences or epiphanies with their readers. A two-section review of the research first describes how authors characterise peak experiences or epiphanies in their works and includes extracts from pertinent works of literature. Second, we question whether peak experiences can occur for the reader and conclude that literary epiphanies shared by authors cannot be guaranteed to produce peak experiences for the reader.

Chapter 3. Peak Experiences and Music

The following quote from William James captures the importance of music as a context for peak experience: "In listening to poetry, drama, or heroic narrative, we are often surprised at the cutaneous shiver which like a sudden wave flows over us, and at the heart-swelling and the lachrymal effusion that unexpectedly catch us at intervals. In listening to music, the same is even more strikingly true" (James 1884, p. 196).

Our literature review for this chapter is therefore replete with references to the peak phenomenon both from a music listener's perspective and from a player's perspective. Correspondingly, our participant experiences are full of wonder and joyful emotion brought about by the connection that is created between composer, conductor, musicians, and audience.

Chapter 4. Peak Experiences in the Creative Arts

Our chapter on peak experience and creative arts pays homage to the link made by Maslow to self-actualisation and creativity. He had observed that peak experiences often arose from aesthetic moments and creativity. In the chapter, we also acknowledge Dewey's theory of [a]esthetic experience that emphasised wholeness and look at a variety of research connected to self-transcendent, peak, and aesthetic experiences, both in various types of creative arts and in audience perception. Artists shared their peak experiences with us, as well as their impressions of flow and peak performance. Also, they reinforced the notion that aesthetic experience involves, above all, connectedness.

Chapter 5. Peak Experiences in Education and Learning

This chapter explores peak experience in education and learning contexts and involves both learners and educators themselves. The literature is discussed in three sections: the first section relates to childhood and adolescent experiences; the second examines peak experience in adult learning; and the third focuses on the teaching literature. Peak experiences are seen as benefitting not only children but also adults and teachers by contributing to workplace sustainability and individual well-being. Our participants were adults, and they shared their peak experiences as children as well as reporting increased motivation and purpose as a result of their adult peak experiences.

Chapter 6. Peak Experiences in Nature and Wilderness

In his book, *Religions, Values, and Peak Experiences*, Maslow recognises how a beholder can "more readily look upon nature as if it were there in itself and for itself, not simply as if it were a human playground put there for human purposes upon it" (1964, 1971). In this chapter, we review a range of literature relating to peak experiences in nature through a variety of environmental settings, including wilderness, forests, and other evocative natural locations. We then share peak experiences from our participants that were similarly generated through engagement with aspects of the natural environment, including with animals. The findings confirm the importance of solitude, yet also recognise that peak experiences seem to be "co-created" in this context through the connection with nature or through an aesthetic appreciation of place, space, or environmental beauty.

Chapter 7. Peak Experiences in Competitive Sport

This chapter begins by unpacking some linguistic concerns, specifically the overlaps between the concepts of peak experience, peak performance, and flow, which are significantly evident in the sport context. A review of literature is attempted in two sections, the first looking at the chronology of these three concepts and the second homing in on felt peak experiences in sports settings. Our participants include high-performing team and individual sportspeople who shared their peak experiences and how these led to learning, increased control, and feelings of connection.

Chapter 8. Peak Experiences in Therapy

This chapter explores the possibility that both therapists and therapy clients have peak experiences during or as a result of therapy interventions. We first provide a review of the literature relating to peak experiences in a variety of therapy settings that emphasise humanistic or whole-person approaches such as Gestalt; a review that also resulted in the exploration of a related term, epiphany. We then present the experiences of several practising therapists who confirmed there are important aspects of therapy that can lead to peak experiences. These aspects can be considered as "core conditions" and include trust, the connection between client and therapist, support and co-creation, and the role that intuition can play.

Chapter 9. Peak Experiences in Executive and Life Coaching

Our own peak experiences whilst coaching led us to study whether other coaches also experience this phenomenon. Our review of coaching literature confirms there is almost no empirical research on peak experiences during coaching, but there is some research on related concepts and experiences for the coachee during the coaching interaction. These include intuitions, shifts in the room, and critical moments. Participants interviewed for this chapter indicated that peak experiences occur through deep connections in the relationship between coach and coachee – what they called "a oneness." The benefit to coaching of the experience was also noted; there is a strengthened connection between the coach and coachee that enriches the relationship, making peak experiences even more likely to occur.

Chapter 10. Peak Experience in Extreme Sport and High-Risk Leisure

In this chapter we focus on peak experiences in extreme risk-taking activities. The review of literature looks at risk-taking in earth-bound activities like rock climbing and mountaineering; air-inspired undertakings such as skydiving and space travel; and water-based pursuits like rafting, channel swimming, or scuba diving. We then present accounts from participants on their encounters with peak experience whilst engaged in some of these risky pursuits. From these accounts, several triggers for peak experience emerged, including connectedness and a sense of being in control.

Chapter 11. Peak Experiences in the Workplace

Notwithstanding the potential of peak experiences for adding value to people's workplace effectiveness and happiness, peak experiences are seldom discussed in this context. Recent researchers have noted how little we know about employee peak experiences and their impact. In this chapter, we review relevant literature, including that on workplace self-transcendence, which, as our participants have indicated, is an important element of team building, cohesion, and subsequent "team togetherness."

Chapter 12. Peak Experiences in Relationships, Love, and Sex

In humanistic psychology, love is regarded as the key to realising human potential. Indeed, belongingness and love are seen as necessary underpinnings in the quest towards self-actualisation, as the pinnacle of that potential. Physical love has also been identified as important in the attainment of peak experiences, and Maslow actually considered that two of the easiest ways of getting peak experiences are "through music and through sex" (1968, p. 75). Peak experiences and music are already discussed in Chapter 3. In this chapter, we are concerned with peak experience in different types of love relationships, including platonic and parental relationships as well as physical relationships.

Conclusion and Insights

This chapter summarises the book across four main sections: in the first section, we discuss the varieties of peak experience, grouping what we call "peak-like" experiences under common headings such as peak performance, flow, or awe and summarising these separately from peak experience itself. To highlight the similarities and differences between the qualities of peak experiences in the different contexts, the second section synthesises the themes that emerged from participant accounts, including the value of connection, physiological impacts, the role of memory, the potential for growth, and the core conditions for attainment of peak experiences. The benefits of peak experiences in relation to positive feelings and emotions are outlined in the third section, and we conclude by identifying emerging research topics in the fourth section.

References

Adams, D., & Beauchamp, G. (2019). Spiritual moments making music in nature: A study exploring the experiences of children making music outdoors, surrounded by nature. *International Journal of Children's Spirituality*, 24(3), 260–275.

Cox, E. (2003). The contextual imperative: Implications for coaching and mentoring. *International Journal of Evidence Based Coaching and Mentoring*, 1(1), 9–22.

Csikszentmihalyi, M. (1990). *Flow: The psychology of optimal experience.* New York: Harper & Row.

Csikszentmihalyi, M. (1997). *Flow and the psychology of discovery and invention.* New York: Harper Perennial.

Davis, J., Lockwood, L., & Wright, C. (1991). Reasons for not reporting peak experiences. *Journal of Humanistic Psychology*, 31(1), 86–94.

Dennis, L. J., & Powers, J. F. (1974). Dewey, Maslow, and consummatory experience. *Journal of Aesthetic Education*, 8(4), 51–63.

Grof, S. (2016). *Realms of the human unconscious: Observations from LSD research.* London: Souvenir Press.

Grove, J. R., & Lewis, M. A. (1996). Hypnotic susceptibility and the attainment of flowlike states during exercise. *Journal of Sport and Exercise Psychology*, 18(4), 380–391.

Hanfling, O. (1992). *Philosophical aesthetics, an introduction.* Milton Keynes: The Open University.

Ho, M. Y., Chen, S. X., & Hoffman, E. (2012). Unpacking cultural variations in peak-experiences: Cross-cultural comparisons of early childhood recollection between Hong Kong and Brazil. *Journal of Happiness Studies*, 13(2), 247–260.

Hoffman, E., & Ortiz, F. A. (2009). Youthful peak-experiences in cross-cultural perspective: Implications for educators and counselors. In L. Francis, D. Scott, M. de Souza, & J. Norman (Eds.), *The international handbook of education for spirituality, care, and wellbeing.* New York: Springer.

James, W. (1884). What is an emotion? *Mind*, 9(34), 188–205.

James, W. (1902–1928). *The varieties of religious experience: A study in human nature.* New York: Longmans, Green & Co.

Kapusta, J. (2018). The self-actualization of John Adams. *Journal of the Society for American Music, 12*(3), 317–344.

Kaufman, S. B. (2018). Self-actualizing people in the 21st century: Integration with contemporary theory and research on personality and well-being. *Journal of Humanistic Psychology.* https://doi.org/10.1177/0022167818809187

Latham, K. (2007). The poetry of the museum: A holistic model of numinous museum experiences. *Museum Management and Curatorship, 22*(3), 247–263.

Leontiev, D. (2008). Maslow yesterday, today, and tomorrow. *Journal of Humanistic Psychology, 48*(4), 451–453.

Marotto, M., Roos, J., & Victor, B. (2007). Collective virtuosity in organizations: A study of peak performance in an orchestra. *Journal of Management Studies, 44*, 388–413.

Maslow, A. H. (1943). A theory of human motivation. *Psychological Review, 50*, 370–396.

Maslow, A. H. (1954). *Motivation and personality.* New York: Harper & Row.

Maslow, A. H. (1959). Cognition of being in the peak experiences. *The Journal of Genetic Psychology, 94*(1), 43–66.

Maslow, A. H. (1962). Lessons from the peak experiences. *Journal of Humanistic Psychology, 2*(1), 9–18.

Maslow, A. H. (1964). *Religions, values, and peak experiences.* London: Penguin Books.

Maslow, A. H. (1968). Music education and peak experience. *Music Educators Journal, 54*(6), 72–171.

Maslow, A. H. (1969a). Various meanings of transcendence. *Journal of Transpersonal Psychology, 1*(1), 56–66.

Maslow, A. H. (1969b). Theory Z. *The Journal of Transpersonal Psychology, 1*(2), 31–47.

Maslow, A. H. (1970a). *Motivation and personality,* 2nd edition. New York: Harper & Row.

Maslow, A. H. (1970b). New introduction: Religions, values, and peak-experiences. *Journal of Transpersonal Psychology, 2*(2), 83–90.

Maslow, A. H. (1971). *The farther reaches of human nature.* New York, USA: Penguin.

Maslow, A. H. (1974). Cognition of being in the peak experiences. In *Readings in Human Development: A Humanistic Approach* (pp. 83–106). Ardent Media.

Maslow, A. H. (1999). Peak-experiences as acute identity experiences. In A. H. Maslow (Ed.), *Toward a psychology of being,* 3rd edition. New York, NY: John Wiley and Sons.

Maslow, A. H. (2011). *Toward a psychology of being.* Connecticut, USA: Martino Publishing.

Maslow, A. H. (2013). *Toward a psychology of being.* New York: Simon and Shuster.

Maslow, A. H., & Hoffman, E. E. (1996). *Future visions: The unpublished papers of Abraham Maslow.* Thousand Oaks, CA: Sage Publications, Inc.

Noltemeyer, A., Bush, K., Patton, J., & Bergen, D. (2012). The relationship among deficiency needs and growth needs: An empirical investigation of Maslow's theory. *Children and Youth Services Review, 34*(9), 1862–1867.

Norwood, G. (2009). Maslow's hierarchy of needs. *A Theory of Human Motivation.* www.deepermind.com/20maslow.htm [Accessed 13 March 2023].

Privette, G. (1981). Dynamics of peak performance. *Journal of Humanistic Psychology, 21*, 57–67.

Privette, G. (1983). Peak experience, peak performance, and flow: A comparative analysis of positive human experiences. *Journal of Personality and Social Psychology, 45*, 1361–1368.

Privette, G. (2001). Defining moments of self-actualization: Peak performance and peak experience. In J. K. Schneider, J. F. T. Bugental, & J. Fraser Pierson (Eds.), *The handbook of humanistic psychology.* Thousand Oaks, CA: Sage.

Privette, G., & Bundrick, C. M. (1991). Peak experience, peak performance and flow: Correspondence of personal descriptions and theoretical constructs. *Journal of Social Behavior and Personality, 6*(5), 169–188.

Schouten, J. W., McAlexander, J. H., & Koenig, H. F. (2007). Transcendent customer experience and brand community. *Journal of the Academic of Marketing Science, 35*, 357–368.

Seligman, M. E. (2002). Positive psychology, positive prevention, and positive therapy. In C. R. Snyder & S. J. Lopez (Eds.), *Handbook of positive psychology* (pp. 3–12). Oxford University Press.

Seligman, M. E. (2018). PERMA and the building blocks of well-being. *The Journal of Positive Psychology*, *13*(4), 333–335.

Senecal, G. (2021). The aftermath of peak experiences: Difficult transitions for contact sport athletes. *The Humanistic Psychologist*, *49*(2), 295–313.

Straś-Romanowska, M., & Kapała, M. (2010). Śmierć Jana Pawła II jako źródło doświadczenia religijnego [The death of John Paul II as a source of spiritual experience]. In M. Straś-Romanowska, B. Bartosz, & M. Żurko (Eds.), *Psychologia małych i wielkich narracji [Psychology of small and great narrations]*. Warszawa: Eneteia Wydawnictwo Psychologii i Kultury.

Street, A. (1991). *From image to action: Reflection in nursing practice*. Geelong, VIC: Deakin University Press.

Whitehead, R., & Bates, G. (2016). The transformational processing of peak and nadir experiences and their relationship to eudaimonic and hedonic well-being. *Journal of Happiness Studies*, *17*, 1577–1598. https://doi.org/10.1007/s10902-015-9660-6

Wilber, K. (1998). *The essential Ken Wilber: An introductory reader*. Boston, MA: Shambhala Publications.

Wilson, C. (2009). *Super consciousness: The quest for the peak experience*. London: Watkins Publishing.

Yalom, I. D. (1980). *Existential psychotherapy*. New York, NY: Basic Books.

1 Peak Experience in Spirituality and Religion

Introduction

In the introduction to this book, we described Maslow's hierarchy of needs and his idea of self-actualisation as a higher level of motivation or of being. However, Maslow later developed "compelling doubts" about the suitability of self-actualisation as a "motivational capstone" (Koltko-Rivera, 2006, p. 304). He had detected a paradox in the relationship between self-actualisation and the self-transcendence inherent in the peak experiences reported by his self-actualised subjects. Maslow noted that, after all the efforts they had invested in the development of their own potential, self-actualisers were also interested in causes beyond themselves. He saw this as a contradiction, since not only were they motivated to develop their own potential, but they were also concerned with supporting others. He compared the kind of self-transcendence he observed, that aims to help those less fortunate, with the "Bodhisattva" state (1970) and viewed self-actualisation as a kind of "bridge" to self-transcendent states, values, and motivation.

As his research continued, he came to the realisation that "self-actualization is not enough" (Maslow, 1961, p. 31) and that it needed to be disaggregated from self-transcendence, the higher level of Being-cognition that he saw as characterising peak experiences. Koltko-Rivera (2006, p. 313) concluded that detaching the construct of self-transcendence and removing its motivational status "provides a means to a deeper understanding of other important constructs and builds bridges between bodies of theory that are currently isolated," including aiding our appreciation of how different people and cultures construe the meaning of life and helping with our understanding the motivational forces of both altruism and religious violence.

Maslow went on to describe peak experiences multifariously as mystical, transcendental, self-transcendent, psychedelic, or unitive events. He saw them as expressions of spirituality, being human by construction but revealing our spiritual nature

> to the extent that all mystical and peak experiences are the same in their essence and have always been the same, all religions are the same in their essence and have always been the same.
>
> (Maslow, 1964, p. 31)

DOI: 10.4324/9781003509219-2

In addition, through his exploration of peak experiences, he believed that organised religion would receive the empirical support it needed. He defined the purpose of religion as to "communicate peak experiences to non-peakers" (1964, p. 24) to satisfy the human need for transcendent experience. Maslow believed his concept of peak experiences with their moments of intense joy, fulfilment, and meaning bridged a gap between the spiritual and the mundane and the religious and secular dimensions of human existence (Hoffman & Ortiz, 2009).

We begin this chapter by defining what we understand by religion and spirituality as contexts for peak experiences. Religion and spirituality can be seen as similar in purpose, but they are very different in practice. Religion is the personal or community-based organisation of belief in God or another supernatural being, while spirituality is the individual connection or experience of wider, transcendental unity. Koenig et al. (2001, p. 18) presented a clear definition of the two that we repeat here:

> Religion is an organized system of beliefs, practices, rituals and symbols designed a) to facilitate closeness to the sacred or transcendent (God, higher power or ultimate truth/reality) and b) to foster an understanding of one's relationships with, and responsibility to, others within a community. Spirituality is a personal quest for reaching understandings about the ultimate questions of life and about the meaning of and relationship with the sacred or transcendent, which may or may not lead to, or arise from, the development of religious rituals and community.

Although spirituality can be viewed as a phenomenon within religious practice, "the search for the sacred and the lived experience of religious life" (Ronkainen & Nesti, 2018, p. 6), it is more commonly seen as a wider construct existing consciously or unconsciously in all people as "an ontological aspect of humanness" (2018, p. 7). Consequently, it can be defined from a religious or a humanist perspective "where personal meaning is derived from whatever people deem to be ultimate and valued in and of itself" (Watson & Parker, 2015). This view of spirituality, as broader than religion, has become dominant in our society, whilst it is still acknowledged that people do have spiritual experiences within their chosen religious frameworks.

In a recent treatise, Hari Narayanan (2021, pp. 25–26) also agrees with the broader interpretation of spirituality that uncouples it from purely religious belief. He pointed out how being spiritual is frequently understood as a religious approach to life and is contrasted with a more materialist or practical approach. Hari Narayanan suggests, however, that religion serves important functions in human life, even if the metaphysical claims are not accepted. Thus, he argues, those who are irreligious "can still fulfil the yearnings such as finding meaning in life or sensing something transcendent" (2021, p. 26). Tanyi, working in the nursing field, also made this distinction arguing that a personal search for meaning and purpose in life may or may not be related to religion: "it entails connection to self-chosen and/or religious beliefs, values, and practices that give meaning to life, thereby inspiring and motivating individuals to achieve their optimal being" (2002, p. 506).

The writing of William James (1902–1928) is important to acknowledge here since his work is seen as the starting point in the study of the nature of religious experience. Following extensive research, James was able to claim a distinction between institutional and personal religion. He found spiritual experiences occurred not only through religious practices but also through non-religious activities such as intense concentration or whilst walking in nature. Furthermore, the experiences were felt as a conscious union with the universe rather than as divine encounters. James subsequently adopted the term "cosmic consciousness" to describe these more secular mystical experiences.

Kruger argues that in James's pragmatic philosophy, religious experiences are reduced to mere experience. Using a phenomenological methodology, Kruger (2020, p. 3) contended that James's influence "pushes the academic study of religion into a focus on peak experience." Employing Heidegger's critique of subject–object dualism (where the subject is the observer and the object is the thing observed), and in particular his rejection of "lived experience" as belonging to that dualism, he considers religious experiences are

> sapped of their power by objective analysis and cultural skepticism, but also by subjective recounting and private interpretation, where everything is merely personal – "that's just my experience" – and shared concerns are no longer possible.
> (2020, p. 3)

Maslow's (1964) research built on James's work. He examined the qualities of leaders such as Abraham Lincoln and Albert Einstein, people recognised for their humanitarian efforts and commitment, to develop the theory of self-actualisation, which at the time he described as the state where the highest level of human growth and attainment were achieved. Later, he discovered that frequent spiritual or peak experiences were a distinctive occurrence for self-actualisers and that these "peakers" were more likely to be drawn towards mystery and awe, to see sacredness in all things and to transcend the ego, the self and their own identity (Maslow, 1976).

Peak experiences, which characteristically involved transcendent states of consciousness, were classified as either religious or secular since they occurred in many contexts. In fact, Maslow described 25 religious aspects of peak experience, arguing that:

> Practically everything that happens in the peak-experiences, naturalistic though they are, could be listed under the headings of religious happenings, or indeed have been in the past considered to be only religious experiences.
> (1964, Appendix A)

Subsequently, Pahnke (1980) offered a nine-category typology of mystical peak experiences: unity; transcendence of time and space; deeply felt positive mood; sense of sacredness; objectivity and reality; paradoxicality; alleged ineffability; transiency; and persisting positive changes in attitude and behaviour. According to MacKnee (1999, pp. 44–47), these nine categories were composed in the belief that they are "universal and not restricted to any specific religion or culture." They can be understood through culture and religion but are also seen as part of general human experience.

We structure the literature review that follows using philosophical debates that seem to challenge Kruger and other religious philosophers. We see this discussion as important both for this chapter and indeed for this book, since the debate highlights the need to attend to contextual and perspectival aspects such as "lived experience" in the analysis of peak experiences as well as in religion.

Literature

Peak experiences, religious experiences, and mystical experiences have all been described differently by different researchers, and this has led to a significant debate about definitions and conceptualisations. Some researchers, like James (1902–1928), have viewed mystical experiences as synonymous with religious experiences, identifying their four characteristics as noetic or cerebral quality, passivity, ineffability, and transiency. Others, for example Hood (2001), differentiate a mystical experience as separate from religious experiences. Watson and Parker (2015, p. 266) point out, "Mysticism is not to be regarded as a religion itself, but the highest expression of all true religions and a means of directly experiencing the supernatural." They cite Woods (1980, p. 20), who describes the mystical experience as "the immediate feeling of the unity of self with God . . . in which the self and the world are alike forgotten, the subject knows himself to be in the possession of the highest and fullest truth."

So, as Adam (2002, p. 801) has pointed out, claims about mystical knowledge are usually seen as having more than merely a subjective validity: "they are thought to pertain to the nature of reality in general." Mystics maintain they have insights into more than their own psychological states, revealing an "object" that is separate and distinct from their own subjectivity.

To look at the different definitions of mystical or peak experiences, we want to contextualise our discussion by reviewing them first in relation to the concepts of perennialism and essentialism and linking this to the work of James. We then look at the significance of constructivist and contextualist viewpoints and examine where Maslow's idea of peak experience fits according to a range of researchers and commentators.

Perennialism and Essentialism in Religious and Spiritual Experience

Perennialism is the idea that there is a shared, *perennial hub of truth* in all major religions. Jones, an American scholar, confirms that perennialists separate completely this primordial wisdom from any expression of it and from any experience of it: "it is the eternal and unchanging Truth that is important, not any experience connected to it" (Jones, 2020, p. 26).

Additionally, according to Taylor (2017, p. 75), perennialism refers to "the claim that there is a common core of basic teachings across religious traditions, and so relates more strongly to the philosophical and conceptual frameworks of traditions." The idea is supported by how perennialists see mystical experiences as proof of God's existence. This was especially prevalent in medieval times when transcendent, mystical states were deliberately induced through religious contemplations (Watson, 2011). Metaphysics researcher, Lowney (2022, p. 8) also suggests that, for perennialists, the object of mystical experience and its unity is the sole focus, explaining that "God is a unity, so mystical experience is contact with that ultimate Reality."

Essentialism, on the other hand, is the idea that there are *essential properties* of religion. Taylor (2017, p. 75) explains how essentialism emphasises "commonalities amongst mystical or spiritual experiences and practices in different traditions." So, in Taylor's view, "essentialism is more experientially or phenomenologically oriented, while perennialism is more philosophically oriented" (2017, p. 75).

Mystical experiences, when viewed from the essentialist position, have been described as "the varied expressions of an identical experience or so many varied expressions of a limited number of experiences" (Almond, 1988, p. 41). James (1902–1928) observed that mystical experiences are frequently beyond description and involve transience, a feeling of overwhelm and have a noetic quality (Yaden et al., 2017). The noetic quality refers to the direct apprehension of knowledge gained from the experience and the understanding that accompanies the mystical experience. Noetic events are "illuminations, revelations, full of significance and importance, all inarticulate though they remain; and as a rule they carry with them a curious sense of authority for after time" (James, 1902/1928, p. 380).

Two illustrations of spiritual or mystical experience are useful here: the first is an example of a deeply religious meditation from a poem of St John of the Cross, the Carmelite friar, where he describes an experience of transcendent ecstasy. The poem stanza is from "Verses written after an ecstasy of high exaltation" (Poems of St John of the Cross, 1951) and illustrates an intense essentialist desire for communion with the divine:

> So borne aloft, so drunken-reeling,
> So rapt was I, so swept away,
> Within the scope of sense or feeling
> My sense or feeling could not stay.
> And in my soul I felt, revealing,
> A sense that, though its sense was naught
> Transcended knowledge with my thought.

The second illustration was recounted by William James, who has been identified as the patron saint of the perennialist argument (Laws, 2005). Here, James shares an experience from a clergyman of the time that epitomises the definition of a mystical or religious experience:

> I remember the night, and almost the very spot on a hilltop, where my soul opened out, as it were, into the Infinite, and there was a rushing together of

the two worlds, the inner and the outer. It was deep calling unto deep – the deep that my own struggle had opened up within being answered by the unfathomable deep without, reaching beyond the stars. I stood alone with Him who had made me, and all the beauty of the world, and love, and sorrow, and even temptation. I did not seek him but felt the perfect unison of my spirit with His. The ordinary sense of things around me faded. For the moment nothing but an ineffable joy and exultation remained. It is impossible fully to describe the experience. It was like the effect of some great orchestra when all the separate notes have melted into one swelling harmony that leaves the listener conscious of nothing save that his soul is being wafted upwards, and almost bursting with its own emotion. The perfect stillness of the night was thrilled by a more solemn silence. The darkness held a presence that was all the more felt because it was not seen. I could not any more have doubted that *He* was there than that I was.

(James, 1902/1928, p. 66, author italics)

The experience subsequently strengthened the clergyman's faith, although interestingly he later says that "never since has there come quite the same stirring of the heart," suggesting it is likely impossible that the same "peak" experience can be repeated. Maslow also commented on the potential for reprise:

My feeling is that if it were never to happen again, the power of the experience could permanently affect the attitude toward life. A single glimpse of heaven is enough to confirm its existence even if it is never experienced again.

(Maslow, 1970, p. 75)

In Rosenblatt's (1977, p. 22) comparison study of the biblical patriarch, Abraham, and Abraham Maslow, he suggests that "according to Genesis, Abraham could speak to and hear God, becoming bound up in fascination in peak moments" and that the mystic and oceanic feelings Abraham had back then actually reflect the peak experiences that Maslow later saw as the significant by-products or characteristics of healthy personalities:

The very beginning, the intrinsic core, the essence, the envisioned nucleus of every known high religion . . . has been the private, lonely, personal illumination, revelation, of ecstasy of some acutely sensitive prophet or seer.

(Maslow, 1970, p. 19)

According to Rosenblatt, Maslow subsumes mystical experiences "under the heading of peak experiences or some other related terminology, such as ecstatic or transcendent experiences" (1977, p. 23), and it seems "as the patriarch Abraham matured personally and, in his faith, (moving from Maslow's D-needs to B-needs), [self-actualised] characteristics developed."

With each peak experience, according to Rosenblatt (1977, p. 23), Abraham moved towards a healthier level but each time with greater faith and sensitivity.

Rosenblatt makes good use of Maslow's frame of reference here, where, as explained in the Introduction, the first four levels are referred to as deficiency needs (the D-needs), and the self-actualisation level involves the Being needs (the B-needs).

Maslow (1964, p. 19) considered that inherent in every known religion has been "the private, lonely, personal illumination, revelation, or ecstasy of some acutely sensitive prophet or seer," pointing out that religions tend to base their validity and function "on the codification and the communication of this original mystic experience or revelation from the lonely prophet to the mass of human beings in general." He further suggested, as Rosenblatt has observed, that such revelations or mystical illuminations "can be subsumed under the head of the "peak-experiences" or "ecstasies" or "transcendent" experiences" (1964, pp. 19–20). Thus, like James, Maslow viewed supernatural, religious revelations as natural human occurrences rather than as evidence for the existence of a divine entity or God:

> [T]hese older reports, phrased in terms of supernatural revelation, were, in fact, perfectly natural, human peak-experiences of the kind that can easily be examined today, which, however, were phrased in terms of whatever conceptual, cultural, and linguistic framework the particular seer had available in his time.
> (1970, p. 20)

In the next section, we examine the more secular nature of Maslow's concept of peak experience in more detail.

Constructivism and Contextualism in Religious and Spiritual Experience

In the previous section, we reported how essentialism points to the commonalities between religious experiences achieved in different religious traditions and the view that such experiences might be universal human experiences rather than proof that a particular religious tradition is true. Constructivism and contextualism imply that religious experiences are filtered through language and culture and through our personal nature.

Constructivism

As mentioned in our Introduction to this book, Maslow was a founder of the humanist movement, and underpinning his work was the importance of individual subjectivity. This emphasis situates him as a constructivist, a theoretical position that contrasts with perennialism and is based on the assumption that the nature of human experience has its foundations in individualism and relativism and the recognition of multiple realities and truths. Maslow was aware that for a considerable time the subject of religious psychology had been off-limits for debate in academia. Like Darwin, he was afraid of ridicule and rejection of his ideas, particularly those contained in his lecture, "Cognition of Being in the Peak Experiences." He was very aware that the experiences he described were secular, yet similar to those described in religious contexts.

Religious educator, Breslauer (1976, p. 55) described the extent to which Maslow's notion of peak experience is a "private participation in a changed awareness of the world." He noted it as an individual experience which is "in essence noncommunicable." Breslauer's analysis of peak experience thus uncouples it from essentialist, organised religion and focuses on its constructivist nature, noting that "because the meaning of the peak-experience cannot be externalized and made public, the problem of religious discourse in general becomes a specific question with regard to it" (1976, p. 55).

In the same year, Horne (1976, p. 279) concurred, explaining how "mysticism is a very private, personal, and individual experience" that, even though it is often described, and we sometimes feel that we recognise the experience as shared, only individuals can report. So, Horne argues, "in these respects mysticism is rather like dreaming, another private experience which we describe to each other." Earlier, Warmoth (1965, p. 19, our emphasis) had similarly explained how "transformations come about through a direct encounter, *unique to the individual, and in his own terms*. The role of powerful communal symbols is minimised and the experience itself becomes a personal symbol."

Taking the constructivist argument even further, Jones (2020) explained that the constructivist position holds that mystical experiences are also shaped by our linguistic influences, "such that the lived experience conforms to a pre-existent pattern that has been learned, then intended, and then actualized in the experiential reality of the mystic" (2020, p. 18).

A secular, yet mystical moment reported by contemporary author, Katherine May, aptly illustrates how her experience has been mediated by the learnt practice of individual meditation:

> By closing my eyes, however briefly, and resting my thoughts on the core of my perception, I can gain some of the peace that meditation brings me. I have come to think of it as prayer, although I ask for nothing, and speak to no one within it. It is a profoundly non-verbal experience, a sharp breath of pure being amid a forest of words. It is an untangling, a moment to feel the true ache of desire, the gentle wash of self-compassion, the heart swell of thanks, the tick tick tick of existence. It is the moment when, alone, I feel at my most connected with others. I can feel entirely separate in a crowd of people, but closing my eyes, I can feel as though I have walked into a river of all consciousness, bathed in common humanity.
>
> (May, 2020, p. 132)

May's self-transcendent, mystical experience as a result of meditation also has a noetic quality, one which James (1902/1928, p. 380) explained as a state of "insight into depths of truth unplumbed by the discursive intellect."

Similarly, Perry et al. (2021) provide a framework for understanding the universality of chanting in certain spiritual practices and the potential of chanting practices to lead to mystical states. The study collected data from 464 participants across 33 countries and indicated that 60% of participants experienced mystical states during chanting. Perry et al. point out that Maslow often noted how peak experiences occur during music listening, because music triggers mechanisms that induce significant changes in mood and emotional experience, "chanting may operate in a similar way, but with a strong emphasis on focused attention, synchronization, and often overlaid with powerful belief systems" (2021, p. 3).

These authors also highlight how some religions promote prosocial behaviour by prioritising others above the Self. They highlight Buddhist traditions as focusing on qualities like compassion and loving kindness:

> Therefore, as well as chanting sounds, individuals may also have intentions during the chanting practice to act compassionately and kindly to others, or to focus attention on the "oneness of the universe," reinforcing community and connection to others. These intentions may enhance the experience of chanting as well as nurturing altered states of consciousness.
>
> (Perry et al., 2021, p. 3)

In addition, Buddhist experiences such as Satori, said to lead to individual awakening, enlightenment, and transcendence (Suzuki, 1961), and the concepts of unity and agelessness identified by Maslow (1961, p. 255) are echoes of the Buddhist notion of subjective isolation, where "the knower no longer feels himself to be independent of the known; the experiencer no longer feels himself to stand apart from the experience" (Watts, 1989, p. 120).

Maslow sometimes mentions the notion of bodhisattvas (those on a path towards bodhi or Buddhahood) when discussing highly self-actualising people (Maslow, 1970). Indeed, Canadian researchers, Birch and Sinclair (2013) point out that there are parallels between Maslow's constructivist description of peak experiences and Buddhist thought. Citing Watts (1989, p. 89), they identify the idea of "letting one's mind alone and trusting it to follow its own nature."

We have therefore classed Buddhism as constructivist because of the emphasis on personal enlightenment. Human experiences are clearly mediated through language, culture, and our own personal experiences throughout our lives. However, as Lucy, one of our participants for this chapter explained, this does not mean everything is relative: Buddhists do believe that there is a universal spiritual "ground" that everything is based on, referred to as "The Law of the Lotus" in the Lotus Sutra (Clarke & Beyer, 2009) and that the life condition of Buddhahood taps into that essential cosmic source.

Lowney (2022, p. 8) has argued that, for constructivists, the "psychological and cultural tools for experiencing and understanding objects are the focus." He explains how strong constructivists advocate "a form of reductionism that supposes the experience is a 'mere' construction rather than an ascent to, or experience of, a higher mode of being" (2022, p. 8). Like Jones (2020), Lowney holds that strong constructivists maintain that mystics in diverse religions have "different experiences because of the differences in their cultures and languages." He suggests, the expectations contributed by different doctrines and religious rites would seem to make up the ingredients that create the mystical experience itself (Lowney, 2022).

The implication, highlighted by Lowney is that, for constructivists, a mystical or peak experience is not one of an ultimate reality but is rather a "psychological and social construction" (2022, p. 7).

Lowney appears to identify a weaker brand of constructivism, which he labels "contextualism." This he suggests acknowledges that "different forms of mysticism do share the same core, but that [this] core is experienced in different ways depending upon the cultural context in which it presents" (2022, p. 7). So, rather than being just constructions of culture, and therefore viewed as all very different experiences, Lowney argues:

> culture might mediate the experience and even shape some aspects of the experience – and it will, at the very least, shape how a mystic is likely to understand and describe his or her experience.
>
> (2022, p. 8)

Contextualism

Philosopher Steven Katz (2004, p. 189) proposed that because there are "no pure (i.e., unmediated) experiences," there is no common core to our mystical experience. He argued that both the experience itself and the form in which it is reported are shaped by the concepts and contexts that the mystic brings to the experience:

> [A]ll experience is processed through, organized by, and makes itself available to us in extremely complex epistemological ways. The notion of unmediated experience appears, if not self-contradictory, at best empty.
>
> (2004, p. 189)

Katz's (1978, 2004) view of mystical experience and its interpretation is, according to Almond (1988, p. 42), also "a more subtle one than that of the essentialists." It creates a "*necessary* connection between context and experience" (author italics). Distinct from constructivism that focuses on individual subjectivity, Katz's religious contextualism therefore enables us to consider the "wide variety of phenomenologically discrete mystical experiences which are due to the cultural and conceptual settings in which they originate" (Almond, 1988, p. 42). Almond further argued that we cannot consider mystical experiences outside of their sociohistorical constraints or indeed separate them from their philosophical–theological environment: that is, they should be determined by the religious tradition in which they occur. They are not "pure, non-relational, unmediated" examples of human experience (Almond, 1988, p. 40).

Katz does not mention secular spiritual experiences, but we would argue that the same "contextual imperative" discussed by Cox (2003) applies to peak or mystical experiences howsoever they are prompted. Like Katz (1978), we believe the historical context lays down the ways in which spiritual experiences are both engendered and perceived.

Stoeber, Professor of Spirituality and Philosophy of Religion, describes how until the late twentieth century, religious scholarship downplayed the sociocultural features of mysticism, "emphasizing the psychological dynamics and an individual, disembodied, and radically transcendent ideal" (2017, paras 1–2). He argues that in an extreme form, "the contextualist perspective suggests that all mystical experiences among traditions are different, given diverse socio-religious categories that overdetermine the experience."

Much earlier, Rufus Jones, the American religious leader, had also argued that there are

> no experiences of any sort which are independent of preformed expectations or unaffected by the prevailing beliefs of the time. . . . Mystical experiences will be, perforce, saturated with the dominant ideas of the group to which the mystic belongs, and they will reflect the expectations of that group and that period.
>
> (Jones, 1909, p. xxxiv)

Developmental theorists, like Maslow, who are also "soft" constructivists (those that Lowney called contextualists), might argue that events have meaning only in the context of the environment in which they occur. Unlike constructivists who hold that the "internal environment of the organism is paramount" (Haynes, 2009, p. 53), a contextualist would be concerned with external, environmental factors. For example, in a seemingly contextualist move, Maslow observed that peak experiences occur "across time, culture, religious tradition, economic class, and gender" even though he was also concerned with the constructivist idea that they are "essentially incommunicable, unstructured, self-validating, beatific moments that can permanently change ones attitude toward life" (1964, p. 75).

An example of how context influences religious experience is described by Rahtz et al. (2021), who studied 67 pilgrims visiting Lourdes seeking rejuvenation for illness or disability. The research explored whether participants had experienced contact with a divine presence or something intangible and otherworldly. Transcendent experiences are a key aspect of pilgrimages to Lourdes, but, in their analysis, Rahtz et al. (2021, p. 3801) acknowledged that the experiences were dependent on the fact they had taken place there, since it is "well known as a therapeutic landscape, where physical, social and human conditions act together to promote healing." They, therefore, recognised its religious significance from a contextual perspective – the divine experience was mediated through Lourdes's historical context as they describe:

> Religious belief is inherently bound up with the significance of the place, and the whole site of Lourdes can be perceived as a "thin space" . . . , a place where there is a close connection between the everyday and the divine . . . where the transcendent can be seen as having broken through into normal life.
>
> (Rahtz et al., 2021, p. 3797)

As we see in the above example of pilgrimages to Lourdes, the relativism of the contextual view takes account of culture, time, and place and gives meaning to individual and societal interpretations of "truth" through what Haynes (2009, p. 54) terms a more "context-sensitive orientation." Contextualist philosophies thus became more accepted because of a dissatisfaction with the focus on individual psychology inherent in the traditional constructivist approaches to cognitive, moral, and faith development.

Peak Experience in Context: Participant Accounts

In this section, we include responses from four participants who have had peak experiences in the context of their religious practice: two in orthodox Christian traditions, one Buddhist, and the fourth who demonstrates a more secular spiritual experience.

Colin is a Baptist minister trained in essentialist Ignatian spiritual direction who explained that this approach fits with his personal teaching as well as his beliefs about God as "Not in our head, but in our heart." He described how in Ignatian spiritual direction, when you work with another person, "it's the Holy Spirit who is the director, not the person. It's staying with the experience, the presence, and the intensity, rather than being analytical."

His introduction to religion really began when he was 15, as a member of the Boy's Brigade – an organisation for young people that has a very strong Christian foundation. He went away on a Boy's Brigade camp. He soon realised some of the boys had already made their own faith commitment, and they met for prayer:

> As part of that I had a sense of the person that they were speaking to in this prayer time although I didn't claim Christian faith at the time. But there was something about it, which intrigued me and called me. And that was the moment for me of reaching out to God.

Colin encountered his first peak experience two or three months later, when he was in a discipleship group to help people get established in Christian faith. In the group, there were about seven young people. It was facilitated by a couple who invited the group to offer their own outloud prayers.

> [A]nd as I prayed, as I attempted to pray to God, one of the things that happened to me was that I went into this sort of almost out of body floating experience – I suppose it was a sort of ecstatic experience, although I'd never have used that word at the time. I wasn't looking down on myself or anybody else; I had my eyes closed, but had a sense of just touching, or being in, a different dimension entirely. And it wasn't just about feeling good – there was something different, almost like heaven and earth had sort of connected in some mysterious way.

He explained his emotions and how he felt joy and an awe that he had never experienced before. He also felt surprised because it was an initial experience. Physically, he felt a bit dizzy: "It felt dizzy and heady; almost like I wasn't quite in my body in the same way. It's very hard to find the words."

As a result of the experience, Colin began his tentative steps, as a teenager, into Christian faith. He described how it was one of those moments "where I tasted or experienced something that helped me get more established and on which I could look back as one of those moments when I would want to say I felt the presence of God."

Colin also shared how that feeling of "being connected" is something that has been repeated over the years, "but actually, that was the first experience, so it stands out. It was, as you say, a peak experience." Later, Colin's Christian faith meant he had to stand up for being a Christian at school, at university, and then eventually responded to a powerful call to Baptist ministry which he is still in 35 years later.

Other similar peak experiences have occurred in times of prayer, and Colin recalled one that stands out for him – a prayerful imagination which he described quite vividly:

> When I was in my early 40s, I went on what is called an Ignatian retreat – Ignatius being one of the pioneers of contemplative spirituality. And in the retreat, I got to the last morning and I was due to see a spiritual director. I was only there, I think, four days and it was near Preston, at Loyola Hall, and I'd seen the spiritual director each day, which is the practice – just for about 20 minutes or half an hour. And I was due to see him later that day. And it was lashing it down with rain. And I sat in the chapel on my own, just attempting to be still before God and reflect and so on. And, as far as I can tell, out of nowhere, came a prayerful experience of . . . I feel quite moved even as I say it – quite tearful actually . . . and in my prayerful experience, in my mind, as it were, I was out on the lawn outside the chapel, dancing with Jesus, a totally twirling sort of dancing, it was that sort of just utterly "going for it" on the grass in the rain.

For Colin, this experience was one of great joy and again, great surprise. He links the experience with essentialist Ignatian spirituality and the concepts of consolation and desolation:

> There is an understanding in Ignatian spirituality of something called "consolation," which is a feeling of inner peace and connection. And then there's something called "desolation," which is the opposite – being disconnected and fragmented and taken down a path which is not of life. And I had what Ignatian spirituality calls "consolation without prior cause." In other words, I hadn't seen a great view standing on a mountain side – and I hadn't been working myself up into a frenzy singing worship songs, and there was no particular explanation for this extraordinary experience to come out of nowhere.

Colin explained the logic behind his peak experience: when something happens between us and God, and by definition God is invisible, it happens in our internal processing, our internal world. Thus, it is a real encounter, but it's internal because God is not physical:

> So, all of this took place in that internal space, but actually it's still a real connection. And I kept with it as well. Again, this is Ignatian spirituality where we talk about staying with the presence of God, however it comes.

He also explained how the lasting effect of this experience has been one of deepening his faith and his sense of being connected with God:

> The lasting effect is that not that long after that, I had a change in my role, which proved to be quite costly in terms of the responsibilities that I was carrying, and the environment I was operating in. It was leading a retreat and healing centre myself, I got called into that sort of role myself and did that for five years.

Colin equates his other peak experiences with religious experience and sees his peak experiences in nature, for example, as the same as his prayerful experiences:

> I no longer see them as qualitatively different; just the starting place is different. My spirituality and theology infers that all things are from God and bear God's imprint, and all things are held by God. It's not pantheism, which is "all things are God," it's "pan-en-theism," using the Greek which means all things are in God, and therefore have the ability to communicate and help us connect with God, even though they themselves are not God.

Ignatius found God everywhere, and in the other peak experiences Colin shared, he explained how he has experienced comparable feelings of joy in familial relationships: "There's something about the old saying 'wherever love is, there is God' – and sometimes, that love is a felt experience, not just a sort of in the head experience or an observer observation." Summing up, Colin expressed how he finds in other people the image of God, again and again:

> That's part of Christian theology anyway, but again, and again, I noticed how much in the experiences that we've talked about, apart from one, there is always something external – a person or more than one person externally in the room, when it's happened. Although the one in the chapel at Loyola Hall, that was me on my own.
>
> But the others – it's either nature or it's other people, or other people are in the room as it happens. The very first one though, was private prayer time of a group of people.

***

34 *Valuing Peak Experience in Everyday Lives*

We also interviewed **Sebastian**, a Roman Catholic, who gave us insights into his understanding about peak experience and religion. Sebastian considers that belief in this essentialist context is such a privileged and private affair that it becomes too personal to discuss in general conversation, although he was content to share his views with us, as it served a purpose in supporting our chapter on religion: "when people push me about religion, unless it's for a specific reason like this book, I get a bit uppity as it's a very, very, private thing."

Belief for Sebastian is sacrosanct. He admits to the fact that there is no evidence of God rather only a personal sense of a higher being or creator. He says that defining what a connection to God means is very difficult as "we only have one side of people's connection to God. We haven't heard from God." He continues by saying that belief would be easy if there were a book which explains how you should feel when you are religious: "we have the Bible, but we don't know how true that is." For Sebastian, belief and faith mean believing in something without any tangible reason or evidence, like life ever after: "Are my dad and Granny really looking down on us? Until we go (ourselves) we never will know."

Sebastian's encounter with peak experience is multifaceted. He shared his story about attendance at Sunday Mass in the Catholic Church. He takes his 90-year-old mother, who is frail and unable to walk very far. For this reason, the priest gives her and Sebastian communion at the front pew, a row reserved especially for them and their family.

Sebastian recalls an incident which touches him deeply, something created through another's kindness:

A Polish lady on crutches was in the queue for communion. I don't know her name, I just know her from church. I touch her and hold her hand as she goes past. She has communion, and then comes over to Mum and kisses her hand (Sebastian became emotional talking about this). It's things like that. I think it's because I know Mum is very religious that I'm glad I'm able to give her that experience rather than sitting in a chair and not being able to get to church. I'm glad I'm able to give her that experience.

A culmination of having a specially reserved row in the church that makes his mother feel special, the priest bestowing kindness by delivering communion at the pew, the respect shown towards his mother by the kissing of her hand by the Polish parishioner, and the peace and tranquillity that emanate from the church were all contributory factors – core conditions almost – to enable Sebastian to feel ineffable joy, an emotionally charged feeling each Sunday as he observes his mother's piety and devotion to God.

In essence, Sebastian is the catalyst to make this happen too. He supports his mother to receive communion by taking her to church; he shows empathy towards the Polish parishioner which enables her to honour his mother. The ambience of the church also has a contributory effect. As soon as we walk into a church or cathedral, we immediately feel settled by that sense of history, people who've gone before, an aura of collective humanity. This environment creates something that enables Sebastian to go into a space in which he observes devoutness in others.

These contributory factors are similar to the core conditions that enable a peak moment of connectedness, co-creation, trust, and rapport (Weijers, 2021). It is a build-up of core conditions which enable Sebastian to experience ineffable joy, a quasi-peak experience through his connection to his mother.

***

Our third participant is **Lucy**, who admitted when we first asked her to do this interview, she thought immediately of Eagle Peak, not the high peak above Yosemite Valley in California so admired by John Muir, but the small mountain northeast of Rājagriha, the capital of Magadha in ancient India. The Eagle Peak was said to be frequented by Shakyamuni Buddha and is symbolic of the Buddha land or the state of Buddhahood.

Shakyamuni Buddha was a wealthy, Indian prince who, in his youth, lived protected by wealth and power. His quest for enlightenment or Buddhahood began after he sneaked out of the palace one day and experienced a moving encounter with the four human sufferings of birth, ageing, sickness, and death.

Lucy, who works in the voluntary sector, shared how her own practice of Buddhism, and its purpose in her life, continues to be the manifestation of Buddhahood.

> Based on bringing forth the state of Buddhahood, I endeavour to take action to relieve suffering in the lives of others so as to create value and peace in my life, family, community and world.

As a Buddhist, Lucy described how she also chants to manifest her Buddhahood and live a valuable and creative life:

> I believe Buddhahood is inherent in my life, and all life: attaining Buddhahood does not mean becoming a special being. In this state, one still continues to work against and defeat the negative functions of life and transform any and all difficulties into causes for further development. It is a state of complete access to the boundless wisdom, compassion, courage, and other qualities inherent in life; with this one can create harmony with and among others and between human life and nature.

Kinoshita and Gakkai (2019, p. 11) describe the life state of Buddhahood as a state of "absolute and indestructible happiness unaffected by circumstantial changes or difficulties" which, although it does not imply freedom from sufferings and problems, "does indicate possession of a vibrant, sturdy life force and abundant wisdom to challenge and overcome all the sufferings and difficulties we may encounter." Most importantly, for Lucy, however, are the words of Daisaku Ikeda – attaining Buddhahood means "to solidify in our lives a spirit of yearning for the happiness of oneself and others, and to continuously take constructive action with that spirit." This, however, seems to bear little relation to the peak experience described by Maslow.

Lucy also explained that she aims to live a life based on the *middle way*, which is described by Kasapa (2021, p. 7) as the middle ground between "attachment and aversion, between being and non-being, between form and emptiness, between free will and determinism." The middle way for Lucy means living a balanced and harmonious life, achieving a state of happiness which is not fleeting but rooted in her own humanity and daily life. Consequently, as she explains, "to talk about peak experiences could seem somewhat counter intuitive." Having said that, however, she clarifies that "Buddhism does equate the state of Buddhahood with the vastness of the universe (and) also outlines the mystic or unseen aspect of life which is not always manifest."

Her most abiding experiences of this vastness, almost resembling Maslow's notion of peak experience, have come when chanting:

> Certainly, when chanting, especially when chanting strongly for something that means a lot to me, I have occasionally experienced this vastness. I remember chanting very strongly just as I was giving birth to my eldest son. The medical team were encouraging me to do so. It was a life and death situation as I was very unwell. I felt very close to death, but I did not feel afraid.

Chanting during her childbirth experience made Lucy feel calm, and it regulated her breathing. She recalls how everything seemed to slow down, and it made her feel very safe and unafraid. However, she continued:

> I do wonder to what extent I felt this way because I was seriously unwell and delirious. Such experiences make me feel great at the time but sometimes sad and dissatisfied at how quickly they pass. I can also feel a sense of nostalgia or even doubt their reality and my own perception of them. Conversely, Buddhism teaches me to endeavour through my daily practice to develop and manifest my state of Buddhahood.

According to Perry et al. (2021, p. 2), the goal of chanting in traditions such as Buddhism is to "promote healing, social connection, and go beyond mundane states of awareness by altering states of consciousness." They describe how in Buddhist traditions, because there is significant focus on qualities like compassion and loving kindness, chanting involves being intentional and focusing attention on community and connection.

Lucy recognises this and acknowledges that a peak experience, as described by Maslow, sounds very similar to the experience of at least three of the ten (inner) worlds, described in Buddhism as a framework for understanding the changeable nature of our moods and, most significantly, the sense of the "possibility inherent in life at each moment" (Kinoshita & Gakkai, 2019, p. 9).

The three inner worlds that Lucy highlights as having similar constructivist qualities to a peak experience are rapture, realisation, and learning. She explains these in some detail:

> Rapture – The life state of heaven is regarded as a condition of joy or rapture experienced when our desires are fulfilled (e.g., we pass our driving test, fall

in love, have a strong spiritual experience etc.). However, such joy is not lasting. It fades and disappears with the passage of time and as situations change. It is transient and fleeting and easily influenced, even controlled and manipulated, by our external environment. So, rapture or heaven is often followed by the state of hell. Therefore, in Buddhism, rapture is categorised as one of the lower inner worlds.

Learning – In this state, we dedicate ourselves to creating a better life through self-reformation and self-development by learning from the ideas, knowledge, and experience of our predecessors and contemporaries. We become more aware of life's transience and seek to perfect ourselves and strive to improve ourselves. It can be quite a lonely and detached state as much as it is given over to *self*-improvement (unlike the state of Boddhisatva which is a state of altruism; given over to helping other people).

Realisation – this is also referred to as a cause awakened when we become aware of some lasting truth through our own effort and observation. Like learning, it is characterised by a striving for *self*-perfection. In its turn this can lead to a state of rapture in the instant, for example, of unexpected discovery.

The other seven inner worlds are hell, animality, anger, hunger, tranquillity, Boddhisatva, and Buddhahood (Mishra, 2019).

Although Lucy explained that talking about peak experiences "seemed somewhat counter intuitive," when we asked if there had been longer-lasting changes because of her experience or if it impacted her attitude towards life, she confirmed that undoubtedly it had:

It was powerful and stopped me from panicking at a very significant point. It was very much a part of my human experience. I welcomed it and would not have been without it. And yet, just as I did not seek this experience, I do not yearn for another one.

Lucy has had other peak-like experiences, "but not as strong: they have felt like markers along the way rather than ends in themselves – often memorable; and always fleeting."

***

Our final participant is **Ny,** who says he has no difficulty in accessing peak experiences, admitting that even as a child he had been keen on understanding the concept. He explained that when aged three or four, he had a real fondness for the film *The Lion King* and felt connected to the music, particularly the Hans Zimmer tracks. He even shared how he can visualise the experience and revisit his peak experience when a child. He would take himself off into his own private area in the garden, stand on a mound, and re-enact a scene with the Zimmer tracks playing in his mind's eye. He felt something spiritual, a connectedness, imagining himself out of his current setting and seeing the world with new eyes. He felt warmth in his stomach and chest with a deep knowing that what he was doing was relatable to his future in some form.

As a teenager his curiosity continued. He enjoyed deep conversations and exploring philosophy with like-minded individuals. In his twenties he put himself into therapy to try to understand and explore the Inner Child model (Capacchione, 1991) and found himself having a series of "lightbulb" moments which reconnected to the child within. He remains fascinated with this model, which has given him meaning in his life: "I found my feet with my family relationships and career choices, removing myself from situations which weren't serving my best interests."

Ny has subsequently developed a timeline that he uses to induce peak experiences. It consists of three steps: mental, spiritual, and physical. The mental steps involve setting goals, writing down what he wants to achieve, and creating vision boards. Ny finds it helpful to journal his thoughts and ideas about what he wants to accomplish. These steps set the foundation for his journey towards peak experiences.

The spiritual step involves opening himself up to new opportunities and allowing them to flow into his life. He connects spiritually to his pursuits and looks for synchronised events that demonstrate that he is on the right path, admitting "these events come in the form of conversations with others that resonate with me, or they may be symbols or emails related to my goals."

The physical step is about taking action towards his goals. Ny says that it is important in this step for him to put the mental and spiritual work into action when the universe affirms that he's on the right path. His beliefs present him with opportunities that require effort to bring about peak experience: "I continually develop and consistently work on myself during this step."

The peak experience is the culmination of the three steps, characterised by a burst of purpose and meaning. For Ny, time stands still, and he experiences a profound feeling of connection, an increase in his self-worth, and how he values himself: "for me, the peak experience is when my inner desires match my outer reality. When the two collide, it causes a peak experience."

Ny's peak experiences are integral to finding his purpose and place in the world. This pursuit has been shaped by his childhood experiences and has resulted in a passion for helping others find their own path in life:

> Peak experiences are like "lightbulb" moments for me. They are brief, intense flashes of insight that resonate with my sense of purpose and direction. These moments are characterized by a profound understanding that is either subconsciously or divinely informed, providing a sudden burst of clarity that illuminates my path. They can be described physically as a warm feeling in the chest, neck and stomach region, a feeling of mild anxiety or butterflies in the stomach region. Hairs standing up on my body, neck, arms and legs.

Through his spiritual and personal journey, Ny has found that peak experiences become more frequent and meaningful, adding "they've allowed me to become more aligned with my authentic self, access my inner truth, and navigate forward with clarity and confidence."

What Is Significant About Peaks in This Context?

In this chapter, we defined religion and spirituality as contexts for peak experiences and acknowledged the contribution of William James as a catalyst for Maslow's interest in mystical peak experience. We have also, in our introductory chapter, highlighted the distinction Maslow came to recognise in his later work (1974, 1976), between the concepts of self-actualisation and being-cognition (B-cognition). This is a distinction that has particular importance for peak experiences in the religious context, since mystical or religious peak experiences would seem to involve B-cognition and yet be quite distinct from the process of, or need for, self-actualisation.

Also, we note that controversy surrounds the relationship between peak experience and mystical experiences, and May (1991) has questioned Maslow's (1964) assumption that they are equivalent terms. May argued that the fundamental difference between a peak experience and a mystical experience was in the latter's awareness of the divine as a unitary being. The awareness of an absolute unitary being is something d'Aquili and Newberg (1998) also considered important in defining mystical experience. This awareness seems to be in addition to the experience of loss of self/other distinctions and the loss of temporality. Their understanding of the relationship between mystical experience and peak experience, as we have outlined earlier, led Benning et al. (2021, p. 3) to conceptualise mystical experiences as "subtypes of peak experience," pointing out that mystical experiences are peak experiences, but not all peak experiences are mystical experiences.

The literature review for this chapter was presented in two parts to recognise the traditional perennial and essentialist ideas in religion and contrast them with more postmodern constructivist and contextualist positions. Two of our participants for the chapter follow essentialist religious traditions: Baptist and Roman Catholic. One is a Buddhist, who we identify as belonging to the humanistic/constructivist tradition. In the two expressions of Christian belief and spirituality, differences in how peak experiences are described are apparent. For example, a sense of awe was mentioned by Colin in several examples, and he expresses a feeling combining reverence and wonder stimulated by the sacred or the divine. For Sebastian, the sacred is a personal sense of a higher being or creator observed through the devotion of others.

In the more humanistic Buddhist tradition, as Lucy explained to us, the state of Buddhahood becomes an individual construction rather than a mystic experience or the desired relationship with a higher being. Also, rather than Buddhists being seen as working to achieve enlightenment and then living in a state of cosmic bliss, the philosophy offers a way to resolve the self-actualisation/self-transcendence paradox Maslow (1970) identified. The Buddhist idea of the "greater self," which is accessed through efforts to develop ourselves as people via self-actualisation (self-reflection, learning from others, studying etc.) stimulates the "Bodhisattva" world – that is the self-transcendent aspiration to be of benefit, support, and encouragement to others. So self-actualisation for Buddhists can be seen as an integral, almost cyclical, part of self-transcendence: a self-transcendent or peak experience can stimulate the breakthrough required for further self-actualisation and that in turn helps us break through the shell of our ego to achieve self-transcendence. So for Buddhists the meaning of a peak experience is in what happens afterwards, what they do with that higher life state to interact with and help others.

Ny shared how as quite a young child he was aware of a spiritual connectedness and shared some profound experiences, and we saw how these have influenced him in adulthood too. Significantly, such a postmodern approach to spirituality can be seen to thrive in European society, and, in England, children's spiritual and moral education is promoted in the educational curriculum via a conceptual framework that seems to encourage peak experiences (School Curriculum and Assessment Authority, 1995):

> A sense of awe, wonder and mystery – being inspired by the natural world, mystery or human achievement.
>
> (1995, p. 9)

> Experiencing feelings of transcendence – feelings which may give rise to belief in the existence of a divine being or the belief that one's inner resources provide the ability to rise above everyday experiences.
>
> (1995, p. 9)

> Tuning – the kind of awareness which arises in heightened aesthetic experience, for example, when listening to music.
>
> (1995, p. 9)

Apparently, more ordinary events in a child's life could also promote a similar sense of unity, for example, through an intense sense of belonging, experienced at a family celebration (Nye & Hay, 1996, p. 148).

Maslow also thought that the teaching of spiritual, ethical, and moral values has a vital place in education. He concluded that educational and other institutions must be concerned with "final values, and this in turn is just about the same as speaking of what has been called 'spiritual values' or 'higher values'" (Maslow, 1964, p. 59).

References

Adam, M. T. (2002). A post-Kantian perspective on recent debates about mystical experience. *Journal of the American Academy of Religion, 70*(4), 801–818.

Almond, P. C. (1988). Mysticism and its contexts. *Sophia, 27*, 40–49.

Benning, T. B., Harris, K. P., & Rominger, R. (2021). Depression and mysticism: Case report and literature review. In *Spirituality in clinical practice*. American Psychological Association.

Birch, R., & Sinclair, B. R. (2013, July). Spirituality in place: Building connections between architecture, design, and spiritual experience. *The Visibility of Research: Proceedings of the 2013 Architectural Research Centers Consortium (ARCC, Spring Research Conference)*.

Breslauer, S. (1976). Abraham Maslow's category of peak-experience and the theological critique of religion. *Review of Religious Research, 18*(1), 53.

Capacchione, L. (1991). *Recovery of your inner child: The highly acclaimed method for liberating your inner self*. Simon and Schuster.

Clarke, P. B., & Beyer, P. (2009). *The world's religions.* London: Routledge.
Cox, E. (2003). The contextual imperative: Implications for coaching and mentoring. *International Journal of Evidence Based Coaching and Mentoring, 1*(1), 9–22.
d'Aquili, E. G., & Newberg, A. B. (1998). The neuropsychological basis of religion: Or why god won't go away. *Zygon: Journal of Religion and Science, 33*(June), 187–201.
Hari Narayanan, V. (2021). Sensing the self in spiritual experience. *Mind & Society, 20*(1), 25–40.
Haynes, C. J. (2009). Holistic human development. *Journal of Adult Development, 16*(1), 53–60.
Hoffman, E., & Ortiz, F. A. (2009). Youthful peak experiences in cross-cultural perspective: Implications for educators and counselors. In *International handbook of education for spirituality, care and wellbeing* (pp. 469–489). Dordrecht: Springer.
Hood, R. W. (2001). Mysticism in the psychology of religion. In *Dimensions of mystical experiences* (pp. 149–152). Brill.
Horne, J. R. (1976). How to describe mystical experiences. *Studies in Religion/Sciences Religieuses, 6*(3), 279–284.
Ikeda, D. *Quotations.* www.daisakuikeda.org/sub/quotations/theme/enlightenment.html [Accessed 17 January 2023].
James, W. (1902/1928). *The varieties of religious experience: A study in human nature.* New York: Longmans, Green & Co.
Jones, R. H. (2020). On constructivism in philosophy of mysticism. *The Journal of Religion, 100*(1), 1–41.
Jones, R. M. (1909). *Studies in mystical religion.* Macmillan.
Kasapa, S. S. (2021). The essence of Buddha-Dharma. *Telangana Journal of IMA, 1*(1), 6–8.
Katz, S. T. (Ed.) (1978). *Mystical experience and philosophical analysis.* Oxford: Oxford University Press.
Katz, S. T. (2004). Diversity and the study of mysticism. In *The future of the study of religion* (pp. 189–210). Brill.
Kinoshita, D., & Gakkai, S. (2019, August 26). *International humanitarian law and Nichiren Buddhism.* https://jliflc.com/wp-content/uploads/2019/12/201909IHLandNichirenBuddhism-1.pdf [Accessed 14 November 2024].
Koenig, H. G., McCullough, M. E., & Larson, D. B. (2001). *Handbook of religion and health.* New York: Oxford University Press.
Koltko-Rivera, M. E. (2006). Rediscovering the later version of Maslow's hierarchy of needs: Self-transcendence and opportunities for theory, research, and unification. *Review of General Psychology, 10*(4), 302–317.
Kruger, M. C. (2020). High on God: Religious experience and counter-experience in light of the study of religion. *Religions, 11*(8), 1–19. Accessed 3/12/24 from https://www.mdpi.com/2077-1444/11/8/388.
Laws, R. W. (2005). *William James and historical mysticism.* Doctoral Thesis, University of California, Irvine.
Lowney, C. (2022). Four ways of understanding mystical experience. In L. Weed (Ed.), *Mysticism, ineffability and silence.* Palgrave MacMillan Press.
MacKnee, C. M. (1999). *A description of practising Christians' experience of profound sexual and spiritual encounters.* Ottawa: National Library of Canada.
Maslow, A. H. (1961). Peak experiences as acute identity experiences. *American Journal of Psychoanalysis, 21*(2), 254–262.
Maslow, A. H. (1964). *Religions, values, and peak-experiences.* Columbus, OH: Ohio State University Press.
Maslow, A. H. (1970). New introduction: Religions, values, and peak-experiences. *Journal of Transpersonal Psychology, 2*(2), 83–90.
Maslow, A. H. (1974). Cognition of being in the peak experiences. In *Readings in human development: A humanistic approach* (pp. 83–106). Ardent Media.
Maslow, A. H. (1976). Theory Z. *Journal of Transpersonal Psychology, 1*(2), 31–47. Reprinted in Maslow, A. H. (1976). *The farther reaches of human nature* (pp. 270–286). New York: Penguin.

May, K. (2020). *Wintering: How I learned to flourish when life became frozen*. London: Rider.
May, R. M. (1991). *Cosmic consciousness revisited: The modern origins and development of a Western spiritual psychology*. Two Totem Press.
Mishra, N. (2019). Long walk of peace: Missing dimensions. *Policy & Practice: A Development Education Review*, (28), 1–20.
Nye, R., & Hay, D. (1996). Identifying children's spirituality: How do you start without a starting point? *British Journal of Religious Education*, *18*, 144–154.
Pahnke, W. (1980). Drugs and mysticism. In J. R. Tisdale (Ed.), *Growing edges in the psychology of religion*. Chicago: Nelson Hall.
Perry, G., Polito, V., & Thompson, W. F. (2021). Rhythmic chanting and mystical states across traditions. *Brain Sciences*, *11*(1), 101.
The Poems of St John of the Cross (1951). The Spanish text with a translation by R. Campbell. Preface by M. C. D'Arcy, S.J. London: Harvill Press.
Rahtz, E., Warber, S. L., Goldingay, S., & Dieppe, P. (2021). Transcendent experiences among pilgrims to Lourdes: A qualitative investigation. *Journal of Religion and Health*, *60*(6), 3788–3806.
Ronkainen, N. J., & Nesti, M. S. (2018). *Meaning and spirituality in sport and exercise*. London, UK: Routledge.
Rosenblatt, H. S. (1977). The humanness of two abrahams. *Journal of Religion and Health*, *16*, 22–25.
School Curriculum and Assessment Authority (SCAA). (1995). *Spiritual and moral development: A discussion paper*. London: SCAA Publications.
Stoeber, M. (2017). The comparative study of mysticism. *Oxford Research Encyclopaedia of Religion*. https://doi.org/10.1093/acrefore/9780199340378.013.93
Suzuki, D. T. (1961). *Essays in Zen Buddhism, first series* (Vol. 309). Grove Press.
Tanyi, R. A. (2002). Towards clarification of the meaning of spirituality. *Journal of Advanced Nursing*, *39*(5), 500–509.
Taylor, S. (2017). The return of perennial perspectives? Why transpersonal psychology should remain open to essentialism. *International Journal of Transpersonal Studies*, *36*(2), 75–92.
Warmoth, A. (1965). A note on the peak experience as a personal myth. *Journal of Humanistic Psychology*, *5*(1), 18–21.
Watson, N. (2011). Introduction. In S. Fanous & V. Gillespie (Eds.), *The Cambridge companion to medieval English mysticism* (pp. 1–28). Cambridge: Cambridge University Press.
Watson, N., & Parker, A. (2015). The mystical and sublime in extreme sports: Experiences of psychological well-being or Christian revelation. *Studies in World Christianity*, *21*(3), 260–281.
Watts, A. (1989). *The way of Zen*. New York, NY: Vintage Books.
Weijers, K. A. (2021). *Peak moments: The experience of coaches*. Doctoral Dissertation, Oxford Brookes University.
Woods, R. (1980). *Understanding mysticism*. London: The Athlone Press.
Yaden, D. B., Haidt, J., Hood, R. W., Jr., Vago, D. R., & Newberg, A. B. (2017). The varieties of self-transcendent experience. *Review of General Psychology*, *21*(2), 143–160.

2 Peak Experiences in Writing and Reading

Introduction

In this chapter, we examine peak experiences associated with writing and reading works of literature. Our motivation for researching such experiences is connected to our own peak experiences in this context, those memorable moments that very occasionally result from engagement with the written word. These are moments of great joy and delight that are stimulated by the writing, particularly of great literary authors. William James commented similarly that:

> In listening to poetry, drama, or heroic narrative, we are often surprised at the cutaneous shiver which like a sudden wave flows over us, and at the heart-swelling and the lachrymal effusion that unexpectedly catch us at intervals.
> (James, 1884, p. 196)

Through examination of the very broad research base, we found that the commentary on works of literature, both fiction and poetry, is replete with parallel terminology used to describe peak experiences. Terms that include:

- "the blazing moment" which is Katherine Mansfield's phrase (Kimber, 2014);
- "the essence of things," the expression Marcel Proust uses in his masterpiece, *À la recherche du temps perdu* (1913–27, p. 909);
- "moments of being," adopted by Virginia Woolf (1985) – experiences of rupture that destabilise consciousness and thereby escape it;
- "spots of time," which is Wordsworth's description of transcendent moments (1805);
- "literary epiphany," highlighted in the work of modernist author James Joyce (1992).

Following the writer and academic Geoff Ward, we consider these terms to be analogous and used to describe the same experience – that is, the peak experience identified by Maslow:

> I believe epiphany and the peak experience – along with transcendent ecstasy, mystical experience, cosmic consciousness, awakening experience

DOI: 10.4324/9781003509219-3

or breakthrough or power consciousness, to give some of the other terms used – merely to be different names for what is essentially the same phenomenon undergone by individuals at varying degrees of intensity.

(Ward, 2011, p. 276)

Ward goes on to say that even if the mystical experience or "oneness with the universe" is absent from the secular epiphany, "it still provides the subject with a moment of profound insight or revelation" (2011, p. 276).

In this chapter, since much of the research of the phenomenon uses the word "epiphany," we also adopt this term, using it as a counterpart to peak experience. Epiphany derives from the Greek word *epiphaneia* and has been used in a secular context to describe a moment of recognition or alteration: "an experience of profound personal transformation resulting in the reconfiguration of an individuals' world assumptions" (Jarvis, 1996, p. 61).

Our review of the research is presented in two sections, Literary Epiphany and Peak Experience and the Reader. Literary epiphany relates to writing and how authors characterise peak experiences or epiphanies in their poetry, for example, by portraying their own experiences or by depicting peak experiences for the characters in their novels. This technique of "literary epiphany" will then be illustrated through extracts from pertinent works of literature. In the second section, the somewhat less examined question of whether peak experiences may occur for the reader is discussed. Following this review of research, we present the peak experiences or epiphanies of our contributors, who are either readers or writers or both.

Literary Epiphany

During our review of the literature, we examined efforts to theorise peak experience in relation to literary writing. We identified a tradition where authors convey their own peak experiences through a technique known as "literary epiphany" and give examples from classical literature to illustrate particular aspects of the phenomenon. To clarify these aspects, we have identified three categories of experiences: the first concerns the historical shift in conceptualisation of epiphanies towards "experiences of secular significance"; the second relates to literary epiphanies as "experiences of recollection"; and the third examines how literary epiphanies are seen as "experiences of revelation."

Literary Epiphanies as Experiences of Significance for Authors

In this category, we recognise the perceived shift in epiphanic emphasis from the sacred to the secular. Nichols (1999), for example, explained a shift from authorial descriptions of epiphany in earlier religious, or Romantic, texts to a Modernist and secular presentation of epiphany where language and imagery are used to suggest significance:

> [Authors] present powerful verbal images that are never "explained"; instead, these epiphanic images are left to "speak" for themselves. In such instances,

cognitive aspects of human experience are transformed, via literary language, into moments of resonance more significant for having occurred in a mind (brain) than for any precise "meaning" they might contain.

(1999, p. 469)

Nichols thus separates modern epiphanies from earlier descriptions or visions of epiphany and characterises them as "momentary manifestations of significance in ordinary experience" (1987, p. 21) rather than liminal or sacred events. In classical epic poetry, the concept of liminality is a vital element of epiphany. According to Risden (2008), epic poets used meetings with divine beings or crossings of other significant liminal boundaries or encounters with elemental aspects of nature "to provide their characters (and thus audiences) with access to information or power" (2008, p. 64). Risden pointed out that the use of liminality highlights the transitional nature of epiphany and emphasises its sense of being on the threshold of something. Taking Nichols's separation a step further, Burke (2010, p. 172) explains how in the literary, "character-based," notion of the word, epiphany involves "a sudden manifestation or perception of the essence or meaning of something" rather than engagement with the divine.

In her book exploring the "space between," Johnson (1992) also differentiated between the depiction of classic "illuminated moments," like the mystical experiences described in St. Augustine or William Blake, suggesting they convey only the fact that a vision occurred. By contrast, Johnson explained how modern authors and poets, for example Wordsworth, intentionally construct the epiphany for readers:

The literary epiphany works upon the reader, forcing him into an experienced moment, while the vision is a literary moment experienced or "read" by the reader from what could be deemed the "outside" of the moment. The writer describes his vision; the reader recognizes the description but does not physically experience the vision.

(Johnson, 1992, p. 8)

In other words, a visionary moment like Blake's is an experience shared with his readers rather than one created for them. Alfred Lord Tennyson (1991, p. 328) shared similar epiphanies in his poem 'The Ancient Sage' for example:

More than once when I
Sat all alone, revolving in myself,
The mortal limit of the self was loosed,
And passed into the nameless, as a cloud
Melts into heaven. I touch'd my limbs, the limbs
Were strange, not mine – and yet no shade of doubt
But utter clearness, and thro' loss of self
The gain of such large life as matched with ours
Were sun to spark – unshadowable in words,
Themselves but shadows of a shadow-world.

To differentiate modern epiphany from the traditional vision-focused epiphanies, Langbaum (1999) introduced four criteria that seem pertinent and chime with Maslow's notion of peak experience:

- The first of these affirms that the epiphany is "not an incursion of God from outside; it is a psychological phenomenon arising from a real sensuous experience, either present or recollected" (1999, p. 44).
- The second states that "the epiphany lasts only a moment but leaves an enduring effect" (1999, p. 44).
- A third criterion relates to the "sudden change in external conditions cause[ing] a shift in sensuous perception that sensitizes the observer for epiphany" (1999, p. 44).
- The fourth relates specifically to literary writing, is that "the text never quite equals the epiphany" (1999, p. 44).

Langbaum summarises the experience of epiphany quite succinctly as "a momentary psychological phenomenon arising from sensuous experience and leaving a lasting effect; a felt shift in sensual perception" (1999, p. 44). Similarly, in Tigges's words (1999, p. 23), such events can "transform a past experience to produce a new sense of significance."

Chappell (2019) also characterises the epiphany but sets out eight conditions, some of which can be seen discussed in the work of Maslow (1962a, 1962b), Privette (1983), Laski (1980), and Weijers (2021). To Chappell, the epiphany must be overwhelming; existentially significant; of value; often sudden or surprising; feels like it comes from the outside; teaches us something new; takes us out of ourselves; or demands a response.

These conditions or directions, Chappell argues, do not all have to be fulfilled in all occurrences of epiphanies. They are, what she calls, "focal case" categories in that the experiences do not need to fulfil all the conditions to still be "clear and central cases of epiphanies" (2019, p. 97). She further suggests there are other "less clear and less central cases, which we might still want to call epiphanies" and that it does not matter where we draw the boundaries around the correct use of the term epiphany: "the central territory of the concept is not threatened by minor demarcation disputes about its borders" (2019, p. 97).

Literary Epiphanies as Experiences of Recollection

In his 1999 essay, Barfoot wrote that in literary terms, there are three interpretations of epiphany: i) the disclosure of the sacred in the mundane; ii) the disclosure of profound significance in the everyday (where the mundane opens to reveal the transcendent); and iii) an experience recalled, like Wordsworth's "spots of time," which tend not to be meaningful at the time but take on meaning when recalled in a new context.

Using an example from Proust (1913–1927), we can follow Marcel's epiphany in the context of taking tea with his mother and see many of the conditions of

Chappell's epiphany bound up in that one experience – the surprise, the overwhelm, the transcendent nature of the experience. We also see a mundane, early childhood experience taking on fresh meaning as it is recollected in a different milieu.

> She sent for one of those squat, plump little cakes called "petites madeleines," which look as though they had been moulded in the fluted valve of a scallop shell. And soon, mechanically, dispirited after a dreary day with the prospect of a depressing morrow, I raised to my lips a spoonful of the tea in which I had soaked a morsel of the cake. No sooner had the warm liquid mixed with the crumbs touched my palate than a shudder ran through me and I stopped, intent upon the extraordinary thing that was happening to me. An exquisite pleasure had invaded my senses, something isolated, detached, with no suggestion of its origin. And at once the vicissitudes of life had become indifferent to me, its disasters innocuous, its brevity illusory – this new sensation having had on me the effect which love has of filling me with a precious essence; or rather this essence was not in me it *was* me. I had ceased now to feel mediocre, contingent, mortal. Whence could it have come to me, this all-powerful joy? I sensed that it was connected with the taste of the tea and the cake, but that it infinitely transcended those savours, and could not indeed be of the same nature. Whence did it come? What did it mean? How could I seize and apprehend it?
>
> I drink a second mouthful, in which I find nothing more than in the first, then a third, which gives me rather less than the second. It is time to stop; the potion is losing its magic. It is plain that the truth I am seeking lies not in the cup but in myself.
>
> (Proust, 1913–27, pp. 48–51)

Marcel has several attempts at replaying the experience, lamenting his failure and sharing his efforts to capture the experience once more until he reaches a perception of the essential nature of the event:

> And suddenly the memory revealed itself. The taste was that of the little piece of madeleine which on Sunday mornings at Combray (because on those mornings I did not go out before mass), when I went to say good morning to her in her bedroom, my aunt Léonie used to give me, dipping it first in her own cup of tea or tisane.
>
> (Proust, 1913–27, pp. 48–51)

Nichols explains how "powerful recollections from childhood can erase years in an instant and provide a way of seeming to live for a moment 'outside' of time" (Nichols, 1987, p. 72). It was this phenomenon that so enthralled Proust and drove his life's work. However, any attempts to repeat the peak experience, despite it being remembered as important and desirable, would, according to Maslow, inevitably be doomed to failure (1959, 1962a, 1962b).

Frick (2001) would call Marcel's experience of the madeleine an example of "symbolic latency," a phenomenon that involves identifying "certain powerful images and emotions of youth and childhood that remain latent in their meaning until brought to fruition through additional experience and emotional readiness" (2001, p. 10). And yet, the very fact that Marcel has had the peak experience (or epiphany) and written a whole classic trilogy around it suggests that it had the power to influence the rest of his life – even if the elusive moment so evaded re-creation.

Langbaum (1999, p. 43) explains how Proust's novel is built upon experiences of what is called involuntary memory, "moments in which the past returns and overwhelms the present." He considers Proust's epiphanies to be closest to Wordsworth's in that they are "mainly delayed epiphanies, epiphanies of recollection, moments triggered by a present event and occurring after the original experience, which was not itself an epiphany." He discusses how the psychological association between present and past events "causes the original experience to return as a delayed epiphany – a moment of recollection in which spatial reality is dematerialized through the free-floating perspective of time" (Langbaum, 1999, p. 43).

Thus, Wordsworth's poetry, like Proust's prose, embodies the idea that peak experiences or epiphanies have a continuing pull on our lives. These lines from Wordsworth's "Daffodils" are the most famous example:

For oft, when on my couch I lie
In vacant or in pensive mood,
They flash upon that inward eye
Which is the bliss of solitude;
And then my heart with pleasure fills,
And dances with the daffodils.

So it appears the daffodils were not just a "one off" epiphany for Wordsworth, rather, just as Marcel's memory of the madeleine sustained him, the lasting memory had the power to nourish and restore Wordsworth's mood. Proust's experience of tasting the madeleine is also a good example of Barfoot's third interpretation, an experience recalled. However, we might question whether it is in fact an example of epiphany or whether it is just how the brain facilitates our sense of smell and makes connections, albeit involuntarily, with the memory. Research (e.g., Buck, 2004) has identified how scents and tastes are detected by receptor neurons in the nose. These send information about scents to the part of the brain called the olfactory bulb just above the nasal cavity, which then sends signals to another brain structure called the piriform cortex where odour recognition occurs.

Chappell (2019) talked about the significance of small things that bring joy – small epiphanies like smelling fresh coffee or seeing a flower – but goes on to argue that it would be too overwhelming for us to have such peak experiences all the time. This, she suggests, accounts for their rarity. Just as Proust wished he could just drink his tea and think "merely of the worries of today" (1913–27, pp. 48–51), Chappell considers "the richness of reality can be overwhelming; and often the cognitive difficulty is evidently not so much to grasp it, as to avoid grasping too much of it" (2019, p. 100). She clarifies how this reduced awareness or sensitivity is vital for our survival, explaining how a lot of what is "potentially epiphanic in our lived experience never makes it into explicit consciousness because it is never attentionally selected." To get on with the quotidian, she says "we need to filter the epiphanic" (2019, p. 101).

Chappell also suggests that epiphanies can teach us new things, or they can merely remind us of what we already know. She points out the difference between aha-moments and wow-moments, arguing that aha-moments are more concerned with "epistemic breakthroughs" and are more "cognitively loaded" than wow-moments. Both give answers to our questions, but wow-moments are like epiphanies in that they may answer questions that we are not asking, or they may just "strike us as deeply existentially significant yet have no clear propositional meaning" at all (2019, p. 102). This might be, she indicates, because the significance of the experience is beyond verbal articulation.

Literary Epiphanies as Experiences of Revelation

The subtitle of Beja's (1971) book on epiphany in the modern novel is *Revelation as Art*. This is important for our understanding of the development of the use of epiphany in the writing context, since previously it had been customary to view "art as revelation." What Beja is implying is that the use of epiphany to reveal aspects of character or plot has become an art form. Thus, the literary epiphany, as a moment of revelation, has been deliberately used as a shaping technique by many modern writers. The epiphanic moment allows them to deepen and enrich protagonists' characters and subjectivity. As long ago as 1919, the short story writer, Katherine Mansfield explained that she used what she called the "blazing moment" to reveal the focus of conflict, crisis, and often irony in her work. A good example of this revelatory "blazing" moment appears in her short story titled "Bliss":

> What can you do if you're 30 and, turning the corner of your own street, you are overcome, suddenly, by a feeling of bliss – absolute bliss – as though you'd suddenly swallowed a bright piece of that late afternoon?
>
> (Mansfield, 1981)

The device of literary epiphany thus intensifies fictional or poetic writing through flashes of sudden clarity and emphasis that can significantly change characters and plots. Authors manipulate their characters to suddenly see things in a new light.

One of the most frequently cited examples of a literary epiphany is presented by Joyce in *A Portrait of the Artist as a Young Man* (1992), where he describes Stephen Dedalus's epiphany, as he observes a beautiful young girl wading in Dublin Bay.

> Her image had passed into his soul forever and no word had broken the holy silence of his ecstasy. Her eyes had called to him, and his soul had leaped at the call. To live, to err, to fall, to triumph, to recreate life out of life! A wild

angel had appeared to him, the angel of mortal youth and beauty, an envoy from fair courts of life, to throw open before him in an instant of ecstasy the gates of all the ways of error and glory. On and on and on and on!

(186)

Frick (2001) summarised Joyce's notion of epiphany as a "subject-object interaction," whereby the manifestation of the epiphany could be seen (or written), first, as an object of experience, that is the physical event that offers itself to the watcher (in our example, the girl wading in the water) and second, to complete the epiphany, as a conjunction made between that object and the watcher (in this case, Stephen) as subject of the experience. Frick explains how the object of the experience acts back on and transforms the subject so that the "distinction and distance between subject and object, between person and environment vanishes" (2001, p. 25). This loss of boundary is evoked in the previous Joyce quote. Psychologists and philosophers such as Wilber (2001) have, according to Frick, "established this vanishing boundary as central to their thought and writing, concluding that there is an essential unity, or a potential for unity, between the person and the environment" (2001, p. 25).

Langbaum has also pointed out that epiphany is a "necessary concomitant of realism" (1999, p. 38) and argues that rather than merely describing an experience, Wordsworth re-created the epiphany for the reader. Thus, as the innovator of the epiphanic mode, Wordsworth influenced twentieth-century authors such as Joyce, although Joyce is usually considered the first to use the term epiphany to denote "a psychological and literary mode of perception" (Langbaum, 1983, p. 341).

Despite Wordsworth's realist reputation, we would argue that such *recreation* is still only his account of his epiphany (whether truly experienced or conjured for his poetry) and that it will not necessarily produce epiphany in the reader. Similarly, as noted earlier, Beja (1971) claims the epiphany is irrelevant to the object or incident that triggers it and may be triggered by a quite trivial object or incident. Tigges appears to agree, explaining that "epiphanies only occur with involuntary memory/a sudden recall (unpremeditated and unmediated)" (1999, p. 20).

In the next section of this chapter, we discuss further how trigger objects and incidents for epiphanies are idiosyncratic, involving direct engagement with the senses and often arising from conscious or unconscious memories of the experiencer.

Peak Experience and the Reader

In the first section, we saw how Joyce, Mansfield, and other early twentieth-century authors used literary epiphanies as techniques of characterisation. In the following subsection, we briefly recap what Nichols (1987) called "rhetorical epiphanies," which may be used overtly as literary devices to promote or provoke epiphany in the reader. However, we will discuss in the second subsection whether a recollected epiphany can produce a peak experience for the reader. We contend that a peak experience or epiphany relies on idiosyncratic memories, and so poets and authors can never be sure that sharing their actual experience or constructing an experience for a character will generate the same peak experience for the reader. There is thus a difference between *sharing epiphanies with* the reader and *provoking epiphanies in* the reader.

Rhetorical Epiphany as Literary Device

Nichols summarised how authors attempt to create epiphanies for readers. He suggests that in a literary epiphany "the isolated moment of one individual's immediate experience becomes *a potential source of value* in the minds of others" (1987, p. 34, our emphasis). Here, Nichols recognises that rhetorical epiphanies help to build a Self or identity for the protagonist or other characters. Biographical events in the story are thus turned into what he calls "verbal archetypes."

According to Tigges, the "epiphanee" (1999, p. 32) can be the writer, a character, a reader, or a combination. In Mansfield's *The Garden Party*, for example, the dialogue is deliberately paused as the character, Laura Sheridan, is invited in to look at the dead body of a workman who lived down the lane. Her epiphany comes from her recognition of the beauty and diversity of life and how death, as closure, is part of that, while the description itself is full of juxtapositions, designed to unsettle or even shock the reader.

> There lay a young man fast asleep – sleeping so soundly, so deeply, that he was far, far away from them both. Oh, so remote, so peaceful. He was dreaming. Never wake him up again. His head was sunk in the pillow, his eyes were closed; they were blind under the closed eyelids. He was given up to his dream. What did garden parties and baskets and lace frocks matter to him? He was far from those things. He was wonderful, beautiful. While they were laughing and while the band was playing, this marvel had come to the lane. Happy . . . happy . . . All is well, said that sleeping face. This is as it should be. I am content.
>
> (Mansfield, 1981, p. 251)

Mansfield's attempt at surprising her readers by involving them in Laura's experience of death and her ensuing revelation could be seen as a privilege, or, as Bidney expresses it, a gift of vision, "when one's feeling of aliveness intensifies and the senses quicken" (1997, p. 1). Also, it exemplifies several of Chappell's (2019) criteria, especially its existential significance, its value, and the surprise and shock it may induce for readers.

In her seminal work on transactional reader response theory, Rosenblatt (1994) suggests that until readers engage with a novel or poem, awakening it with their own blend of interest and experience, the text will lie dormant:

> The reading of a text is an event occurring at a particular time in a particular environment at a particular moment in the life history of the reader. The transaction will involve not only the past experience but also the present state and present interests or preoccupations of the reader.
>
> (1994, p. 20)

A text is therefore brought to life only by readers remaking it through their own unique interpretation. Rosenblatt further argues that the text should not be confused with an entity existing apart from the author or reader, since the transaction is between the reader and what he/she senses the words are pointing to:

> The paradox is that he (sic) must call forth from memory of his world what the visual or auditory stimuli symbolize for him, yet he feels the ensuing work as part of the world outside himself. The physical signs of the text enable him to reach through himself and the verbal symbols to something sensed as outside and beyond his own personal world. The boundary between inner and outer world breaks down, and the literary work of art, as so often remarked, leads us into a new world. It becomes part of the experience which we bring to our future encounters in literature and in life.
>
> (1994, p. 21)

The text and the reader's own affective inputs can thus be seen as interacting flexibly with implicit and explicit memories so that the activity of reading simultaneously involves interactional mental processes and representations resulting in different emotions and motivations (Burke, 2010). Burke captures this cross-cortical nature of literary processing in a new term, "oceanic cognition' and gives the example of the twentieth-century beat-generation poet Allen Ginsberg recalling his reading of *Ah! Sunflower* by William Blake in the 1940s. Here Richman (1985) is recounting Ginsberg's reflection on how, during his reading of the closing lines of the poem, he suddenly went into an altered state of consciousness:

> My body suddenly felt light, and a sense of cosmic consciousness, vibrations, understanding, awe, and wonder and surprise. Kind of like the top of my head coming off, letting in the rest of the universe connected to my own brain.
>
> (Richman, 1985, p. 60)

Langbaum (1999, p. 55) argued that "the richness of sensuous texture" of creative writing makes it possible for readers, such as Ginsberg in this example, to participate in the epiphany, because they feel the interplay on their own senses. He explained how, in many instances of rhetorical epiphany, an author does not "tell the reader the story but plays upon him (sic) as though he were a musical instrument – making him move through a series of associations that will produce the epiphany in him" (1999, p. 48). Even though this is not entirely borne out by our own research, Langbaum, claimed a reader's response to an epiphany devised by the author, can be quite powerful and the emotions aroused can go beyond the scope of the literary work itself.

Reader Epiphanies as Individual and Personal

In this section we want to question further whether writing about a peak experience, either by sharing it or constructing it, produces an epiphany or peak moment for the reader.

Acknowledging Damasio (1999) and the link between bodily experience and cognition we affirm that, since peak experiences involve bodily sensations, emotions, and intuitions, these are also ways of knowing that inform our reflecting and thinking. Thus, by recalling their own feelings and emotions during a peak moment, authors are able to write in a way that creates an epiphany for the characters in the novel or poem.

More recently, literary scholar Nigel Fabb (2021, p. 2) has explained that literature has a special status in relation to what he terms "experiences of ineffable significance," including the possibility that the representation of a character having such an experience "can trigger a similar experience in the reader." He discusses the quite rare experience of reading that involves sudden feelings of coming to know something "very significant but which cannot be described in words" (2021, p. 2). Such experiences, he explains, might even be associated with "emotional arousal, such as chills or tears."

Fabb (2021) also confirmed that literary epiphany could be seen as elaborated surprise, achieving its effects by either violating our expectations or trying to be seen as inconsistent with our existing knowledge. Proposing a unified account of how such experiences could occur, Fabb (2021, p. 3) questions what cognitive processes might lead them to be considered "full of significance and importance" and why the knowledge gained from them is sometimes described as "inarticulate or ineffable." He suggests this could be triggered by surprise. However, he also argues that the occurrence of such significant reader experiences, and their rarity, must depend on "*the contribution of context*" (our emphasis) and is why different readers will have different reading experiences.

This emphasis on the "transient and contingent factors associated with the moment of experience, the environment, the experiencer's body, the experiencer's cognitive context" (Fabb, 2021, p. 5) suggests to us that elements of significance, surprise, or shock could be produced for individual readers at any point in the book, not necessarily via the reading of an author's planned epiphany, however genuine. Dutoit (1999, p. 98) similarly stressed how seeing is different from reading and explained how an epiphanic moment is linked with unconscious and involuntary "seeing," as opposed to the conscious reading of the visual representation.

Barfoot, in the same vein, confirmed that literary epiphanies are "first literature and then epiphanies" and asked to what extent examples of epiphany in poetry, for example, are designed to create effect (1999, p. 65) rather than recounted as true experience:

> As readers we are not in the position of knowing to what extent moments of insight, which we might be inclined to describe as epiphanic, have been stage managed by the poet: the rhetoric of casualness, of accident and incidental occurrence, which one finds in Wordsworth and Coleridge is still a rhetoric and no more guarantees the "genuineness" of an event of an emotion outside the text of the poem than . . . more deliberate rhetoric
>
> (pp. 65–66)

In further attempts to theorise the epiphanic phenomenon, Beja (1971) introduced two terms, "incongruity" and "insignificance," as definitional criteria. Incongruity, as a concept, encompasses the idea that "an epiphany is irrelevant to the object or incident that triggers it" (1971, pp. 16–17), while Beja's second term implies that an epiphany can be triggered by a trivial object or incident with no particular significance. If this is accurate, then the fact that epiphanies can be generated by irrelevant and inconsequential objects or events suggests to us that authors' very carefully constructed literary epiphanies may be missing the mark for their readers. Even though we may appreciate the portrayal of the epiphany and even identify with it, we will not *experience* it unless it produces a real-world surprise for us – it cannot be experienced vicariously. For as Langbaum explained: "involved in all epiphanies is both discovery and the shock of recognition – recognition of the self in the external world" (1999, p. 57). Reading someone else's shock of recognition, we would argue, cannot produce that feeling for us. It has to be ours. The "spot of time" identified by Wordsworth is a spot in one person's time, one person's memory or consciousness – made sublime not by reading another's words, however carefully constructed, but by connection with something individual and personal that makes us feel our past. It may be a memory, it may be conscious or unconscious, but it has to be ours.

Peak Experience in Context – Participant Accounts

In this section, participants who each have meaningful relationships with literature, either writing or reading, share their experiences.

Sarah Taylor, who we will meet again later in Chapter 8, recalled the time she bought a book that was totally alien to her normal reading taste, yet it seemed to seek her out. She began reading it but initially hated what it was saying. For some reason, it was so provoking to her that she threw it across the room several times. But when she reached one particular chapter, something told her just to keep going. She was reading about a man's life and his connection to God or spirit, and how once when he was in a cinema, he got up and went to a bookshop and bought a book and then went back to the cinema. In the chapter, he recalled how the book he bought on that day totally changed his life.

It was when Sarah read that, it totally "freaked her out" because she had done the same thing herself – left a cinema, gone into a bookshop, bought a book, and returned to the cinema. She got goosebumps and started shaking. Then, as she continued to read, questions which her mother had failed to answer when she was a child were answered; questions about existence were satisfied in a way that made total sense. Everything fell into place. Sarah hit a wave of ecstasy, and the whole world seemed to disappear for a moment; she melted into everything, and everything melted into her.

Sarah thinks that at that moment she experienced a oneness with the universe, a total melding of everything. She felt no fear, nor was she scared anymore. There was a complete understanding of who she was, what she was, and why she was there.

This account is interesting because Sarah's experience provoked an emotional response in her that went beyond the scope of the book she was reading. Endorsing Fabb's (2021) theory, the surprise Sarah experienced was not produced deliberately by the author of the book as a "planned epiphany" but was contingent on her environment and her own cognitive context.

***

Alison Fure is a field ecologist and blogger who writes nature blogs and chapbooks. Also, she leads wildlife walks and, more recently, soundwalks that involve listening to the environment. In 2020, she did the famous walk undertaken by the nineteenth-century poet, John Clare from Epping to Northborough. Alison is a huge fan of Clare's work, and here we see how her peak epiphany moments from her readings of Clare are interlinked with her sense of place and passion for nature:

> When I read something profound, I want to "ground-truth" it. It is usually connected to the natural world in some way and becomes part of a "read-see-write" or "read-see-perform" as some of my creative work is performance.

So when Alison reads the works of John Clare, she identifies strongly with the places he describes and wants to make those journeys and see those places. She says there are "features that connect us over time and belong to us such as drove roads, national trails and footpaths. They are quiet, traffic free, vegetated, unlit and used only by wildlife." This identification is especially strong for her when she reads lines such as "Enclosure like a Bonaparte let not a thing remain, It levelled every bush and tree and levelled every hill And hung the moles for traitors" (Clare, 1986). As an ecologist, Alison, measures hedgerow biodiversity and recognises the newer enclosure hedges as they are often low in species diversity, straight rather than haphazard, and not as thick as ancient hedgerows.

Alison recounts her peak experience on the first day of her recce for retracing John Clare's famous walk from Epping. The experience occurred when she was physically standing outside the old asylum at High Beech where John Clare was interned, when she actually sensed his presence there. She saw him seated by the pond in the cobbled garden and noticed his face at the window, "in belligerent mood, looking at the unchanged landscape, wanting to go out unaccompanied."

She explains how the build-up to this experience must have been her many years of reading the complete works of Clare and visiting his house in Helpston. Alison conveys how his poem "Journey Out of Essex" had a particular influence on her wanting to undertake the walk, as she knew many of those places herself. However, Clare's route had changed over time, and it was not possible to walk the exact route: "For me, this was now a great perambulation of 140 miles, not the 80 miles that Clare undertook."

Also, Alison notes how physically she learnt a new way of walking during this time and describes this as a peak experience:

[A] kind of release of the hips, a swagger. It is not something that happens when you are studying maps or puzzling about the best route or hating Huntingdon for its abuse of its station with the concrete flyover. It happens when all that lifts, and lifts when least expected – and only when you hit the open road. It gives heightened awareness, a vivid technicolour. I am not tired, I have no needs. I walked 24 miles from Hertford North to Baldock arriving without feeling anxious, wet, cold, hungry, just thrilled at seeing the Clothall Road and its tumbleweeds.

Moreover, Alison shares how when she rereads the original texts of her own writing at that time, she is "transported to those moments and it plays like a film. I can smell the Owl pub, I re-find the riding crop, buried under leaves in Bury Hill Wood."

For Alison, the realisation that the landscape of Epping Forest has not changed in 200 years is also very special: "John Clare walked around these same trees in Bury Hill Wood." Also, she took a list of actions to complete on the walk: these were mentioned by Clare in "Journey Out of Essex and are exemplified in her own poem "Out of Epping." For example, Alison had walked through an industrial estate realising she was at the end of the walk and remembered: "I hadn't found an acorn, but then suddenly there it was – a magical moment when a semi-mature oak was found on the grass verge."

Alison explains how "ground-truthing" is the process of confirming, by direct observation *on the ground*, the reality of a situation, as opposed to what other intelligence or data reports about it. She describes it as "finding the location and turning it inside out – smelling it, touching it and watching the juice ooze out. Older landscapes give up their truths more readily than highly modified ones."

She explains how when she read Jane Jacobs's exploration in the *Sidewalk Ballet* (Jacobs, 1961, p. 71), she wanted to look for evidence of those street dynamics in her own neighbourhood and then write or express them in another way as a performance. Alison shares that peak experiences prompt her creative writing, explaining that they are something that "often switches on during a visit to a site," but then the writing, the "fleshing out," is undertaken on the journey home and the fine-tuning undertaken immediately after: "It can only happen when I am alone, not when there are lots of voices around me. It is a solitary activity." For example, she says, "I wrote the key words of *Beating of the Bounds* in a café immediately after the group walk with Radical Stroud, and I wrote the prose on the train going home."

Other peak experiences connected to reading or writing are recalled as well. Last year, Alison decided to visit the demesne of another favourite author and musician of hers, the late Roger Deakin. Deakin wrote *Waterlog*, a sensual account of his wild swimming experiences, and Alison remembers particularly how he described his swim through the lode at Wicken Fen. She was so inspired that she had to "ground-truth" his reminiscences by holidaying at his farm, staying in a caravan at Walnut Farm in Suffolk, and playing his music: "I swam and swam in his moat with the ovipositing blue damsel flies," she says, "and I felt like a warrior."

Alison recalled other peak-like experiences when she saw 20,000 bats leaving caves in Cuba or 6,000 greater mouse-eared bats leaving a church in Slovakia. But she explains that these experiences involved feelings of awe or wonder rather than the empowerment she felt after reading John Clare and walking in his footsteps or wild swimming in Deakin's moat.

***

Christine Eastman is an academic and writer focusing on how literary works can be used as a pedagogical tool. She explains how teaching others how to read in order to write has been her entire professional life's work. Her books (Eastman, 2016, 2018) examine how the reading and study of essays and novels can enhance student learning and how literary works can transform coaching practice.

Whereas Alison identified strongly with particular authors and the places they mobilise, Christine recognises the power of "becoming one with a character." She says that "although it can be harrowing and painful at times," and gives examples such as Mary in *The Rector's Daughter* (Mayor, 2021), "the experience of being on an emotional rollercoaster and vicariously living in another era is the most stimulating feeling imaginable. One abandons oneself fully into the consciousness of a fictionalised entity which is a privilege."

Christine's first peak experience when reading involved identification with James in Roald Dahl's *James and The Giant Peach*, which she read when she was nine or ten years old. This experience involves the memory of her physical surroundings and her identification with the character of James:

> I remember exactly where I read it – on my parents' enclosed back porch, and when – in the growing dusk after a summer job of working on a farm, and I remember the excitement of loathing the gargoyle aunts and desiring James to overcome his seemingly insurmountable adversities. James epitomised the underdog for me, and I have always rooted for the underdog. I experienced a kaleidoscope of emotions: anger, fear, wonder, hatred, hope and relief.

Christine explains how her main motivation for reading is the desire to escape into another world:

> Entering into another world is bliss. In the absence of a fully functioning time machine, a supremely well-crafted book is the nearest thing we have to enable us to travel into the past. Naturally, entering into the emotional consciousness of a fictional character is a joy and honour. Great writers who are able to offer us this opportunity are gods to me.

The experience of reading has also given Christine a "why" as an educator. She says:

> I am evangelical about pioneering the use of literature to resolve organisational challenges: an engagement with literature hones our voices and makes us more reflective, sensitive, and confident practitioners of whatever field: there is wisdom between the pages of many books, and my role is to guide students to mine it. Problem solving is a valuable by-product of the simulative experience. Using fiction in coaching (and overall, in any discipline) enables students to reflect better on their lives. Literary texts are essential sources of data for comprehending other people and their motivations, thus they can help us solve problems.

Christine explains how inspiring it was when she shared Willa Cather's short story "Ardessa" (1973) with her master's sales students. Here she shares how the students had an epiphany or cognitive aha experience during their engagement with the text:

> I was thrilled to find a group of young to middle aged salesmen connecting with a fictional secretary (Ardessa) who has been demoted in her newspaper office job because of her lazy attitude to the work and bullying behaviour to younger female staff. The students perceived her as unable to adapt to a VUCA environment: she was out of her depth in this new volatile, uncertain, changing and ambiguous world. The story, written over 100 years ago, contained a multitude of contemporary themes the students wanted to pursue. The character Ardessa did not have a peak experience, but the students did. Some, for the first time, could see how fiction has a valuable role in organisational coaching and, in particular, leadership coaching.

Christine compared her own experiences with literature with her epiphanies in response to music. The first chords from Bryan Ferry's *Avalon*, for example, have her "re-experiencing the world as an innocent and hungry teenager again." She goes on to explain how peak experiences derived from music seem more ephemeral: "they are the exquisite connections with the younger 'you' and are different from the more lasting experiences of entering into a fictional character's universe."

***

Our final interview was with **Liz Wright,** whose PhD research involved imaginative ways to use fantasy and speculative literature for creating new leadership development models.

Liz explained how the two things she enjoys most about reading are i) the ability to absorb herself into another world, escaping from the current world and 'actually being in another world, a different world and experiencing that' and ii) getting ideas and enlarging the mind:

Reading literature is to put yourself in the mind of somebody else. And then you can imagine different things that you might not have imagined before. I enjoy that.

Also, she identified a third aspect, "it gives you more empathy into other people's situations or into the lonely human condition." Liz considered how reading is a bridge to other people's experiences and perceptions and a way out of our loneliness:

We are islands and what reading does is give us little ferries or bridges so that we can cross over into other people's islands and see the world from their perspective. And some of the bridges are quite big, like some of the classics, and they really change the way you see things. And some of the bridges are just little, tiny foot bridges, or tiny ferries and you can get a glimpse of another world without too much influence on your thinking or your feelings.

When she first considered peak experience, Liz was thinking of the best experience she has had rather than a sense of great uplifting joy or oneness with the universe. In the context of writing and reading, she has had very positive experiences – things that have changed her, but she shared how she had not had one where she had felt any sort of joy or transcendental awareness, which are the terms that she would equate with peak experience:

Certainly not in writing anyway. I don't think writing has been an area for me to achieve great joy. But I've cried when I've read books sometimes. When I look back on it, I can remember feeling awe or feeling huge sort of sorrow for some characters – Black Beauty (Sewell, 1877) being my first, I think. Plus, there's been massive amounts of influence from certain books, but I've never felt a sense of transcendental joy from reading. Nothing that's really lifted me.

Liz explained how reading is not about joy for her, but she acknowledged that she does get joy from being in the countryside or looking at flowers or a beautiful garden or listening to birds. She confirmed she wouldn't get that kind of joy from reading. What she would get from reading is

a peak experience in terms of opening my mind and seeing other people's experiences and suddenly understanding more – that to me is a wonderful thing. And that's why I do it – it's understanding and seeing and perceiving differently.

She thus believes the role of writing and reading is to "change the way you think, or it gives you the tools to think."

So, for example, Wordsworth's poem, what that does is give you a tool. In other words, he could be saying, "this is what happened to me, this is how I use my sensations of awe and this is how you could do it too." So, in other words, it's giving a mental tool.

Liz moreover wondered whether we need to experience something awesome through our senses but because in reading we are not actually using our senses, but rather using our mind, we cannot elicit awe from reading: "Maybe we must experience it directly through our senses – actually take it in in a physical way rather than a cognitive one."

Echoing Langbaum's observation that "the text never quite equals the epiphany" (1999, p. 44), Liz thinks that "maybe we're looking at two different things. Awe and transcendence are emotional sensations that come directly from our senses, whereas reading is a cerebral activity."

She recalled contexts where peak experiences may occur:

> So, let's just think about all the things we derive awe from being in nature, seeing nature, experiencing the wind on your face, and the perfume from flowers, or a huge cathedral perhaps might give you a sense of awe – a cathedral will have a certain smell, a certain air or certain feel to it. But I've got to say, I just haven't had that experience with literature.

Liz further reflected on whether, because a peak experience is a transitory sense of joy, literature hampers or obstructs the joy because it is more permanent. She explained how she has gone back to *Jane Eyre* all her life and thought about parts of it and has also thought about different aspects of Lord of the Rings or other books: "You know, with some books you go back and you think about it, and you perceive things differently each time."

The feeling of recognition Liz had when reading *Jude the Obscure* is another example. It gave her a sense of realisation about the impact of parenting:

> I just felt a real sense of recognition of the sort of chaos of the family situation and the amount of stuff coming through from the past. And intergenerational transmission of angst from previous generations was very strong for me in Jude. It made sense to me in terms of thinking about my own family and some of the things that they went through. Again, that's hardly a peak of peak experience – but it taught me an awful lot.
>
> So, it didn't give me a sense of awe even though it gave me a real sense of insight, and a real desire to make literature work for people, and to use it as a resource – as a greater resource than it currently is – and to make it accessible to everyone. Which is what I tried to do with Lord of the Rings in my PhD thesis – to use fantasy literature as a way of solving problems, and to have a more structured way of doing it. Because otherwise, it just doesn't always go anywhere. Let's give it a vehicle.

Liz then recalled Edwin Muir's poem, "The Horses," where he writes about the aftermath of an atomic war where people are giving up on everything, and then all of a sudden, a herd of wild horses come and live with them and give them renewed hope for the future:

> It's a wonderful poem that really makes you think about what things might be like, how we would cope and what is the role of animals. There are so many

things that we can reflect on in literature that it isn't necessarily good or bad. It's the furniture of our mind, I suppose. Maybe that's how literature works. It furnishes the mind with models and ideas that we come back to if they are sufficiently deep.

Liz could therefore see the utility value of literature but then questioned what evolutionary purpose a peak experience or a sense of joy or awe gives us. She could recognise the peak experience in terms of the birth of a new baby or a relationship – a joy in bonding. But queried whether this joy gives us an evolutionary tool like stories do. Then she shared an insight – perhaps peak experiences have a primal evolutionary purpose and through the senses are connected to how we survive as a species: awe and peak experiences may be connected to bonding and ultimately surviving – direct bonding with nature, bonding with the physical world, bonding with our environment:

> Maybe all transcendental sensations are more about providing the glue that sticks us to our lives, stick us to our place, stick us to our environment, stick us to each other or our home whereas stories are more an evolutionary tool that help us make sense, anticipate what is to come, think about possible options, understand our enemies. In which case you wouldn't expect joy to come necessarily from stories.

Asked where music would fit in this theory, Liz admitted that she does have more a sense of awe with music, "but then music is not filtered, not explained or shared in writing."

> There's that piano music by Shostakovich that he wrote for his son and it's very moving and very beautiful – or if you listen to one of Beethoven's symphonies or his concertos. I really love Vaughan Williams' *Fantasia on a Theme by Thomas Tallis*. Again, it's because music is coming directly via the senses – and that's why you don't get the same with literature because there are cognitive filters interfering with how you receive literature. Awe can come through art and music, nature, sport and sex, as they engage directly through your senses.

Later in the interview, Liz shared her very first feeling of awe – seemingly a Wordsworth moment which she just recalled as she looked at the yellow of the daffodils outside the window:

> I was about five and living in Salisbury. It was on the Earl of Longford's estate and so my mother let me go to school on my own in that safe environment. I remember one day on my way home going into a field of amazing buttercups and feeling an immense sense of awe at the beauty of one particular buttercup – the nature of it, the colour, the shininess and the intensity of it and thinking how intensely beautiful it was.

She emphasised how this example illustrates the importance of direct experience for children. Reading, writing, film, television, virtual reality, and even acting are all filtered experiences:

> You need to strip away everything that stands in the way of the perceiver and the awe. It's got to be naked experience without any filters. A raw immediate experience – you've got to experience it in that moment for yourself without anything in-between and then it touches the emotions.

Liz also raised the question of whether the ability to enjoy peak experiences could relate to personality type. How we experience situations and events may vary for different people she proposed: "because a peak moment for one personality type might be experienced totally differently for another, it's another filter, perhaps, that you could overlay on your peak moment." She wondered, for example, whether her experiences are different because she is an ENFP in Myers Briggs terms, whereas someone with a different combination of Myers Briggs- type indicators may experience more real joy from reading. She moreover felt it would be interesting to do some research with ACAI, the Coaching Adaptation Innovation Inventory, to see whether peak experiences are described differently by adapters or innovators:

> Perhaps there are filters or lenses that change the nature of our experience – and whether we call it peak, or whether we experience it as peak, depends on our personality and cognitive style, and perhaps even our attachment style as well. So, some people might have peak moments where they experience the sheer joy of living, while other people might consider a peak moment to be something that enlarges the mind, which I do, and which gives you a whole new perspective as if you're breaking new ground or climbing to the top of a mountain and suddenly seeing a new vista. But that's not transcendental although it is very satisfying and very thought provoking, and I come back to it in my mind again and again.

The Significance of Peak Experience in This Context

After researching many of the interpretations and terminologies of peak experience in the context of writing and reading literature, we found that "literary epiphany" is the term most widely used to describe what writers attempt when constructing peak experiences for their readers. Sometimes, our participant readers used the word "awe" in the context of peak experience, which, as mentioned in Chapter 1, has some religious connotation. Its meaning, according to *The Merriam-Webster Dictionary*, is an emotion that combines veneration and wonder inspired by authority, the sacred, or the sublime.

In the chapter, we explored extracts from some well-known authors who were moved to embrace literary epiphany in their work following their own physical engagement with a peak experience. We saw Proust's obsession with the sensual taste of the madeleine from his childhood, Wordsworth's experience of surprise with the sight of a host of daffodils, and Joyce's image of a beautiful girl wading in Dublin Bay.

After looking at some of the ways in which classical authors have rendered literary epiphany for their audiences in the first section, in the second section, we reasoned that the most significant aspect of literary epiphany may be the author's aim to promote peak experiences in the reader vicariously. The author mediates between his or her own experiences, or those invented for the characters in the text, attempting to convey the immediacy of the trigger event and so elicit a subsequent response.

Kien (2013, p. 578) argued that the "recurring, longitudinal but unpredictable characteristic of remembering the epiphanic moment as it erupts throughout one's life" can lead to descriptions of epiphanies that imply they have a life of their own. Additionally, the seeming emotional urgency of an epiphany can compel us to try to return over and over again to the epiphanic moment. But we have seen how Proust and other writers struggle to convey their peak-like epiphanies to readers but with little avail. This is because, as noted by our participants, when writers relay the epiphany via the written word it "interrupts" the immanence of the material world and the intensity it embraces. Such second-hand epiphanies are moments of connection shared by the author, but they are not necessarily received by the reader when engaging with the literature. Indeed, while explicating this literary device, we discerned that even the most carefully crafted literary epiphany cannot be guaranteed to produce a peak moment for the reader. As Maslow emphasises, "we cannot command the peak experience. It happens *to* us" (1962b, p. 87, Maslow's italics).

In the theoretical literature, Nichols implied that epiphany is cognitive: "the act of the mind noticing its own activity" (1999, p. 468) and pointed to literary epiphany as an authorial device used to herald a turning point for a character or plot. In real-life contexts, however, we would argue that epiphanies are not so cognitively imbued. They are not episodes of the *mind noticing* but are instead the *body experiencing*. We would argue that if an epiphany, as we have contended, is to be consistent with Maslow's notion of peak experience, it has to have, as a core condition, something much more visceral. Accordingly, like Johnson who argued that an epiphany is "an insight *shared with* rather than *created within* the reader" (Johnson, 1992, p. 10, our emphasis), evidence from our participants suggests that peak experiences occur only during reading if the written material triggers a memory or emotion for them. This was evident in Sarah's "wave of ecstasy," where a direct sensory or somatic recall was activated. It seems that, only if that idiosyncratic prompt is perceived physically can the peak be experienced.

We presented four accounts of peak experiences in this context, and these seemed to confirm our reasoning. Each of our participants got a lot of insight and understanding from reading, but they did not report transcendental or peak experiences, unless they were allied with some sensual activity, such as being in nature, wild swimming, or listening to music. Although they appreciated the peak experiences shared by authors as literary epiphanies, they did not automatically share the experience as "peak" or as an epiphany for themselves. We would argue that this is because the relayed experience is something specific to the author, and it loses its veracity in the sharing. Because of the idiosyncratic nature of peak experience, a reader (like Sarah in this chapter, e.g.) might pick up on some other aspect of a poem or book that has more particular resonance and reality for them – and the author could never realise it was "peak material" at all.

One participant, Christine, recognised the power of identifying with characters in literature and engaging vicariously in their lives. She talked about the kaleidoscope of emotions that she has sometimes felt when reading. None of our participants, however, mentioned that they had peak experiences generated through writing, although there is some research to suggest that writing is a positive experience. Fatemi (2004, p. 65), for instance, asked whether writing could trigger peak or similar positive human experience and what factors influence their occurrence. Of the 270 undergraduate students enrolled in writing classes, 44% reported experiencing at least one peak experience or a similar positive human experience as a result of writing: participants described their peak writing experiences as the flow of words, peak performance, clarity, disappearance of negative states of mind, an enhanced sense of power, and the process of writing as its own reward.

References

Barfoot, C. C. (1999). Milton silent came down my path: The epiphany of Blake's left foot. In W. Tigges (Ed.), *Moments of moment: Aspects of the literary epiphany*. Atlanta, GA: Rodopi.

Beja, M. (1971). *Epiphany in the modern novel*. Owen.

Bidney, M. (1997). *Patterns of epiphany: From Wordsworth to Tolstoy, Pater, and Barrett Browning*. SIU Press.

Buck, L. B. (2004). Olfactory receptors and odour coding in mammals. *Nutrition Reviews, 62*(suppl_3), S184–S188.

Burke, M. (2010). *Literary reading, cognition and emotion: An exploration of the oceanic mind* (Vol. 1). Routledge. ProQuest Ebook Central. https://ebookcentral-proquest-com.oxfordbrookes.idm.oclc.org/lib/brookes/detail.action?docID=957895

Cather, W. (1973). Ardessa. In *Uncle valentine and other stories*, with Intro by Bernice Slote. Lincoln, NE: Universtiy of Nebraska Press.

Chappell, S. G. (2019). Introducing epiphanies. *Zeitschrift für Ethik und Moralphilosophie, 2*(1), 95–121.

Clare, J. (1986). *John Clare: Selected poetry and prose*. Edited by M. Williams & R. Williams. London: Methuen.

Damasio, A. R. (1999). How the brain creates the mind. *Scientific American, 281*(6), 112–117.

Dutoit, T. (1999). Epiphanic reading in Ann Radcliffe's the mysteries of Udollpho. In W. Tigges (Ed.), *Moments of moment: Aspects of the literary epiphany* (Vol. 25). Atlanta, GA: Rodopi.

Eastman, C. A. (2016). *Improving workplace learning by teaching literature: Towards wisdom*. New York: Springer.

Eastman, C. A. (2018). *Coaching for professional development: Using literature to support success*. London: Routledge.

Fabb, N. (2021). Experiences of ineffable significance. *Beyond Meaning, 324*, 135.

Fatemi, J. (2004). *An exploratory study of peak experience and other positive human experiences and writing*. PhD Thesis, Texas A & M University.

Frick, W. B. (2001). Symbolic latency. *Journal of Humanistic Psychology, 41*(3), 25.

Jacobs, J. (1961). *The death and life of great American cities*. New York: Random House.

James, W. (1884/1969). What is an emotion? In *Collected essays and reviews* (pp. 244–275). New York: Russel & Russel.

Jarvis, A. N. (1996). *Taking a break: Preliminary investigations into the psychology of epiphanies as discontinuous change experiences*. Amherst: University of Massachusetts.
Johnson, S. H. (1992). *The space between: Literary epiphany in the work of Annie Dillard*. Kent State University Press.
Joyce, J. (1992). *A portrait of the artist as a young man*. London: Penguin.
Kien, G. (2013). The nature of epiphany. *International Review of Qualitative Research, 6*(4), 578–584.
Kimber, G. (2014). *Katherine Mansfield and the art of the short story*. New York: Springer.
Langbaum, R. (1983). The epiphanic mode in Wordsworth and modern literature. *New Literary History, 14*(2), 335–358.
Langbaum, R. (1999). The epiphanic mode in Wordsworth and modern literature. In W. Tigges (Ed.), *Moments of moment: Aspects of the literary epiphany*. Atlanta, GA: Rodopi.
Laski, M. (1980). *Everyday ecstasy*. Thames and Hudson.
Mansfield, K. (1981). *Selected stories*. Oxford: Oxford University Press.
Maslow, A. H. (1959). Cognition of being in the peak experiences. *The Journal of Genetic Psychology, 94*, 43–66.
Maslow, A. H. (1962a). Lessons from the peak-experiences. *Journal of Humanistic Psychology, 2*(9), 9–18.
Maslow, A. H. (1962b). *Toward a psychology of being*, 2nd edition. New York: Litton Educational Publishing.
Mayor, F. M. (1924/2021). *The rector's daughter*. Rare Treasure Editions.
Nichols, A. (1987). *The poetics of epiphany, nineteenth-century origins of the modern literary moment*. Tuscaloosa: The University of Alabama Press.
Nichols, A. (1999). Cognitive and pragmatic linguistic moments. In W. Tigges (Ed.), *Moments of moment: Aspects of the literary epiphany*. Atlanta, GA: Rodopi.
Privette, G. (1983). Peak experience, peak performance, and flow: A comparative analysis of positive human experiences. *Journal of Personality and Social Psychology, 45*, 1361–1368.
Proust, M. (1913–1927). *Remembrance of things past*. Volume 1: *Swann's Way: Within a Budding Grove*. The definitive French Pleiade edition translation by C. K. S. Moncrieff & T. Kilmartin (pp. 48–51). New York: Vintage.
Richman, R. (1985). Allen Ginsberg then and now. *Commentary, 80*(1), 50.
Risden, E. L. (2008). *Heroes, gods and epiphany in English epic poetry*. Jefferson: McFarland.
Rosenblatt, L. M. (1994). *The reader, the text, the poem: The transactional theory of the literary work*. USA: SIU Press.
Sewell, A. (1877). *Black beauty*. London: Jarrold & Sons.
Tennyson, A. (1991). The ancient sage. In A. Day (Ed.), *Alfred Lord Tennyson: Selected poems*. London: Penguin Books.
Tigges, W. (Ed.) (1999). *Moments of moment*. Atlanta, GA: Rodopi.
Ward, G. (2011). Super consciousness: The quest for the peak experience (2009). In C. Stanley (Ed.), *Around the outsider: Essays presented to Colin Wilson on the occasion of his 80th birthday* (p. 274). Alresford: John Hunt Publishing.
Weijers, K. (2021). *Peak moments: The experience of coaches*. Unpublished Doctoral Thesis, Oxford Brookes University.
Wilber, K. (2001). *No boundary: Eastern and Western approaches to personal growth*. Shambhala Publications.
Woolf, V. (1985). A sketch of the past. In J. Schulkind (Ed.), *Moments of being* (2nd ed.). New York, NY: Harcourt Brace & Company.
Wordsworth, W. (1805). The Prelude XII, [Lines 208–261] "Daffodils" (Wordsworth 1984, 303f.).

3 Peak Experiences and Music

Introduction

Music is one of the contexts most discussed in relation to peak experience. Maslow argued that peak experiences can be triggered by "great aesthetic moments, particularly of music" (1962, p. 9) and connected peak experiences in music with the classics: "great joy, the ecstasy, the visions of another world, or another level of living have come from the classical music – the great classics" (Maslow, 1968b, p. 168).

The literature reveals, however, that other genres of music also invite peak experience. For example, Green (2015, 2021) tells us that the phenomenon of peak experiences is a popular topic among indie music fans, adding that such experiences in this genre are quite specific; experiences are especially memorable, influential, and "even pivotal for the individuals involved" (2015, p. 333). Similarly, contemporary music performers talk of their awareness and encounters with peak experiences. The band Oasis, for instance, professed that when they come together, they make people feel something that is indefinable that people never, ever forget (Whitecross, 2016). Sara Cox, a BBC Radio 2 disc jockey, once made a similar comment about singer-songwriter Katy B when listening to her single, *Under My Skin*. She concluded the artist gave us "a moment," which, if not interpreted as a peak experience, was definitely a moment to be remembered and cherished. Even *University Challenge* (Caldwell, 2021–2022) referred to peak experiences in episode 18/37. Its host, Jeremy Paxman, reported Marilyn Monroe's response to hearing Rachmaninov's *Piano Concerto No. 2* in the film *The Seven Year Itch*, which arguably points to a peak experience: it shook her and made her feel goose-pimply all over.

We have already discussed in earlier chapters that linguistic struggles are prevalent when participants are asked to describe their peak experiences. This difficulty in articulation arises in music too. David, one of our participants and a former second violinist with the Royal Philharmonic Orchestra, verbalises the dilemma:

> It seems quite difficult to put it into words, in fact to find the right words at all. It sort of diminishes it. You can describe a certain amount but there's more that I can't describe that is inside, bound up with feelings.

David's experience corresponds with Fabb (2021, p. 17), who describes this phenomenon as "structural ineffability," a type of representation that is "too fine-grained

DOI: 10.4324/9781003509219-4

for verbalization." Similarly, Lavaysse (2002) saw no necessity to make sense of her experience as a singer by trying to verbalise how she felt. She merely maintained that the feeling was indescribable and bore no comparison to anything else.

Green (2015) also recognised the failures of language when his participants simply said "whoa" as descriptive of their encounters, thus capturing the intensity with which their peak music experiences were felt and the revelation and connection experienced. Indeed, one of Green's participants notes: "I probably called them pinnacle experiences, but whatever you want to call it there's these nodes of awesomeness" (2015, p. 345).

The word "polysemy" is seldom used in the English language. It means the coexistence of many possible meanings for a word or phrase, and it undoubtedly applies to the concept of peak experience. Certainly, in the music context, the vocabulary of peak experience is substantial. In this chapter, therefore, we not only acknowledge the synonyms for peak experience but also concede and define the differences between peak experience and the related concepts of peak performance and flow.

Review of Literature

In this review, we begin by assembling related concepts, since the lexicon of synonyms for peak experience in this context is very varied. Whereas a number of researchers have worked with Maslow's (1968a) notion of peak experience (e.g., Lowis, 1998, 2002; Lavaysse, 2002), Gabrielsson and Lindström preferred not to use the peak experience nomenclature, since peak experience is defined by "moments of highest happiness and fulfilment" (2010, p. 120). Instead, they wanted to explore the often-significant negative feelings that music can induce and so preferred the term "strong experience of music." Lamont (2011, p. 232) also noted the differences between strong experiences of music and peak experience, again highlighting that peak experiences are always deemed positive, whereas the term "strong experiences of music" enables research into negative experiences as well.

Similarly, Green (2015, p. 334) recognised the similarity between the terms but used "peak *music* experiences" to differentiate from Maslow's peak experience. In this way, he intended to relegate the psychological theories integral to Maslow's concept. Green further noted that what he called peak music experiences could also be seen as "epiphanies," the "interactional moments that leave marks on people's lives and in which personal character is manifested" (2015, p. 338). He argued, however, that epiphanies seem qualitatively different from peak experiences, since they are retrospective and reflective. In the writing and reading context, we saw how epiphanies can be used as a device in literature for sharing or introducing significant experiences. Such reflection or sharing of experiences often provides a resource for what Giddens (1991) called the "reflexive project of the self."

Schafer et al. (2014) used the term "intense music experiences" in their qualitative research, aiming to analyse the effects music has on the course of people's lives. These authors confirm that according to Maslow, "peak experiences can have permanent after-effects and add meaning to life permanently changing how we view our lives" (Schafer et al., 2014, p. 527). Pathak (2017) similarly supports the idea that music can add meaning to our lives. Drawing on findings from a qualitative study, he argues that what he also terms "intense music experiences" have the capacity to make individuals mindful of their basic values and goals, such that they manifest as meaning in their lives even after the experience has passed.

Another term widely used, and discussed in other chapters, is awe. Paquette (2020, p. 171) talks of awe using terminology not dissimilar to Maslow in his description of peak experience, suggesting that music can evoke a powerful sense of immersion and being transported and that listening to music "can be a powerful path for experiencing awe."

Flow, as an aspect of peak experience, is also commonly studied in the music sphere. It is often mentioned in experiences where individuals are so involved in playing, jamming, or practising that nothing else seems to matter. For example, De Manzano et al. (2010, p. 301) examined flow during piano playing and found flow to be "a state of effortless attention, which arises through an interaction between positive affect and high attention." However, it is noted that some confusion has arisen following Csikszentmihalyi's (1990) references to peak experience as a flow state. Misunderstandings occur because common to both peak experience and flow are factors such as loss of ego and the unperceived passage of time. In flow, "every action, movement and thought follows inevitably from the previous one, like playing jazz" (Kotler, 2014, pp. 20–21).

Bakker's (2005) study is one example where peak experience and flow are linked in the research. Bakker found that when music teachers are absorbed in their work and enjoying the moment, they reported more flow experiences, increasing the opportunity of a higher frequency of comparable peak experiences among their students. Bakker moreover suggested that teachers experience more flow when their students have more peak experiences. The study is robust, yet it is apparent that Bakker's (2005, p. 36) references to flow as a peak experience may have caused some confusion.

Similarly, Kirchner (2011) and Groarke and Hogan (2016, 2020) suggest that features of peak experiences during music listening align the listener with flow-like states of consciousness and a reduction of self-consciousness. In their study of the Eudaimonic FML scale, Groarke and Hogan (2020) offered a robust measure of peak experience, flow, and transcendence in music listening, explaining that peak, strong, or intense emotional experiences in music listening have also been understood by reference to physiological responses such as chills, thrills, and frisson (2020, p. 2). They confirm that "intense musical experience initiates a shift in consciousness where stressors and negative affect are replaced with strong positive feelings" (2020, p. 2).

Ford et al. (2020), in their qualitative study, also found that the ways a musician experiences flow are important, impacting emotional connectedness and interpersonal relationships. In a systematic review of the topic, Chirico et al. (2015) noted a special relationship between music and flow. They outlined the flow experience as both a "trait" and a "state" within three musical domains: composition, listening, and performance.

These accounts highlight the difference between flow and peak experience, although as Seligman (2002) noted, individuals might describe the flow experience in similar terms, as total immersion in an activity, loss of external distractions, loss of a sense of time, and loss of self-consciousness. However, as Collins stresses, a peak experience "is neither synonymous with nor in any way a necessary dimension of flow state experiences" (2010, p. 75). Echoing Maslow (1994), he confirms that characteristics of peak experiences include:

> an emotional "rush" or "charge," ego transcendence, and revelations of new awareness sometimes associated with religious rites. A peak experience might come on very quickly, and only occur for a brief instant. Other times, however, peak experiences extend beyond the initial rush and conclude with a plateau phase that might last for minutes, days, or weeks.
>
> (Collins, 2010, p. 75)

Collins's (2010) own experiences seem to indicate that flow states are closely related to *context*, and peak experiences are related to an expanded understanding of *content*:

> [M]usically induced flow states seem closely related to rhythm through their repetitive patterns. Furthermore, peak experiences might be similarly related to content and melody, as peak experiences appear as the highest expressions of meaning, understanding, and reality.
>
> (2010, p. 80)

The remainder of this review examines research on peak experiences when either making and performing music or listening to music.

Peak Experiences During Music-Making/Performing

As suggested earlier, the study of peak experience during music-making appears to focus on musicians' experiences of flow. Indeed, Whaley et al. (2009, p. 460) noted that "relative to other areas of music psychology . . . the study of peaks has not attracted as large a body of research." However, we found some relevant research that concerns experiences closer to Maslow's idea of peak experience.

Panzarella's (1980) study is one of the earliest to focus on music and peak experience. The study involved 103 participants' experiences of music or visual art. Using content and factor analysis, Panzarella reported that peak experiences involved four phenomenological factors: renewal, motor-sensory, withdrawal, and fusion-emotional experiences. Motor-sensory was particularly associated with music. In addition, temporal stages were displayed, beginning with "cognitive responses and loss of self; climaxing with continued loss of self, and motor-responses; and subsiding with emotional responses, self-transformations and stimulus specific responses" (1980, p. 69). The outcomes attributed to peak experiences were vivid, stimulating memories, enhanced appreciation, and permanent effects that involved "more positive self-feelings as well as improved relationships with others" (1980, p. 69).

In her doctoral thesis, Lavaysse (2002) examined the peak experiences of six professional singers. Through a qualitative heuristic methodology, she discovered that her co-researchers had not spoken about their peak experiences whilst performing to anyone else and that they were actually "relieved to finally be able to discuss peak experience" (2002, p. 6). Earlier, Simons (1977) had noted the great potential for self-actualisation and peak experience in an adult choral choir. However, she cautioned that if progress towards self-actualisation is inhibited by some basic needs not being met, either during rehearsals or in concerts, peak experiences are unlikely to occur.

Cohen's (2009) study also explored peak experience in a choral setting. She explored 44 participants' experiences from a joint inmate/community volunteer choir at a minimum-security prison. Survey data suggested that participation led to peak experiences, with momentary disappearance of stresses as well as a sense of accomplishment, especially for inmates. This grounded theory analysis included comparing themes with relevant literature and suggested that choral music experiences have potential for personal transformative and interpersonal change in prison choir contexts. Similarly, Sutherland & Jelinek (2015) used a grounded, participant-centred approach to explore the experiences of executive students in three choral-conducting masterclasses. His findings suggested potent learning including impact on the relational dynamics of leadership and a positive impact on the professional practice of participants.

Marotto et al. (2007) studied peak performance in an orchestra and in particular the concept of group-level peak performance. They were careful, however, to distinguish peak performance from peak experience, arguing that "by definition all peak performances are peak experiences" but that the opposite does not hold true (2007, p. 390). In confirming that not all peak experiences are peak performances, they explain how the bliss and joy involved in peak experiences of nature or during religious meditation, for example, are not action-oriented like peak performances in music. Rather than being passively absorbed in contemplation of an object as in nature, in music there is absorption in active performance. As a consequence, during such performance, musicians can transcend their normal level of performance and experience the joy and rapture associated with the peak experience (2007, p. 390). Thus, Marotto et al. consider peak performances to be action-oriented aesthetic experiences, whereas peak experiences are more passive aesthetic experiences. This active versus passive distinction is totally comprehensible when considering the spontaneity of peak experiences and the fact that they "just happen," as Maslow frequently points out.

Having made the close association between peak performance and action, Marotto et al. conclude that the nature of a group orchestral-level peak experience involves transcending the normal level of performance. At both the individual and group levels, orchestral members were "for a time transported by each other and to an experience variously labelled as flow, timeless-ness and aesthetic experience" (2007, p. 409).

The results from Green's (2015) study suggest that peak experiences in music, as in any other context, are dependent upon the merging of the subject's susceptibility and their environment. Using interviews with five amateur/part-time performing musicians, Green showed that peak music experiences have a lasting effect. His participants used expressions such as it "changed my life," "blew my young mind," and "this is awesome." They shared how motivation is part of their narrative in describing a peak music experience, demonstrated by their desire to learn new instruments and even get involved in the music industry. These shifts, for example, to instrumental music when previously lyrics had been more important, appeared to be influenced by participants' peak music experiences. The participants interviewed in Green's (2015) study, therefore credited their peak music experiences with moments of influence, inspiration, and motivation.

Green (2015) moreover confirms that peak music experiences are interactions that stir up important and intense feelings and meanings that affect us deeply. He compares the effect of peak experiences with other epiphanies that make us reflect on who we are, and what we want, "enabling people to remember and reproduce their tastes and values, making them important to self and group identity" (2015, p. 334).

In their grounded theory study of a related phenomenon, "intense musical experience," Schafer et al. (2014) studied six people who have had experiences as performers and seven as listeners. Their aim was to investigate potential long-term effects of such intense experiences on people's way of life. They found that intense musical experiences promote shifts in consciousness such that stressors and negative effects are replaced with strong positive feelings. Participants felt inspired to exploit their full potential. The study moreover highlights the motivational effects of peak experiences on the listener and performer. Although harmony was felt strongly during an intense musical experience, any feelings of disharmony left them with the motivation to achieve a balance:

> They remembered the positive experience and all the positive feelings that had accompanied it. The memory of the harmony gave them power and confidence, improved their mood, and made them forget thoughts of problems and worries.
>
> (2014, p. 534)

Schafer et al. (2014, p. 528) concluded that their research provided valuable hints at the potential long-term motivational effects of intense musical experiences.

Peak Experiences During Music Listening

As noted earlier, peak music experiences not only happen for the performer, via an action-oriented encounter, but also affect listeners through a more passive experience.

In the earliest of two studies, Lowis (1998, 2002) researched how listening to music induced peak experiences in 74 college staff. The staff had previously completed questionnaires based on Maslow's descriptions to ascertain their histories of peak experience and were then played taped music. The findings emphasised that participants who had a previous connection with a piece of music had enhanced potential to have a peak experience and that "significantly more reports occurred with upbeat music than was the case with gentle music" (Lowis, 1998, p. 203). This finding suggested a link between participants' associating the music with previous events in their lives.

Lowis's (2002) study used a similar research method, but with 102 college staff, most of whom had previous peak experiences in a music context. Participants completed a Musical Involvement and Reaction Questionnaire (MIRQ) to gauge their musical ability and connection, and findings suggested those who measured high on this test were more likely to encounter a peak music experience.

Gabrielsson (2001, 2011) and Gabrielsson and Lindström (1994, 2003, 2010) have written about emotions and strong experiences with music. Their work is derived from research with 900 participants who provided descriptions of their strongest experiences. Content analysis was used to generate seven central categories: general characteristics, physical reactions and behaviours, perception, cognition, feelings/emotions, existential and transcendental aspects, and personal and social aspects. Results have been shared in a number of publications, and Gabrielsson (2011), for example, explains the value of strong experiences in music as a resource for self-therapy and self-realisation; insights into the meaning of life and existence; increased value of relationships, insights into the value of music; and increasing inspiration, motivation, and interest in music.

As suggested earlier, Gabrielsson's (2001, 2011) explanations of strong experiences in music echo Maslow's account of peak experiences. Groarke and Hogan highlight these similarities noting how Gabrielsson's strong experiences are described as:

> life-enhancing, giving rise to intense, frequently positive emotional experiences, a change in attitudes and thoughts, spiritual insights and reflections on humanity, momentary loss of self-consciousness, increased hope and self-esteem, and can have therapeutic benefits.
> (Groarke & Hogan, 2020, p. 1)

Similarly, Solberg and Dibben (2019, p. 371), in their analysis of peak experiences with electronic dance music, imply that Maslow's peak experiences and the strong experiences examined by Gabrielsson (2011) are each "moments of intense pleasure, most frequently described as emotionally powerful and accompanied by physical sensations."

Like Gabrielsson and Lindstrom, Lamont (2011, 2012) also studied strong experiences with music. Her work refers to "engaged listening experiences" involving the audience and how passive enjoyment of music leads to peak music experiences. She shares a potent account of one participant who had been listening to Mozart's *Requiem*:

> The music is so powerful that it leaves you unable to not be moved; it's haunting, beautiful and packed with such strong emotion, it's just impossible to not be left moved by it. It physically affects me even to listen to it now – as soon as I hear the strings and woodwind in the Introitus my spine tingles!
> (Lamont, 2012, p. 586)

Lamont further explains that descriptions of pleasure evoked by listening to music parallel earlier findings about ways in which music affects the body and the brain:

"listeners reported thrills, shivers down the spine, piloerection (goosebumps), tears, and other physical responses that have been found in previous research" (2011, p. 241).

Lamont's work into music listening (2011) and performing (2012) highlighted different patterns of response when considering performance as a separate activity from listening.

> Performing often includes a high proportion of negative as well as positive emotions... and requires a high level of skill. It has the potential to generate more connections to others, both other performers and the audience.
>
> (2012, p. 587)

Lamont (2012) also expresses how motivation affects the performer. Thirty-five university students reported their strongest, most intense experiences of performing and illustrated that such experiences provided them with "valuable and overwhelmingly positive memories of performing which they can draw on to sustain their motivation for music" (2012, p. 589).

Benzecry and Collins (2014) researched whether cultural consumption, such as listening to opera, is a *sui generis* experience. They found highly committed opera fanatics in Buenos Aires explicitly distinguished between their pure experience of the music and the class-based consumption of opera that involved joining in conventional applause without really understanding the music. The authors describe the peak experience in detail:

> The opera fanatic closes his or her eyes during the aria. The listener tunes out the surrounding people to concentrate on how the soaring soprano voice feels inside his or her own body. It is an intensely inward experience, although not quite in isolation: There is a connection "from diaphragm to diaphragm," as one interviewee puts it, from the vocal apparatus of the singer to the body of the hearer. It is hearing not just with one's ears, brain, and nervous system; it is all of these, the bodily arousal of emotions as well, but above all a response to the singer's voice that sets the hearer not exactly singing himself or herself but resonating with the singer's voice. At the peak moment, the sound goes right through you, it makes you weak in the knees, it makes you feel you are melting.
>
> (2014, pp. 309–310)

Findings suggested that the operatic peak experience is individually intense but also involves bodily "copresence" that intensifies mutual awareness and emotional experience so that participants become absorbed into their common object of attention and feel a very strong emotion about it.

Cultural and Well-Being Aspects of Peak Experience and Music

In Rana's (2006) cross-cultural study, also with students, 65.7% of British and 48.7% of Pakistani participants reported having one or more peak experiences when either listening to or playing music or both. Rana's quantitative results point to the universality of peak experience since ethnicity appeared not to be related to the antecedents of participants' peak experiences of music. However, similar to Privette et al. (1997), some results indicated that inner emotional and mental responses to those peak experiences varied: "although peak experiences of music are not limited to particular ethnic groups, the mental and emotional effects of these differ in some ways between these two groups" (Rana, 2006, p. 150).

In another study of peak experiences of music and subjective well-being, Rana et al. (2009) hypothesised that "it would not be surprising if peak experiences of music were also associated with subjective wellbeing" (2009, p. 43). Passive music involvement is known to reduce stress hormones in some circumstances. Data from questionnaires completed by 12 British and Pakistani participants indicated that experiences inspired by music were not restricted to a specific demographic group. Features that impacted the nature of the peak experiences included the type of music participants heard, whether they were alone or with others, and the type of people there at the time. Also important was the distinction between recorded music and live performance and listening versus performing music.

Several studies have hinted at a link between music, health, and well-being. However, Douglas (2019) agreed with Rana et al. (2009) that there are still very few studies examining the impact on well-being of playing or listening to music. Douglas's research found that music listening and playing can fulfil "many functions that contribute to both hedonic and eudaimonic wellbeing – influencing mood regulation and positive emotions" (2019, p. 132). Also, he explored the effect of playing an instrument both as a soloist and with others. A comment from Jim Hunt, the British saxophonist, illustrates this impact:

> I think your sense of self, your sense of wellbeing is intrinsically linked with your music. You're looking for transcendence that you can't really control. You don't know when it's going to come and when it does, it's the most exhilarating feeling you can have, and for a second you take your hands off the saxophone and it feels as though it's playing itself. And it's very difficult to recreate that – and yet you want it again and again.
>
> (Murray, 2020)

More recently, Harney et al. (2022) conducted a systematic review of music listening as an intervention that can be self-administered for the possible reduction of anxiety. Twenty-four controlled studies were considered, and 21 were used in the resulting meta-analysis, where it was determined that music listening is effective for reducing anxiety in a range of participant groups.

Peak Experience in Context – Participant Accounts

In this section, six participants involved in making and performing music share their experiences.

David Lyon's first music peak experience was in the Royal Albert Hall in 1976. He was playing in the second violin section of the Royal Philharmonic Orchestra

(RPO), performing Prokofiev's *Romeo and Juliet* suite, conducted by the Russian conductor, Yuri Temirkanov. He had never heard that piece played so brilliantly. It was not only a peak music experience for him but also a peak performance for the entire orchestra, echoing Marotto et al.'s (2007) description of the group-level peak performance.

David considers Temirkanov to be supremely skilled. When he first came over to the UK "he was like a breath of fresh air." Unable to speak much English, Temirkanov inspired every player with his hands, his eyes, his body language, and managed to entice magic from each player to produce electrifying performances. David recalls numerous enthusiastic comments from other players who thought it to be the finest performance for a long time: "just awe-inspiring, it really stuck in my mind." We are again reminded of Paquette's description of awe: "our encounter must be with something vast" (2020, p. 7). David felt elated, excited, fulfilled, and proud to have been part of such an occasion, so much so that he can revisit and visualise exactly how he felt some 40 years later.

David is not sure if it was a timeless experience, as, by its very nature, music exists in time, and a performance comes to an end. But those feelings of elation, generated by that experience continued. He doesn't remember trying to qualify his feelings at the time but having reflected on it, his memory is not so intense as the exact experience but intense enough to be able to visualise and enjoy it. David's recollections resonate with Maslow's (1962, p. 14) observation that "some of the effects or after-effects may be permanent but the high moment itself is not." The impact on him was that, even though he had "upped his game" when joining the RPO, there were levels of performance, even with a top-performing orchestra that could still go beyond but might depend heavily upon having a conductor with the calibre of Temirkanov.

David explained there are hundreds of conductors who achieve good but not inspiring performances. They may know the music well, but they can neither communicate it nor indicate what they want. An inspiring performance doesn't always happen – rather like a peak experience. According to David, Temirkanov's strength was that he spoke so little and communicated with his face, his hands, his eyes, to tell the orchestra exactly what he wanted. Everything was just "there" in his body language. He created the magic of the performance that was felt by the entire orchestra. Each individual player was focused with an intensity that resulted in a collective brilliance. David said that you could sense the feeling that something special was about to happen.

The role of the conductor in creating peak experiences is not David's experience alone. Other musicians recall concerts conducted by Bernard Haitink (Bridcut, 2020) and say of him that "there's an aura around him which I feel deserves the word radar; there's an inexplicable pulse and everyone feels it."

David described the sensation that accompanied his peak experience in music as an "uplift" on both an emotional and intellectual level. This extended to a gut feeling, which was hard to describe; the more he tried to encapsulate and describe his feelings, the more elusive it became. He pointed out that although language can be very precise in many areas, it certainly did not apply to peak music experiences. He considers that terminology and expressions can become debased by inappropriate use, for example, how many times do we hear someone say, "that was amazing" or "that was fantastic" when what they are describing was simply good. David's understanding of having a peak music experience transcends language: "you know something special has happened." He says that its effects are visible on the faces of those with whom you have shared the experience but attempts to put it into words merely detract from it.

The impact of David's experience taught him that however high a level of achievement any musician has reached, there is always something more to attain, as yet unknown. A level of experience beyond our known capacity. He thinks that until you have had such an experience, you are unaware that there is an unknown, intense level to attain. Since becoming aware, David has had more music peak experiences which generate similar feelings, varying in intensity because of different circumstances and situations. He remembers a very remarkable performance of Brahms' first symphony with conductor Kurt Masur. Masur too inspired a level of involvement and camaraderie from the whole orchestra which generated the level of excitement and intensity so often absent. David remarked that "you get so many 'run of the mill' performances – good performances but just lacking in that extra 'something' that really brings it to life."

Peak experiences have increased David's awareness and appreciation of an ever-expanding range of nuance and subtlety, stimulated by playing with the RPO where a higher level of technical expertise was demanded. Throughout his first year of working with them, David admits that he was working at a raised level which made him try that much harder. In fact, he was unconsciously working towards self-actualisation as a musician, and in fine-tuning his level of performance he agreed that he was much better placed to experience a peak music experience. Through the realisation that he had to "up his game," David admitted this opened up the possibilities of greater and more intense music experiences:

> Obviously there must be a limit somewhere but there is a whole range of stuff that you might not have been aware of until you get to that stage when you've really got to pull yourself up to the level that is around you.

On a much smaller scale, in a string quartet, for example, David said you know when you've done a good performance. You can see it on one another's faces, you don't need to say, "that felt good" as you know that it was good: "You just know that there has been that experience, and you can see that you've shared it."

Also, we discussed sharing a desk as a violinist. Both desk violinists play the same music; so sharing a desk is intimate but can be problematic. For example, some violinists want to write in the fingerings which differ from player to player. What suits one person doesn't necessarily suit another, and this tension can be a hindrance to achieving a peak music experience. David imagined that the synergy he felt with his desk partner in the performance of *Romeo and Juliet* (conducted by Temirkanov) must have contributed to his peak music experience.

***

Our next participant is **Graham Sheen**, former principal bassoonist with the BBC Symphony Orchestra for 34 years. We were especially keen to explore Graham's experience when playing the *Rite of Spring* by Stravinsky (BBC, 2013), an evocative pagan dance, electrifyingly atmospheric and featuring the infamous opening bassoon solo. If the audience is gifted with a peak experience from simply listening, how does the bassoonist, who has created the entire mood, feel?

When asked about his peak music experiences, expecting Graham to say how exhilarating it was to play the opening solo, his initial response was to think about orchestral playing; everyday issues like having the correct reed for the job and the technical aspects of performing. Regarding *The Rite*, he simply said:

> It's not that hard as long as you set yourself up to be able to do it. You are alone and have to begin the piece and set the mood. You are playing this special role, which is very, very unusual for the bassoon. Hard to think of any other pieces when the bassoon starts absolutely alone, it's pretty much unique.

Graham explained that to overcome technical challenges, he used a special crook to get to the high notes more easily. He made the difficult practicalities sound easy but doubted that he experienced a peak experience because the technical factors required intense focus:

> When I played *The Rite*, I was much more unlikely to have one of those peaks because the reality of the situation was quite difficult. It's an intensely practical moment. You've got to start this thing off right and not mess up so you can't take any chances so that tends to be the focus. It only lasts about 15 seconds.

The opening to *The Rite* involves only a small section of the orchestra. Graham explained that all the strings are just quietly sitting for most of it, listening, "so there is a sort of high feeling of attention and concentration on what the bassoonist is doing." Graham prepared his reeds, choosing the right one at home, but almost without exception would choose another for the performance, having analysed the effect the reed had when in the room with other people in the orchestra.

It was only through persistent questioning and feedback that we were able to ascertain that the approach to this solo started about three or four days before rehearsals: mental preparation for the solo, choosing the right reed and crook, and visualising playing the piece on the day. On the day, the conductor quietens the audience and gives the bassoonist a nod to start:

> I don't have to start as I can take time and just sort of breathe into it and let it go. You have to create a sound that seems as though it's coming out of the ground with this paper-thin reed that you just breathe into. I think of putting the listeners at ease.

Graham explained that, despite all the technical challenges, the solo had to sound:

> like something happening in a prehistoric time; a simple bone flute that someone's doodled on. This simple pentatonic melody has to have that kind of simplicity despite the fact that you're wading through a sea of difficulties playing in that register. To have the control is quite complex.

As a musician, Graham concurs with Douglas (2019, p. 135), who stresses that "music provides an opportunity for musicians to present themselves to others, to express identity – an aspect of eudaimonic wellbeing." What preoccupies musicians most of the time in an orchestra, he says, is communicating and playing together: "It's the sideways concentration. The difference between professionals and amateurs is that professionals play for each other."

When asked how his colleagues reacted to his performances of the *Rite*, he said the entire orchestra was banging their stands in appreciation after the performance:

> That's the most important thing. In the end you play for each other. I think the excitement of having all your colleagues, really, really applauding and then for weeks, the next week and beyond, colleagues coming up to you and saying that was incredible. As experienced professionals they would know what it was like to have to hold the thing together all on your own so there's an appreciation of the challenge.

Graham's dialogue reflects words used by Marotto et al. (2007, p. 409): "orchestral members were for a time transported by each other and to an experience variously labelled as flow, timeless-ness and aesthetic experience." His experience echoes their observation, noted earlier, that the action-oriented nature of music-making more often leads to highs of peak performance than the transcendence of peak experience.

When asked how feedback, such as "what you did there was absolutely bloody marvellous" or "wonderful beginning, lovely solo," made him feel, Graham conceded:

> All these little moments are like electrical impulses – they are mini peak experiences. . . . and now I realise that too was a sort of physical thing, like a buzz in the chest.

He confessed that had he been wired up to some kind of medical experiment, his heart, blood pressure, and adrenalin would probably have gone off the scale, but he was able to turn that to his advantage. He thinks that some musicians use nerves negatively, yet for the most successful musicians, nerves have to be positive: "you have to be able to turn that into something otherwise we wouldn't survive."

Graham also shared how the three- or four-day mental build up to the concert, the technical challenges, and using adrenalin to his advantage, all contributed to his peak music experience when playing *The Rite*. His peak experience was a combination of every element. Each was integral to producing the final piece in the jigsaw, including praise from his colleagues and fellow musicians for weeks after the performance.

Graham's belief in attaining the very best performance he can muster is inspired by Gallwey (1987) and the concept of the "Inner Game," which involves recognising Self 1 (the conscious self, which Freud called the "Super-ego") and Self 2 (the unconscious self). Gallwey's concept helps people to achieve excellence in various sports (e.g., tennis, golf, skiing) and in other fields such as music. It mentally prepares them to perform well.

When coaching students, Graham believes that too much focus on Self 1 obstructs getting to a sort of higher level. This belief is also evident when he is composing. He maintains that he experiences an extension of knowing something in the back of his mind and "being able to use that Self 2." When reviewing his work, he noticed he was able to analyse it as a third person, spotting a lot more detail:

> I notice a lot more detail derived from the original theme than I'd imagined or I'd consciously seen. There were a lot more elements in it that Self 2 had just done. When I went back to revise it, I could see a lot more in it. I would say that was a peak experience – starting with a blank piece of paper and ending up with a performance of the variations with four bassoons at the Guildhall. It's one of the most exciting things I think you can do in music, apart from playing the bassoon in an orchestra.

Graham's third recollection of a peak music experience was in the context of playing with four other prestigious musicians in an impromptu wind quintet concert at a New Year's Eve party. He recalled:

> I remember it being completely effortless – sight-reading with amazing players of that quality. It seemed so easy – everything was just happening. First rate players getting together, drinking, playing, and having fun. That whole time just worked and there was a sort of electricity about the thing.

Graham explained that years of practice enabled the freeing-up of his hands on the instrument, almost shifting into an unconscious behaviour led by Self 2. His hands knew what to do.

In a way Graham considers this is what effective practice is; setting up a foundation of reactions and sequences which allow him to operate the instrument in a certain way so that he is able to get beyond the mechanical process of technique and see a different sort of shape while being in flow. But additionally, he described how playing with other exceptional musicians enabled the peak experience to happen and suggested some core conditions for him: "the people with you have to be right, whatever that means for the situation." On that occasion, Graham explained, the people were very exciting musicians he had worked with in different circumstances, and the location was wonderful – about 100 people at a party in a big old house: "everything was just right. All the factors were there."

***

Steve Hamilton, our third participant, is one of London's leading session saxophonists and a member of Noel Gallagher's group High Flying Birds. It was an easily recalled moment for Steve when we asked him about peak experience:

> [I]t is what I call "fuzzy head" – and I've never really met anyone else who feels it or admits to it. I remember from a very early age, about six or seven, when someone came round to the house and played with a Tonka toy of mine. If was as though they had some sort of tenderness about them or were simply gentle. I would go into this blissful state and my head would just zing like total euphoria.

Fuzzy head is a delightful expression and the first time we have heard peak experience described this way. It seems that a trigger for Steve fuzzy head is something to do with a sense of kindness and gentleness, which he responds to. He gave us another example:

> [T]he other day someone was doing a WhatsApp video of the house as we're moving. He was working for the removal company and had such a gentle manner about him that I could have had a conversation for hours, but my head was just fuzzy . . . it's really weird. I was just walking around the house, talking to him and he had such a nice manner . . . I'm getting it now, just thinking about it. The most random kind of moments catch with me. Is it common?

We talked about how easy it seems for Steve to recall those fuzzy feelings, which reflect Maslow's (1962, p. 14) assertion that "some of the effects or after-effects may be permanent." They are absolutely permanent in Steve's case.

Steve attended the Guildhall School of Music college in London, which gave him a formal classical education, but he is at his most prolific when improvising as a commercial player rather than reading music. He recalled a time when he was in Perth, Scotland, with the band, and for some reason he was nervous about playing a three-minute ad-lib improvised solo called "The Right Stuff." He'd played it numerous times before and recalled:

> It was near the end of the set, and I was trying to bargain with myself that it's gonna be all right, but my sax was cold. However, as soon as I started playing one note – I'm getting that fuzzy feeling again – the emergence of it, and I got into this melange of sound. I loved every second of it. And afterwards I thought "why on earth was I worried about that?" I don't really know what happened but the whole time I was playing I was loving it. It was as though I was flying around in the air – really lovely phrases and I remember thinking "did I actually just do that?"

We asked Steve if he had that "fuzzy head" when both reading music and improvising, and he immediately recalled a gig in New York around 2000. He was playing on a Radiohead album with an eight-piece horn section which he called "the perfect storm." The band, people who were put together with limited soundtrack time, created harmony and an unforgettable atmosphere, no doubt enhanced by the environment. They were playing at the Roseland ballroom; an iconic building where Duke Ellington, Otis Reading, and other Motown and jazz stars have performed:

> I played one tune, the first of the set, improvising around some sort of thematic framework and it just worked. When we went on stage the atmosphere was unbelievable. You're reacting to other people's reactions but in that moment – and again I'm getting a bit of a tingle about it – it was so phenomenal. I played there a couple of times since but never with that incredible atmosphere. I was outside myself kind of thing. It would be an incredible thing if everyone could experience that.

It would seem that Steve is responding to not only the expertise of the musicians and the iconic building but also the audience's response and reaction. Not only did Steve have the peak "fuzzy" sensation, but it seems so did the audience.

We then asked Steve to further elaborate his sensations with "fuzzy head," and he explained:

> I really wish I knew so that I could bottle it as it's an incredible feeling and something you don't want to let go of. The only thing that's important is to keep that feeling. There's something very comforting and secure about it.

Steve's description of how the experience passes, "without you realising its passed . . . it's like everything else is still going on but time is standing still," echoes Maslow's (1959, p. 50) observation that "in all the common peak experiences . . . there is a very characteristic disorientation in time and space."

Additionally, Steve introduced a new aspect of peak experience – the sense of gentleness in others, which acts like a trigger to an emotional response. It seems to be a part of him that has a fuse, waiting to be ignited as though it has a life of its own. Steve agreed:

> I think and feel it's the other person's energy I'm connecting with, the energy around me. When I'm on stage it's a different kind of fuzzy head but it's a moment where I've got to where I want to get to, and kind of gone way past it and surprised myself.

We questioned Steve about the difference between the two fuzzy heads – the one triggered by someone's tenderness and the other that he identifies as everything being in place in a music setting that made him perform at an unprecedented level, triggering a peak experience:

> There are so many points of energy in, for example, a 10-piece band on a stage; so many variables that it's very unlikely that it would happen again. So many people's emotional energies are generated in that contact, that

environment and assembly of players, the temperature of the place, the atmosphere, the sound etc. I think it's incredibly rare for it to happen and it's happened to me because of so many determining factors. I think in those moments all these factors collide to become perfect. It's such a personal thing like someone playing with my Tonka but really gently . . . it just slows things down a bit and it occurs to me that only the tenderest moments trigger it with me.

***

Our fourth participant is **Anthony Baldery**, an organist, pianist, teacher, and choirmaster.

Anthony believes his work as choirmaster defines who he is as a musician. An instrumentalist is concerned with phrasing, breathing, and linear thinking, but keyboard players, however, as accompanists, are forced into thinking about other parts – sopranos, altos, tenors, and basses when leading the choir. Anthony considers this to be analogous to playing a Bach chorale and bringing parts in at the right time.

Anthony believes that a peak experience is a shared experience:

> It's the unexpected. You work, prep and plan, and then it's the unexpected thing around the corner that you weren't looking for necessarily. It's a bi-product and it's that recognition, across everybody, young and old, that "Ahhh, that was good." And nothing needs to be said but there is that body posture that tells you that was all right. And it might be just alright, or it might be absolutely fabulous.

Anthony's thinking resonates with Maslow's. He believes peaks are achievable, but "you don't set out to achieve them," something he learnt when teaching both adults and children:

> Peaks are just a bi-product and that is obviously the pay-off. The "ooh, I wasn't expecting that." Somehow it just happens, something just enables it. With the adults it's introducing new things, things they probably thought they couldn't do.

When asked how these experiences make him feel, Anthony simply said "proud" – a pride embraced on several levels. The first, he said, is when everything comes together, and he feels all the effort was worthwhile. He builds trust with local choirs by introducing music from the 1950s and 1960s. The singers know the lyrics and tunes, removing the need for music sheets so all the non-music readers are happy. He then introduces some John Rutter or the *Messiah* to really take them to a new level:

> Part of my make-up is that I do not see barriers. I don't see restrictions on people: they might struggle with reading of words or notation but there are ways around that. It happened recently when the sopranos sang brilliantly

with conviction. I'd been asking for that for weeks and it was all of a sudden – bang! – every one of those people was prepared to sing at that pitch and not crumble because they saw a note above the stave. All of a sudden it was wow, brilliant, thank you, a peak!

Anthony admitted how excited he felt when those moments happened, moments that made him smile involuntarily:

I can't help grinning when that happens. I smile, I can't stop it because it's wow, I wasn't expecting that. They must see it as well and at those moments I can't help but be absolutely excited about it. It's just an elation. It just grabs you!

When we talked about Anthony the organist, he remarked that studying under Colin Walsh from Lincoln Cathedral for four years takes his playing to a different level – an understanding way beyond where he was at university. His peak experiences involve the organ, organist, and an awareness of the building and space:

[A]nd you're playing to that space and time. There's a piece I'm learning, *Toccata and Fugue in D minor* by Bach, not the famous one but the one in the Dorian mode. It has a manual change and is marked in by Bach, which is rare. I asked Colin how long to wait before that change and he said, "ask the building"!

Anthony explains that in a cathedral you might wait a little bit, giving that chord time to disappear before continuing, and it's a good reminder to listen to the building:

With the organ you're in it, and in a completely different space to the audience as it depends where you sit in the building as well. That's exciting, the idea of colour, registration, tempo, phrasing, articulation – all those things are combining to produce the best effect you can possibly achieve.

When asked about his peak experiences playing the organ, Anthony said that the experience is similar to being choirmaster:

It's the same sort of thing really – it's when it all comes together, all that breaking down of individual parts and layers, which takes a huge amount of time. When I'm practising, I'm hearing my best sound and then eventually joining things together like we do in choir. It takes a long time, but the proof is whether you can play it in front of anybody – at a concert or a service. So that's the light bulb moment – when I'm glad I did all that hard graft, hours and hours and hours!

***

Philippa Lowe has enjoyed playing music since she started learning the violin at age five. Music, she says, makes her feel alive and vibrant: "I am incapable of keeping still when I hear music." She not only finds great joy in playing but also relishes the creativity of making music with fellow musicians: "critically it is about having fun and being free to express and feel my feelings."

Philippa's peak musical experiences have been multiple and memorable including one she describes as a 12 year old, when she performed in a choir alongside Sir Peter Pears as the soloist in Benjamin Britton's St Nicholas:

> I can see the amazing concert hall, hear the sounds and recall how I felt. When Sir Peter Pears' incredible voice rang out for the first time, it was a truly amazing moment. I was completely awestruck at the purity and beauty of his voice and was utterly moved by the sound. I heard the voice, I felt it run through my body, all senses tingled and it was all consuming – I was swallowed up by the experience like a wave washing over me. I never realised anything could sound so beautiful.

Philippa confirmed that music allows her to be free and express her feelings and give her new insights. Such expression has recently become evident in music improvisation. Encouraged by her violin teacher, Andrew Hodges, she now experiments with free music improvisation to push her musical boundaries and open her mind to any possibility of expression:

> I am able to access underlying feelings and emotions more directly than via language. I have had almost out of body experiences when I totally free my mind and just let the bow play whatever it likes. The less I think about it the more meaningful the experience. If I try too hard to replicate the experience it doesn't work.

Going back to gain more understanding, we asked Philippa if she was able to deconstruct a process before improvising:

> To prepare myself I pick up either my Violin or Viola, I shut my eyes and look into the back of my head and bring an image of a scene I know looking across a bay to a cave entrance. I put the bow on the string and see what happens. Sometimes I've gone for ages just playing a single note and I patiently wait to see what follows. I don't go searching for anything but I do try to clear my mind and stay in that "altered state of consciousness."
>
> The experience is like my head is talking to my heart. On one occasion I had been having a very emotional week and my playing felt like a great guttural scream but without the associated sore throat! It was a very calming and re-balancing experience. It didn't feel like a troubled mind but an exercised mind – letting go and free.

She goes on to describe how the experience is like is a private conversation with her subconscious.

I can play how I feel, even if I don't start by knowing how I feel. Then I can express or better understand how I am doing, through new insights. The free music improvisations are never the same – what is consistent is that they reflect the mood I am in and will reveal insights into how I really am feeling, whilst if when I started, I wasn't really sure as my head was too full of the activities of the day to really notice how I was doing.

***

Katy Moses-Hamilton is an ardent yoga practitioner, who also shares her peak experiences with us in the therapy context. She confirmed that "so many of peaks are combined with music." Katy is married to Steve Hamilton, the saxophonist. They have been together for almost 25 years, and much of their life involves music, gigs, and festivals. Katy's peak experiences are of particular interest as they relate to the passive role of the music listener rather than the active music player.

Katy went on to describe seeing Steve play with Noel Gallagher, at a Manchester gig:

> I stood looking out at 16,000 people as he played *Don't Look Back In Anger*, which has become the sort of Manchester theme tune since the bombings. And that was a peak experience – really overwhelming. It made me think: do musicians get that peak experience several times during a really great gig? I certainly had it there.

She remembers being an Oasis fan at age 15, and now, all of a sudden, she knows Noel Gallagher:

> [W]e're mates and I'm standing by the side of the stage watching him at his best, in his home city, singing the song that is Manchester's adopted song, looking at people's faces. They were sobbing and screaming, singing along. That's another interesting point actually: the peak experiences I've had at gigs – there's a lot that goes into that. It's not as simple as I love this song, all the variables need to be correct for peaks to happen in the music situation. I go to about 100 gigs a year – music and festivals are my great love and that's why I go – to get a peak experience. It's that feeling.

We asked Katy what she was experiencing physically when she has that peak experience, and she explained she has her own expression for peak experience; the feeling that she calls "fizzy nose." This is almost the same as her husband Steve's "fuzzy head."

> It's almost like a feeling of wonder, like is this really happening – this is fucking amazing. And often you're at a festival with a friend and that heightens it. I get the fizzy nose and my heart beats faster – I'm sure if you were to put a tracker on it my heart rate goes up. You kind of forget about everything else – you are actually in the moment, in the present and you're

not thinking what to say next, or what are they going to play next, who are we going to meet later, where are we going to sleep, which club are we going to go to? It's just that you're right here and this is the only thing that's happening in this moment.

Katy also made a comparison between yoga and music and how they both made her feel in the peak moment:

It's like a higher state of consciousness in the band/festival/gig/music situation which is empowering and makes you feel the extremities of your body. The yoga one is calm, probably by design. One is on a mat in a room and the other is with 100,000 people at Glastonbury where, actually, it may be the situation you find yourself in that contributes to the feelings – as other people around you are having a similar experience. It's a very energetic high, just like the chord Noel Gallagher plays as he starts in *Look Back in Anger*, or the chord the Killers play in *Right Side*.

What Is Significant About Peaks in This Context?

In this chapter, we began by recognising the range of terms used in the music context to describe phenomena similar to peak experiences. Often, these terms have been devised to take account of the feelings and emotions that music can arouse that extend beyond the joy and transcendence that epitomise Maslow's idea of peak experience. Strong experiences of music and intense musical experiences were two examples we found in the research. Also, we looked at the fairly recent conflation of flow with peak experience, which has resulted in a concentration of research on flow in various music contexts.

For our six participants it would seem that shifting into higher levels of performance, almost becoming "super-self-actualised," stimulated peak music experiences for them. David talked of "upping his game," which infers a higher level of musical prowess; Graham talked of higher levels of performance when Self 2 comes into play, freeing Self 1 from conscious thought and action to operate the instrument in a state of unconscious competence. Anthony talked of taking his playing as an organist to a different level. Philippa also explained how music allows her the freedom to express feelings and gain new insights, something that has really taken flight in her recent experiments with music improvisation.

Something else we have observed from our participant responses in this context is their visual recognition of the physical expressions of peak experience, particularly facial expressions. We have seen how three participants mentioned this. David, for example, shared how the effect of a peak experience may not be possible to put into words but is visible on people's faces. Anthony explained how he felt excited when peak moments happened and couldn't stop grinning when it happened. Graham recalled how, when Barenboim directed concertos from the piano, "the sensation of him playing, and his dark eyes boring into you" managed to convey exactly what he wanted just by looking. Graham's words reflect those of

Sutherland & Jelinek (2015) participants who also felt connected through eye contact "like there were little strings between us" or in a bubble with the other people "with eye contact, communicating, feeling the energy" (2015, p. 298).

Notably, there are three aspects of our participants' responses to music peaks that reflect the core conditions required to create a peak experience (Weijers, 2021). The first is *connectivity*. Both David and Graham expressed that their encounters were dependent on either the conductor or other musicians. Through their charisma and body language, some conductors were able to create the core conditions for a peak music experience to happen, encouraging the orchestra to dig deep into their mastery to perform at their best and produce electrifying performances.

This response was driven by a second condition, *trust* between conductor and player and trust between musicians in the co-creation of something exquisite. Anthony's core condition for stimulating a peak experience is framed around trust in the relationship with his choirs. He resists the urge to put boundaries around their abilities and, instead, challenges them with new music which "ups their game" as singers.

Trust was also evident in the third condition, the *co-creation* of peak music experiences when playing in a string quartet or wind quintet. The experiences of our participants were wholly reflective of the joyous, momentary yet memorable peak experiences described by Maslow (1971, p. 176) "the great joy, the ecstasy, the visions of another world, or another level of living." Katy expressed the joy of co-creating peaks at gigs or festivals with other members of the audience and the energy emanating from the bands, a three-way process. Steve also agreed that the three-way process is core; the expertise of the musicians, the audience's response and reaction, his performance, and even a fourth, the iconic building and environment. Steve introduced a new term for peak experience, "fuzzy head," which is triggered either by sensing gentleness in others, which he finds comforting, or by his emotional response when everything is "just right" in a music setting which empowers him to perform at an unprecedented level.

Another aspect concerns feedback, also identified by Weijers (2021). A different type of feedback experience was recalled by Graham when the comments he received from fellow musicians, weeks after his peak performance, prompted a reflective peak experience. This peak experience was not a transcendental, unexpected encounter but was both important and memorable, similar to the taste of the madeleine for Proust. This reflected peak experience was acknowledged by Maslow (1959, p. 65) when he explains: "he remembers the experience as a very important and desirable happening." In a way, all peak music experiences are reflective as the memory retains the feelings, and, on reflection, the encounter becomes again a visceral, relived experience.

All the musicians interviewed for this chapter concurred that peak music experiences cannot be brought about by choice; they simply happen. Anthony, for example, believes peaks are achievable but that we don't set out to achieve them: "Peaks are just a bi-product," he says.

There is something about a performance coming together, they all agreed, that intensifies the possibility of a peak music experience. They each used words such as "putting it all together," "when everything/it all comes together," aligning with Marotto et al.'s findings that preparation for peak performance in this context leads to peak experience (2007, p. 407):

> During a peak performance, one transcends his/her normal level of performance and experiences the joy and rapture associated with the peak experience.
> (Marotto et al., 2007, p. 390)

References

Bakker, A. B. (2005). Flow among music teachers and their students: The crossover of peak experiences. *Journal of Vocational Behavior*, *66*, 26–44.

BBC. (2013, June 14). *Prom 4: Les Siècles – the rite of spring*. www.bbc.co.uk/events/e3pmbp, also www.youtube.com/watch?v=vO6Yvi-jKgU [Accessed 13 January 2023].

Benzecry, C., & Collins, R. (2014). The high of cultural experience: Toward a microsociology of cultural consumption. *Sociological Theory*, *32*(4), 307–326.Bridcut, J. (2020, September 28). Bernard Haitink, the enigmatic maestro. *BBC2*. www.johnbridcut.com/filmdetail.php?film=45

Caldwell, B. (Director) (2021–2022). University challenge, Episode 18/37. *BBC2*. www.bbc.co.uk/programmes/m0011gnw

Chirico, A., Serino, S., Cipresso, P. Gaggioli, A., & Riva, G. (2015). When music "flows". State and trait in musical performance, composition and listening: A systematic review. *Frontiers in Psychology*, *6*(906), 1–14.

Cohen, M. L. (2009). Choral singing and prison inmates: Influences of performing in a prison choir. *Journal of Correctional Education*, *60*(1), 52–65.

Collins, M. (2010). Music and personal experience: Flows and peaks. *Journal of Integral Theory & Practice*, *5*(2).

Csikszentmihalyi, M. (1990). *Flow: The psychology of optimal experience*. New York: Harper & Row.

De Manzano, Ö., Theorell, T., Harmat, L., & Ullén, F. (2010). The psychophysiology of flow during piano playing. *Emotion*, *10*(3), 301.

Douglas, K. (2019). "Without music, life would be a mistake" – the impact of music listening and playing on hedonic and eudaimonic wellbeing. *Paper presented at the 5th Annual Applied Positive Psychology Symposium*, High Wycombe, UK.

Fabb, N. (2021). Experiences of ineffable significance. In E. Ifantidou, L. de Saussure, & T. Wharton (Eds.), *Beyond Meaning*. Amsterdam: John Benjamins Publishing.

Ford, J. L., Vosloo, J., & Arvinen-Barrow, M. (2020). "Pouring everything that you are": Musicians' experiences of optimal performances. *British Journal of Music Education*, *37*(2), 141–153.

Gabrielsson, A. (2001). Emotions in strong experiences with music. In P. N. Juslin & J. A. Sloboda (Eds.), *Music and emotion: Theory and research* (pp. 431–449). New York, NY: Oxford University Press.

Gabrielsson, A. (2011). *Strong experiences with music: Music is much more than just music*. New York, NY: Oxford University Press.

Gabrielsson, A., & Lindström, S. (1994). May strong experiences of music have therapeutic implications? In R. Steinberg (Ed.), *Music and the mind machine. Psychophysiology and psychopathology of the sense of music*. Berlin: Springer Verlag.

Gabrielsson, A., & Lindström, S. (2003). Strong experiences related to music: A descriptive system. *Musicae Scientiae*, *7*(2), 157–217.

Gabrielsson, A., & Lindström, S. (2010). Strong experiences with music. In P. N. Juslin & J. A. Sloboda (Eds.), *Handbook of music and emotion: Theory, research, applications* (pp. 547–574). New York, NY: Oxford University Press.

Gallwey, W. T. (1987). *The inner game of tennis*. Toronto: Bantam Books.

Giddens, A. (1991). *Modernity and self-identity: Self and society in the late modern age*. CA: Stanford University Press.

Green, B. (2015). I always remember that moment: Peak music experiences as epiphanies. *Sociology*, *50*(2), 333–348.

Green, B. (2021). *Peak music experiences: A new perspective on popular music, identity and scenes*. Abingdon, Oxon: Routledge.

Groarke, J. M., & Hogan, M. J. (2016). Enhancing wellbeing: An emerging model of the adaptive functions of music listening. *Psychology of Music*, *44*, 769–791.

Groarke, J. M., & Hogan, M. J. (2020). The eudaimonic functions of music listening scale: An instrument to measure transcendence, flow and peak experience in music. *Frontiers in Psychology*. https://doi.org/10.3389/fpsyg.2-2-.566296

Harney, C., Johnson, J., Bailes, F., & Havelka, J. (2022). Is music listening an effective intervention for reducing anxiety? A systematic review and meta-analysis of controlled studies. *Musicae Scientiae*, *27*(2). https://doi.org/10.1177/10298649211046979

Kirchner, J. K. (2011). Incorporating flow into practice and performance. *Work*, *40*(3), 289–296. https://doi.org/10.3233/WOR-2011-1232. IOS Press.

Kotler, S. (2014). *The rise of superman*. London: Quercus Publishing Ltd.

Lamont, A. (2011). University student's strong experiences of music: Pleasure, engagement, and meaning. *Musicae Scientiae*, *15*(2), 229–249.

Lamont, A. (2012). Emotion, engagement and meaning in strong experiences of music performance. *Psychology of Music*, *40*(5), 574–594.

Lavaysse, L. (2002). *Professional singers describe peak experiences that arise during public performances*. Dissertation, California Institute of Integral Studies.

Lewis, M. J. (1998). Music and peak experiences: An empirical study. *Mankind Quarterly*, *39*(2), 203–224.

Lewis, M. J. (2002). Music as a trigger for peak experiences among a college staff population. *Creativity Research Journal*, *14*(3 & 4), 351–359.

Marotto, M., Roos, J., & Victor, B. (2007). Collective virtuosity in organizations: A study of peak performance in an orchestra. *Journal of Management Studies*, *44*, 388–413.

Maslow, A. H. (1959). Cognition of being in the peak experiences. *The Journal of Genetic Psychology*, *94*, 43–66.

Maslow, A. H. (1962). Lessons from the peak-experiences. *Journal of Humanistic Psychology*, *2*(9), 9–18.

Maslow, A. H. (1968a). *Toward a psychology of being*, 2nd edition. New York: Van Nostrand.

Maslow, A. H. (1968b). Education and peak experiences. *Music Educator's Journal*, *54*(6), 72–171.

Maslow, A. H. (1971). *The farthest reaches of human nature*. New York, NY: Penguin.

Maslow, A. H. (1994). *Religions, values, and peak-experiences*. New York, NY: Penguin.

Murray, O. (Director) (2020). BBC. *Ronnie Scott and his world-famous jazz club*. BBC4 www.bbc.co.uk/programmes/m000pjcm [Accessed 14 November 2024]

Panzarella, R. (1980). The phenomenology of peak experiences. *Journal of Humanistic Psychology*, *20*(1), 69–85.

Paquette, J. (2020). *Awestruck*. CO, USA: Shambhala Publications Inc.

Pathak, V. (2017). Effects of intense musical experience on way of life. *Indian Journal of Positive Psychology*, *8*(2), 252–257.

Privette, G., Hwang, K. K., & Bundrick, C. M. (1997). Cross-cultural measurement of experience: Taiwanese and Americans' peak performance, peak experience, misery, failure, sport, and average events. *Perceptual and Motor Skills*, *84*(suppl_3), 1459–1482.

Rana, S. A. (2006). *The positive psychology of music*. PhD Thesis, University of Leicester, UK.

Rana, S. A., Tanveer, S., & North, S. C. (2009). Peak experiences of music and subjective wellbeing. *Journal of Behavioural Sciences*, *19*(1–2), 41–57.

Schafer, T., Smukalla, M., & Oelker, S. A. (2014). How music changes our lives: A qualitative study of the long-term effects of intense musical experiences. *Psychology of Music*, *42*(4), 525–544.

Seligman, M. E. P. (2002). *Authentic happiness: Using the new positive psychology to realize your potential for lasting fulfilment*. New York, NY: Free Press.

Simons, H. (1977). Leading adult choral-singers toward self-actualization. *Choral Journal, 17*(5), 11.

Solberg, R. T., & Dibben, N. (2019). Peak experiences with electronic dance music: Subjective experiences, physiological responses, and musical characteristics of the break routine. *Music Perception: An Interdisciplinary Journal, 36*(4), 371–389.

Sutherland, I., & Jelinek, J. (2015). From experiential learning to aesthetic knowing: The arts in leadership development. *Advances in Developing Human Resources, 17*(3), 289–306.

Weijers, K. A. M. (2021). Peak moments: The experience of coaches. *Submitted in Partial Fulfilment of the Requirements of the Award of Doctor of Coaching and Mentoring*. Business School. Oxford Brookes University.

Whaley, J., Sloboda, J. A., & Gabrielsson, A. (2009). Peak experiences in music. In S. Hallam, I. Cross, & M. Thaut (Eds.), *The Oxford handbook of music psychology* (pp. 452–461). Oxford, UK: Oxford University Press.

Whitecross, M. (Director) (2016). Oasis: Supersonic. *Shown on BBC Two*. www.bbc.co.uk/programmes/b09ksl9g

4 Peak Experiences in the Creative Arts

Introduction

For the purpose of the chapter, we see creative arts as including any art- or craft-based occupation that evokes a creative process in an individual. This would include painting, drawing, sculpture, textile or ceramic arts, dance, performing arts, and even hairstyling.

Maslow (1963, p. 4) made a link between creativity and his theory of self-actualisation, expressing the view that "the concept of creativeness and the concept of the healthy, self-actualising, fully-human person seem to be coming closer and closer together and may perhaps turn out to be the same thing." He noted too that peak experiences appear to emanate from "great aesthetic moments," from "bursts of creativeness," and from "great moments of insight and of discovery" (1962, p. 9) and described these as:

> especially joyous and exciting moments in life, involving sudden feelings of intense happiness and wellbeing, wonder and awe involving an awareness of knowledge or higher truth as though perceiving the world from an altered and profound awe-inspiring perspective.
>
> (1962, p. 9)

Also of specific interest for this chapter is Dewey's explanation of an aesthetic experience. In the context of art, the word "aesthetic" traditionally means the philosophical reflection of art in how it is both created and experienced. However, Dewey (1990 [1934]) argued that all elements of our being "are merged in *[a]esthetic* experience" and contended that these elements of being are "so completely merged in the immediate wholeness of the experience that each is submerged – it does not present itself in consciousness as a distinct element" (Dewey, 1990 [1934], pp. 278, 274]). By rethinking art experience in terms of this more broadly defined aesthetic experience, Dewey hoped it would enlarge the domain of art and integrate it more fully into the real world (Latham, 2007). This "wholeness" is also a part of Maslow's definition of peak experience, and so we may, for the purposes of this chapter, attempt to link the concepts of "aesthetic experience" and "peak experience."

DOI: 10.4324/9781003509219-5

Following publication of his hierarchy of needs in the 1940s, Maslow was still concerned that the self-actualisation level did not explain why self-actualised people still behaved badly (Morrison, 2018). Eventually, he found what he thought was a resolution and so updated the hierarchy to include an extra motivational need, beyond self-actualisation. Raab (2014, p. 188) describes how Maslow connects this meta-motivation with *B-(being) creativity*, that is, creativity that arises from being motivated by a higher level of growth and explains how Maslow's other type of creativity, *D-(deficiency) creativity*, "is a type of creativity that arises from an individual needing to fill a gap due to an unmet primary need or the need for affirmation, acceptance and/or love" (2014, p. 188).

Maslow called this higher level of growth "self-transcendence" (Koltko-Rivera, 2006; Maslow, 1969). However, he died before he could publish his work on self-transcendence, and his final thinking on the hierarchy was neglected for some decades, not receiving any extensive attention until 2006, when Koltko-Rivera published a review of the updated hierarchy of needs that included self-transcendence at the top. Koltko-Rivera considered this to be a more accurate reflection of Maslow's theory, noting there are advantages to be gained from rectifying the theory:

> [I]ncorporating self-transcendence into Maslow's hierarchy of needs gives us a theoretical tool with which to pursue a more comprehensive and accurate understanding of human personality and behaviour.
>
> (2006, p. 313)

In Maslow's (1969) analysis, the next step for self-actualised individuals would be to connect their self-actualised identity towards making a positive impact on the world. When they do this, they get a kind of "high" from it, which Maslow called a self-transcendent peak experience (Koltko-Rivera, 2006; Maslow, 1969). Self-transcendent peak experiences, in which our potential is connected to making an impact on the world, are, according to Maslow, addictive and self-reinforcing, and the self-transcendent person is motivated to pursue more of them (Koltko-Rivera, 2006). Consequently, it can be seen that self-actualisation and self-transcendence are very closely associated, since, as Morrison (2018, p. 3) later argued, to achieve their next self-transcendent peak experience, individuals may need further self-actualisation: "In this way, self-transcendent peak experiences fuel self-actualization."

To position the accounts of the participants who shared their experiences for this chapter, we first review relevant literature connecting or relating to self-transcendent, peak, and aesthetic experiences in the creative arts. Following this, we explore participants' first-hand accounts of the artistic experience, peak, aesthetic, and transcendent, and how those experiences are interpreted.

Self-Transcendent, Peak, and Aesthetic Experiences in the Literature

As noted earlier, Maslow (1969) viewed self-transcendence as the highest level of motivation (beyond self-actualisation). For him, doing impactful work is the stimulus for self-transcendent peak experiences and the fuel for self-actualisation (Koltko-Rivera, 2006).

Self-Transcendence Through Creative Arts

In the creative arts, transcendence is manifest when either the experience of the creation or the observation of the art or artefact results in feelings that extend beyond the personal self. Four examples from the research literature demonstrate this phenomenon in action.

1) Diamond et al. (2020, p. 609) conducted a phenomenological study examining the creative engagement of Holocaust survivors in Israel. Thirty Holocaust survivor visual artists were interviewed, and two major themes surfaced. The first theme, turning outward, describes how, beyond the world of threat, a "realm of wonderment at the world beyond the self" is enhanced through art. A second theme, identified as "connecting with the world and others through creative experience," relates to the way in which art can provide an emotional experience of connection. The authors suggest the themes point to an emotional state of self-transcendence as "fundamental to survivors' artistic experience" thus shedding fresh light on "the redeeming potential of art in the face of trauma" (2020, p. 609).
2) Drawing on interviews with exotic dancers, Barton and Hardesty (2010) found that the dancers' descriptions of flow and peak experiences suggested a transcendent fusion of the "I" and the "me." The dancers described self-transcendent and even spiritual experiences as they performed, results which the authors saw occurring as a result of the unique combination of elements present in strip bar environments: "specifically the lights, music, movement, nudity, and performance"(Barton & Hardesty, 2010, p. 289).

    Barton and Hardesty's participants reported experiencing "a kind of transcendent bliss while dancing" (2010, p. 289). They felt a form of transcendental unity with something larger than the self. For example, April, a 23-year-old student working towards a bachelor's degree in psychology, shared the following experience:

When I'm on stage and I'm there dancing I feel the most spiritual I've ever felt and, a lot of my songs, they talk about God. A lot of people think that's sacrilegious, but not to me. I used to wear crosses around my neck all the time when I danced. I mean I loved it, I loved it, I just felt something just soaring all through my body. Something was! It's like the only time I felt connected, almost like at church.

(2010, p. 289)

3) In his study of the meaningfulness of work, Morrison (2018) provides an anecdotal illustration of self-transcendence in the context of creative work. In this example, Morrison explains the experiences of Rachel, who is a top hairstylist in

Georgia, USA. In Rachel's description, we can recognise the process involved in Maslow's (1969) hierarchy: from an initial degree of self-actualisation achieved by fulfilling her potential as a stylist, to the connection and making a difference in the lives of others, and then, after making a difference, "she has a self-transcendent peak experience, and she's motivated to pursue more self-transcendent peak experiences" (Morrison, 2018, p. 3).

This is how Rachel described getting a sense of meaningfulness from her job:

> I get a kind of buzz or high from using my skills to really transform a customer. One time, a woman came in after she'd divorced her husband for having an affair. She was really sad. I did a great job on her hair – so good that I took a picture of it for myself. When she looked in the mirror, her mood completely turned around. She thanked me profusely, and told me that I'd given her the confidence to see a romantic future for herself even after her divorce. That was a big buzz; I get buzzes like that only every month or so, but there are lots of little versions of that same feeling that I experience throughout the week, and that's what keeps me going, keeps me working harder on being better at what I do.
>
> (Morrison, 2018, p. 3)

4) Wang et al.'s (2023, pp. 788–789) exploration of how art as part of a consumer experience induces a state of self-transcendence includes discussion of how self-transcendence involves the "fading away of the subjective sense of one's self as an isolated entity" (p. 778). As a consequence, the authors note how purely personal pursuits become less important. They suggest that art transcends thoughts of self-centred indulgences, arguing that the art experience stimulates a mental state of self-transcendence that subsequently "reduces the focus on one's own desires and shifts attention away from the self" (2023, p. 289).

Aesthetic Experience Through Creative Arts

As mentioned earlier, Dewey's definition of aesthetic experience does not equate to the more traditional definition that relates to appreciation of the fine arts. Rather, he believed aesthetic experience is not reserved for art galleries or concert halls but permeates ordinary activities too. In fact, Dewey's aim was to incorporate the continuity that exists in all human experience, including the aesthetic experience.

To clarify his ideas, Dewey (1934) identified three different forms of experience notwithstanding that they form a continuous whole:

1) the general everyday continuum of interactions and events;
2) a specific and meaningful interaction or event;
3) an experience distinguished by reaching of a stage of fulfilment or consummation.

The third type of "highpoint" consummation is, Dewey argues, an essential aspect of an aesthetic experience (1934), but it merges with general experience and is integrated with it, just as specific events are intermingled. Thus, aesthetic experience is not a special form of experience reserved for fine art!

Another important feature of aesthetic experience for Dewey is the absence of closure. Dewey (1934) writes:

> [C]onsummation is relative; instead of occurring once for all at a given point, it is recurrent . . . For as we turn from reading a poem or novel or seeing a picture the effect presses forward in further experiences, even if only subconsciously.

Following Dewey, Barrett (2007, p. 115) argues that creative arts practice involves the "intensification of everyday experiences from which new knowledge or knowing emerges," and confirms that "knowledge produced through aesthetic experience is always contextual and situated." Barrett (2007) explained how in Dewey's thinking the process of attributing meaning and value in artistic practice, and in its contemplation, is necessarily experiential.

Summarising the basic traits of an aesthetic experience, Dewey identified completeness, involving an organic wholeness; uniqueness where there is unity, a singular quality difficult to describe because it is not like any other experience; and unifying emotion even though there are no separate things called emotion in it (Jackson, 1998). Dewey argued that it is only through the knowledge gained by the artist through everyday living and activity that it can be expressed through and embodied in the artwork via creative practice. Thus, "action, feeling and meaning are one" (Dewey, 1980, p. 35). Jacob (2018, Intro) similarly emphasised that in Dewey's aesthetics it is the experience that matters and that through Dewey's understanding we are able to see that "both the artist and viewer contribute to making art. Such aesthetic experiences enable us to make meaning and, thus, grow."

Dewey frequently talks of emotion and spontaneity in the pursuit of achieving an aesthetic peak experience in the creative arts. He discusses these dimensions at length, concluding that "emotion is essential to that act of expression which produces a work of art" (1934, p. 71).

Dewey believed that the spontaneity of art lies in complete absorption in the subject matter and is characteristic of aesthetic experience. In a letter Van Gogh wrote to his brother, he said that "emotions are sometimes so strong that one works without knowing that one works, and the strokes come with a sequence and coherence like that of words in a speech or letter" (Dewey, 1934, p. 85). Dewey emphasised that this spontaneity is evident when actors lose themselves in their roles, and painters' strokes come with a sequence and coherence.

Relatedly, Van Deurzen-Smith (2014) introduces inspiration as part of the artistic process. Inspiration, she suggests, has as its starting point communion with the universe. Having taken in a message from the universe, she can communicate the message to others. This creates an ongoing a connection between herself and her creation, a chain reaction whereby the audience becomes subject to the object of creation and by extension herself as artist. The result is a holistic engagement between universe, self, other, and creation, which

> shows the importance of factoring in the act of being inspired, as it brings with it a sense of connectedness to something external, rather than one's creative project being a solely personal endeavour . . . the finished project is the initial object of judgement and not the artist herself.
>
> (2014, p. 79)

She shares how she noticed clients referring to inspiration as a moment already experienced. They saw it as a trigger point for them to begin a project but noted that it "seemed to lose its impact once the work had begun" (2014, p. 84). These feelings expressed by Van Deurzen-Smith's clients are similar to descriptions of peak experience – transitory moments of richness or ephemeral experiences.

Peak Experience Through Creative Arts

In Maslow's unpublished papers, there are notes concerning our aesthetic needs. He describes what he sees as a variety of aesthetic impulses that are subjective, introspective, and conscious responses that cannot be described in words and must be experienced to be known. He reported how some phrases are commonly used to describe this type of experience:

> [P]eople frequently report such sensations as a faster heartbeat, a holding of the breath, feelings of fascination and mental absorption, sensations of sharp pleasure, and cold shivers moving up and down the back. Indeed, I have often thought that the aesthetic experience may share a similarity with what physiologists call "sensory shock." For example, this encompasses a person's set of responses when suddenly immersed in ice-cold water.
>
> (Maslow & Hoffman, 1996, Location 802)

From his observations, Maslow (1968) suggested that much of what we have learnt from peak experience studies could be transferred directly to the area of creativity and creative attitude. Common qualities of absorption, intrinsic value, rich perception, disorientation in time and space, and freedom from usual fears and anxieties are analogous for both peak and creative experiences.

These qualities have been recognised by other researchers too. Hanfling, for example, has described the aesthetic aspect of peak experience, as

> an experience to be prized very highly . . . arresting, intense and utterly engrossing; that when achieved it seizes one's whole mind or imagination and conveys whatever it does convey so vividly that the result is delight and knowledge.
>
> (1992, p. 115)

Marotto et al. (2007) also suggest that "both the aesthetic and the peak experience describe the state of individual engrossment in which a sense of time is lost."

Such experiences are inclined to be short-lived and transitory with profound and enduring consequences which "may include a deepened understanding of self and the relationship of one's self to the world" (2007, pp. 389–390).

Privette (1983) discusses how peak experiences can be found in activities that seek excellence, including the creative arts. Bennetts (1998, p. 211) also suggests that creative individuals may be more predisposed to the peak experience: "the ability to recognise the beauty and truth in that which is created, is the aesthetic sense, and is crucial to artists if they are to be able to portray the 'truth' of that which is seen." Additionally, Marotto et al. (2007, pp. 389–390) claim that they can be prompted by a large variety of triggers, including "moments of inspiration or discovery, unity with nature, exercise and movement, love and sex and *aesthetic perceptions, particularly in the performing or fine arts*" (our italics).

In the context of performing arts, Panzarella (1980) studied the phenomenology of aesthetic peak experiences. He interviewed 103, generally well-educated respondents in the aesthetic media in art galleries and concert locations and concluded that 90% of the participants reported some lasting effects, creating vivid and continually stimulating memories. These findings concur with Maslow's (1962) assertion that some of the effects or after-effects of peak experiences may be permanent. Participants in Panzarella's (1980) study reported an intense joyous experience when listening to music or looking at visual art. They experienced an enhanced appreciation involving more positive self-feelings, as well as improved relationships with others, and a boost of optimism.

In their study of peak experiences, Yeagle, Privette, and Dunham claimed their results bolstered Maslow's "position of universality of the peak experiences" (1989, p. 529). Descriptions of peak experiences were collected from 29 exhibiting artists and compared with data from a comparison group of 123 university students. All participants described and rated their personal experiences of highest happiness. There were no significant differences in the two groups' accounts of peak experience, and their responses were consistent with other subjective descriptions of peak experiences.

Peak and Aesthetic Experiences in the Audience Perception

According to Dewey (1934), the value of artistic expression is in the ongoing transactional dynamic through which the experience is created and perceived. Latham notes that, in line with his overall definition of experience, Dewey defined aesthetic experience as "occurring not just in the presence of art or 'beauty,' but in the presence of something that causes the reaction one has in this situation" (Latham, 2007, p. 253). Latham further suggests this might be "any kind of situation for any person, and varies from person to person" (2007, p. 253).

Dewey's seeming democratisation of the aesthetic experience is also evident in Jacques Rancière's (2009) idea of an audience of emancipated spectators. In Rancière's work, spectators, particularly in the theatre, are recognised as actively creative and responsible, so much so that he argues our notions about the act of viewing need to change to see spectators as "both distant spectators and active interpreters" (Rancière, 2009, 13). According to Breemen (2017), Rancière's ideas suggest all people have a right to be heard, yet a struggle is needed to challenge the division between actors and the audience. This struggle is visible in the theatre, especially in participatory performances (Breemen, 2017, p. 301), where both theatre makers and audiences together create a space for critical reflection. Seen in this way, theatre as both an aesthetic act and an event in the everyday life could fulfil an important role in a democratic society.

Rancière (2009) therefore considers that the spectator role should not be seen as a matter of secondary importance but as a necessary element actively creating the conditions and the content for performances. However, there is an inconsistency in this argument. The audience or the spectator is necessary for the art to be perceived as art in the first place, but at the same time they are separated from the capacity to plan or execute the creative act. As Breemen (2017) points out, a performance cannot proceed without its spectators, even though the audience has no real influence or role.

Van Deurzen-Smith (2014), drawing on what Sartre (1943) called "the look of the Other," suggests that when an artist is conscious of the audience's gaze, there comes a realisation that their subjective art has been made "object" by the onlooker or spectator. In this encounter, the artist becomes the object of the audience's subjective experience and "the meaning that the artist has expressed within her work is suddenly no longer in her control and is open to interpretation by the audience" (Van Deurzen-Smith, 2014, p. 83).

A similar paradox could be identified in relation to the display context of creative art, which also adds to the audience subjective experience. Szubielska and Imbir (2021) report that the situational context of an art gallery, for example, contributes to the intensity of the aesthetic affective experience and the appreciation of the artworks displayed. During a study in which aesthetic emotions were measured, these authors found that participants viewing installation art in a contemporary gallery were "more positively aroused, the source of their emotions was to a greater extent automatic than reflective, and their emotions were considered as more important than those which viewers felt in a laboratory setting" (2021, p. 6).

Japanese scholars, Pelowski and Fuminori Akiba (2011) sought to establish the nature of a transformative aesthetic experience for both the artist and the viewer/spectator. They began by recognising the traditional aesthetic experience as "state of selfless, pleasurable and harmonious mastery involving the successful reception and assimilation of art information, that might be equated to a peak moment of epiphany or insight itself" (2011, p. 81).

Also, they identify how throughout history people have been stirred by works of art, expecting almost to be elevated by them. Such stirrings and accounts of transformation or epiphanies abound and are collectively known as aesthetic experiences encompassing, for example, states of heightened awareness (Ferree, 1968), consummation (Maslow, 1959; Dewey, 1934), enlightenment (Shusterman, 1997), and cognitive development (Dewey, 1934).

According to Pelowski and Fuminori Akiba (2011, p. 81), an aesthetic moment for the viewer has traditionally involved a "flattened conception of the experience of art," where perception and evaluation are in harmony, and they experience what

Maslow (1959) terms a peak experience that appears to reaffirm existing conceptions and identities. These authors argue that this traditional aesthetic experience tends to preclude the possibility for art to mark and transform lives, focusing as it does, "exclusively on the moment of 'aesthetic' insight or peak of harmonious pleasure and contemplation itself" (2011, p. 81).

As already intimated, Dewey (1934) argues for an alternative approach to aesthetic experience involving recognition of disruption based on the viewer's personal beliefs and identity, and to this end Pelowski and Fuminori Akiba (2011), recognising that there are two distinct aesthetic states – facile "recognition" and the more active meta-cognitive "perception," offered a five-stage process model based on Dewey's work.

The model clarifies the stages leading to transformation and provides an alternative model of art perception and transformative aesthetic experience. The first stage accepts that people have pre-expectations of art based on their pre-existing schema. Drawing on Dewey, Pelowski and Fuminori Akiba (2011, p. 82) explain that by focusing exclusively on informational assessment, "the significance or meaning of an artwork becomes implicitly located outside of the viewer, where it can be received and assessed but is itself fixed and unchangeable."

The second stage recognises that for the viewer there is often cognitive rejection or discrepancy that falls short of their expectations. Through this disruption of what is expected, new thinking about a piece of art takes place, triggering reflection, acceptance, and self-change. Pelowski and Fuminori Akiba (2011, p. 84) suggest that in this stage "a viewer returns to cognitive mastery with a new set of expectations or schema as a direct result of their perception of art." The third stage is where viewers are able to process their experience and make it part of their life. Without the process of disruption, reflection, and meta-cognitive change, these events will not include the necessary component of self-modification and so "leave the viewer without any understanding of the significance of the preceding event" (2011, p. 92).

Stage four then looks at the empirical study of this process. The authors state that if we, as viewers, focus only on the peak conclusion of epiphany or assimilation of art information, "we are left with no means of assessing art experience other than for pleasure or formal assessment" (2011, p. 93). Stage five summarises the process suggesting three phases of art viewing: i) an initial, self-reinforcing mastery phase involving assessment of formal elements, ii) an abortive, self-protectionary escape phase, encompassing a period of meaninglessness and loss of understanding, not unlike the low point on the Kubler-Ross change curve (1969), and iii) a final, fundamental shift in assessment from the informational plane to a meta-cognitive mode of "experiential" interpretation (Pelowski & Fuminori Akiba, 2011).

Funch (1997, p. 42) views the possibility of researching transformation through an aesthetic experience with a certain amount of scepticism, saying that "if appreciation of a specific work of art has an impact on the viewer's life . . . it would be difficult, if not impossible, to give evidence of such influences through empirical studies." However, we are optimistic about our challenge for this chapter, which is to interview creative artists with the hope that we can uncover their peak aesthetic experiences.

Commenting on research in the arts, Landy (1984) similarly reports that research is diverse and difficult to define. However, he observes that creative artists can be seen as researchers even as they are engaged in the process of making art. They use qualitative, historical, and aesthetic methods and often engage in a reflective rather than purely empirical processes, "implying a search for the unique case" (1984, p. 89). Researching the peak aesthetic experiences of our participants using phenomenological interviews could similarly be seen as fitting this more reflective pattern.

Peak Experience in Context – Participant Accounts

The first of our participants is **Tanya Poole,** an established international artist. When discussing the essence of a peak experience, Tanya recognised she had many examples of peak experience, experiences realised through three bodies of work: *Thozama and Rose, The Whispering Spring,* and *The Night Guide.* These bodies of work and their provenance are discussed and referred to throughout our interview.

Tanya believes that a painting is an object in the world, a kind of crystallisation of time made up of many, many moments; an image she perceives as a sort of contemplative mode. For Tanya, there is something about a painting and the process of having brought it together which is very similar to a peak experience. She says:

> It's taking all of that stuff and distilling it into an extraordinarily intense thing. You can say that of both a peak experience and a painting when considering everything that goes into the framework of an exhibition, and the formal aspects of painting: scale, technique, colour and format. All of these things you use to construct coming into one moment, like a peak experience.

In each of her three bodies of work, Tanya constructed three "chapters" and allowed them to come into conversation with each other. She says, "I'm a little nervous around polarising thought, and I find working around a three-way thing is much better for thinking through." This three-dimensional perspective sheds light on her interpretation that her experiences are shared between herself through her self-awareness, participants, and a kind of outside eye witnessing as if it were somebody else observing in a certain way:

> I'm always interested and immersed in the outward eye because it clarifies so much for me. I'm thinking painting, I'm thinking walking and it's a tremendously complex web for me as I do a lot of stuff intuitively and laterally. To pull something right out of it and look with a perspective that I don't really have is extraordinary.

Tanya believes a characteristic of her work embraces a transitional value when being observed in the context of growth and development. This perspective aligns with Privette and Bundrick's (1991, p. 171) definition of peak performance, "transactive, clearly focusing on self, as well as the valued object." Additionally, Tanya's inclusion of these three chapters in her work appears to reflect Van Deurzen-Smith's (2014,

p. 84) chain reaction, resulting in holistic connections between herself, the other parts of the creation, and the witnesses to the whole body of work. It is the starting point in her communion with the universe which acts as the subject to her object.

Tanya describes her peak experiences as "aha" moments. She constantly queries her surroundings and is always asking questions that perhaps are never answered, yet in this constant state of thinking suddenly answers come together in a crystallisation:

> [A]nd there's a little bit like . . . O fuck, yes, right . . . all of those little questions, those little intertwined thoughts suddenly come into one focus or one moment and that moment is so distilled that it kind of explodes.

When her thoughts land and something clicks, Tanya gets an overwhelming sense of "that's what it's all about," a message that makes her feel awe and excitement. Her peak experience lies not in the physicality of actually painting but in each aspect of her three individual chapters, which in turn become more distilled and explosive because she has experienced that "aha" moment.

Tanya is also a second dan black belt in karate and recalls a memorable peak experience which came to her in the *dōjō*. She says she must have been very adrenalated, fearlessly pushing herself into a fight which seemed to last for an hour but in reality was only minutes and seconds. This experience in the *dōjō* led her to create an exhibition called *Thozama and Rose*. Central to the success of this exhibition were the relationships between Thozama and Rose, two women karate practitioners and Tanya herself. The creation of this exhibition took place in the context of a post-apartheid South Africa. The *dōjō* was one of the few places where a sense of race, class, and hierarchy is stripped away. People are thrown together in this environment which gave rise to a sense of Tanya connecting with herself, finding out who she is, and what she represents. By immersing herself into that experience Tanya experienced "aha" moments of realisation and growth, which she aligns with peak experiences.

The after-effects of a bout of a fight between Thozama and Rose were projected by video onto two centrally hung panels in the exhibition space. The images were life-size and simply showed their heavy breathing and panting until their breath returned to normal. On the wall of the gallery, Tanya had painted 19 big portraits of others aged from 7 to 60 years in the *dōjō*. Tanya explains:

> Every single one of those 19 portraits looks directly at you. Everything is very, very raw. You really are being asked as a viewer to conjure up that stuff from who you are and how you connect; how you observe yourself, how can we observe the world? I'm hoping by my discipline to prompt these kinds of questions. And also, prompt a sense of the extraordinarily magical, the beauty of the aesthetic of art and painting.

The three chapters of this body of work are first, the video work; second, the audience (the portraits); and third, a series of ten paintings showing various stages of Thozama and Rose engaging with each other as they entered and left the *dōjō*. This third aspect was caught by still camera, which together with the eye of the video camera was embedded as the observational aspect with the audience. The idea, Tanya explains, is that we become what we observe. This project was two years in the making.

Another exhibition, called *The Whispering Spring*, is, Tanya says, "where I am and who I am." She informally calls it "the shes, the bees and the trees." The setting was a palaeontology dig in South Africa, a group of seven women including a paleobotanist and a paleoentomologist. The women all had a close relationship with one another. They excavated fossils which had not seen the light of day for 275 million years, and this gave Tanya an overwhelming sense of profound connection with herself and the whole team. Her peak experience, similar to the *Thozama and Rose* exhibition, was that sense of connectedness with the environment and the people. Again, this exhibit was in three chapters. The first was huge portraits of the women's faces (the shes) in the field which created a sense of intelligence and transcendence, enabling Tanya to find a new space. The second was a large-scale aspect of about ten trees, viewed as if lying at the bottom of the forest looking up through them. And the third chapter was 167 individual paintings of aspects of bees which were installed as a swarm into the gallery space. Tanya explains:

> The seven women researchers were the observers and through them I was then allowed to observe this crazy timespan of 275 million years. And to observe myself cracking open a rock, dropping into this time chasm which was absolutely extraordinary – a privilege, and you've got this element of being looked at as well.

Tanya's peak experiences arise from her absolute immersion into the artistic medium, almost becoming the medium. Her inspiration comes from world and environmental issues such as the political situation in South Africa in *Thozama and Rose*, and the #MeToo movement, which was gaining popularity at the time of *The Whispering Spring*. The scientists and researchers had experienced various manifestations of the resistance to the #MeToo movement, something they talked about and connected with. Tanya's art represents her feelings and thoughts about such issues. Describing *The Whispering Spring* Tanya says:

> I like the way the bees become the Universe. Without them, we're fucked as a world. It makes us put ourselves into the timeline of existence.

The Night Guide is Tanya's third piece of work for exhibition. She moved to France from South Africa with her family and was wandering through the hedgerows, noticing the complicated and intricate small ecosystems at work. She had a peak moment again. She remembers thinking:

> I need to be here. And when I came here it was reinforced by this crazy experience in nature when I kind of just . . . the boundaries between myself and what was surrounding me dissolved and for lack of a better phrase it was an

overwhelmingly spiritual experience. It was extraordinary. And those experiences . . . *The Night Guide* is about finding out about who I am with spaces, and how I'm connected here.

For this project she wanted to imagine being a moth and see how the moth sees – to envision, empathise, and put herself into another creature's environment. The three chapters of this exhibition project are a suite of outsized moth paintings; the moth's habitat, depicted as electric blue undergrowth in the moonlight; one large-scale painting of the moon, a 2.5 × 1.5-metre painting at one end of the gallery.

The Night Guide primarily takes the form of several huge moths, which Tanya finds very ephemeral and feminine, occupying a space between dark and light:

> I love the fact that when you look closely, they are definitely brilliant, even though they are often seen as the drab cousins of the butterfly. And of course, they actually do their job better than the butterflies. They're super pollinators and they're amazing. And I love the exchange between them and the pale flowers in the night, the exchange between them and the moon – and, because my head works like this, I see the black and white as a lack of knowledge or how we gain and access knowledge. And there's this lovely crackle of feminine energy in me that responds to this stuff.

Next to these outsized moths lies the dark undergrowth and the forest at night, a kind of deep electric blue "a connected, strange matrix that the moth is kind of coming through." Tanya's senses become heightened by tuning into what it's like to emerge at night, to feel their energy, and to fly in the dark which she then represents pictorially.

Then there is the moths' relationship with the moon, which Tanya captures in this work, describing it as "reflecting light off of the sun onto this weird little orbiting planet, which the moths respond to because they are evolved to look for light, to look for pale flowers."

> And the primary feeling in this exhibition is this sight. I'm looking where I'm going, and there are these eye metaphors circling around all of this which I love! That's where my peak experience happens. It's through my eyeballs. And that's where I get the out of body experience; it's blinding. It almost takes away that visual intensity by blowing out the boundaries; how you think your body is. It's extraordinary.

We asked Tanya to tell us how she felt physiologically when she visualised and relived that explosion. She explained that she visualised the experience both within and outside of herself:

> I was walking through the forest in the context of moving to a country that I don't know. The light shining through the forest is very different from South Africa. The light is almost horizontal, picking up all the spider silks spun from

tree to tree to tree. As I moved everything shimmered and glittered around me as if I was in one complex and joyous web and I suddenly realised I was in someone else's home. Not my home but what I wanted to be my home.

I felt a desire to escape my boundaries as a human. I wanted to become more animal and understand that I am as much a part of nature as the spider or the tree or the fungi that live under the forest floor and all of that came together. I called it the eye trap. And the beauty of those spider silks and that shifting light in that moment just nearly demolished my mind. I wasn't big enough to contain it. And the physical sense of it. I had to close my eyes. I had this gold around me, and the gold just exploded inside in my chest and up behind my eyeballs. As a visual metaphor it almost felt like my boundaries in my body just didn't exist anymore. And at that point I was completely as one. I was a creature in that entire, entangled Gaia. That experience was so pure and it was about my eyes and light and too much light. It was uncontainable and beautiful.

Tanya reiterates that her painting of a moth is three metres wide and not its actual size. At the moment of seeing the real moth she experienced an "aha" moment or peak experience:

It's like "what the fuck? This is the most extraordinary thing I've ever seen!" I'm beside myself with intensity, looking at this moth under the microscope, through a lens or just in my hand. The beauty, complexity and intricacy of it. I then try to describe that experience to somebody who hasn't seen the moth themselves but I'm saying to them "look how I saw this moth because it will make you look at it differently and it's really incredible." So, if I've painted a 3-metre-wide moth, I can conjure for the viewer a similar experience with my painting as I had with my moth.

On top of that I do have these other experiences. I don't know if you would call them peak experiences or being in flow, it happens in the process of working itself and then you get lost and you come out of it, and you've lost a day. You've lost your sense of time or become so immersed that you've entered a different world. You come out of it and it's beautiful but exhausting and exhilarating and it's a very, very privileged place to be able to access. And I access it all the time. This is my world.

All of Tanya's work portrays a representation of the self, the other, and the universe in the three aspects of each work. For example, in *The Whispering Spring* the awareness of the other is represented by the observers, seven women watching; the awareness of the self is Tanya, exposed to fossils from 275 million years ago, and asking where she fits into this phenomenon. And the portrait of the trees is the universe, looking down and giving a holistic view of everything. Her peak experiences are present through each stage of her work but more noticeable when something "lands" or "clicks." It happened when she moved to France and realised "this is where I need to be." Her peak experiences are absolutely visual not ascribed to brushes and ink. The 'aha' moment happens when she is walking in the fields, forests, or in the *dōjō*, a moment which seems to be driven by these contexts but enriched by her connections and relationships with people.

Tanya's relationships and connectedness to people, nature, the environment, and her artistic medium are key to making all three chapters happen in each of the three pieces of art she described for us. She feels no fear of immersing herself into situations without knowing how they might affect or change her. She feels confident to venture into the unknown, accompanied by the mutual trust and connectedness in her relationships with participants in the co-creation of her art: "it is people enjoying and valuing each other and having a sense of mutual values about life and energy and purpose."

There is trust in her relationships with her participants, her audience, who feel safe to go to a place of vulnerability and take a risk. Trust allows them to feel safe, and safety gives permission to become open and to partake in experiencing life as a moth, for example. Tanya hopes that observers may also have their own peak experiences, making meaning, and achieving "aha" moments through her work:

> That's another really very, very strong context for this work. I would say that my art-making, making a piece, is almost like trying to recreate that moment for somebody else.

In her transformation and intensification of everyday experiences into art via the interpenetration of herself, objects, events, and even audience, Tanya embodies Dewey's notion of aesthetic experience and the democratisation of art.

***

Our second participant is **Barty (Andrew Barton)**, an award-winning professional hairdresser, critically acclaimed as hairdressing royalty. Known as Barty, his energy, charisma, and vigour are visceral. When introducing the concept of peak experience, his expression became animated, his eyes shone with enthusiasm, and his immediate recognition of the phenomenon became evident.

His instant recollection of a peak experience was when cutting one particular client's hair. The shape of the head at the back, the movement of the strands suddenly struck him as familiar. All senses were engaged. The hairline at the back of her hair, the feel of the hair though his hands, the sight of something familiar, the engagement of mind and body released an energy and awareness that he remembered some years later. He asked his client "Have I cut your hair before?" She replied, "Yes, 10 years ago."

There was another experience that Barty was reluctant at first to express, but his feelings and emotions on recalling the encounter were visible. He talked of a particular client whom he saw weekly. They had built up trust and a very strong bond with one another through discussions over a hairdryer. Sadly, she passed away. Barty found this out only when her husband called him to ask if he would fulfil her request for him to style her hair in her coffin. This request was an enormous stretch for Barty, as he was going to see and then touch a dead body for the first time in his life. He was somewhat taken aback but realised that the trust and relationship with his now deceased client had to be honoured and valued "she wanted me to look after her." He agreed, providing her husband was also present.

The moment of entering the mortuary seemed surreal. He found himself talking out loud, having a conversation with her, almost picking up from the week before when chatting about developments on Coronation Street. He describes it as "quite a remarkable experience":

> I just became very respectful of her wishes, and I think it brought a lot of meaning. It meant something to me that she wanted me to do that and to make her look beautiful. She was lying in the coffin and her hair was not clean, so I used a dry shampoo. I had to go through a whole process of thinking what do I take with me. Is it respectful to use a hair dryer as they don't have loud machinery in that type of place?
>
> And what was nice afterwards, was that her husband said let me take you for a pint. We went to the local pub and just sat and had a pint. It was fascinating chatting to a man who I'd never really met before. . . . He was someone I'd never had a relationship with – but I had because she had been telling me about him for over ten years!
>
> I saw this as a peak experience as it was taking me out of the usual aspects of my life, and to a different emotional state that I had to go through. So, it was a peak experience because I learnt things from it about myself and about the relationship I have with human beings when I'm doing their hair. So yes, I think it was a peak experience.

The meaningfulness that Barty felt is akin to hairdresser Rachel's experience described in Morrison's (2018) research.

Barty also shared that there have been situations where he has looked after famous celebrities and prime ministers, such as Lady Thatcher, whose hair he styled a couple of times. He recalls:

> That was a peak experience because it took me away from my normal behavioural attitudes and responses. I felt unsure how to respond in the situation and ended up leaning back on my normal behaviour. So, part of that was stimulating laughter and humour, and also relying on my northern working-class roots which I use a lot in certain relationships.

We asked him how he senses such a peak experience, and he admitted to experiencing a kind of adrenalin rush ignited by a fear of failure and his own preconceptions of celebrity status. Barty questions himself about this fear of failure, knowing that he can create amazing hair:

> But it's all wrapped up in the emotional state they're in rather than just me. Because they're bringing so much of their ego. So, it's not so much doing their hair but satisfying their ego.

Barty thinks the fear of failure is also linked to his reputation "because I've got some level of fame" and admits that his ego is at play too. When clients come to him for the first time, their expectations are usually very high, but he admits modestly "after all, they are only a pair of scissors." More significantly, Barty has come to realise that it is the relationship the client and hairstylist develop together that yields the results they both seek, explaining:

> Over the years I've grown confident to talk to a stranger, coming to me for the first time, about things like weight issues, around finding out a little bit more about why they're not taking good care of themselves. It's usually wrapped up with a lot of issues about emotions. You know too that hairdressers relate the story that we're told more than gynaecologists or psychologists – it's rather like being a doctor! It's a bizarre relationship that you sit in a chair in front of a mirror, and you start talking to this complete stranger who's doing your hair.

Barty is adamant that his peak experiences have been learning experiences too. For example, although he felt the loss of his client acutely, and that of her husband, the experience of doing his client's hair in the mortuary taught him to be more resilient around death. The trust built in that relationship gave Barty a sense of pride and made him feel good about himself: "something quite magical came. She had wanted me to arrange her hair post-mortem, and that says a lot about the meaning of the relationship that some clients have with their hairdresser."

Barty's peak experiences come from 30 years of dedication to the profession: "I'd get home mentally and emotionally worn out. After a full day behind that chair with 10–12 clients, I'm absolutely spent. There's nothing left to give." Over the years, however, Barty has learnt to put in boundaries around his working conditions to protect his homeostasis:

> I think the fence I've learned to put around myself is around not doing it every day. It's about a day being as organised and as mechanically perfect as possible. Any interruptions to that day will throw me off balance. I need to be focussed. That includes the temperature of the room, the volume in the room and I have to work in the same position every single time. I can't cope with any change of light that's going on around me and noise too. I just realise what the parameters are and the conditions to make it work.

These boundaries are almost core conditions for Barty to be able to perform at his very best whilst maintaining his professional integrity.

Barty's recollection that he'd cut a client's hair before is reminiscent of the sensory experiences discussed in our chapter on Peak Experiences in Writing and Reading. Each of the senses plays a significant part in the stimulus for a peak experience. Interestingly though, Barty then used that recollection to reminisce with the client, thus creating the trust that is all important in his work and which is further exemplified in his posthumous hairstyling experience.

***

Our third participant is **Fiona Haygreen,** a freelance artist and businesswoman. We asked Fiona what a peak experience meant to her, and she explained that when she is painting she tends to ignore her surroundings and gets into an almost flow like state:

> I forget about my environment. I'm so in the moment that I forget everything else, lose time almost, and nothing else seems to matter. I don't notice anything around apart from the concentration that I'm giving to the painting I'm doing.

Fiona describes two types of paintings, one where she is really focused on a project and knows exactly what she wants to achieve and another for relaxation, which she says is almost like meditation:

> When you meditate you try to shut out all the disruptions. I just copy a nice picture in water colours, just for me and my own pleasure. I feel my tension and anxiety levels come down and I'm not stressing. It's another way of closing off the world. I'm completely focussed on the painting that I don't really notice what's going on around me, almost in a bubble of what I'm doing.

Fiona's description of her experience of losing her sense of time when concentrating on her painting seems less like a peak experience and more like Csikszentmihalyi's idea of flow. Csikszentmihalyi (1990) studied artists during his doctoral research and documented how they were particularly prone to experience intense focus while painting. During the process of painting, they entered into what many of them described as a zone of intense, pleasurable focus. Csikszentmihalyi even characterises the flow experience as an exceptional mental state, where "an individual is engaged with an activity as if nothing else mattered" (1990, p. 4).

***

Our fourth participant, **Andy Secombe,** is an actor and author. He began our interview with his recollection of Sir John Gielgud's thoughts about peak experience:

> Gielgud said the reason we all get involved in this business is that we're all expecting that transcendental experience which happens very rarely. That's the hook that keeps you going because you're looking for that "ahhh" moment on stage.

Andy's own peak experience came six months into the run of *The Invisible Man* in the West End of London in the 1990s. A key factor in this experience was a technique recommended by Stanislavski that involved giving a character a life outside the play. This helped Andy to concentrate and stay in character.

The character Andy was playing was Squire Burdock, and in his first entrance he would come on and make it different each night: "I'd come from a party or from just having dinner or whatever I felt like that day and this gave a new continuity to the character, plus I didn't come on stage cold."

One night he walked on stage, and he knew something had happened:

It was as though I wasn't being the character anymore. It was as though someone else had taken over and what was happening was completely effortless. I was watching myself as if from above, and I felt an absolute freedom from anything – it was a sort of transcendental experience. I had this extraordinary connection with everyone in the audience. People on the stage were looking at me slightly funny but I felt like I was the play – not in a narcissistic way but I felt I was sort of "being" the play.

Andy's experience carried on through the play, and although he thought it had to eventually stop, the feelings got deeper and deeper, resulting in massive cheers from the audience when he came on in the second half:

It was quite bizarre. It had never happened before like that, and I just sort of let go and dissolved into it. The play just sort of happened through me and it was a wonderful experience. Walking on stage was just like "I am this character." I am Squire Burdock. There was no difference between me and him. We were the same person.

Dewey (1934) highlighted how when actors lose themselves in their roles they become more spontaneous. This is something Andy had clearly worked on and now owned.

The cast too had experienced something extraordinary and asked Andy what had happened:

I had no answer, but it was a wonderful, amazing experience. I was completely shattered. Really, really tired as though some great energy had come through me. I actually felt that the audience was following my every thought. We were all in the same space, but I was at the centre, like a storyteller. Everything had a newness and a truth. There was a huge feeling of euphoria. I couldn't explain what had happened and I didn't want to talk about it but just bask in the afterglow – the wonderful sense of peace. I'd come through something and felt as though I'd been changed by the experience and wanted to sit with that and not talk to anyone. People who talk about enlightenment say that unless you've experienced it you can't explain it. I think I came close to experiencing what that felt like.

In their research, Loveday et al. (2023, p. 1456) similarly found that actors achieve peak performance through preparation processes that allow self-efficacy and the ability to perform freely. They also found that such performances involved connection and a heightened state "where actors felt like they cognitively and physically lived as their character."

***

Peak and flow experiences are in evidence not only in the professional lives of artists but also in the pursuit of creative hobbies such as crafting and DIY. **Louella,** our next participant, enjoys many forms of creativity. She recently took a course on chicken-wire sculpture and made a beautiful goose. She feels that hobbies can trigger a playful peak experience and felt enormous joy and pride in finishing the goose. Joy and happiness are qualities of a peak experience, and, as Maslow agued: "it has a cosmic or a godlike, good-humoured quality, certainly transcending hostility of any kind. It could easily be called happy joy, or gay exuberance or delight" (1968, p. 91).

On reflection, however, Louella thinks creating the goose and the whole experience could also be called a flow experience as described by Csikszentmihalyi (1990). When enjoying a hobby such as flower-arranging or gardening, she expressed how time flows past her without her noticing how long she has been engaged in the activity.

Similarly, **Dan Walmsley,** who we meet again in the sporting context, also experienced an impromptu experience in relation to creativity:

> I was painting my daughter's room, cutting in between the ceiling and the wall, listening to some trance music. I remember my tongue coming out as I was painting a line. It was perfect and I couldn't stop. Usually what happens is that I would think about it and then go off and make a smudge. But here I wasn't in control of it – and when I say I wasn't in control I must have been at some level, but my brain seemed to switch everything off that I needed to worry about and put me into kind of auto-like state. I don't know.
>
> I think it's spontaneous and fascinating. The brain must power down to get rid of all that self-doubt because as soon as you start to doubt yourself it's over. The brain is so primitive, it wants to keep you safe.

At that moment Dan was completely focused on the line of painting and could think of nothing else. The trance music in the background reduced his sense of time and place, creating the right conditions for a flow experience to happen, and when he stopped, he recognised that euphoric peak moment:

> Wow, I can't believe I just did that! That was amazing. In that moment I wasn't feeling anything, it was focus and afterwards, just that rush of Wow!

It is interesting to note that Dan uses the word "rush" to describe his experience, a term borrowed from the sporting field, rather than the "aha," "peak," or "transcendent" – terms used by other participants in this creative arts context. This variance in terminology can be noted across the different contexts and will be discussed further in our Conclusion chapter.

What Is Significant About Peak Experiences in This Context?

In this chapter, we examined peak experience and related theories in the context of a variety of creative arts. Our review of the literature focused on the links that Maslow (1963) made between creativity and his theories of self-actualisation, self-transcendence, and peak experience. We reviewed Dewey's (1934) idea of aesthetic experience. We found the theory of particular relevance to the participant interviews gathered for this chapter. The idea that aesthetic experience is a transaction between all that is present in any given moment and signifies the connectedness of all events and objects in the world (including our own situation and current perceptions) is very powerful.

One of the overriding factors that our participants have in common is their relationship with their art and their connectedness with the medium and the art form. Tanya illustrates this by describing how she immerses herself into her medium and virtually transforms herself into the object of her art, losing all sense of physical boundaries. Through her use of a three-dimensional, "three chapter," perspective she epitomises Dewey's aesthetics. Her artistic interpretation ensures that experiences are connected and shared between (i) herself – through self-awareness; (ii) participants – active contributors to the artistic endeavour; and (iii) the audience – what she calls "a kind of outside eye witnessing as if it were somebody else observing in a certain way." Andy also exemplified this ability to transform into the object of his art and fully become the character he was playing.

Barty, by contrast, achieves connectedness and his peak experiences through developing trust and unity with his clients. He recalled a sensory memory (in a similar way to Marcel when he tasted the Madeleine) when he recalled cutting one individual client's hair. The shape of her head and movement of her hair appeared familiar to him. This sensory memory was very powerful for Barty. It released an energy and awareness that is still an enduring memory and something that contributes to positive emotions and his subjective well-being.

Fiona experiences her unity by entering into a timeless zone of intense pleasure, similar to the flow state. In fact, all our participants experienced some kind of flow when immersed in their art and when working intensely, losing all sense of awareness of their environment. Dan's flow experience, for example, turned to peak experience when he stopped to reflect. Bakker's (2005) study similarly linked the flow experience with peak experience. Here flow is characterised by the three underlying dimensions of absorption, work enjoyment, and intrinsic work motivation and is often seen as a precursor to a peak experience.

There seems to be a direct connection too with participants' states of mind. They often lost track of time by entering into a seemingly altered state of consciousness or trance-like state which led to experiences of "harmony and self-realization" (Schafer et al., 2014, p. 525). These trance-like states are invited by an absolute focus on their art, reminiscent of Maslow's notion of self-transcendence and the diminishing sense of self. Thus, the common qualities of absorption, disorientation in time and space, and freedom from anxieties identified by Maslow (1968) were also evident in the peak creative experiences shared by our participants.

References

Bakker, A. B. (2005). Flow among music teachers and their students: The crossover of peak experiences. *Journal of Vocational Behavior*, *66*, 26–44.

Barrett, E. (2007). Experiential learning in practice as research: Context, method, knowledge. *Journal of Visual Art Practice*, *6*(2), 115–124, Intellect, Bristol, UK.

Barton, B., & Hardesty, C. L. (2010). Spirituality and stripping: Exotic dancers narrate the body ekstasis. *Symbolic Interaction*, *33*(2), 280–296.

Bennetts, C. M. (1998). *Traditional mentor relationships in the lives of creative people: Towards an aesthetic understanding*. Doctoral Dissertation, University of Sheffield.

Breemen, A. (2017). Performance philosophy: Audience participation and responsibility. *Performance Philosophy*, 2(2), 299–309.

Csikszentmihalyi, M. (1990). *Flow: The psychology of optimal experience*. New York: Harper and Row.

Dewey, J. (1934). *Art as experience*. New York: Capricorn Books.

Dewey, J. (1980/1934). *Art as Experience*. New York: Perigee.

Dewey, J. (1990/1934). Art as experience. In J. Boydston (Ed.), *The later works 1925–1953* (Vol. 10). Carbondale, IL: Southern Illinois University Press.

Diamond, S., Ronel, N., & Shrira, A. (2020). From a world of threat to a world at which to wonder: Self-transcendent emotions through the creative experience of Holocaust survivor artists. *Psychological Trauma: Theory, Research, Practice, and Policy*, 12(6), 609.

Ferree, G. (1968). The descriptive use of "aesthetic experience". *Journal of Aesthetic Education*, 2(2), 23–35.

Funch, B. S. (1997). *The psychology of art appreciation*. Copenhagen: Museum Tusculanum Press, University of Copenhagen.

Hanfling, O. (1992). *Philosophical aesthetics, an introduction*. Milton Keynes: The Open University.

Jackson, P. (1998). *John Dewey and the lessons of art*. New Haven: Yale University Press.

Jacob, M. J. (2018). *Dewey for artists*. University of Chicago Press.

Koltko-Rivera, M. (2006). Rediscovering the later version of Maslow's hierarchy of needs: Self-transcendence and opportunities for theory, research, and unification. *Review of General Psychology*, 10(4), 302–317.

Kubler-Ross, E. (1969). *On death and dying*. New York: Simon & Schuster.

Landy, R. L. (1984). Conceptual and methodological issues of research in drama therapy. *The Arts in Psychotherapy*, 11, 89–100.

Latham, K. F. (2007). The poetry of the museum: A holistic model of numinous museum experiences. *Museum Management and Curatorship*, 22(3), 247–263.

Loveday, K., Neumann, D. L., & Hassall, L. (2023). The peak performance experience in professional screen acting. *Current Psychology*, 42(2), 1456–1466.

Marotto, M., Roos, J., & Victor, B. (2007). Collective virtuosity in organizations: A study of peak performance in an orchestra. *Journal of Management Studies*, 44, 388–413.

Maslow, A. H. (1959). Cognition of being in the peak experiences. *The Journal of Genetic Psychology*, 94, 43–66.

Maslow, A. H. (1962). Lessons from the peak-experiences. *Journal of Humanistic Psychology*, 2(9), 9–18.

Maslow, A. H. (1963). The creative attitude. *The Structurist*, 3, 4.

Maslow, A. H. (1968). *Toward a psychology of being*, 2nd edition. New York: Van Norstrand.

Maslow, A. H. (1969). The farther reaches of human nature. *Journal of Transpersonal Psychology*, 1(1), 1–9.

Maslow, A. H., & Hoffman, E. E. (1996). *Future visions: The unpublished papers of Abraham Maslow*. Sage Publications, Inc.

Morrison, M. A. (2018). Increasing the meaningfulness of work with motivational self-transcendence. *International Journal of Existential Psychology and Psychotherapy*. Special Issue: Proceedings of the 2016 Meaning Conference, pp. 1–16.

Panzarella, R. (1980). The phenomenology of peak experiences. *Journal of Humanistic Psychology*, 20(1), 69–85.

Pelowski, M., & Fuminori Akiba, F. (2011). A model of art perception, evaluation and emotion in transformative aesthetic experience. *New Ideas in Psychology*, 29, 80–97.

Privette, G. (1983). Peak experience, peak performance, and flow: A comparative analysis of positive human experiences. *Journal of Personality and Social Psychology*, 45, 1361–1368.

Privette, G., & Bundrick, C. M. (1991). Peak experience, peak performance and flow: Correspondence of personal descriptions and theoretical constructs. *Journal of Social Behavior and Personality*, *6*(5), 169–188.

Raab, D. (2014). Creative transcendence: Memoir writing for transformation and empowerment. *Journal of Transpersonal Psychology*, *46*(2).

Rancière, J. (2009). *The emancipated spectator*. Translation by G. Elliott. London & New York: Verso.

Sartre, J. P. (1943). *L'être et le néant: Essai d'ontologie phénoménologique*. Paris: Gallimard.

Schafer, T., Smukalla, M., & Oelker, S. A. (2014). How music changes our lives: A qualitative study of the long-term effects of intense musical experiences. *Psychology of Music*, *42*(4), 525–544.

Shusterman, R. (1997). The end of aesthetic experience. *The Journal of Aesthetics and Art Criticism*, *55*(1), 29–41.

Szubielska, M., & Imbir, K. (2021). The aesthetic experience of critical art: The effects of the context of an art gallery and the way of providing curatorial information. *PLoS One*, *16*(5), e0250924. https://doi.org/10.1371/journal.pone.0250924

Van Deurzen-Smith, S. (2014). Creative inspiration and existential coaching. *Existential Analysis 25*(1), 79–88.

Wang, Y., Xu, A. J., & Zhang, Y. (2023). L'Art Pour l'Art: Experiencing art reduces the desire for luxury goods. *Journal of Consumer Research*, *49*(5), 786–810.

Yeagle, E. H., Privette, G., & Dunham, F. (1989). Highest happiness: An analysis of artist's peak. *Psychological Reports*, *65*, 523–530.

5 Peak Experiences in Education and Learning

Introduction

This chapter explores the value of peak experiences in learning and educational settings. Maslow believed peak experience to be integral to learning, suggesting "the experience of awe, mystery, wonder, or of perfect completion, as the goal and reward of learning as well, its end as well as its beginning" (1968b, p. 695). In addition, he argued, educators themselves need to be encouraged to value peak experience, contending that, through the recognition of peak experiences during the learning process, both cognitive and personal growth can take place simultaneously. Maslow (1968b, p. 693) thus sees peak experiences as developmental and to be cherished in children's learning processes: "above all, we would care for the child, that is enjoy him and his growth and self-actualization."

Maslow predicted that individuals needed to at least achieve satisfaction in each of the lower stages of his needs hierarchy to reach self-actualisation. Later, however, as mentioned in our introductory chapter, he suggested that peak experience could be achieved without moving through the stages of the hierarchy, so transcending them (Maslow, 1970a). He reported how most individuals, including children, could experience intense peak episodes, confirming that people having peak experiences were not necessarily all self-actualised people. However, researchers exploring constructivist developmental psychology in the years since Maslow's death have questioned the idea that children can have peak experiences of the same transcendent nature as mature adults. We will report on peak experiences as a childhood phenomenon where appropriate in this chapter.

In our search for peak experiences in different learning settings, we adhere to the definition of peak experience set out in the Introduction – a quite fleeting sensation of peace, harmony, and oneness that is both *felt* physically in the body and metaphysically as a memorable and personally significant incident. Nonetheless, as in other contexts, we have also encountered different definitions, especially in the literature concerned with children's learning, suggesting that children's peak experiences may be qualitatively different from those of adults. Thus, in the chapter we will comment on related concepts as well.

We begin the next section by reviewing the extant literature, first surveying research relating to children and adolescents. Then we focus on literature relating to

DOI: 10.4324/9781003509219-6

adults, teachers, and other educationalists. This section also acknowledges research into potential differences across cultures in relation to peak experience. Following the review of literature, we report on examples of both childhood and adult peak experiences shared by educationalists working in a variety of learning contexts. We then draw some conclusions in our final evaluation section.

Literature

Since children and adolescents are the primary recipients of education and learning in our society, we begin our review of the literature with this demographic. However, it should be noted that Maslow died in 1970, before he could begin any systematic research on this topic, and it was more than ten years after his death that any study concerning childhood peak experiences was published.

Peak Experience in Childhood and Adolescent Literature

Maslow discussed at length the role that peak experiences might play in children's education. He acknowledged there was, at that time, no research on childhood peak experiences, but he thought there were "enough anecdotes and introspections and memories to be quite confident that young children have them, perhaps more frequently than adults do" (1968b, pp. 693–694). He also argued that we must learn to

> treasure the "jags" of the child in school, his fascination, absorptions, his persistent wide-eyed wonderings, his Dionysian enthusiasms. At the very least, we can value his more diluted raptures, his "interests" and hobbies, etc. They can lead to much. Especially can they lead to hard work, persistent, absorbed, fruitful, educative.
>
> (1968b, p. 695)

Maslow considered that such recognition of their experiences would teach children to value rather than suppress their "greatest moments of illumination, moments which can validate and make worthwhile the more usual trudging and slogging and 'working through' of education" (1968b, p. 694).

Following up on Maslow's theories, Robinson (1983) and Armstrong (1984) subsequently argued that children are capable of ecstatic experiences, although they perceived their weaker language skills may hamper research into such phenomena. Interestingly, both authors reported that religious history has many examples of epiphanies occurring in childhood.

Luber (1986) also studied the peak experiences of children and adolescents and identified that older children were the most likely to recount peak-type experiences. In her research, Luber used Maslow's definitions although she also noted a phenomenon she calls a "pre-peak" experience where there is a great intensity of positive feeling that goes beyond just happy feelings but does not reach the transcendental nature of the peak experience as defined by Maslow. The collated experiences from Luber's (1986) study were categorised as i) happiness or a feeling pleasure; ii) having a strong sense of satisfaction or pride in a person or thing; iii) reaching a plateau, based on Maslow's definition of this phenomenon, of serenity and calmness in response to the miraculous or the awesome; iv) "pre-peak" where feelings were not quite transcendent but more than merely happy or proud; v) transcendent – a true peak experience of intense joy.

In Schlarb's (2007) study, mainly conducted with adult women, their recollected childhood peak experiences were reported as being suppressed or even ignored, which in turn had a negative emotional or psychological impact especially as they got older. Schlarb concluded that it is likely that, as children, his respondents may have been having insights into and an appreciation of a reality that was "spiritually mature beyond their years," and thus much of their experience went unnoticed. Schlarb determined that this may result in adults failing children on a fundamental level of personal development, since recognition of such peak experiences could offer parents, teachers, clergy, and therapists "an opportunity to connect with the children in their lives at deeper levels that would have positive lasting influence" (2007, p. 260).

Schlarb's research further suggested that when children were trying to make sense of the world, they expected to turn to their parents for understanding and validation of any childhood peak experiences. However, because their experiences were of such a "subjective and profound nature it was difficult for their parents or peers to pay it tribute to the degree that participants felt adequate" (2007, p. 261). In this study, the drive for external validation revealed the shortcomings of what Schlarb refers to as the "insular nuclear family."

In 2010, Canadian researchers Scott and Evans reported how what they identified as childhood "peak experiences" have also been described using a range of different terms, including "flow" (Csikszentmihalyi, 1988), "quantum change" (Miller & C'de Baca, 2001), and "non-ordinary experiences" (Nelson & Hart, 2005).

According to Miller and C'de Baca (2001, p. 258), quantum change happens when individuals undergo "a radical re-organization in values and behaviors." They categorised change as either a noetic experience or a brief mystical experience. The noetic is a transforming revelation, a profound "aha" experience leaving the individual dumbfounded. The mystical experience, also referred to as an epiphany, is equally transformative, explicitly transpersonal, and includes "the sense of being acted upon by an Other" (2001, p. 257). Both experiences share similar characteristics of vividness, surprise, benevolence, and permanence. The vividness of the experience includes profound emotion combined with the certainty that something happened – something unexpected, often uninvited, and almost always considered positive. The effects are enduring, and the aftermath includes profound shifts in values, relationships, emotions, and behaviour. This permanence is unlike peak experience, which Maslow acknowledged did not necessarily produce lasting change (Miller, 2004).

Ultimately, Scott and Evans (2010) classified 13 different types of childhood peak experiences, admitting that there was overlap, and that some participants reported more than one kind of experience. The categories are listed as interpersonal joy, nature, aesthetics, external achievement, skill mastery, prayer, dream, philosophical musing, uncanny perception, near-death experience, recovery from illness, materiality, and developmental milestones.

Such multiple accounts of childhood peak experiences had emerged initially in Hoffman's, 2003 and 2007 research with young Japanese participants, where it was confirmed that childhood peak experiences occurred among both Western and Eastern young people alike. This work resulted in categories of peak experience for young people being developed.

Later, Ho et al. (2012) conducted a cross-cultural study where they compared Hong Kong Chinese with Brazilian students' childhood peak experiences. Using measures of autobiographical memory to look at cultural variation in these two generally collectivist societies, the authors presented findings that appear to confirm the importance of context in understanding peak experiences. They asked students to recall a childhood peak experience and give a self-rating on its enduring impact. Both groups of students most often reported events involving interpersonal joy. The next most frequently reported event was external achievement in the Hong Kong group, with developmental landmarks being second in importance for the Brazilian group. The findings of this cross-cultural research found interesting cultural variations from two essentially community focused, collectivist societies.

In relation to the cultural influence on peak experiences, Maslow believed that, although experienced across cultures, peak experiences are interpreted by each person within the framework of their own cultural or personal belief system. However, he considered that ultimately there must also be a point where each individual is unchained from the influence of their environment. Maslow (1968c) thus reasoned that people who transcend their culture are not alienated or separated from it, rather they are not exclusively defined by their immediate environment or have an overidentification with it. Venter (2016) recognised this and reported that one of the main things that inhibit personal growth is culture. He viewed culture as important but claimed that it is vital for people to be independent of, or to transcend enculturation, or else cultural forces may distort the way they see the world so that they identify themselves only as the culture prescribes. Venter confirms that "without distortion of their own cultural identity or developing crippling insecurity, they can identify and side with other people, different groups, entities, causes and nationalities" (2016, p. 4).

More recently, Haberlin (2017) has researched the peak experiences of second-grade gifted students in a general classroom. Using Arts-Based Educational Research, the children were asked to create self-portraits with captions to illustrate their peak experiences. Analysis revealed four main themes: (i) teachers have a direct impact on students' peak experiences; (ii) peak experiences occurred when students were being praised or recognised; (iii) students experienced peak states when engaged in intellectually challenging activity; and (iv) they reported peak experiences from creative accomplishments such as drawing. The catalytic influence of teachers and the presence of recognition and positive attention echo Schlarb's earlier findings in 2007 and prompt Haberlin to query whether teachers are familiar enough with peak experiences and with Maslow's work.

A two-year study conducted by Adams and Beauchamp (2019, p. 1) also revealed that primary-aged pupils can experience "extraordinary, transcendent or what might be called spiritual moments." Their experiences were the result of making music with their teachers in outdoor rural locations in Wales. The authors attribute the findings to the value of outdoor learning in supporting creativity and describe how the children seemed to enter a "heightened reality that included bonding with nature and each other" (2019, p. 11).

There appears to be little research that looks at peak experience as defined by Maslow, in either the college or the university context. However, Raettig and Weger (2018) studied how learning can be a shared peak experience for students. They equated peak experience with flow, adopting Csikszentmihalyi's classification and describing it as an "optimal or peak experience characterized by intense, enjoyable involvement in an activity" (2018, n.p.). Their subsequent research with students from six undergraduate psychology courses found that the experience of flow is correlated with interest in course content and the amount of contribution within the learning group. By showing an interest in course content, participating in open discussion, acknowledging the competence of others, and sharing the learning experience, students would communicate effortlessly and facilitate each other's thought processes. Fostering such an environment was seen as crucial when looking to increase academic achievement, reduce drop-out rates, and improve subjective well-being.

This short review suggests there has been more interest in childhood peak experiences than in adolescent and young adult peak experiences. However, by encouraging students of all ages to realise their potential, teachers can fulfil what Maslow (1971) called "value education," a process of promoting all-round development – intellectual, social, physical, moral, and spiritual – which ultimately leads to self-actualisation in adulthood and, potentially, more peak experiences.

Peak Experience in Adult Learning Literature

Maslow's views of education expanded following his development of the hierarchy of needs. At the apex of the hierarchy was self-actualisation, and that began to take priority as the culmination of human fulfilment. Maslow believed that: "the goal so far as human beings are concerned is ultimately the 'self-actualization' of a person, the becoming fully human, the development of the fullest height that the human species can stand up to or that the particular individual can come to" (1968a, p. 74). In relation to education, this pinnacle can be thought of as "helping the person to become the best that he is able to become."

The view of self-actualisation accompanying maturity appears to suggest that there might be more peak experiences in older learners. In her research, Neto (2015), for example, noted that people who engage in lifelong learning increase their likelihood of reaching self-actualisation. She moreover argued that the learning environment is important:

> The conditions of the environment must be accommodating in order for an individual to reach self-actualisation – in some cases this takes many years, as those lacking nourishment in a lower tier of Maslow's hierarchy of needs are ruled by those concerns.
>
> (Neto, 2015, p. 19)

This observation conceptualises the self-actualisation needs as involving selflessness and maintains that it is only when the other lower-tier needs have been met sufficiently are humans able to be more selfless and altruistic. Thus, we can share food when we have enough food, and we can love more completely when we feel loved.

Maslow's proposal that peak experiences come more to self-actualised people involves a shift, as individuals move beyond the self-limiting position of physical needs towards a broader more all-encompassing awareness. Such shifts in world view are often framed as peak experiences (Polnitsky, 2012) or, as predicted by Maslow (1971), glimpses of the transpersonal beyond the limitations of the ego.

Here we are not concerned with an in-depth discussion of the nature of the transpersonal but just noting the connection between Maslow's original theories of self-actualisation and the subsequent constructivist developmental theories that develop this idea. For instance, Maslow's hierarchy culminates in the need for self-actualisation, but later he added the requirement for self-transcendence that accords with the later stages in models proposed by, for example, Wade (1996), Wilber (2000), and Cook-Greuter (2004).

Maslow links transcendent peak experiences to lack of consciousness of time and space, where "the dichotomies, polarities, and conflicts of life tend to be transcended or resolved" (1971, p. 74). Also, he considered the possibility of transcending our separateness as the ultimate human condition, where the move from dependence, through independence, to interdependence become the acknowledgement of our essential unity and connectedness with all life's energy: "The peak experience seems to lift us to greater than normal heights so that we can see and perceive in a higher than usual way" (1971, p. 72). Consequently, Maslow's ideas heralded the development of subsequent stage theories (e.g., Loevinger, 1976; Kegan, 1994) and the ensuing attempts at integration by Wade (1996) and Wilber (1999, 2000).

Despite successive research on self-actualisation and adult cognitive development, the question still remains: can people have peak experiences only if they have achieved self-actualisation or transcendence to higher levels/stages of development? The only clue we have is in Wilber's work in this area. He suggests that, as human development is a "massively complex, overlapping, non-linear affair" (1999, pp. 291–292, 2000), peak experiences may occur at different stages or on different lines of development at different times and, as we aim to demonstrate in this book, in different contexts.

There have been several attempts to identify useful principles of educational design or application that could enable conditions for peak experiences or transformative experiences within learning contexts. Yacek and Gary (2020, p. 217), for example, argue that what they term "epiphanies" are "a central means for transformative moral and intellectual growth." These can be promoted in the classroom through an "ethos of epiphany," which they describe as

> a genre of transformative experience with three distinct phenomenological dimensions: a disruption of our everyday activity, a realization of an ethical good or value, and an aspiration to integrate this value more fully into our lives.
> (2020, p. 217)

Peak Experience in the Teaching Literature

Maslow was passionate about education and argued that if teachers learned to value peak experiences as great moments in the learning process, this value can be transmitted to children. He particularly championed arts education as ways to approach and understand peak experience, explaining that:

> I think that the arts . . . are so close to our psychological and biological core, so close to this identity, this biological identity, that rather than think of these courses as a sort of whipped or luxury cream, they must become basic experiences in education. I mean that this kind of education can be a glimpse into the infinite, into ultimate values.
>
> (1971, p. 72)

Consequently, peak experiences are identified as benefitting not only children but also teachers by contributing to workplace sustainability and individual well-being. Based on his own personal experience as a Steiner teacher in the United States, Evans (2016) assumed that all teachers would have intrinsic experiences that could be described as peak experiences. He proposed that a study of peak experiences in teachers would cultivate a positive awareness of the phenomenon and inspire a new generation of teachers who would "embody moral presence worthy of emulation by children" (2016, p. 2). He suggested that the best outcome of education is the emergence of moral individuals and teachers who model intrinsic moral presence, a suggestion underpinned by Maslow (1971), who perceived that self-actualising individuals are known by their ethical, progressive action.

Evans's (2016, p. 188) empirical research suggested that teachers who have peak experiences are "less likely to burn out and more likely to see themselves as good teachers." Over 80 percent of the teachers Evans surveyed, all of whom were Steiner trained, testified that peak experiences contributed to them staying in their teaching roles. They frequently demonstrated high human potential and were confident that they were becoming good at their work: "With every peak experience the teachers often felt inspired, imbued with a sense of meaning, and connectedness" (2016, p. 188). The teachers felt themselves to be witnessing a "higher force" which was being revealed through them. Inspiration was also reported, spurring teachers into action. Some felt a divine guidance in the form of images or words that were spoken to them from a "transpersonal horizon," sometimes giving "pedagogical direction for the entire year" (2016, pp. 177–178). Spontaneity was common with unplanned utterances or ideas that came mid-lesson. An empathic stance was commonly reported between teacher and student, each comfortable in contact with the other" and working subtly with the "space between." Evans concluded that many teachers found peak experiences helped them sustain themselves within their chosen profession. They felt an improved relationship with their students as a result of such experiences, and this provided "sustenance and often life altering results" (2016, p. 180).

Evans's study further suggested the potential for teachers to transform themselves:

> By developing capacities of meditation, contemplation, and self-reflection, by developing intrapersonal and interpersonal skills, teachers enter on a path

of development and actualize a truly human individuality. Therefore, self-actualization becomes the modus operandi and peak experiences the phenomena that will give the self-reflecting teacher knowledge of their own development.

(2016, p. 192)

In particular, Evans moreover claims that teachers working within the Steiner pedagogy have a multitude of peak experiences: "These teachers use contemplative practice and self-reflection to cultivate intrinsic qualities of empathy, love, and dialogic competence" (2016, p. 194).

Evans's thinking appears to echo the commonplace interpretation of Maslow's early theory, whereby achievement of self-actualisation was thought to result in more peak experiences. However, as explained in Chapter 1 of this book, Maslow's later idea was to differentiate peak experiences, with their attendant transcendent qualities that anyone could achieve, from self-actualisation, which retained its place at the top of the needs hierarchy.

Researchers in Israel, Klein and Ninio (2019, p. 903) examined the key experiences of school principals. They explained how these experiences occur suddenly and leave "strong emotional or conscious impressions" on people, which in turn affect their perceptions and behaviours over time. These authors also equate key experiences with peak experiences and identify their unexpected nature as "inducing a quick, one-time impact that is intense, surprising, exciting and liberating." Klein and Ninio also considered how key experiences can lead to turning points that involve changes in behaviour following the experience, suggesting that often such turning points lead to improved happiness and mental health: people subsequently find more meaning in their lives and expand their self-concept. This in turn influences their values and beliefs and longer-term actions (Yair, 2009).

Klein and Ninio's evidence suggested that "unplanned, one-time, foundational key experiences are followed by significant changes in principals' perceptions of their role and of their functioning, particularly their managerial functioning" (2019, p. 913). These changes were not seen as alternatives to cumulative learning, which is derived from ongoing work experience, "instead they are considered as an additional layer of learning" (913). Klein and Ninio conclude that helping principals with their awareness of the existence of the key experience phenomenon could encourage them to discuss the experiences publicly "and without hesitation." This they argue will "promote improved utilization of the insights from key experiences" (2019, p. 915).

Even more recently, Waterhouse, as first author of Waterhouse et al. (2021), explained how his peak experiences happened during intensive periods of weekend teaching. Waterhouse recalls how in the final session of a long teaching weekend, students shared personal and professional challenges prompted by a chosen image. Reflecting on his experiences, Waterhouse found that "heightened moments of illumination and shared insight between teacher and graduate students were generative, intensely gratifying and imbued with deep connectivity" (2021, p. 1). Of particular note is the idea that there is an "afterglow" to these peak experiences that stretches across time and continues to shape educational viewpoints:

> Peak moments can be times of breakthrough when an overt sense of connection with students diminishes one's doubts, or on some occasions, focuses them into sharp relief.
>
> (2021, p. 3)

The example provided in Waterhouse et al.'s paper highlights creative techniques usually reserved for working with adult learners. However, these techniques are often employed in a Steiner setting too, for example, working with pictures, and the importance of "placing the pictures on display earlier in the day as a point of curiosity and reflexivity for students and then using this curiosity to engage students' interpretive potential in the class" (2021, p. 4).

Following an exercise with the pictures there was silence, but not an empty silence, and the "emotional texture" of the moment was recorded:

> [I]t was laden richly with meaning and memory, emotion and reflection. We had finished, but no one moved, and no one spoke. Somehow a small community had formed, it recognised what had happened – and just for that moment, it didn't want to disband.
>
> (Waterhouse et al. 2021, p. 5)

This powerful group peak experience is something worthy of further research to explore similarities and differences with individual peak experiences. Our first thoughts are that although a powerful group experience appears to generate a peak moment for everyone in the group, individuals will each experience a peak moment uniquely personal to them.

Our review of the literature has shown research being undertaken in a number of learning settings. However, to shed more light on the phenomenon of peak experiences in these contexts, we now present a number of first-hand accounts.

Peak Experiences in Context: Participant Accounts

Our participants were all adults working in some aspect of education: two adult learning specialists/university lecturers, a leadership coach, a Steiner teacher, a primary teacher, and a head teacher. Most also had experience of working and/or studying in other countries. Their insights help to bring the concepts discussed earlier into sharper relief and demonstrate the relevance of peak experience in this context. Also, participants were asked to recall any childhood peak experiences, either in a learning setting or elsewhere.

Our first participant is **Sue Fontannaz**, a team leadership coach who explained how her earliest professional peak experience occurred when she was working with an entrepreneurial team of early career professionals transitioning from graduate positions. Having worked in education and learning settings for over 25 years, she had observed that shifts in people's thinking allowed new insights to be realised. Such shifts gave rise to personal growth for students and increased confidence. This was particularly noticeable in one particular team dialogue, which she reports "encouraged new insights to emerge, together with the sharing of diverse perspectives." The physical sensations that accompanied this peak experience were a sense of calmness and acceptance that demonstrated to Sue that we all have the capacity to find solutions between us.

The experience impacted her view of life, reinforcing the belief that "we share a common humanity and that we have more in common than our differences." Sue describes the experience as expansive, giving her a sense of joy and generosity in witnessing the innate capacity for human growth. It reminded her that we each see the world differently and that by listening and witnessing other experiences, "we in turn expand our understanding of the world." Thus, she sees the peak experience as about expansion and connection rather than as change and making the world seem more related. As a result of these experiences, Sue has learnt to challenge her assumptions and the judgements of others.

Sue has also had other peak experiences and explained how each one builds on the previous sense of connectedness and being in the world:

> [E]ach time, I am reminded of the innate human spirit that we all share and how generative it can be when we choose to see beyond our differences.

This sense of connectedness is also reflected in her work with groups, especially those where there is no competitive agenda. Here she experiences a sense of correspondence where no individual feels the need to rise above another and where "we value being together, rather than competing against each other." From these experiences, she gains a sense of contentment through enjoying the company of others: "with genuine dialogue about things that matter to us."

Sue shared how some peak experiences are not of the same intensity as those where we are in the presence of someone who is sharing their deep thinking. But even these less intense peaks generate a similar sense of contentment and well-being through being in what she calls "a space of authentic relatedness." Such peak experiences for Sue are a reminder that these moments are "fleeting and often pushed out of reach by the stresses of every day." She finds the epithet, "live for the moments that you can't put into words," resonates greatly with her and concludes by stressing that peak experiences "can't be chased – merely invited into our lives by creating the space for them to arise." This last reflection was also observed by Maslow (1962, p. 87) when he highlighted how "we cannot command the peak experience."

Thinking about peak experiences in her childhood, Sue expressed how much the peak moments she shared with her pony fostered her awareness of shared experience. She was introduced to feelings which she sees as affecting her readiness to encounter peak experiences later in her working life. She remembers her feelings then as

> the contented end of day. Stable moments, of listening to the contented chewing of hay or eye contact in the unhurried moment.

The contentment she felt with her pony was also characteristic of other childhood memories. She describes, for example, swimming underwater as giving her a sense of "space and freedom" and similarly the joy of watching an albatross glide over the middle of the ocean, where "time is suspended." These early childhood experiences were meaningful and important to her and are suggestive of how Armstrong (1984) and others viewed the significance of such experiences.

***

Sarah Elliott, our next participant, has been a Steiner class teacher for most of her adult life but did at one time work in mainstream secondary education. She finds the Steiner philosophy of freedom, as a basis for spiritual education, fits with her own philosophy. What she most enjoys about her work now is that she can look at herself in the mirror each morning and know she is doing the right thing, that is, "making a difference to the life of children and thereby the future of humanity."

Sarah describes one of her first peak experiences in the educational context as occurring in July 2003, when she first met her Class One at the Steiner Kindergarten in the west of Ireland. She had been appointed to be their class teacher starting in September and recalls how the experience occurred while one little girl was telling the class all about her pets. Sarah describes that peak experience as

> being in a "tunnel of time" – as if there are rays of blue-white light raying all around me from far behind and vanishing to a point invisibly far in front. It's an experience of infinity. I feel infinite. I feel infused with infinite certainty.

Like the Steiner teachers interviewed by Evans (2016) where feelings of self-worth were increased, the experience made her feel an incredible confidence and energy – knowing that she was doing the right thing:

> [S]omething that is not just doing something but achieving your destiny. I think I became quite driven. It confirmed to me that the world is a place that speaks; that life contains signposts if you are open to them.

Sarah does not remember any specific physical sensations accompanying the peak experience on that day, but as she was in front of a group of children, she was aware she had to maintain a normal exterior. There were, however, longer-lasting psychological and attitudinal changes. She explains how the experience encouraged her to continue to try to open herself to the "activity of the supra-sensible world in everyday life and to know that as I move through life there is another stream of life that is moving towards me."

Other peak experiences have been similar but not so intense. For example, Sarah suggests "the more intense experiences tend to accompany bigger life changes." The main transformation that happens for her is that when peak experiences occur, she knows that she has found the thing that she ought to be doing. For example, in 2001 in the library of Steiner House in London, she had another "tunnel of time" experience in which she realised that all the streams of all the things she had done in her life were leading her to this point.

Since then, she has had other experiences that she describes as "golden thread experiences":

> When I experience a golden thread, I know that it is something that I have to follow. These (experiences) tend to be leading to things that will nurture my development in some way.

Sarah considers that although a peak experience is something that happens spontaneously:

> It is also possible consciously to develop this faculty: I practice a form of silent meditation, sometimes called a "Centring Prayer." The practice is to still everything that normally blocks out our connection to infinity.

The childhood peak experiences of our participants appear to endorse Maslow's proposition that children have the capacity for epiphanies and peak experience. Sarah confirms that as a child she had frequent childhood peak experiences:

> I would describe them as times when my soul soared like a bird. For example, I would go to a particular place above the village and experience the imminence of the whole landscape.

As a consequence, she used to write poetry and explained to us how she has always been a spiritual person: "It's not something that I've really had a choice about because the spiritual world has always found me." She concludes by recalling the words of Rudolf Steiner (Guttenhöfer et al., 2004, p. 15) that inform her practice:

> We must eradicate from the soul all fear and terror of what comes to meet us from the future. We must look forward with equanimity to whatever comes and we must think only that whatever comes is given us by a world direction full of wisdom. It is part of what we must learn in this age; namely to act out of pure trust in the ever-present help of the spiritual world. Truly nothing else will do if our courage is not to fail us. Let us discipline our will and let us seek the awakening from within ourselves every morning and every evening.

Steiner's philosophy and his principles relating to human nature and spiritual growth suggest areas of convergence between his beliefs and Maslow's later theories of self-actualisation and plateau experience.

***

Leni Wildflower's peak experiences could be seen as less rarefied and intense than Sarah's but no less valuable. As a university lecturer who is now a learning consultant, Leni has had peak experiences that she believes have aided her own development considerably. She taught human development for ten years at a high school in the United States and then taught at a university for 30 years, latterly as Director of Knowledge Based Coaching. She first had a peak experience when she started teaching in a girls-only school in Los Angeles, when students told her how much of a difference she was making in their lives – particularly the personal and emotional difference. She describes that experience as "wonderful" because she was making a life transformation for the girls: "Most simply, I was answering questions about what happens in adolescence for girls and many of them had not felt comfortable talking to their mothers about these subjects."

Leni explains how the experience made her feel different about herself as well: "Yes, on days when it all seemed dreary, an email from a student telling me I changed her life – that made my day." She describes the physical sensations that accompanied the peak experience as

> the heart opening up, crying more easily (not for any negative reason), being excited (I'm dancing around the kitchen more!).

She considers that as a result of her peak experiences she is "much more oriented to how people function, what is important to people, how to be a skilful communicator and how to really listen to other points of view." The longer-lasting psychological changes or ways in which the experience impacted her view of life and attitude towards life also impacted the way she now seems to care less about money. She feels freer.

> I am more attached to the wilderness. I have been able to let go of people and situations that have troubled me. I've let go of resentments. And, maybe most importantly, I have accepted what I can't change in my life.

Further peak experiences have generated similar responses: "I am increasingly moved by trees and countryside and mountains." As a child she remembers taking a hike down a shallow canyon when she was about 9 years old. She explains how she "Loved it! The feel of the soil and getting very dirty, and sliding down sandy/muddy places." The memory of these special experiences has influenced her subsequently, as since then she has done a lot of backpacking, camping, and hiking.

In the 1980s, Leni walked across the United States for peace, taking part in the Great Peace March and describes her feelings:

> In the middle of states like the Midwest, it would feel like nothing was happening and I asked what I was doing walking down miles and miles of endless cornfields. Then I'd be reminded – a train whistle would blow and I would look over at the engineer giving us a "high five." There's nothing like that experience.

She notes that these later experiences were different because they were more oriented to experiencing something that someone did to inspire her. Leni's most recent peak experience outside of education has been when she found out her grandson has been born: "I was teaching in California. My son was in Canterbury hospital with his wife. My son phoned and said, 'Hi grandma!' Hearing the news filled me with such joy."

***

Judith Smith has worked as a teacher and as a university lecturer and is very well-acquainted with the British educational system. Both her parents were employed in learning situations, and she says she more or less grew up in a staffroom. However, she confirmed that, at that time, she was "not remotely interested in becoming a schoolteacher or a lecturer."

Then something happened that changed her point of view. After graduating she was engaged to be married and decided she should get a job where she could use her studies and thought: "Maybe a role as a schoolteacher might work." As part of the requirement for her PGCE, student teachers needed to observe in a school near their home. It was here that she had her most profound peak experience in the educational context. She was observing the headteacher with a class in the library where he was explaining Aesop's fables. Suddenly, he asked her to take over and explain the fable of the "Fox and the Crow":

> I can still see the library classroom with sun pouring in from one side. The children had become *my* class in the moments I stood up to take over as teacher. Suddenly all reticence about teaching had vanished and I was "at home" doing what I knew how to do . . . I felt transformed, I belonged, I was empowered and at the end of the lesson the headmaster told me that I had a job in his school once I had completed my PGCE.

Somehow, Judith's entire life has been transformed by teaching that one lesson. For the first time in her life, she knew what her future would be. She would be a teacher.

Since that time, she has been working in a variety of educational and learning situations at both school and university levels. She is now an academic, reviewing academic journals and working in the educational field as a mentor and coach to PhD students. She enjoys learning with her students and the mutual, shared knowledge that ensues.

As an educationalist, she has studied Maslow's theories and observes similarities between her current motivation and personality and his account of self-actualising creativeness. Maslow highlights "a certain kind of humour; a tendency to do anything creatively; for example, teaching and so forth" (Maslow, 1970b, pp. 160–161).

A different peak experience context offered bittersweet memories for Judith. Her much-loved husband was unfaithful in their marriage. However, as she points out, "I was no longer a timid child lacking in ambition. My schoolchildren made me strong. As a role model to them, I wanted them to believe in themselves and be the best they could be." She became capable of sharing excitement and talking to children as if they were her family, and their well-being mattered profoundly to her. The physical experiences that accompanied her peak experience were the forerunners to a profound series of physical and psychological changes as she felt stronger. The experience taught her that she could overcome adversity.

Judith has encountered many other peak experiences since the first one. They have taught her not to cower in fear from life's problems and be more open to bringing about some fundamental changes in directions that she would never previously have thought possible. The major change in her is that she felt she was always meant to be involved in education. But there have been other major changes in her outlook since her first peak experience, for example, in relation to her mental and physical health. She recalls going for an interview for a main-scale post in a school and being told that she was "too gifted for that job," which would result in a disruption in the staffroom as she would not fit in. Although upset at the time, Judith is simultaneously very grateful for the change in outlook it prompted, which meant that she had to learn to aim higher. A second example of aiming higher was when she was told she should definitely seek promotion to a senior post as soon as possible, either at the current school or elsewhere. This peak experience left her feeling overjoyed and empowered. Her world was filled with colour, purpose, and strength. Somehow these peak experiences opened up possibilities that she has had never entertained.

There have been many other peak experiences in different contexts. Judith recalls the love she felt for her husband and then her partner. She recalls peak experiences in discovering a friendship which introduced her to the artistic work of Charles Rennie Macintosh, visiting places where Macintosh's work could be seen and enjoyed in all its glory. She now has prints in her lounge and profoundly enjoys them still. As a young woman she was a passionate dancer to Motown Music and an ardent badminton player: both gave her moments of peak experience. Walking in the Lake District and in Switzerland also gave her moments which she describes as "pure bliss when time has stood still, and I am in awe of the world."

These peak experiences were breathtaking and empowering but in a different way from those associated with her career in education and learning settings. Somehow, she was not accessing them in the depth of her being where she acknowledges there lay a darker side to her character. Her honesty is compelling when she admits that deep inside her being, there was a recurrence of depression that afflicted her childhood and her divorce. Nonetheless, even in those darkest moments there was empowerment: "I have confronted those realisations and I grow stronger and set horizons further every day."

A final peak experience for Judith is tinged with sadness. In 1998, her father died in her arms. She knew he was dying but took his head to rest upon her, an intimate and meaningful moment between father and daughter: "He smiled as I thanked him and said goodbye."

Judith thinks that without these peak experiences her life would be dull and monotonous. They have shaped her existence, and she firmly believes that they will continue to do so. Moments of sheer bliss continue to enliven her life, and she is rediscovering life in all its empowerment, enabling her to better understand her personality and revive her motivation to live a life that is useful to humankind.

***

Emma is a primary school teacher and someone who immediately connected with the notion of Maslow's hierarchy of needs in the context of education. She explained that before children's cognitive and developmental needs can be met, their education needs to be built from the ground up; their physical needs need to be met. Children need to feel safe and secure in the classroom environment. When feeling secure they are able to make mistakes in safety and progress by learning from their mistakes without feeling inadequate. Esteem needs, she suggested, are scarcely present and only encountered when physiological and safety needs have been met.

We asked Emma how she, as a teacher, has encountered peak experiences. She identified the point at which children feel safe and secure (the first two elements of Maslow's hierarchy) and then suddenly understand something she's been teaching them. At first, Emma was unclear about the exact meaning of a peak experience but soon accessed memories when we described the phenomenon as an "aha" moment, a light bulb moment, or the potential "wow" factor in teaching. She immediately connected with the light bulb moment, especially in maths lessons when the children suddenly "get it." We asked her to describe that moment and if possible, visualise the context, her feelings, what she saw and experienced when the children were unexpectedly enlightened.

> It's like this realisation that they've got it right. This look dawns across their faces when I tell them they have the right answer. They're proud, really proud and really often surprised . . . "I've got it Miss, I've got it!." I feel I've done the right thing and that I'm doing my job well. It generates momentum in the classroom. Up until that point it's been a bit sticky to start but when we're on the right road, when we have this lightbulb moment with a couple of the children, they are able to help others who then help others to get the lightbulb moment.

Emma's description of such a momentum is discussed by Bakker (2005) when he talks of contagion between teacher and pupil. Each child feeds the other with enthusiasm and a sense of engagement. They are in flow, and ultimately this results in peak experiences. Emma agreed it was contagious and "spreads like wildfire sometimes." She puts this down to the children explaining to one another in their own language: "they have better ways to explain to their friends than I have." They feel very pleased with themselves when they understand and "get it" rather than experiencing the mental barrier that is there before clarity emerges.

The children's "wow" moments make Emma feels she's in the right job. Seeing the children so excited gives her additional confidence to tackle the next challenge in teaching. The children's "aha" moment similarly gives them increased confidence as well:

> We've all got a renewed passion in the classroom. They're so pleased and proud to show me what they've done or written. If they buy into their education and learning, they're more likely to buy into the future. If I can get them hooked into space, for example, in the science lesson, they become really enthusiastic and gain enormous enjoyment from learning.

***

We end this section with some thoughts about peak experiences and education from **Colin**, a Baptist minister and mentor who shared his spiritual peak experiences in Chapter 1, and from **Sandra**, the headmistress of a high school in the UK.

Colin commented on his awareness that peak experiences and other emotional responses are not necessarily the same and identified how he had noticed a sense of awe, rather than anything transcendental, when watching professional educators at work:

> Two standout things. One is my sense of awe at those that work in children's education, and one is the experience of watching governors of a school, and the professionalism there – the attitude and the values of the teaching staff that I was able to see . . . just their whole approach was so devoted to the well-being and brilliant development of the children. Just their sheer professionalism was something that actually left me and still leaves me, genuinely awestruck. And then layered with that, is my wife who has been involved in special needs education for many years, having started out as a reception teacher, and the experience of watching her day by day do the same thing. Just the depth of her skill and ability to work with children with many, many challenges, multiple challenges, socially, emotionally, physically, mentally, and just the sheer dedication, and the skill that goes with it.

Sandra similarly believes that teaching as a profession potentially provides lots of peak experiences, even in the most challenging of schools. Her own peak experiences are linked with observing pupils and seeing their understanding grow:

> I think it's that euphoric response, that epiphanous moment when they get it, that joy of them getting it for the first time, that lightbulb moment of eureka.

Like Emma, Sandra recalls pupils' physical responses as "something to behold, when you can literally see the lightbulb moment illuminate their faces. The penny drops and you see the 'aha' moment."

Johnson (2023) explains how, for a child, after that peak learning insight is attained, then he or she "actualizes" that "peak" for the rest of his or her life:

> It would be the same for learning how to ride a bike or any other task we master. There's that "insight moment" (peak experience) of "getting it." Once gotten, that peak result is now a part of the developed repertoire.
> (Johnson, 2023, p. 152)

The peak experiences Sandra identifies seem to be what Luber (1986) described as "pre-peak" experiences, which are not quite the transcendental peaks defined by Maslow but still go beyond "just happy." Relatedly, such childhood peak experiences would be described by Scott and Evans (2010) as external achievement, or skill mastery, or developmental milestones, all of which are valid and important childhood landmarks.

For pupils to experience such moments, Sandra says, it is down to the teacher's ability to be creative:

> [I]t's not a case of teaching it louder or saying it again, rather you have to have that constant, on the spot, creativity even when delivering the same content or piece of knowledge. Because that eureka moment won't come in the same way for every child.
> That creativity is really, really satisfying, and intrinsically satisfying, I love it! It's extrinsically satisfying when I see it working in the classroom.

In her early days of teaching, Sandra remembers she had physical reactions: "the excitement of your blood pumping and your heart going, and a deep-rooted satisfaction from knowing that yes, that's worked." There was definitely a feeling of euphoria but not for her own benefit but for the children's. She explains how being in the classroom was a special time for her:

> I don't get that physical response anymore, but that doesn't mean I'm not feeling it. I still love the creativity of planning lessons, planning resources, being in the classroom. Being in the classroom I describe as being my golden time.

What Is Significant About Peaks in This Context?

In this chapter we presented an overview of peak experiences in educational contexts. A review of the literature revealed gaps in our understanding of children's and students' peak experiences particularly and whether they have transcendent or more non-transcendent peaks. However, there seemed to be a consensus that by encouraging children of all ages to talk about their peak-like experiences, educators can support development in intellectual, social, physical, moral, and spiritual spheres, which it could be argued will lead to self-actualisation in adulthood.

In our exploration of adult tertiary education, we realised that a question still hangs over whether individuals have peak experiences only after they have achieved self-actualisation or whether the two concepts are not really linked. Self-actualisation was seen as a precursor to the theoretical development of the many stages of development models discussed in cognitive development literature, whilst peak experiences seem to occur at any stage in human life.

Above all, this chapter hints at the link between peak experiences and well-being. Evans (2016) found that teachers who have peak experiences see themselves as better teachers who are more connected and motivated to stay in their teaching roles. This sense of connectedness was also observed by Sue and Judith in this chapter. They too reported increased motivation and purpose as a result of their peak experiences.

The experiences of our participants also seem to bolster the observation that there are at least two types of peak experience that could be referred to as transcendent and non-transcendent. The transcendent experiences were identified by Miller and C'de Baca (2001) as epiphanies which are quite out of the ordinary, mystical, and overwhelming. Sarah's peak experience where she describes a "tunnel of time" could fall into this category and chimes with Evans's (2016, p. 40) research with Steiner teachers in the United States. Such transcendental experiences may be connected to their training in mindfulness practices and other reflective and contemplative techniques.

The non-transcendent peak experiences seem similar to what Miller and C'de Baca call "insights," which have a sense of continuity and "follow from the person's development rather than being an intrusion into it" (2001, p. 19). They reveal new perspectives or ways of thinking, new realisations, and understandings occurring within the realm of everyday experience. These non-transcendent experiences, often experienced in childhood, comprise very deep feelings of empathy and positive connection with other beings that are significant components of self-actualisation and result in a greater capacity to identify and communicate with others (Neto, 2015).

These joyous feelings can still be described as "peak" because of the boost they give to the recipients, but more accurately we suggest that this type of peak experience should be called a "non-transcendent peak experience." Most of our participants have recalled this type of "peak-like" experience. Examples of these are Sue's memory of "stable" contentment with her pony, Leni's "high-five" from the train driver, and even Sandra's response to spontaneous creativity in the classroom. However, participants have not specifically differentiated these more common non-transcendent experiences from their transcendent experiences, which they have possibly had less frequently.

In this chapter, besides adult experiences, we also learnt about children's peak experiences. These, as some commentators argue, could be seen as less transcendent. However, the times when the children suddenly "get it," as Emma and Sandra recount, are important examples of learning from experience. Schlarb's (2007) research is particularly useful in this regard, suggesting that children may have insights and peak experiences that go unnoticed by the adults in their lives. Schlarb concluded that adults are failing children by not recognising their peak experiences and seizing opportunities to connect with them at a deeper level. We saw from some of our participants that a childhood peak experience can have a lasting and positive influence, and so identification and acknowledgement of these experiences during school years could be beneficial.

References

Adams, D., & Beauchamp, G. (2019). Spiritual moments making music in nature: A study exploring the experiences of children making music outdoors, surrounded by nature. *International Journal of Children's Spirituality*, *24*(3), 260–275.

Armstrong, T. (1984). Transpersonal experiences in childhood. *Journal of Transpersonal Psychology*, *16*(2), 207–230.

Bakker, A. B. (2005). Flow among music teachers and their students: The crossover of peak experiences. *Journal of Vocational Behavior*, *66*, 26–44.

Cook-Greuter, S. (2004). Making the case for developmental perspective. *Industrial and Commercial Training*, *36*(7).

Csikszentmihalyi, M. (1988). The flow experience and its significance for human psychology. *Optimal Experience: Psychological Studies of Flow in Consciousness*, *2*, 15–35.

Evans, P. G. (2016). *Peak experience in educational encounters: A phenomenological-hermeneutic study*. PhD Thesis, California Institute of Integral Studies, USA. ProQuest.

Guttenhöfer, P., Wright, J., Oswald, F., Hamilton, K., Bhanumathi, M. K., Rubisz, H. et al. (2004). The initiative circles of the pedagogical section in New Zealand and Australia. *Journal for Waldorf/Rudolf Steiner Teachers*. www.waldorflibrary.org/images/stories/Journal_Articles/NZJournal2004.pdf [Accessed 9 September 2021].

Haberlin, S. (2017). Using arts-based research to explore peak experiences in five gifted children. *International Journal of Education & the Arts*, *18*(24).

Ho, M. Y., Chen, S. X., & Hoffman, E. (2012). Unpacking cultural variations in peak-experiences: Cross-cultural comparisons of early childhood recollection between Hong Kong and Brazil. *Journal of Happiness Studies*, *13*(2), 247–260.

Hoffman, E. (2003). Peak experiences in Japanese youth. *Japanese Journal of Humanistic Psychology*, *21*, 112–121.

Hoffman, E., & Muramoto, S. (2007). Peak-experiences among Japanese youth. *Journal of Humanistic Psychology*, *47*(4), 524–540.

Johnson, D. (2023). *Minding Maslow's mystery* (Vol. 2). Independently Published.

Kegan, R. (1994). *In over our heads*. London: Harvard University Press.

Klein, J., & Ninio, R. (2019). School principals' key experiences and changing management patterns. *International Journal of Educational Management*, *33*(5), 903–918.

Loevinger, J. (1976). *Ego development: Conceptions and theories*. San Francisco: Jossey-Bass.

Luber, M. (1986). *Peak experiences: An exploratory study of positive experiences recounted by children and adolescents (Maslow, Erikson)*. Doctoral Dissertation, Bryn Mawr College.

Maslow, A. H. (1962). *Toward a psychology of being*. Princeton: Nostrand and Co.

Maslow. A. H. (1968a). Music education and peak experiences. *Music Educator's Journal*, *54*(6), 72–75, 163–171.

Maslow, A. H. (1968b). Some educational implications of the humanistic psychologies. *Harvard Educational Review*, *38*(4), 685–696.

Maslow, A. H. (1968c, July) A theory of metamotivation: The biological rooting of the value life. *Psychology Today*, 38–39, 58–61.

Maslow, A. H. (1970a). *Religions, values, and peak-experiences*. New York: Viking Compass.

Maslow, A. H. (1970b). *Motivation and Personality*, 3rd edition. New York: Addison Wesley Longman, Inc.

Maslow, A. H. (1971). *The farther reaches of human nature*. New York, NY: Viking.

Miller, W. R. (2004). The phenomenon of quantum change. *Journal of Clinical Psychology*, *60*(5), 453–460.

Miller, W. R., & C'de Baca, J. (2001). *Quantum change: When epiphanies and sudden insights transform ordinary lives*. London: Guilford Press.

Nelson, P. L., & Hart, T. (2005). *A survey of recalled childhood spiritual and non-ordinary experiences, age, rate and psychological factors associated with their occurrence*. www.childspirit.org [Accessed 27 July 2023].

Neto, M. (2015). Educational motivation meets Maslow: Self-actualisation as contextual driver. *Journal of Student Engagement: Education Matters*, *5*(1), 18–27.

Polnitsky, C. A. (2012). *Prosocial shifts in worldview: Promises and challenges of growth and transformation*. Master's Thesis, Smith College, Northampton, MA. https://scholarworks.smith.edu/theses/859

Raettig, T., & Weger, U. (2018). Learning as a shared peak experience: Interactive flow in higher education. *International Journal of Applied Positive Psychology*, *2*(1), 39–60.

Robinson, E. (1983). *The original vision: A study of the religious experiences of childhood*. New York: Seabury. career development. Palo Alto: Davies-Black.

Schlarb, C. W. (2007, December). The developmental impact of not integrating childhood peak experiences. *International Journal of Children's Spirituality*, *12*(3), 249–262.

Scott, D. G., & Evans, J. (2010). Peak experience project. *International Journal of Children's Spirituality*, *15*(2), 143–158.

Venter, H. J. (2016). Self-transcendence: Maslow's answer to cultural closeness. *Journal of Innovation Management*, *4*, 3–7.

Wade, J. (1996). *Changes of mind: A holonomic theory of the evolution of consciousness.* Suny Press.

Waterhouse, P., Creely, E., & Southcott, J. (2021). Peak moments: A teacher-educator reflects (with colleagues) on the importance of heightened moments of teaching and learning. *Teaching and Teacher Education, 99,* 103275.

Wilber, K. (1999). *One taste: The journals of Ken Wilber.* Boston: Shambhala Publications.

Wilber, K. (2000). *Integral psychology: Consciousness, spirit, psychology, therapy.* Shambhala Publications.

Yacek, D. W., & Gary, K. (2020). Transformative experience and epiphany in education. *Theory and Research in Education, 18*(2), 217–237.

Yair, G. (2009). Cinderellas and ugly ducklings: Positive turning points in students' educational careers-exploratory evidence and a future agenda. *British Educational Research Journal, 35*(3), 351–370.

6 Peak Experiences in Nature and Wilderness

Introduction

From her 28 descriptions of where peak experiences may be generated, Laski (1980) found that one of the main contexts or settings that triggered peak experiences was being in nature.

Based on the power of nature identified much earlier by, for example, the English romantic poets in the early 1800s, this is probably not surprising; as Aaltola (2015, p. 284) reminds us, these poets believed that in nature we gain a sense of "interconnectedness, more significant and real than human culture." Hence, we see that the elevated reaction to a peak experience, felt whilst participating in some form of outdoor recreation or retreat, has captured the imagination for many years.

A quote from Scottish naturalist, John Muir likewise captures the effect that being in nature has on people: "I only went out for a walk and finally decided to stay until sundown, for going out, I discovered, was actually going in" (cited in Wolfe, 1938, p. 427). Being in nature is only in part about experiencing a sense of place and exploring the physical nature surrounding us. As Muir found on his walks, there can also be a meditation-like exploration of ourselves that contributes to a developing awareness of the relationship between the external body and the internal where the body seems to vanish and "the freed soul goes abroad." He found walking in nature a means of making meaning, of awareness and understanding, and noted in his journals that forests, mountains, and desert canyons are holier than our churches.

Historically, the natural world was also seen as "an antidote to the ills of industrialisation," bringing psychological benefits through spending time in natural settings (McDonald et al., 2009, p. 372). Similarly, Nukarinen et al. (2022) describe how environmental psychology research has shown engagement with the natural environment to have restorative and stress-ameliorating effects. So, alongside the aesthetic and spiritual attraction, human engagement with the natural world is also seen as a way to increase well-being and prosocial behaviours. As an example, according to Laski (1980, p. 12), Mary Wilson, wife of a former British Prime Minister, reported how in 1974, alone on a beach in the Isles of Scilly, she had what she described as "a mystical experience . . . a most extraordinary experience as if I was dissolving." She felt at one with the past and the future, and all the anxieties

DOI: 10.4324/9781003509219-7

of the world seemed to disappear. More recently, Mathers and Brymer found that such experiences in nature can have long-lasting, significant effects:

> [A] profound experience with nature can encourage a new understanding of self, redefine relationships with others and nature as a whole, and promote meaningful and intentional decisions and behaviours.
>
> (2022, p. 10)

As in other contexts, a variety of different terms have been used to try and capture the essence of the experiences felt in nature. Chenoweth and Gobster (1990) referred to aesthetic experience in nature, concluding that even if aesthetic experiences are not all "peak" ones, they "stand out from the ordinary experiences of everyday life and are worthy of greater attention from those concerned with the effects of the environment on the well-being of its human inhabitants" (1990, p. 7). In a similar way, Storie and Vining (2018) referred to peak experiences in the natural world as environmental epiphanies, describing them as experiences that shift the fundamental relationship between self and nature. Drawing on Maslow's concept of peak experience, Gee also discussed what he called the "unique power of a moment in the wilderness," terming these emotionally charged recollections "wild epiphanies" (2010, p. 1).

At this point, we note that Maslow did not elaborate on the topographical metaphor of "peak" experiences and included very little about the role of nature in fulfilling psychological needs (Marshall, 2003). However, he did comment on the transcendent value of being in nature for the perceiver who can

> more readily look upon nature as if it were there in itself and for itself, not simply as if it were a human playground put there for human purposes upon it. In a word, he can see it in its own Being (as an end in itself) rather than as something to be afraid of or something to wish for or to be reacted to in some other personal, human, self-centered way.
>
> (Maslow, 1964)

This was most likely the nearest Maslow came to discussing nature. He envisioned it as inducing a "higher" psychology that could be transpersonal: "transhuman, centered in the cosmos rather than in human needs and interest" (Maslow, 1968, pp. iii–iv).

Peak experiences in nature take place in a variety of environmental settings including being experiences in and on water, encounters with wild animals, as well as observations of sunsets and mountains (McDonald et al., 2009, p. 371). Castelo et al. (2021, p. 1) have also defined nature broadly and included stargazing on a clear night, watching the sunset over the ocean, and hiking through a national park. In this chapter, we also keep our scope all-encompassing. We review a range of literature on peak experiences and then share peak experiences from our participants that were similarly generated through engagement with aspects of the natural environment.

Review of Literature

A focused literature review uncovered research relating to peak experiences and analogous concepts in a variety of natural settings, particularly wilderness (McDonald et al., 2009; Ashley, 2017) and forests (Williams & Harvey, 2001) but also in encounters with animals (DeMares, 2000; Curtin, 2006). Such experiences have led to a variety of feelings and emotions being identified.

Wilderness

McDonald et al.(2009, p. 371) defined wilderness as "a large area of uninhabited land containing native plant and animal communities that had been relatively unaffected by modern civilization" (2009, p. 371). Adapting their research from Maslow's instructions to his participants, they asked their Australian participants to use their own words to describe a peak experience in a wilderness setting. Then, using content analysis, they identified seven themes that characterised peak experience in this context. Aesthetic quality was the most common theme with sunsets, forests, mountains, and valleys being picked out as the most significant natural features (2009, p. 376):

1) Aesthetic qualities – where the focus of attention is absorption in the aesthetic qualities of the wilderness setting.
2) Being away – an escape from the pressures, people, distractions, and concerns of the human-made world.
3) Meaningful experience – the experience is significant to the individual's life.
4) Number of peak experiences – the peak experience recalled is only one of a number of positive and profound moments experienced in wilderness settings.
5) Oneness – connectedness – feelings of connection or belonging generated by the wilderness.
6) Overcoming limitations – a sense of overcoming limitations such as overcoming pain or renewing depleted energy resources.
7) Heightened awareness – a deeper understanding of world/self/life occurring during or shortly after the experience.

Being away from pressure and people was a key theme for McDonald et al.'s participants, moreover, they cited tranquillity and absence of time constraints as important. Also, they pinpointed their peak experiences as meaningful, valuable, and of importance to them going forward and experienced a connectedness or "merging with or being at one with the wilderness, world or universe" (2009, p. 378). There was also a link between peak experiences in the wilderness and spiritual expression, particularly through the valuing of the natural environment and withdrawal from the human-made world with all its pressures and distractions.

McDonald et al. consider that a key aspect of peak experiences in this context is the lack of intrusions and distractions which occur in wilderness, "coupled with its visually arresting landscapes" (2009, p. 381). Interestingly, these authors conclude that a vital part of the wilderness experience is undertaking risk. This aspect will be considered in more detail in a later chapter.

Earlier, Cumes's (1998, p. 15) summary of the research literature at the time revealed similar characteristics of wilderness experiences. He identified particular emotional changes in people participating in extended journeys or treks into wilderness settings and classified these changes under the heading "wilderness rapture." Ten possible transformations were identified, many of which correspond to the empirical findings of McDonald et al. (2009):

1) Being or feeling more like our true self;
2) An appreciation of awe, oneness, wonder, transcendence, or a peak experience;
3) Humility and the realisation that any control we think we have over nature is an illusion;
4) Becoming more pleasant and affable with fellow trekkers;
5) A connection with nature and a sense of comfort in her surroundings;
6) A sense of renewal and vitality, feeling less cluttered, and more mindful and focused;
7) An appreciation of solitude. This experience was often described as the most powerful aspect of the trek;
8) Major lifestyle shifts on returning such as changing occupations. These may be attempts to align the outer self or persona with inner needs. Intimate contact with wilderness can bring people closer to an appreciation of what is really true for them;
9) Release from bad habits or addictions. These could be past patterns of undesirable behaviour, such as substance dependency;
10) Many participants experience a sense of loss or depression when they return home. This phenomenon is what Cumes calls re-entry depression that may be a result of having been in an altered or elevated state of consciousness, followed by a rude awakening upon being propelled back into a normal state of awareness.

Several researchers have looked at emotions such as awe and wonder in relation to wilderness and open spaces (e.g., Schroeder, 2002; Bethelmy & Corraliza, 2019). Bethelmy and Corraliza's (2019) quantitative study focused on transcendence and sublime experience and found two factors of sublime emotion towards nature – awe and inspiring energy. Both, they say, feed the emotional bond with nature. But they define awe as "feelings of fear, threat, vulnerability, fragility, and respect for nature, which is perceived as vast powerful, and mysterious" and inspiring energy as "the feeling that awakens a sense of vitality, happiness, freedom, and unity between the self and the natural world" (2019, p. 9). These different emotions, it is argued, promote differing responses to the natural world.

As well as awe and similar emotions, early research by Kaplan and Talbot (1983) also identified that participants had a higher likelihood of self-realisation and awareness as well as improved self-esteem. Other researchers who have identified similar transformations include Gee (2010), who reported research with individuals who, when young, were mandated to attend a wilderness-based residential programme. Remembered experiences were compared with observations by counsellors who facilitated the excursions into the wilderness, and the findings included descriptions of improved mental well-being that had welcome implications for therapeutic interventions. Ashley (2017) also confirms how wilderness can be a place for human transformation, with the wilderness experience increasingly being recognised as both restorative and a positive contributor to psychological well-being.

More recently, Naor and Mayseless (2020) focused on positive transformations taking place in the wilderness, which they identify as peak *transformative* experiences (our emphasis). Their inclusion of the word "transformative" suggests peak experiences may have an effect that is more lasting and powerful than just a joyful feeling. This research was concerned with the process of personal transformation that took place when participants experienced nature in a new, more meaningful way. Fifteen participants aged between 28 and 70 years were interviewed, and findings suggested peak transformative experiences were the result of moments of profound insight, which in turn were a step in the process of personal growth and "deeply related to a lifelong significant issue" (2020, p. 881). The aesthetic qualities of the wilderness setting and being away from pressures, people, distractions, and concerns of daily life were key elements of that experience. Findings thus revealed the centrality of nature in the process of transformation, the importance of free choice, and the potential for "harnessing transformative peak experiences in nature for human development" (2020, p. 866).

Naor and Mayseless go on to argue that despite accepted definitions of the peak experience as "a momentary, short, and surprising experience seemingly distinct from one's life," their phenomenological analysis had enabled them to reveal a broader scale of peak experience "as part of a life process" (2020, p. 880). These authors also confirm that in wilderness settings participants experienced "hardship and dissonance as integral to their peak experience" and that this involved both "positive and negative emotionally laden experiences" (2020, p. 880).

The feeling of arousal also appears to be a key feature of wilderness immersion, especially that involving risk of some kind. Indeed, Ashley (2017) has developed a "wilderness experience pathway schema" that includes arousal of the senses. In this model, entering and encountering the wilderness setting produces arousal, where the senses are heightened. This in turn evokes physical, emotional, and cognitive responses which, it is argued, can lead to a variety of benefits including attitudinal and behavioural changes. According to Ashley, in the evocation phase, we may also get "a sense that we are not strangers or outsiders but instead belong there." This suggests we cross not only physically into the wilderness but also psychologically, resulting in shifts in our perception of time with people reporting "a sense of timelessness as they become more attuned to natural rhythms" (Ashley, 2017, p. 33).

Mountain Peaks, Trees, and Forests

According to Cornell (2011), the founder of *Sharing Nature Worldwide*, intense moments with nature heighten awareness and promote a true and vital understanding of our place in the world: "When people are quiet and receptive, fully immersed in nature, insights on the real purpose of life reveal themselves" (2011, p. 31). The powerful emotions aroused in nature, Cornell reminds us, resemble how Maslow (1964) described peak experiences: "feelings of intense happiness and well-being" which often involve "an awareness of transcendental unity."

In their study of transcendence in forest environments, Williams and Harvey (2001, p. 256) observed the sense of timelessness as a feature of the experience. Their research involved 131 people who visited, worked, or lived in forests and who described their transcendent moments through written responses to open-ended questions. Analysis of these responses suggested there may be at least two distinct forms of transcendent experience that occur: the first is the feeling of insignificance – a feeling that is quite commonly reported by our participants in this book (e.g., Paul, in this chapter). The second is a strong sense of compatibility and familiarity. Further findings highlighted the transcendent, aesthetic, and restorative functions of nature which are commonly reported in other literature (e.g., Cumes, 1998; Ashley, 2017). Williams and Harvey (2001, p. 256) concluded that natural landscapes are unique and complex systems comprising "matter, energy, human purpose and action" and that every element of the system is perceived, interpreted, and altered in what they call the "human-environment transaction."

Relatedly, Castelo, White, and Goode found that exposure to nature increases a sense of transcendence, which in turn "increases people's willingness to take actions that benefit other people" (2021, p. 1). Their quantitative study revealed how nature can lead to emotional and cognitive benefits plus enhanced concentration, reduced stress, or improved mood. These aspects have been identified in earlier research too (e.g., Ulrich et al., 1991, Abraham et al., 2010, and Hartig et al., 2011).

An emphasis on humility and understanding also comes from being in nature and was noted by the American philosopher and poet, Emerson (1996), who claimed that "in the woods, we return to reason and faith":

> There I feel that nothing can befall me in life, no disgrace, no calamity . . . Standing on the bare ground, my head bathed by the blithe air and uplifted into infinite space, all mean egotism vanishes. I become a transparent eyeball; I am nothing
>
> (1996, p. 29)

Emerson is suggesting here that when we are separated from human civilisation, we are pure and without distractions, we are able to see the world as it truly is. Often, such experiences have been described as encompassing intense and often mystic qualities and are frequently compared to religious experiences.

In his book subtitled *Walking Meditations on Literature, Nature and Need*, Marshall (2003) describes how he used Maslow's hierarchy of needs as a framework to record his own account of the role nature played in his journey towards peak experience. Alongside Maslow's structure, he used Walt Whitman's 52-verse poem, *Song of Myself*, to inspire and record a series of 52 mountain hikes. Having achieved and written about the other needs in the hierarchy, Marshall uses the poem as his guide towards the final stage: self-actualisation. Ultimately, he draws together his experience of being "both the climber and the climbed," noting that the "conflation of self and mountain has been my main conceit throughout, and I've been engaged in a sort of self-ascent, progressing up the life zones of psychological needs" (2003, p. 240).

Many authors have connected peak experience with the sense of space that being outdoors offers. Ramyar (2020), for example, has drawn on Maslow to emphasise that the experience of space could provide the right environment for euphoric mental states to occur. He explains how peak experience is perceived holistically and felt through different elements or in different layers (Maslow, 1968, p. 71). Talking about the purity of space in a Persian garden, Ramyar suggests that a strong involvement in the process of experiencing the space "creates a distortion of the sense of time and a loss of self-consciousness" (2020, p. 243) and might be related to spiritual transcendence "as a feeling of connectedness and unity with other people, life, nature, and the like." Ramyar likens this to Maslow's (1968) observation that "the experience of space could result in a kind of perception providing a moment accompanied by a euphoric mental state."

Muir, cited earlier in this chapter, describes the exhilaration of his tree-top ascent during a storm. He spent several hours in the tree and experienced enhanced sensitivity and sensory stimulus due to the movement of the tree caused by the wind. The peak he experienced resulted in an increased perception of organic wholeness of the tree and the storm, and he records how "never before did these noble woods appear so fresh, so joyous, so immortal" (Muir, 1961, pp. 187–197).

Animals

In our earlier chapter on peak experiences in education, Sue shared how, as a child, she had experienced peak events with her pony. These experiences echo what Hart (2000) observed that "the horse offers a peak experience, perhaps unmatched by any other, with a totally unique physical experience while in a joyous social environment" (Hart, 2000, p. 94).

Such joyous experiences with animals are also reported in other research. For example, DeMares and Krycka (1998) explored peak experiences triggered by dolphins and whales. In their qualitative study, six participants revealed the underlying structure of their experiences, suggesting that oceanic encounters with dolphins and whales can lead to a sense of harmony, connectedness, and a sensation of coming alive. Participants described having direct eye contact with these animals and reported that their peak experiences were triggered when the animals seemed to have initiated the contact or indicated some kind of desire for communication. The peak experience generated by this connection was so powerful for some participants that they forgot about the potential danger in the situation.

DeMares and Krycka (1998, p. 161) made the claim that wild animal encounters trigger peak experiences and feelings of transcendence because "the persona of the experiencer is not dominant." They explain that it is almost as though "the experience, always spontaneous, is so intense that it overrides the normal state of 'being'." This finding supports what Maslow said about transcendence too:

> These moments were of pure, positive happiness when all doubts, all fears, all inhibitions, all tensions, all weaknesses, were left behind. Now self-consciousness was lost. All separateness and distance from the world disappeared as they felt one with the world, fused with it, really belonging in it and to it, instead of being outside looking in.
>
> (1962, p. 9)

Rames's (2016) study also focused on how interactions with dolphins affect people. In the research with 99 adults, Rames collected experiential responses to scuba diving with bottlenose dolphins and compared them with diving without the animal interaction. Participants who interacted with the dolphins expressed more tranquillity and connection to nature, to themselves, or the Divine, and some appeared to have peak experiences as defined by Maslow.

Peak Experiences in Context – Participant Accounts

The peak experiences shared in this section are our participants' recollections of peak events in the context of the natural world. Sometimes, these experiences occur through apparent solitude in wilderness settings, or sometimes they are co-created through a perceived connection with animals, nature, or through an aesthetic appreciation of place, space, or environmental beauty.

Colin, who we met in Chapter 1 in the context of Religion and Spirituality, recalled significant peak-like experiences in nature as well. He described one such experience when he was on a camping trip with a friend, and they were passing through Austria. They stopped by a stream, with mountains above, and he described how the experience was just a deep feeling of inner gratitude for what he was seeing impacted by "just the sheer stunning beauty of the scenery."

Colin further explained how he has had these experiences often because his major obsession in nature is kingfishers:

> Every time I've seen kingfisher, I'm totally grateful and *awestruck*. But there have been a few sightings which have been "heart in mouth," I've been deeply moved, grateful. There's just a beauty. It's exquisite – the back of a kingfisher with that iridescent blue. You cannot really explain it. And I'm feeling it now. It's just so wonderful, gorgeous, and reminds me of the beauty that's everywhere.

The feeling of being *awestruck* is discussed in detail by Paquette (2020, p. 6), who explains how over time the meaning of awe has shifted and is now used to describe positive experiences and a feeling that comes "when we're in the presence of something so vast or profound that it transcends our understanding of the world." Paquette suggests it might come from seeing a beautiful vista or from "countless other things." The common thread, however, is that we feel overwhelmed in its presence. Thus, it could be argued that being awestruck is similar to having a peak experience or that it is indeed a type of peak experience.

***

Dan Walmsley, who we also meet in the sport context and in creative arts, explained how during wilderness experiences while he was living with tribes in Canada, he noted how they are hugely allied to the environment: "everything has its place and is connected. Everything is a ritual." He had experienced that sense of connectedness himself:

> [T]hat being at one with everything – paddling across a lake, paddling rhythmically with others for 15 hours, you feel it. There's nothing else going on so you're completely connected to your environment.

In his early work, Maslow (1964) noted the possibility that psychedelic drugs, such as the psilocybin contained in some fungi, might produce peak experiences in some circumstances, suggesting that perhaps it may not be necessary to wait for peaks to occur by good fortune. Dan admitted that when he was younger, he experimented with psychedelic drugs such as magic mushrooms. He vividly recalls one such hallucination while in Canada. He shared how he literally felt connected to everything around him: "Complete oneness. I couldn't explain it, I was part of it. I was the woodland" and how that experience stays with him:

> Now fast forward 20 years. When you're in that flow moment or peak experience there is nothing else. It's wholeness. We're all atoms, aren't we? All part of the same thing in this crazy world that we live in. And it's that connection to that place, and around us.

During our interview, Dan went on to explain how the idea of connection fascinates him:

> We're sitting in this woodland right now and I know from working for years in the woods that the trees communicate with each other through their roots for glucose to feed mycelian to get things out of the ground. And they know if a tree is under attack. In these woods behind me, these trees put on a growth spurt because they knew those trees were under attack. That's connectedness.

***

Wildlife photographer and ecologist, **Jo Cartmell** explains how she became interested in photography when her children were teenagers, and she started meditatively wandering along local streams and meadows in solitude. Here she might encounter an ethereal light, a water vole, a Roesel's bush-cricket, a banded demoiselle damselfly, or a marbled white butterfly. It was during these wanderings that she had her first peak experience in nature which for me was undoubtedly due to awareness becoming like a clear blue summer's sky without a cloud (thought!) obstructing reality.

Jo's peak experiences began after practising the Rinzai tradition of Zen Buddhism and also attending a Buddhist Society where she met her teacher Ven. Myokyo-ni, who talked about the interconnectedness and interdependence of all things. She recalls particularly a talk by Ven. Soko Roshi (head monk at Daitoku-ji Monastery) speaking about the self-awareness and connection. Also, she remembers how, during a walk in a woodland at a Summer School, Ven. Soko Roshi left the group to pay his respects to a nearby tree whom he bowed to:

> This was a life lesson which has remained with me and I now bow in deepest gratitude to trees, water voles, great green bush-crickets . . . after spending time with them.

Jo recounts how Zen is a slow process of maturation through many years of meditation practice (both sitting and walking) and physical daily life practice (giving yourself wholeheartedly into whatever is being done at that moment without being distracted by thoughts): "When thoughts arise you simply go back to washing up, gardening, cycling, washing the floor and repeat the process each time thoughts arise."

In her recollections of her childhood, Jo describes visiting the water meadows and brooks within a few minutes' walk from her home. She liked to do this in solitude. She delighted in encounters with water voles, kingfishers, and sticklebacks and loved to look at the wildflowers, butterflies, and grasshoppers in the water meadows. She enjoyed her grandmother's wildflower meadow. She remembers being immersed in nature since she was old enough to walk, and it has always given her a sense of joy, wonder, awe, calm, and bliss.

She wrote this account of a peak experience at the age of 16:

> There was no mist to this early morning. The air was beautifully clear, the sky a golden hue from the gleaming sun on the horizon. The grass flashed and glistened as the beads of dew caught the golden light. The brook running alongside a meadow resembled a ribbon of running diamonds. As far as you could see there seemed to be a new freshness.

When asked for a more detailed description of the experience and how it made her feel, Jo said:

> At first, I felt as though I might be alone in having this kind of experience, but over the years, I have learnt that it is cross-cultural. I felt joyful, a profound sense of peace and was totally alert. It was a blissful experience which made me realise that there is a magical aspect to life which we enter into when we die and that we journey on. My heart was bubbling over with joy, yet I also felt calm and there was no sense of a separate self.

Jo was also reminded of the experiences shared by wildlife cameraman Rolf Steinmann whilst working in Alaska: "He talks about how difficult life gets when you've been in the zone – Mother nature's zone – and suggests that the problem with this magic zone is that it's intense like a drug."

After her peak experiences, Jo feels deep gratitude and humility towards nature, being part of nature, and close to animals and birds. She explains how during her peak experiences the world seems a different place. The experiences have fostered an attitude of reverence towards the natural world, and she says she now has more love and compassion for her "wild kin." As a consequence, she has been motivated to lobby government and social media followers to make changes for the benefit of the nature of which we are all part.

> Their problems became my problems, because I regard them as kin and resolved to help them by highlighting their issues: chalk streams, water voles, wildflower meadows, nightingales.

In recent years, Jo has become aware of the concept of "thin places" which has its origin in ancient Celtic tradition. The Celts spoke of thin places, like caves or wells or other special sites, where the boundary between the mundane and magical was permeable. Thin places are referred to in Celtic mythology as places where the veil between worlds is lifted. So a thin place might be felt as one where the membrane between the spiritual and the physical worlds are particularly fine and where we might see and experience something of another world, another time, and have a peak experience.

Zen practice also offers a kind of thin place, a place where we can discover that there is fundamentally no separation between ourselves and others, that what we seek is always so close, always right here. But, as Jo reminded us, "we cannot achieve this by an act of will. It happens when we are not seeking such an experience and usually when we most need it." She gives an example:

> I had gone to Wittenham Clumps and was walking on the Clumps in solitude when the light changed. For a moment there was a sense of standing at a portal, of immersion in another reality, and of becoming that which was before me. A feeling of timelessness, interconnectedness and bliss.

When reading Native American works, Jo says it is clear that they have had the same Zen-like, thin place peak experiences – they are captured in an extract from a Lakota poet about the sun, stars, moon, rocks, animals, and plants that ends with a line something like:

> I am all these things, the only separation that exists is in the mind.

Jo shares that she has had about seven thin place, peak experiences in local areas over the past 20 years: on two old Roman settlements, on a tree-lined lane, a close encounter with a fox family and hare (https://nearbywild.org.uk/

nearby-wild-close-encounters-with-fox-family-and-hare/), whilst standing by a small woodland plantation ride with a multitude of wildflowers, and walking along a lakeside path beneath trees. They are always the same kind of feeling of deep, otherworldly interconnectedness where sense of self and other disappears. There is always a sense of timelessness and of it being a portal moment. I usually bow with deep gratitude for them.

> Life is now a continuous journey of joyful discovery and I am never quite sure what is going to happen, or the magical wildlife encounter that I may experience next in this world full of flux and change.

Also, she added that her recent thin place experiences have helped her through the grieving process after the sudden and unexpected death of her husband: "It seems grief opens up thin places when we are at our most bereft and lonely, or walking in solitude."

Jo concludes that it would be wonderful if everyone could experience solitude and feel at ease being alone, so that they can experience thin place moments in the natural world. This, she says, would help to solve "over-consumption, consumerism and the pollution of our pale blue dot, as thin place moments foster humility and compassion. It would make us live more wisely, with reciprocity and reverence towards Mother Earth and our wild kin."

***

Paul Andrews is an environmentalist and citizen scientist who writes children's books under the name Paul Noël. His approach to nature is one that Cumes (1998) would classify as humility, based on the understanding that any control we may think we have over nature is just an illusion.

This humility is linked to Paul's early and very keen interest in astronomy that then developed into an interest in a far wider range of science subjects. He has come to realise that he most enjoys exploring the universe and everything about his surroundings from the perspective of what Carl Sagan (1994) referred to as "a human primate living on a pale blue dot." A photograph of the earth from space inspired Sagan to write his *Pale Blue Dot*, and the seeming insignificance of mankind engendered in that picture also inspires Paul and is captured in the following Sagan quote:

> There is perhaps no better demonstration of the folly of human conceits than this distant image of our tiny world. To me, it underscores our responsibility to deal more kindly with one another, and to preserve and cherish the pale blue dot, the only home we've ever known.
>
> (Sagan, 1994, p. 13)

Paul's interest in astronomy grew when he was a teenager, and he remembered his first awareness of the vastness of the universe when watching the Apollo 11 moon landing: "That probably kicked off my interest in science and especially astronomy." He then studied for an environmental science degree in his thirties after being involved with Friends of the Earth in his twenties.

Looking back Paul has realised that, from his peak experiences, he has developed a growing awareness and understanding of our cosmos. He shared how this *cosmic consciousness* has matured: "that interest in what I call a cold, dark and empty universe, in the human terms we have had given to us by evolution to experience our surroundings, has developed over time:"

> I see things from the perspective of being in the universe looking at this particular pale blue dot rather than just walking on its surface looking out. It does make me feel a bit non-human sometimes. . . . In the simplest of terms, at a certain point in time and space, matter and energy has come together in a configuration pattern that is me. From a simple construction of matter and energy to a more complex one and after hopefully a few more revolutions of the sun and not too soon I will become a simpler configuration of matter and energy.

This description by Paul, this strong sense of belongingness and being part of the universe, is very like Maslow's (1969) view of cosmic consciousness:

> [It's] a special phenomenological state in which the person somehow perceives the whole cosmos or at least the unity and integration of it and of everything in it, including his Self. He then feels as if he belongs by right in the cosmos. He becomes One of the family rather than an orphan. He comes inside rather than being outside looking in. He feels simultaneously small because of the vastness of the universe, but also an important being because he is there in it by absolute right. He is part of the universe rather than a stranger to it or an intruder in it.
>
> (Maslow, 1969, pp. 63–64)

Paul reflected on how his cosmic experiences have helped motivate him or helped solve problems. His broadened world view also enables him to query everything, and he doesn't understand why others accept so much without questioning. Talking about life and death, he says there is no need for religion or spirituality:

> [A]s the universe just is and we only have ourselves and each other for a short time. Taking that one step further you could say that I have been dead, then alive and will be dead again at some point or the matter and energy that I am was in state A, became state B and will return to be state A again.

Over his lifetime, Paul has grown more aware and has tried to see things from a point of view of "a consciousness not bound by the ten kilometres or so of thin blue and green ecosystem that we live in."

> We are literally stardust, we won't have this particular configuration for very long (our consciousness and physical self) and therefore it's time to realise that we only have each other in this cold, dark, empty universe.

Paul hopes that what he terms "this particular biological unit" continues to function as it is for as long as possible: "If I get to be like James Lovelock, the environmentalist and scientist, I would be very happy." In the meantime, he deems that

> [a]s the highest level of consciousness currently alive, to our knowledge, humans must observe the planet and nature going through changes over time and learn to live within the bounds of both. We must question ourselves as a species and come to terms that we must restrain our numbers, where we live and our resource use over time.

Paul's first peak experience in nature was well before Carl Sagan wrote his book. He describes how in the 1970s he was driving to a car club meeting in the countryside in Sussex when he had a tyre burst. Friends in a second car took him to a pub in a small village nearby to phone to call for a recovery vehicle. Long after the pub closed, he was still waiting for the recovery in the darkness, in a strange village with no streetlights. It was almost completely black and made him feel very alone. He describes his peak experience as a unitive feeling of being: "adrift in an ocean of emptiness in human centric terms, but in an ocean of something in universal terms."

Paul has had other peak experiences in nature as well; one of the most notable ones being watching swifts and swallows at different times. The swifts reminded him of spitfires flying with their grace and agility, but then he remembered "evolution honed their form long before humans thought up a fighting aircraft."

For Paul, the theme of connectedness is prominent, as are the indications that nature, particularly the night sky and space, induces feelings of insignificance and the realisation that although our life on earth is transitory, we have obligations to future generations. Reviewing these recollections, we might contend that Maslow's criterion for peak experience that sees it as enduring seems to aptly capture the nature of Paul's experiences too:

> Peak experiences are . . . perceived and reacted to as if they were in themselves "out there" as if they were perceptions of a reality independent of man and persisting beyond his life.
>
> (Maslow, 1959, pp. 52–53)

***

Our next participant, **Nicole Clough**, has been working with a nature conservation charity, and, for her, what is important is feeling "immersed and connected with the world and beyond." She also feels the sense of insignificance which Paul and others have experienced as part of being in nature. Nicole encapsulates this feeling in terms of peak experience: "a sense of oneness and the enormity of everything past, present and future." She describes how she also experiences relationships:

> Whilst I tend to seek vastness, I also seek oneness and connection with non-human animals, and to a lesser extent with plants. My emotional and

psychological response is similar or the same but to varying degrees. Essentially, I am brought to the moment, as the importance of time recedes, and I gain perspective through my connection.

In their research, Diebels and Leary (2019) similarly found that believing in oneness is associated strongly with feelings of closeness and a connection with nature. In addition, from a psychological perspective, they suggest: "believing in oneness may have important implications for people's identities, values, and worldviews, as well as for how they behave toward other people and the natural world" (Diebels & Leary, 2019, p. 464).

Nicole has always found herself to be deeply guided by nature and expresses her deep concern for the state of nature:

> My peak experiences offer me clarity and rejuvenation, which help with problem-solving and resilience. But, with this perspective I also find acceptance which is part of the constant process of grieving I have for our planet as we know her.

She shared how her earliest peak experience was whilst sailing on a tall ship across the North Sea, at the age of 17. She described how she spent a lot of time on boats and at sea as a child but that this was the most "at sea" she had been. She explained how she was at an age when she was exploring who she was as a young adult and how she felt and thought about the environment and our culture. She describes how she was on shift in the middle of the night when it was "blindingly dark, and the only sounds were those of the sea, our ship and her sails." She explains how night shifts felt special: "peaceful, contemplative but always with the huge sense of responsibility for the safety of the crew asleep below being in your hands." At one point, Nicole's shift buddy took the helm while she took some time out on the stern deck:

> On the stern I sat down to take the night in; I was blown away by the stars which were so thick and deep, like I'd never seen before, and I felt a deep sense of gravity versus weightlessness; the air was cold and fresh; and the waves were so huge that when down in a trough you couldn't see beyond the crests, which seemed even taller than the height of our ship! It was the first time I was deeply moved by vastness and could feel my own insignificance.

The main sensations Nicole noticed involved "bodily presence," which, she said "shifted between being pushed down into the deck of the ship and being weightless, moving towards the stars." She was purely in that moment.

Although she doesn't remember there being a conscious change in outlook, now she can observe that from that time she has sought out that sense of vastness and insignificance. She explained how "it continues to inspire me, move me, feed my soul and help me find purpose in life. As for many people, the night sky is my go-to when seeking perspective and calm, as is water." Looking back, however, Nicole can see now that her world view changed around that time, and she knew that her endeavours, particularly regarding career aspirations, had to be towards something greater than her own needs.

Nicole has also had peak experiences in other settings and gives the following examples:

1) *Wild swimming in the Tuichi River, a wide Amazon tributary river with a very strong current and solo walking on the Pennine Way, to then navigate off the path to wild camp at Fountains Fell tarn at 2,100 feet:*

Whilst both the swimming and the walking/camping experiences were in nature, the physical and mental achievements of these situations contributed to the emotional and spiritual response to them. Both were hugely physically demanding for me, pushing me to the limits of my fitness, stamina and mental strength; and the awareness of the potential to do myself harm heightened my perception. This combined with the exhilaration of being immersed in the elements of nature, and my vulnerabilities as a human being very apparent, made for very powerful experiences.

Nicole referred to the physical and mental challenge of her wild swimming and also solo walking and explained how these activities push her to her physical and mental limits but also heighten her awareness and perception. Thus, they have become rewarding and positive experiences for her.

2) *Music: whilst creating and playing music; and also, in experiencing exceptional music played live:*

Whilst inherently different from nature, in music there is a crossover in terms of connectivity and being in the moment. Music is also primal, with the hearts, minds and bodies of those present resonating in sync, together. And the playing of it is meditative and at its best can be transcendental. For me in those moments, my mind, my hands and my guitar merge, everything is flowing and there is no room or need for thoughts, not even to tell my fingers where to go or what notes could or should come next.

Nicole moreover made a connection between her childhood peak experiences and her subsequent career choice. This link between children's peaks and subsequent careers has been identified by Scott and Evans (2010, p. 149), who found that childhood peak experiences appear to function as "focusing lenses" since people come to see their childhood peak experiences as clarifying their future life path; they are a "directional impetus for a vocation or career." Of course, it could be that the very act of looking back at childhood peak experiences means they are now viewed as what Scott and Evans (2010, p. 149) describe as "a seed for the future" or as having "a visionary quality giving a clear picture of a life path and direction."

Thinking about childhood peak experiences, Nicole further explained that if she had any at all, they were very simple ones with no conscious recognition that such experiences are special. She has water- and sky-based snippets of memories: "the night sky, sound of the waves, the sea so dark, except for the phosphorescence, and the fresh, cool air." She recognised as she was completing our interview that "these beautiful times as a child are so clearly linked to my experiences as an adult!"

> I have never really thought about the experiences I have had in these ways – I have just sought them or come across them, enjoyed and valued them, then kept them tucked in my heart and memory for when I need to draw strength from them. I think more thoughts are yet to emerge from that realisation.

So for Nicole just thinking about her peak experiences for our research had been a very enlightening exercise. In the literature we found that people are often unaware of the term peak experience, and yet they can describe many memorable moments of awe or ecstasy. Maslow particularly noted this phenomenon: "I now suspect they occur in practically everybody, although without being recognized or accepted for what they are" (1962, p. 10).

***

Clare Josa, an engineer and marketing director, who we meet again in Chapter 11, gave an evocative example of a peak experience whilst wild swimming in a glacial river in Italy after white-water rafting:

> And it was just the bliss-zone taking me back into that oneness. The feeling of that ice-cold water, once I'd got over the cold shock . . . that feeling of the flow, that feeling of the ancient-ness of the water that's flowing past me, that's ever changing. And it really felt that everything that I'd been thinking of and worrying about in that moment, were completely irrelevant. And the smell, taste and feel of the water was just pure joy. I could have stayed there for hours. It was the power of nature and how we're all a part of it. It took me straight back into a peak experience. And I said to myself, "I have to do more of this."

Clare explained how there is very little thinking when the peak experience is happening, as it is being processed on a physical level, not cognitive. However, recalling her experience, she says she can go back to it instantly:

> It's not as intense as being there, but I can get quite close. I can hear the river, and I can hear the people in the distance. I can feel, and I can smell it.

And if right now, if I just close my eyes, I can just go back there. Again, I'm doing that thing. I can feel my heart, my feet are on the floor. It's there for me and that becomes an anchor. And nothing can take that experience away. It doesn't matter what life throws at me. We've got those experiences and we've got a body memory of them. We can go back to them. It might be a diluted form, but they can never be taken away.

***

Andy, who we will also see again in Chapter 11, explained a peak experience he's had when snorkelling on holiday. He says he didn't really know it was a peak experience until he thought about it afterwards. He was in Hawaii with his wife and remembers a swim with dolphins. They were out on a boat, and Andy swam out on his own, quite a distance from the boat, bobbing about with his snorkel and separated from the group.

Like the participants in DeMares and Krycka's (1998) study, Andy's encounter with dolphins led to a sense of connectedness.

I put my face in the water to start swimming and I was surrounded by dolphins and had a complete "wow" moment. They slowly started to dive, and I was just alongside them as though I was completely accepted as one of them. It was one of those lost in the moment, magical never to be forgotten experiences. They were just there, and it's stuck in my mind forever. Once they started to swim off, I knew I had to surface but they treated me as though I were one of their own. It was amazing. It was as though I was part of their pod. A weird but lovely, unbelievable sensation.

The strangest thing for Andy was that the group on the boat had been unsuccessfully looking for dolphins, and he swam out and just found he was surrounded by them. These moments in nature, associated with peak experience, have been a theme throughout our chapters.

What Is Significant About Peak Experiences in This Context?

In this chapter, we have been exploring nature-inspired peak experiences with help from both the extant research literature and from participants who have kindly shared their experiences with us. After initially examining some of the terminology, such as environmental epiphanies, used in this context to describe peak-like experiences, we presented summaries of literature relating to experiences occurring in wilderness, forests, and other related outdoor spaces. In addition, we found a variety of literature focusing on peak experiences during encounters with animals. Our participants' peak experiences were also all stimulated by the power of the natural world: the night sky, thin places, rivers, or connections with animals.

The literature suggested that reactions to peak experiences in nature are almost always transformative and can be powerful enough to have lasting effects. They are also found to be restorative and, in many cases, therapeutic. Indeed, we found that peak experiences in nature very much share the three key characteristics described by Privette (2001):

1) Peak experiences can lead to increases in personal awareness and understanding and may serve as a turning point in people's lives;
2) Peak experiences generate positive emotions and are frequently intrinsically rewarding;
3) During a peak experience, people feel at one with the world and often experience a feeling of transcendence and of losing track of time.

McDonald et al. (2009) also pointed out that peak experiences as a result of being in nature have an impact on well-being. This could be as a result of escaping from people and pressures of everyday life, the feelings of oneness that are generated, and a deeper understanding of the cosmos and its relationship to our lives. In many instances, these observations were confirmed by our participants as well.

All of our participants referred to the connectedness that being in nature gives them, and this echoes Storie and Vining's (2018) findings that, as well as the aesthetic, there are also intellectual, realisation, connection, and awakening responses. Certainly, our participants felt the connectedness of merging with nature and the universe. In one example, the feeling of connection aroused by a sense of place (Ramyar, 2020) was something that Jo experienced through visiting thin places, where she experienced feelings of "timelessness, interconnectedness and bliss."

For Dan, Paul, and Nicole, there was a distinct sense of connection and being at one with everything generated by immersion in the natural environment here on earth, and also, for Paul particularly, there was a more transpersonal awareness of the vastness of space, what Maslow (1969) termed "cosmic consciousness." These experiences sometimes led to feelings of humility, insignificance, and timelessness and the realisation that life on earth is transitory.

References

Aaltola, E. (2015). Wilderness experiences as ethics: From elevation to attentiveness, ethics. *Policy & Environment, 18*(3), 283–300.
Abraham, A., Sommerhalder, K., & Abel, T. (2010). Landscape and well-being: A scoping study on the health-promoting impact of outdoor environments. *International Journal of Public Health, 55*(1), 59–69.
Ashley, P. (2017). Mapping the inner experience of wilderness. *International Journal of Wilderness, 23*(1), 31–37.
Bethelmy, L. C., & Corraliza, J. A. (2019). Transcendence and sublime experience in nature: Awe and inspiring energy. *Frontiers in Psychology, 10*, 509.
Castelo, N., White, K., & Goode, M. R. (2021). Nature promotes self-transcendence and prosocial behavior. *Journal of Environmental Psychology, 76*, 101639.
Chenoweth, R. E., & Gobster, P. H. (1990). The nature and ecology of aesthetic experiences in the landscape. *Landscape Journal, 9*(1), 1–8.
Cornell, J. (2011). The importance of deep experiences in nature. *Legacy, 22*(3), 30–33. https://clearingmagazine.org/archives/3161

Cumes, D. (1998). Thoughts on the inner journey in wilderness. *International Journal of Wilderness*, 4, 14–18.
Curtin, S. (2006). Swimming with dolphins: A phenomenological exploration of tourist recollections. *International Journal of Tourism Research*, 8(4), 301–315.
DeMares, R. (2000). Human peak experience triggered by encounters with cetaceans. *Anthrozoös*, 13(2), 89–103.
DeMares, R., & Krycka, K. (1998). Wild-animal triggered peak experience: 137 Transpersonal aspects. *The Journal of Transpersonal Psychology*, 30(2), 161–177.
Diebels, K. J., & Leary, M. R. (2019). The psychological implications of believing that everything is one. *The Journal of Positive Psychology*, 14(4), 463–473.
Emerson, R. W. (1996). *Essays & Poems* (Vol. 29, p. 10). New York: Library of America.
Gee, C. M. (2010). Wild epiphany: Turning child and youth care inside out. *Relational Child & Youth Care Practice*, 23(4).
Hart, L. A. (2000). Methods, standards, guidelines, and considerations in selecting animals for animal-assisted therapy. In A. H. Fine (Ed.), *Handbook of animal-assisted therapy: Theoretical foundations and guidelines for practice* (pp. 81–97). San Diego: Academic Press.
Hartig, T., Berg, A. E., Hagerhall, C. M., Tomalak, M., Bauer, N., Hansmann, R., . . . & Waaseth, G. (2011). Health benefits of nature experience: Psychological, social and cultural processes. In *Forests, trees and human health* (pp. 127–168). Dordrecht: Springer.
Kaplan, S., & Talbot, J. F. (1983). Psychological benefits of a wilderness experience. In *Behavior and the natural environment* (pp. 163–203). Boston, MA: Springer.
Laski, M. (1980). *Everyday ecstasy*. Thames and Hudson.
Marshall, I. (2003). *Peak experiences, walking meditations on literature, nature and need*. Charlottesville: University of Virginia Press.
Maslow, A. H. (1959). Cognition of being in the peak experiences. *The Journal of Genetic Psychology*, 94(1), 43–66.
Maslow, A. H. (1962). Lessons from the peak-experiences. *Journal of Humanistic Psychology*, 2(1), 9–18.
Maslow, A. H. (1964). *Religions, values, and peak experiences*. London: Penguin Books Limited.
Maslow, A. H. (1968). *Toward a psychology of being*. Princeton, NJ: D. Van Nostrand.
Maslow, A. H. (1969). Various meanings of transcendence. *Journal of Transpersonal Psychology*, 1(1), 56–66.
McDonald, M. G., Wearing, S., & Ponting, J. (2009). The nature of peak experience in wilderness. *The Humanistic Psychologist*, 37(4), 370–385.
Muir, J. (1961). *The mountains of California*. Doubleday-Anchor.
Naor, L., & Mayseless, O. (2020). How personal transformation occurs following a single peak experience in nature: A phenomenological account. *Journal of Humanistic Psychology*, 60(6), 865–888.
Nukarinen, T., Rantala, J., Korpela, K., Browning, M. H., Istance, H. O., Surakka, V., & Raisamo, R. (2022). Measures and modalities in restorative virtual natural environments: An integrative narrative review. *Computers in Human Behavior*, 126, 107008.
Paquette, J. (2020). *Awestruck: How developing a sense of wonder can make you happier, healthier, and more connected*. Boulder, CO: Shambhala.
Privette (2001). – cited in other chapters.
Rames, A. E. (2016). *Playing with dolphins and calling it research: A mixed-methods study investigating human emotional well-being and experiential responses to interacting with dolphins*. Doctoral Dissertation, Sofia University.
Ramyar, R. (2020). Learning from tradition: The role of environment perception layers in space making – the case of the Persian Garden. *Journal of Urban Management*, 9(2), 238–249.
Sagan, C. (1994). *A pale blue dot*. New York: Random House.
Schroeder, H. (2002). Experiencing nature in special places: Surveys in the north-central region. *Journal of Forestry*, 100(5), 8–14.

Scott, & Evans (2010). – details in Education chapter.
Storie, M., & Vining, J. (2018). From oh to aha: Characteristics and types of environmental epiphany experiences. *Human Ecology Review*, *24*(1), 155–180.
Ulrich, R. S., Simons, R. F., Losito, B. D., Fiorito, E., Miles, M. A., & Zelson, M. (1991). Stress recovery during exposure to natural and urban environments. *Journal of Environmental Psychology*, *11*(3), 201–230.
Williams, K., & Harvey, D. (2001). Transcendent experience in forest environments. *Journal of Environmental Psychology*, *21*(3), 249–260.
Wolfe, L. M. (1938). *John of the mountains: The unpublished journals of John Muir*. University of Wisconsin Press.

7 Peak Experiences in Competitive Sport

Introduction

We begin this chapter by acknowledging the linguistic confusion mentioned in our introductory chapter, where we noted Privette's (1983) argument that, in sport, especially, the term peak experience is regularly used interchangeably with flow or peak performance.

In her 1983 paper, Privette compared peak experience, peak performance, and flow, identifying important attributes which they share: absorption, valuing, joy, spontaneity, a sense of power, personal identity, and involvement. She moreover identified some distinguishing features: peak experience was found to be mystic and transpersonal; peak performance was transactive and focused on the self and the valued object; and flow involved fun.

Reviewing Privette's work and that of other researchers, McInman and Grove (1991) considered the characteristics of the three constructs of peak experience, flow, and peak performance and argued they are in fact all sub-categories of the overarching, umbrella concept they called *Peak Moments*. To support their argument, they drew out characteristics that were present in at least two, if not three, of these constructs and found seven commonalities: absorption; detachment; emptiness or loss of ego; ecstasy and euphoria; larger or more powerful energy; a perception of time either slowing or speeding up; a sense of unity with the environment (1991, p. 343). These were the shared characteristics they claimed characterise the umbrella concept of peak moments.

In their review of peak moments in sport, McInman and Grove (1991) also stressed the definitional problems. They confirmed that overlapping features made definition quite difficult. Their review examines four earlier attempts to shed light on the phenomenon: positive experiences (Landsman, 1968), aesthetic peak experiences (Panzarella, 1980), peak experiences (Thorne, 1963), and feeling and performance (Privette & Bundrick, 1987).

In this chapter, because of the ambiguity in the literature relating to peak experience, and taking account of the nature of athletes' experiences, it is impossible for us to exclude discussions of peak performance and flow. All three constructs are integral and closely intertwined. The conflation of constructs also illustrates the reciprocity of sensations between them, so that when sportsmen and women talk about their

DOI: 10.4324/9781003509219-8

extraordinary encounters they may, in fact, be referring to peak experience or peak performance or flow. In this chapter, we therefore aim to illuminate the power generated by peak experiences, perhaps in the guise of peak performance and flow.

In the next section, we present a detailed examination of the literature relating to peak experience and the composite concept of peak moments to highlight any potential development of the concepts. Examples of felt peak experiences from the sport literature are also included before we give our detailed exposition of our own participant sportspeople's accounts of their peak experiences.

Review of Previous Research

This review is divided into two sections. The first explores attempts to disaggregate the seemingly overlapping concepts of peak experience, peak performance, and flow in the sports context. The second section provides some examples of peak experiences from the sport literature.

Peak Experience, Peak Performance, and Flow in the Sport Literature

In one of the first studies of how Maslow's notion of peak experience manifested in the sport context, Ravizza (1977) focused on how the phenomenon was experienced by 11 athletes associated with team sports and nine with individual sports. The findings echoed 19 of Maslow's qualities of peak experience, including peak experience as a unique, non-voluntary, transient, spontaneous experience; the result being a temporary transcendence of the usual self, replaced by a sense of union or harmony with the environment. Most athletes felt a strong feeling of belonging or a harmony with the world; they felt fearlessness and a feeling of control; there was a time–space disorientation; fusion of the self on all levels; total, effortlessness concentration on the sport activity and awe and wonder at the "perfection" of their experience. Furthermore, the experience was self-validating for the individuals regardless of the outcomes of their competitions. The athletes also felt that someone or something was "moving" them. This feeling resonates with Murphy and White's (1978a, p. 5) contention that the transpersonal and mystical side of peak experience happens, and yet coaches and athletes tend not to "burden us with exhortations about the spiritual things they are doing."

Murphy and White believed that sport has much to teach us about peak experiences. Through examining athletes' reports on inward knowing and transcendence, they found perceptions of something profound – an athlete's sense that something "secretly supports the superficial mental being and enables it to persevere through all labours, sufferings and ordeals" (1978b, p. 127). When athletes are pursuing their passion, something happens; similar to what happens in Zen archery where "you do not let go of the bow string, it just happens" (1978b, p. 25). Murphy and White (1978b) explain further that in both religion and sport, the purpose of just letting go is to achieve a higher level of functioning or what Privette (1983) would call optimal functioning. In addition, Murphy and White also noted the feelings of fusion and unity during a peak experience: union of mind and body, a sense of inner unity, a oneness with teammates, even a feeling of unity with the cosmos. The perception of time is akin to Maslow's observations: the athlete's sense of time is altered, often perceived as moving either more swiftly or slowly: "great athletes, for example – may merely be blessed with basal brainwave firing significantly slower than that of the general population" (Murphy & White, 1978b, p. 44).

According to research carried out by Privette and Bundrick (1991) with 123 college students, there are three distinguishing qualities that differentiate peak experience from peak performance and flow: fulfilment, significance, and spirituality. Peak performance had two distinguishing characteristics, full focus and a sense of self, whilst flow could be distinguished through play, outer structure (i.e., a task), and the importance of other people. These authors described peak experience in sport in particular as involving the upper limits of joy, with positive feelings, ecstasy, happiness, and satisfaction: "peak experience is intense joy, a moment of highest happiness that stands out perceptually and cognitively among other experiences" (1991, p. 171).

In 1999, Thornton, Privette, and Bundrick reported on a study designed to examine peak performance and self-actualisation. They argued that peak performance is an optimal experience that "parallels and is among a person's closest approximate to self-actualisation, an optimal personality constellation" (1999, p. 253). Interestingly, Maslow had alluded to such a reciprocal relationship when describing peak experiences as "states of pure success" (1962b, p. 47). Attempting to differentiate peak performance, Privette had earlier observed how it is identifiable and measurable and refers to a superior level of functioning regardless of the type of activity. In addition, she argued, "although the performance does not necessarily exceed that of other people, it surpasses what could be predicted for a person in a particular situation" (Privette, 1983, pp. 323–324).

Gallwey's publication, *The Inner Game of Tennis*, was an attempt to unravel the mental aspects of peak performance. Gallwey recognised that the intrusion of conscious thought was a hindrance to success in sport and recommended that players improve their performance by attending to their psychology or inner game (1986). Based on his own observations as a tennis player and coach, Gallwey suggested that "every game is composed of two parts, an outer game and an inner game." The outer game is played against an opponent while the inner game takes place in the mind of the player: "it is played against such obstacles as lapses in concentration, nervousness, self-doubt and self-condemnation . . . all habits of mind which inhibit excellence in performance" (1986, p. 11).

Gallwey noticed how players could get in their own way by becoming discouraged by an inner critic he called "Self 1." Failure to deal with Self 1, he argued, means that "Self 2" (the player's body and subconscious mind) is not able to execute what it knows how to do instinctively (Gallwey, 1986, p. 18). He then suggested that players entering "the zone" of being fully absorbed in the game with total focus and awareness in the moment without interference from Self 1 would perform better. Gallwey thus advocated that winning the inner game is about quieting Self 1 through focus and awareness, and then Self 2 becomes more conscious and more present, enjoyment increases, "and the gifts are being given" (1986, p. 14).

Although not referred to as such by Gallwey, in the sport and performance psychology literature, the unconscious state he studied has typically been referred to as "flow" (Csikszentmihalyi, 1990; Jackson & Csikszentmihalyi, 1999). Flow is a state characterised by complete absorption in a task, present mindedness, lack of self-consciousness or fear of failure, the merging of action and awareness, time distortion, the paradox of control (feeling in control while letting go), and knowing precisely what to do moment by moment (Csikszentmihalyi, 1990; Nakamura & Csikszentmihalyi, 2002).

The conditions for the occurrence and continuation of flow according to Csikszentmihalyi (1990) are clear goals and feedback; balance between challenges and skills; the merging of action and awareness; concentration on the task; a sense of potential control; loss of self-consciousness; an altered sense of time; and an autotelic (self-rewarding) experience. More recently, according to Stoll (2019), the corresponding outcomes for athletes experiencing flow are enjoyment, increased motivation, the development of skills in the long run, and decreased or increased performance.

Despite earlier attempts by Privette and colleagues and McInman and Grove to distinguish between the concepts of peak experience, peak performance and flow, recent commentators have continued to conflate the terms. For example, in their study of surfers, Morgan and Coutts (2016) investigated flow as a measure of peak experience. These authors maintain that peak experience is often reported in sport, describing the feeling as "like you are on top of the world" (2016, p. 203). Participants in their study identified four of McInman and Grove's characteristics of peak moments: (i) absorption in the activity, (ii) emptiness by becoming one with the activity and losing oneself, (iii) the perception of time either slowing or speeding up, (iv) the sense of unity with the self via the freeing-up from self-consciousness. Their participants also described flow as "being in the zone," manifested as a positive relationship between peak experience and intrinsic motivation. Coincidentally, Csikszentmihalyi also identified flow as the state which also induces intrinsic motivation, illustrating the symbiotic nature of the two states of peak experience and flow. Morgan and Coutts (2016) clearly support the links between flow *or* peak experience and performance, which, they maintain, are of interest to research on surfing, concluding that measures of peak experience might provide information about the "sustaining of positive experience and safe participation in physical activity pursuits" (2016, p. 215).

O'Brien and Kilrea (2021, p. 314) looked at the positive effects of unitive experience on the mental health and well-being of athletes. They define unitive experiences as "spontaneously occurring states of consciousness characterized by a sense of unity or 'oneness' that transcends sensory or cognitive apprehension." Using a quantitative methodology, these authors demonstrated that athletes scoring high on a unitive experience measure actually scored lower on sport-related anxiety but higher on subjective well-being and motivation measures.

Earlier, Young and Pain (1999) had described the heightened states of consciousness attained during participation in sport as "the zone" or a "flow state," which seem to be universal phenomena across sport. Similar to Maslow's and McInman and Grove's descriptions of peak experience, Young and Pain say that the zone can be likened to a "diverse range of phenomena covered by the umbrella terms of ecstasy, transcendence or altered states of consciousness in sport participation" (1999, p. 22). These authors explain that these umbrella terms include the various concepts of "peaks" – peak moments, mindfulness, peak experience, and flow, assimilating these concepts to define the zone. Young and Pain moreover identify that in sports psychology literature, the terms flow and zone are, in fact, used interchangeably and synonymously. Due to the blending of the various peaks into the zone or flow, we can assume that the conditions for flow are therefore pertinent to being in the zone.

Felt Peak Experiences in Sports Settings

The kind of peak experience felt by athletes is memorably described by Jonny Wilkinson, the England player who scored a breathtaking drop goal in the 2003 Rugby World Cup:

> I actually got lost in that moment, I didn't know where I was . . . it felt like a surreal, dream-like situation . . . I want to keep it exactly as I remember it, which was one hell of an experience.
>
> (Bech, 2013)

Some 18 years after that astonishing drop-kick goal in 2003, Wilkinson (in Thomson, 2021) recalls his sensations:

> I don't remember being present for the kick . . . I can feel it and see it, but I just wasn't in my body for it. As it went over, I kicked back in and my body sort of went. It's gone, it's gone over. The best moment of my rugby life. That's been the secret of the journey since, just to find that space. You just want to pause that, bottle it . . . that's the one.

Wilkinson's recall of his encounter is memorable and illustrates the power of peak experience as a significant moment in his life. For an experience to be remembered in such fine detail ten years after the event, and then re-recalled almost two decades later, illustrates the impact this peak experience had on Wilkinson, and for him, the uniqueness, rarity, and importance of this phenomenon.

We can also note how Wilkinson's feelings are similar to those identified in earlier research literature. He describes his feelings of "getting lost in the moment," which can be interpreted on two levels. First, there is an implication that Wilkinson was experiencing a sort of emptiness, absence, and misplacement in the moment, explained by McInman and Grove (1991) as a sense of loss of self, a feeling of abandonment, and devoid of any reference point. Second, there was timelessness or an altered perception of time, often associated with an altered state of consciousness. In this state, time has no rational meaning and can either fly past or slow down. Wilkinson also remembers the sense of not being present for the kick, suggesting he was experiencing a sense of detachment. According to McInman and Grove (1991), individuals are detached not only from their surroundings but also from themselves in what could be called an out-of-body experience: seeing oneself from an observational perspective whilst participating in the activity.

Croucher (2021), reporting for the BBC, describes how British triathlete Alex Yee also recalled an out-of-body experience: "I felt like I flowed in that race. It's almost like an out-of-body experience. Everything feels, not effortless but, very present. It's indescribable." Yee's use of the word indescribable could be interpreted as euphoric, a state of ecstasy and total enjoyment. Both Wilkinson and Yee appear to have been totally absorbed in their experiences. Absorption is produced by intense concentration, when athletes are entirely focused on the task in hand, which often challenges their skillset, a characteristic of flow.

Heery's (2003) study in Japan, exploring peak or mystical experiences in the practice of Aikido, detailed experiences of the inner and outer worlds of three senior black belt Aikido masters and teachers. It revealed deeper layers of meaning that exemplify the kind of experiences recorded much earlier by Maslow. The following narrative records their visceral experience:

> Palms joined just below the navel, throat open and relaxed, sound echoing from deep within the body, each cell resonating, physical vibrations expanding out from the core a single note, heart opening, thoughts receding . . . there is only the unquenchable light and joy, molecules of moss, water, air, flesh, and bone resonating in perfect harmony.
>
> (Heery, 2003, p. 147)

Participants in Heery's study reported flow experiences which provided an "inside out" rather than an "outside in" perspective. They likened their experience to transpersonal and transformational changes, inviting the spirit to awaken. Other relevant findings included activating internal energies and changes in subjective experiences of space and time with frequent peak experiences after the age of 50.

In his research into contact sports, Senecal (2021, p. 301) asked participants to describe the greatest experience they have ever had during their sport career. Their narratives all expressed profound levels of joy, ecstasy, and fulfilment:

> [M]any participants expressed that few, if any, experiences in their lives outside of sport could match the magnitude of enjoyment, elation, or euphoria uncovered in these moments of sports "highs."

Indeed, many of Senecal's participants said they have had many peak experiences in the sporting context and that it would be hard to choose only one.

Senecal's (2021) work on the aftermath of peak experiences for contact sport athletes identifies the influence of Maslow's general category of peak experience on the development of Csikszentmihalyi's notion of flow. Flow, Senecal argues, is "a more specific manifestation of self-transcendence, tied back to some form of performance and linked to the act of pushing the limits of our ability" (2021,

p. 296). He also claims it is "in the process of self-transcendence and limit-seeking that the truly sublime nature of peak experiences are manifest." Senecal explains, however, that in the case of contact sport athletes such a limit-seeking and self-transcending tendency "is likely to take the form of pushing oneself past pain, fear, and bodily harm" (2021, p. 297).

In the next section we present accounts of six participants' peak experiences, taken from recorded interviews with modern-day athletes.

Peak Experience in Context – Participant Accounts

Our first participant is **Ali Hollest,** a marathon runner and endurance athlete who set a record in September 2020 as the first person to achieve Snowdon Six-Ways, an overnight marathon of some 18 hours.

For Ali, a peak experience in sport "just happens":

> There's nothing that you've done differently than what you've done before; there's nothing that you've particularly focussed on and if anything, you're not focussed on anything at all. All the experiences that you've had, all the lessons, all the coaching, all the negative failures, all the positive successes come together for a period of time, and the goal of what you're trying to do "just happens."

Ali adds that when it's over, and it's happened a couple of times: "your jaw just hits the floor. I've done it, I did it. Where's it gone? The feeling of something that's not going to last forever."

The fact that Ali describes his experience as inhabiting a space without focus excludes the possibility of his experience being either peak performance or flow. It was a peak experience that happens unpredictably, as Maslow, Murphy and White, and others have reported in their research and as Wilson (2009, p. 51) described: "sometimes they seem to happen of their own accord, out of the blue, as it were."

When asked if "just happens" was timebound, Ali answered "yes" and recalled a running experience on the track in 2014:

> One guy was always 8 to10 seconds in front of me, per lap, and that's a big chunk for a lap. In this one lap, coming round the final bend, I remember almost coming out of myself and running past him, cruising past him; not even breathing, just so relaxed, obviously working hard yet it didn't feel like I was doing anything. I felt as though I was floating past this guy. I've got this vision of almost looking at me from behind, running around this corner. I'd never beaten him on a lap, and he looked at me as if to say, "where the fuck did that come from?"

Ali remembers trying again and again in the following weeks to find what allowed him to do that lap but never managed to repeat it. Ali's experience resonates with Schuler and Brunner's notion of flow (2009, p. 173): "flow functions as a reward of the running activity, which leads to the desire to perform the activity again."

Ali can vividly remember the feeling of flow and again the feeling almost an out-of-body experience that transcended time. Elements of disassociation or detachment from one's surroundings, and absorption and perceptual distortions such as perceptions of time experienced during flow, are similar to hypnotic states (Grove & Lewis, 1996). Ali is convinced that his training, marathon experiences, and the environment were contributory factors in setting up the conditions for something special to happen. Yet, despite the conditions being in place, Ali admitted you can't just say it'll happen:

> What I mean is when you try to make it happen, and you say, right I'm going to get into flow, you're not going to do it. You're almost aggressively trying to make it happen. But if you can set the environment right and control everything you can, and put yourself in the environment where it could happen and go with it, then it might very well happen again. When it does happen, like an out of body experience, it is amazing.

Ali explained how whenever anyone talks about flow, he just goes straight back to that amazing moment in 2014, to that thing that "just happened."

Asked what he was thinking during his experience, Ali said:

> You try to not think about things when running hard as traditionally, it tends to put things off course a bit. I felt that sense of relaxation, bearing in mind that I'm running as fast as I possibly can, and all these emotions and feelings are going on in my head while I'm still running. You're working at a very high heart rate and at a high effort level. If you're looking to incorporate something like that, it makes you slower. Whereas this time around I was feeling all these emotions. I was aware of the emotions but, excuse the pun, I ran with it. I kind of let it all happen. I didn't change anything but just let it happen and went with it. I remember this conscious thought of "Don't change. Don't let it go. Don't do anything. Don't fuck it up! Don't lose this feeling, make sure you hold onto it" which isn't what you would normally do. Normally it would be "Keep your cadence high, keep your heel high." Fuck all of that. Just keep doing what you're doing. And I just cruised past this guy.

When asked about what he was feeling, Ali replied that in a sense he was feeling so much that it wasn't feeling it at all, but he felt light as though he was able to stretch like he'd never stretched before. He described the feeling as simply moving as if he were really well-oiled, not clunky but smooth. He hesitated as though trying to find the right words. "I felt light and empowered."

The experience was so powerful that Ali believes it has had an ongoing impact on him:

> Out of all the other things that I've done, this one corner is the highlight of my running career. If anyone looks at my sporting history, they'd ask what about x, y, and z. Yes, they were all great, but that one bit is the key that unlocked something.

Ali also spoke about team peak experiences. He remembers playing hockey at school, in what he describes as a "ridiculously high-performing team," winning championships at the national level with athletes who achieved international status. He recalls "real, deep subconscious understanding of one another," connectivity and trust being the core elements of their success both on and off the pitch. Ali's peak experiences of success with that team resemble a significant growth experience, the euphoria of winning with teammates who knew each other so well that they "had each other's backs"; they intuitively knew where to place the ball and reacted instinctively through a mutual understanding of one another which led to a particular type of peak experience:

> [T]hat experience, that team, that learning with those people, that connection, that synergy and knowing that someone's got your back. We're all in this together, we've all got the same goal, the same plan. There's no one person, it's all about us as a unit – that journey of success and failure I would consider is a peak experience for me.

So Ali's team experience was less of a peak experience and more a growth experience. The whole period of growing together as a team was a developmental experience that impacted on him, making him who he is today. He explained that the experience with that team of amazing people, that lasted for over 12 years, reached an unbelievable goal with all the highs and lows that entail. He considers that the team experience was very much a peak learning experience rather than an isolated peak experience and was a very different experience to running on the track.

We then talked about Ali's peak experiences doing the Snowdon Six-Ways challenge – 18 hours and 21 minutes of constant running with a support team for each leg. One was seeing a clear sky with the moon shining on the lake as they descended. All four runners stopped for a second as they took in an amazing sunset, remaining silent in wonder. Their experience resonates with Paquette's (2020, p. 116) observation that "awe often occurs as a result of something in our external world that overwhelms our senses – a beautiful sunset, a magnificent mountain, or the night sky above." Ali said it felt like a truly special, memorable moment; there was harmony and connectivity with an element of performance, but more so the unconditional trust between them had helped him get up the mountain. It was a magical experience, a collective "something happened" as time stood still. He doesn't recall stopping but continued jogging even though the act of running was the last thing on his mind. There was an out-of-body experience which he can still visualise. All he felt was pure happiness, one of the amazing feelings he can still sense to this day and that has become part of his legacy, part of who he wants to be.

Ali explained how the Snowdon Six-Ways was a complete peak experience "right up there with any experience I've ever had." Everything was planned down to the last detail from the equipment to the nutritional plan. Everything was in place to invite a peak experience to happen. Again, it was a shared experience built through mutual trust and connectivity with teammates, a sense of adventure, and a reflection of life: "you're up, you're down; you're cold, you're hot; you're hungry, you're full. The only difference with life is that I was happy all the time. I loved every single step of that challenge."

Snowdon remains a special place for Ali. He learnt to connect with mountains through training courses and mountain walking, but only through Snowdon Six-Ways did he appreciate its beauty. Regardless of weather conditions, the relentless rain and wind in Wales, he was prepared, capable, and trusted the team. He felt totally connected with the mountain, again echoing Paquette's (2020, p. 98) sentiments: "take in the full experience and allow yourself to feel a sense of deep and grateful awe for being able to witness this." Ali remembers looking back at the mountain for 20 seconds and taking it all in:

> Thank you, I'm ready. I'm not going to fight you but work with you. This was a connection of understanding each other and the respect I felt towards the mountain. I think, going through that process of getting that connection sounds so "hocus-pocus" but it's not because that's how it happened. But it was definitely a point in time when I knew "you've got this, it's nothing major, it's fine. You're doing a really good thing, you're going to enjoy it, you've got respect for and from the environment." So that was a real turning point.

Paquette (2020, p. 89) records how "mountains inspire us, mystify us, and instil us with a profound sense of awe." He moreover explains how over time the meaning of awe has shifted and is now used to describe positive experiences and a feeling that comes "when we're in the presence of something so vast or profound that it transcends our understanding of the world" (Paquette, 2020, p. 6). Paquette suggests it might come from seeing a beautiful vista or from "countless other things." The common thread, however, is that we feel overwhelmed in its presence. Thus, it could be argued that being awestruck is similar to having a peak experience or that it is indeed a type of peak experience.

***

Rugby is **Kevin Harris**'s passion. He was involved with the sport both as a player and as a coach in local clubs, and his peak experiences arise from feedback from youngsters who he's trained and who often tell him "you don't realise the impact you've had on me." Kevin finds these comments immensely rewarding and gave an example: he saw someone waving at him from a car and realised it was a former coachee he had trained since a young boy but who was now an adult:

> He took hold of my hand and gave me a massive hug and said "without you I wouldn't be doing what I'm doing. I thought I was just playing rugby, but it was so much more than that. It's changed my life."

This left an enormous impact on Kevin, not immediately but progressively:

> [T]his is the peak of it, you can have more of an impact on people than you ever truly understand. And it's often just giving a little bit of time. I wasn't expecting it, it was really lovely and it's the impact it's had on me and

166 *Valuing Peak Experience in Everyday Lives*

my thinking from that moment. It happened about 10 years ago and still stays with me. He couldn't have been more thankful in that moment, it felt wonderful.

Kevin recalled how giving the boys time, all those years ago, has impacted him and given him peak moments; boys who he made sure got to the training if their parents were busy, boys who may have gone in a different direction in life had he not given them care and consideration he is now acknowledging and thankful for. Kevin revealed:

One day I opened up the local paper and there was a big picture of him – he was a soldier and had been killed in one of the Afghan wars. That moment just got me. In that second something came to me that he'd had a better short life than the crazy long life he would have had as he was going the wrong way. And somehow that felt good. I know that sounds awful, but he'd become a soldier and was really, really good at it. And I think the discipline of the rugby and being around a team obviously just helped him think differently because he was one step away from going to prison.

It seems as though Kevin's peak experiences are through his recollections of youngsters he's coached in rugby and how they've grown and developed. He's observed how they have become self-actualised, become their very best self, and achieved something in life. Thus, Kevin's peak experience is triggered by how they've got there through his influence and support. Kevin's experience is reminiscent of Fatemi's (2004) study results, where 90 percent of respondents reported that their peak experiences had a permanent memorable affect.

We then talked about the difference between peak experience and peak performance, which Kevin thinks are quite different and are revealed in one of his memories of being a rugby player:

[W]hen I was playing rugby, for a moment, everything seemed to just stop. It was quiet. I was probably as mentally and physically fit as I've ever been and in my early 40s. I was an experienced captain and for some reason this day the ball felt much larger than usual. It landed in my arms, and I was fending people off and getting through tackles but in my mind, I knew I was going to get there. I knew I was going to score from the moment the ball landed in my arms. I have no idea why. Looking back, I could hear the crowd cheering and everything seemed perfect. Almost being guided through and I knew I was going to get there – a bit like Jonny Wilkinson. I could see it play out before it actually happened. And it was amazing. It felt as though the whole thing had stopped – as if all the people were just frozen and I just had to do whatever I needed to do to score.

Until we had our interview, Kevin admitted that he would have been unable to give these moments a label but:

they definitely sit in my list of buckets of great things that have happened in my life. I hadn't appreciated that they were a peak of anything. Looking back, I often draw on these experiences.

Kevin then recalled another experience which made him burst into tears of joy: "it's making me want to cry now, the thought of it, you know. Such a brilliant, brilliant moment in my life that I don't think I'll ever experience again." This was a team experience and one he will never forget. As captain of the team, he knew it was down to him to create belief for everyone in a game against their rivals:

> I gave a speech at half time to the team, which inspired them, and that collective effort was brilliant. Everyone got behind that moment, and everyone seemed to find that extra one percent. Mentally you have to adjust to say to yourself we're not losing this, we're winning this to make the distinction that you're not giving in and going for it. And as captain I had to up my game so everyone else could up theirs. So, you find an extra five or ten percent. It gives you another part of you that you didn't know you had . . . it was a peak moment for the team . . . everyone still talks about it . . . that was 22 years ago and it's still part of our lives and conversations, and the things we talk about as friends. I can remember the blood pumping around me as though it was going at 1000 miles an hour . . . everyone was just hugging each other and it was just a magic, magic moment. It's contagious.

Kevin summarised our interview by quantifying that there were two peak experiences for him: the collective team effort, which he thinks was more of a peak performance, and the coaching effect; to play a part in another human being's direction that's helped them with the course of their life through rugby. He simply said "amazing"!

***

Our third participant is **Guy Disney,** a former captain in the British Army who is now a successful steeplechase jockey.

Guy's moments of euphoria, his peak experiences, stem from his army training. Rigorous training and discipline acquired in the army enabled Guy to develop his own style of leadership:

> My culture is looking down not up – I'm interested in the team. The worst thing you can do is behave like a dictator: the guys in your team have experience to draw on too. I'm given a directive from above, I make a plan, take it to my guys and ask their opinion which was often similar to mine which I kept to myself. I ran with one of their ideas and they felt completely empowered with it. They owned it and felt part of the decision-making cycle.

Guy has a positive attitude to challenges. He loves contingency planning, breaking down each aspect of new tasks, leaving no stone unturned in preparation. He says, "I'm not a believer in luck, I think you should break down the scenarios as much as possible and understand that things can go wrong." He uses visualisation to focus on the intense effort that is required to achieve a successful outcome. Guy's internal dialogue reminds him of what he needs to do to achieve a level of perfection that enables him to move to the next chess piece of his internal map: "I role play scenarios. I role play meetings; what are they going to ask, what will they want to know? I definitely game-plan a lot." Risk is assessed and procedures put in place to avoid unnecessary risk although, as he also says, "you cannot control the uncontrollable."

A veteran of two deployments in Afghanistan, Guy recalls that a lot of time was spent training in Norway, spending time with "guys who'd been there, getting information out of them the whole time, and not just listening but practising it, running through it time and time again." Guy's notion of peak experience is, therefore, quite definitely linked to the performance of his team. Guy recalls the feelings of euphoria after firefights; gunfights, which he thinks are an adrenaline rush. He recalls, "the moment contact starts a huge amount of adrenalin is released which dissipates the more you do it, as the body acclimates to it."

Guy experienced euphoria not only on the battlefield but also at Sandown and Aintree when he returned to his teenage love of horses and decided he wanted to ride again. Despite losing the lower half of his right leg in the first deployment in Afghanistan, he wanted to ride not just for pleasure but to compete – and win. He used his "how to" toolkit to ensure that all contingencies were covered and to give himself the best chance of success as a competitor.

We contacted Guy after watching the television programme *Against the Odds* (Martin, 2022) and seeing the rapturous expression on his face when he crossed the finishing line and won the Royal Artillery Gold Cup in 2017. He looked utterly ecstatic. He radiated happiness and joy and seemed to embody what we discerned as a peak experience. Typically, and modestly, Guy recalls:

> At that time, I felt completely euphoric but for me, unfortunately it doesn't last very long. It's very much about on the horse, coming back into the winner's enclosure and then it's gone by the time I'm off the horse. I feel quite awkward celebrating success, I don't like praise that much and I'm not trying to come across as too humble, but I think there's a lot of factors that build into that moment in terms of other people involved.

The fact that this euphoric moment was short-lived is reminiscent of Maslow's (1962a, p. 14) description of peak experience: "I found all peak experiences to be transient experiences – temporary not permanent. Some of the effects or after-effects may be permanent but the high moment itself is not."

Another peak experience for Guy was on an expedition to both the North and South Poles as part of a team of injured veterans after Afghanistan. His philosophy came into play yet again, "it's about finding the strengths and weaknesses of each individual in the team and being brutally honest about them and then breaking that apart." He succeeded in reaching both Poles, but the moment of exhilaration at the North Pole was a team experience. He explained how the ice was still moving and slowly drifting away from 90 degrees north, but the team got in a line and walked onto it together using the GPS, grinning uncontrollably at each other with an incredible sense of achievement.

Guy's attitude to life is unassumingly simple:

> Everybody should find something engaging, it's just a case of finding it, and demystifying it. Find everything you can about it and break it down as much as you can by doing due diligence on it.

***

Our next participant, **Amy Williams** (MBE OLY), is an Olympic Skeleton champion. Originally a runner, in 2022 she began training in skeleton, a sport which challenges the racer to hurl themselves down an ice shoot on a sled, travelling at up to 90 miles per hour with only a visor and a helmet for protection. She was a member of the Great Britain team at the 2010 Vancouver Olympic Games, winning a gold medal to become the first British individual gold medallist at a Winter Olympics for 30 years.

Amy confesses to lacking a competitive nature as a child, yet says: "I wanted to be the best runner I could in the 400m and I always wanted to do my very best." An introduction to skeleton at an Army Ice Camp, however, changed her mind when her internal dialogue dictated "I could be really good at this." She gave us a sense of what it feels like to be on the bobsled:

> I felt fear, adrenalin, joy, all high emotions, the buzz – wind rushing past my face. You lie on the sled, and someone pushes you off. The first time was like being in a washing machine. Bruised black and blue with a top speed of 140 km or 90 mph, with a four or five g-force on your face and body. The run is almost two metres high. All senses are poised, listening to the speed on the ice, feeling the speed in your body with quick steers left and right. There are between 14 and 19 corners to navigate with the visor rattling against the ice. It was a tough track in Vancouver, 60 mph on corner three – inches too late in turning and you'd miss the veer. I was exhausted at the end.

It was only when Amy got off her skeleton sled after four runs and everyone was cheering that reality set in. She hugged her coach and asked, "where did I come?" "You're Olympic champion," he replied:

> And I think then, sort of immediately, I was thinking what do I do now? Everyone's looking at me. I'm naturally a shy person and then it's that "BOOM! WOW!" Everything you've worked for over the past however many years. And that kind of real moment hitting you.

Such an achievement comes with sacrifice and at a personal price. Amy trained in Austria, dedicating herself to a strict regime over five winter months without friends and family but failed to qualify for the 2006 Olympics. This disappointment fuelled her dedication to qualify in 2010. Amy decided to train hard for four years; no alcohol, or chocolate, in bed by 9:00 p.m. with orange juice. She focused totally on her goals and the challenges ahead, explaining:

> Years of practice come into play – trial and error. Coaches and sports psychologists help. You ignore all noise and control the controllable. I really had to ignore the distractions and noise and block it out to focus.

We can deduce that Amy had a set of core conditions to get to the top of her game and so encounter peak moments. Apart from the enormous success of winning a medal, Amy remembers another massive WOW factor at the Winter Olympics in Vancouver:

> A massive peak for anyone and any athlete getting to the Olympics is the opening ceremony. It sort of hits your chest as you walk in. You have the Olympic rings on you and your teammates around you. You're behind your Union Jack flag, you walk into the biggest arena of your life – it's all kind of dark because they've dimmed the lights – you've got 1000's of people around you and you know the world's media is watching you. And I think for me that was huge, huge BOOM, WOW! Already this is one of my top three experiences of my life. That was a real boost which sums up that whole WOW experience of being at the Olympics.

The third peak experience for Amy at the Olympics was getting her medal on the podium:

> You're singing the national anthem and your emotions are everywhere, both relief and disbelief and a strange calmness that you knew you could do it but you've actually gone and done it, all swarmed up in the WOW moment. It's a moment in history when I've given my whole life to getting this medal.

Several times Amy used the words "BOOM" and "WOW" to describe her feelings, which we asked her to articulate more fully:

> I now definitely live my life from that pit feeling in my stomach. I tell people to do what your gut is telling you because that's always the right answer. So, I guess it's sort of the two places, the WOW factor, when you've achieved something, it's right there in my chest then almost like, having to make decisions is right down in the pit of my stomach.

Amy also described the physical feelings in her body when on the sled, sensations she likened to those times when we are driving a car on autopilot:

When you slide down a track, even though you're super-concentrated on all your steers on every single corner, you almost get to the bottom of the track and it's like "oh . . . how did that happen?" Like, I almost lost concentration there and now I'm at the bottom of the track. It's that lovely, unbelievable experience.

We always say that you and your sled need to become one, you can't fight against it, you need to have enough tension in your body to hold your perfect body position. If you're too tense and rigid, the sled will just skid. If you're too floppy, you'll just flop around on the sled . . . and then it's that balance of feeling everything through the sled. We feel the vibrations of the ice. We feel the pressure of the G-force through the corners. You feel it all through your body – you have all your peripheral vision, your senses as most of the time your head is pinned on the ice. So, all of your senses come into play.

Amy also shares how her "out of body" experiences are quite exceptional:

Having that wonderful "at one with your sled" feeling is that you're almost sliding without the sled underneath you, and that's a really hard kind of thing to teach. Sometimes it just sort of happens – once every 3–5 weeks or you might get it in a race, definitely in my last run at the Olympics, the last bit of the track was definitely almost like an out of body experience. Blink, and I'm at the bottom. That's a kind of rare kind of feeling, I guess. It's amazing when it happens, it doesn't happen that often: you can't make it happen, it just is a natural thing.

Amy's descriptions of a sudden feeling of being at one with the sled, of sensing an almost out-of-body experience, something that is rare and happens spontaneously, all echo Maslow (1962a, p. 13):

Peaks come unexpectedly, suddenly they happen to us. You can't count on them. And, hunting them is a little like hunting happiness. It's best not done directly. It comes as a by-product – an epiphenomenon, for instance of doing a fine job at a worthy task you can identify with.

***

Our fifth participant, **Anna Hemmings**, is a British marathon kayaker who competed internationally in the 1990s and 2000s, winning six world championships. She retired in 2009 and is now a motivational speaker and leadership coach, advising on high performance and resilience.

When we explained peak experience to Anna, she immediately linked it with being in the zone, saying:

Being in the zone is when you have a sense of freedom, when things are happening on autopilot. . . . If I was racing an Olympic distance of 500 meters start to finish, the gun goes and I'm so present that I don't even have to think about strategy. I have a race plan and all technical aspects, but I don't really think about that – it just happens automatically. I'm so in the moment and free that everything's flowing. My mind and body are in sync. It's a joyous place I guess, because you're performing at your best and allowing the mind and body to take over really without too much thought.

Anna didn't think, however, that she could get into the zone without the many hours of practice and setting up all the conditions to get there. She explains:

Not every race I did was I in the zone. I think it depends upon your mental state. If you're stressed or too nervous or got too many things going on in your head, you can't be that present. You have to be able to free your mind so that you can just go. You can do all the hours of practice you want to be ready physically but if your mind isn't present enough or free enough, I don't think you get into that peak state. It's not just about the practice. It's also about your mental state.

Anna also acknowledged that a small dose of nerves is needed for peak performance, but a highly nervous state is totally undesirable: "you don't want to be super relaxed, but you don't want to be pounding away, shaking." She said she had a variety of different strategies for coping, but essentially it was important to prevent the nervous state before it happened. Visualisation, for example, played an important part. She focused on the imminent race that she wanted to win rather than previous races:

I'd use mental imagery to help me prepare my mind and body by visualising the peak state and visualising myself on the start line, mentally and emotionally. How I wanted to feel, how I would be thinking when I was doing the race, what would that look like, visualising the race strategy, so helping to prepare my mind to get into that state, before I've got there. I've practised it physically but I'm also visualising it, imagining what happens. When I was able to see that happen in my mind's eye, exactly the way I wanted it to happen, perform how I wanted to perform and win, I felt confident and that allowed me to turn up on race day and be less nervous. I knew I was ready. I knew I could do it. I could see myself do it and I just had to put it into action. So, there was a real inner belief. When you can see it, you can believe it which gives you confidence.

Breathing techniques were also useful to help stay focused and fully present in the moment. Diaphragmatic breathing was her preferred technique to calm her – breathing in for a count of four and out for six with no hold of the breath:

If I needed to relax a little bit more, then a round of ten with a slightly longer out breath on six. That was a really powerful tool that I used. But other than that I guess understanding the thoughts going through my head, what was causing me to feel like this.

Other contributing factors to her success included working with a sports psychologist for 16 years and techniques like neurolinguistic programming for state management which Anna describes here:

> When I've had a really brilliant state, this is the state I want to be in, so let's anchor it to recreate a state and be able to create it in an instant. But when I'm visualising that's a slightly different nuanced state. And what I want to be able to do is see the next race happen how I want it to happen so that's slightly different. Yes, we did do something around let's create a state that I've experienced before, or a new one.

A "peak" for Anna means a mixture of joy and relief at the end of races:

> [Y]ou're on a high. That's emotion based I suppose – a mix of euphoric emotions. I'm sure I've had moments post-race, even in the middle of some races. I can't really pinpoint anything specifically – adrenaline flows and it's exciting and it's a risk when you do something that's a little bit dangerous and you're surviving. You're barely thinking, it's just happening. But it is a moment where there's very little thought it's just all clicking into place and going. And at the end probably comes the euphoria because you've crossed the finishing line.

A final interesting aspect of Anna's successes is the work she undertook with neuro feedback. About ten years ago she went to Toronto to train with one of the leading psychologists on how visualisation affects performance. She was working with athletes who had electrodes placed on the brain which was connected to a computer. She trained the athletes to create the "visualisation" state, her passion, and was intrigued see the brain light up really strongly when doing visualisation. Neuroscience has now been developed to the point that brain states can be trained and recalled by athletes.

Anna explained how neurobiology entails training the physiology to calm adrenaline and the autonomic nervous system. Breathing techniques are also important, and software is available to check heart rate variability to ensure a coherent heart rhythm state called bio feedback. She described how neuro feedback is looking at brain feedback and the neural pathways to the brain so alpha state, beta brainwaves, and different brainwaves can also be measured:

> What athletes are doing is training the neural pathways so you're getting feedback every time you're generating alpha brainwaves or beta or whatever it is you want to be creating. Your brain is getting feedback so it's going "this is how I create alpha; this is what I need to do, I'll do it again." So we practice and then you can recreate those certain brainwave states that create those peak experiences. I don't know how to measure if it's a peak experience, but I know that you can teach someone through neuro feedback technology to create a certain brainwave state. And so if a peak experience is associated with a certain alpha or beta waves, you can train someone to recreate that. That's what people are doing in sport.

This fascinating research puts in question Maslow's observations that peak experiences "just happen." It now seems we may be able to recreate the peak experience through neuroscience (Gold & Ciorciari, 2020).

***

Our final participant is **Keith Haynes,** a head coach in competitive swimming. We discussed his peak experiences as a swimmer and as a coach. His most memorable peak experience as a swimmer was at regional championships. Keith was swimming against two big regional rivals:

> Of the thousands of races I've swam over 25 years, this race just stands out above all the others. I don't remember having any concept of time and didn't feel fatigue at all. I was very conscious of my rival all the way through it and he became my motivation. There was almost a feeling of elation, almost superhuman. It was a stand-out swim for me and has always stayed in my mind – memorable, still with me, and something I'll never forget.

Keith told us about his peak experience as a swimming coach. He recalled a relay race where four girl swimmers had achieved finals they weren't expecting to make and something the club had never achieved:

> The girls swam phenomenally – the fastest times they could possibly swim. My peak experience was as though I was swimming every stroke with them. I was physically shaking and giddy with excitement because they were doing so well. My heart seemed to be beating faster and I just sort of exploded at the end of the race.
>
> It's a short-lived experience but something that stays with you for a long time and that you can look back on and draw from.

The fact that Keith identifies his experience as a short-lived suggests a peak experience and not peak performance or flow. Although such experiences cannot be engineered, he works incredibly hard to motivate his swimmers both at the poolside and at the planning stages of their development. Visualisation is important, as it challenges them to replicate their frame of mind from their really good performances and remember what they were thinking and feeling.

Paquette (2020, p. 164) noted that experiences of awe can not only be inspiring to us "but can even be contagious." Similarly, Keith's experiences whilst watching others racing could be considered an example of "contagion." For example, Keith shared how he had been so excited when another coach seemed to erupt with joy when his swimmers won the gold medal at British Championships. Keith recalls, him "launching out of his seat, papers going everywhere, banging his hands on the table, pumping his fists in the air – he has to have had some kind of peak experience."

What Is Significant About Peaks in This Context?

Several themes emerged as important in relation to peak experiences in this context. We highlight four: connectedness, learning, control, and visualisation.

Significant for all our participants was a sense of connectedness. Ali mentioned connectedness when talking about team spirit both on and off the hockey pitch and also during the truly memorable moment on Snowdon created by harmony and connectivity with the team. Amy felt an intense connection, a sense of being at one with her sled which Anna also endorsed with her kayak. This sense of being at one is also highlighted in Chapter 10 where we discuss high-risk leisure, and Dodson (1996) is cited, explaining about the extended self in mountain biking, where she and the bicycle seem to become one.

A type of "vicarious" peak experience was reported by some participants in the sport context. It was evident in Kevin's experience of coaching young rugby players and receiving feedback from them; Keith felt as though he were swimming stoke by stroke with his swimmers, and Guy's connection with his teams provided the backbone for his resilience toolkit.

Also linked to the feeling of connectivity with others was the sense that some peak-like experiences led to learning and growth. These experiences are fuelled by trust and occur principally when playing with others in team situations. Frick (1990, p. 78) calls such learning experiences "Symbolic Growth Experiences" and claims they provide "very strong support for the existence of a self-actualizing force in human personality." Schindehutte et al. (2006, p. 350) also suggested peak experiences promote "growth as an aspect of self-actualization and optimal emotional functioning." The peak experiences Ali felt with both hockey and Snowdon teams meant they learned and grew together, reaching unbelievable goals and creating unforgettable growth experiences. Ali's dialogue suggests that these reflective experiences allow him to look back on them as educational experiences rather than as isolated, individual peak experiences. Guy also stressed the importance of teamwork to his own learning, almost refuting his own individual success and laying the credit quite firmly at the door of his supportive teams. Kevin too endorsed this common aspect of growth through coaching and developing others to reap the satisfaction of their success in life.

All participants stressed the importance of preparation to up their game and be in control as much as possible. They each demonstrated how they put in motion discipline, goals, and the groundwork necessary to facilitate winning. Ali also set up the conditions for flow and ultimately a peak experience to happen, controlling everything he could control so that conditions were right. Several participants spoke of controlling the controllable, a cognitive aspect of creating a winning formula to excel. Preparation was key, and no detail was overlooked. A second aspect of their preparation is the need for awareness of not only Self 1 but also non-cognition Self 2 as described by Gallwey (1986). Guy also took nothing for granted and researched every aspect of his challenges to ensure he had everything covered to guarantee success.

Visualisation was also part of preparation and control. Guy role-plays scenarios to predict the outcome, and Keith encourages his swimmers to visualise previous successes to fast forward into future events. Anna is also passionate about visualisation and trains athletes on how to achieve more success through this skill. The upshot of their success is simple: find a passion, find the time, space, and focus to start; avoid intrusions from others, and notice how time flies when you become engrossed and challenged.

Throughout this chapter we have been aware of definitional inconsistencies. Our participants confirmed our belief that the overlapping features of peak experience, peak performance, and flow might make clear definitions problematic at times. Our aim was to illuminate the power generated by peak experiences, and we hope that in doing so we have also presented the nuances of definition relative to the sporting context. We have distinguished how peak experience was short-lived but very memorable; how sustained effort led to experiences of flow; and how various types of preparation led to anticipated peak performances.

References

Bech, D. (2013, November 22). Rugby world cup 2003: Jonny Wilkinson recalls "that kick" against Australia. *The Independent*, www.independent.co.uk/sport/rugby/rugby-union/news-comment/rugby-world-cup-2003-jonny-wilkinson-recalls-that-kick-against-australia-8956710.html [Accessed 15 November 2024].

Croucher, B. (2021). www.bbc.co.uk/sport/triathlon/57051888 [Accessed 14 May 2021].

Csikszentmihalyi, M. (1990). *Flow: The psychology of optimal experience*. New York: Harper and Row.

Dodson, J. (1996). Peak experiences and mountain biking: Incorporating the bike into the extended self. *Advances in Consumer Research*, *23*, 317–322.

Fatemi, J. (2004). *An exploratory study of peak experience and other positive human experiences and writing*. PhD Thesis, Texas A & M University.

Frick, W. B. (1990). The symbolic growth experience: A chronicle of heuristic inquiry and a quest for synthesis. *Journal of Humanistic Psychology*, *30*(1), 64–80.

Gallwey, T. (1986). *The inner game of tennis*. London: Pan Books.

Gold, J., & Ciorciari, J. A. (2020). Review on the role of the neuroscience of flow states in the modern world. *Behavioral Sciences* (Basel), *10*(9), 137.

Grove, J. R., & Lewis, A. W. (1996). Hypnotic susceptibility and attainment of flowlike states during exercise. *Journal of Sport and Exercise Psychology*, *18*, 380–391.

Heery, B. (2003). *Awakening spirit in the body: A heuristic exploration of peak or mystical experience in the practice of Aikido*. Doctoral Dissertation. Retrieved from ProQuest: UMI 305247877.

Jackson, S. A., & Csikszentmihalyi, M. (1999). *Flow in sports: The keys to optimal experiences and performances*. Human Kinetics Books.

Landsman, T. (1968, April). Positive experience and the beautiful person. *Presidential address delivered to the Southeastern Psychological Association*.

Martin, S. (Director) (2022, April). *Against the odds* (ITV, Series 1 Episode 6). www.itv.com/hub/against-the-odds/10a1454a0022 [Accessed 13 April 2022].

Maslow, A. H. (1962a). Lessons from the peak-experiences. *Journal of Humanistic Psychology*, *2*(9), 9–18.

Maslow, A. H. (1962b). Notes on being-psychology. *Journal of Humanistic Psychology*, *2*(2), 47–71.

McInman, A. D., & Grove, R. G. (1991). Peak moments in sport: A literature review. *Quest*, *43*, 333–351.

Morgan, J. D., & Coutts, R. A. (2016). Measuring peak experience in recreational surfing. *Journal of Sport Behaviour, 39*(2), 202.

Murphy, M., & White, R. A. (1978a). *The psychic side of sports*. Reading, MA: Addison-Wesley.

Murphy, M., & White, R. (1978b). *In the zone: Transcendent experiences in sport*. England: Penguin Books Ltd.

Nakamura, J., & Csikszentmihalyi, M. (2002). The concept of flow. In C. R. Snyder & S. J. Lopez (Eds.), *Handbook of positive psychology* (pp. 89–105), Oxford University Press.

O'Brien, K. T., & Kilrea, K. A. (2021). Unitive experience and athlete mental health: Exploring relationships to sport-related anxiety, motivation, and well-being. *The Humanistic Psychologist, 49*(2), 314.

Panzarella, R. (1980). The phenomenology of aesthetic peak experiences. *Journal of Humanistic Psychology, 20*(1), 69–85.

Paquette, J. (2020). *Awestruck*. CO, USA: Shambhala Publications Inc.

Privette, G. (1983). Peak experience, peak performance, and flow: A comparative analysis of positive human experiences. *Journal of Personality and Social Psychology, 45*, 1361–1368.

Privette, G., & Bundrick, C. M. (1987). Measurement of experience: Construct and content validity of the experience questionnaire. *Perceptual and Motor Skills, 65*(1), 315–332.

Privette, G., & Bundrick, C. M. (1991). Peak experience, peak performance, and flow: Correspondence of personal descriptions and theoretical constructs. *Journal of Social Behavior & Personality, 6*(5), 169–188.

Ravizza, K. (1977). Peak experiences in sport. *Journal of Humanistic Psychology, 17*(4), 35–40.

Schindehutte, M., Morris, M., & Allen, J. (2006). Beyond achievement: Entrepreneurship as extreme experience. *Small Business Economics, 27*, 349–368.

Schuler, J., & Brunner, S. (2009). The rewarding effect of flow experience of performance in a marathon race. *Psychology of Sport and Exercise, 10*(1), 168–174.

Senecal, G. (2021). The aftermath of peak experiences: Difficult transitions for contact sport athletes. *The Humanistic Psychologist, 49*(2), 295–313.

Stoll, O. (2019). Peak performance, the runner's high and flow. *APA handbook of sport and exercise psychology*. Volume 2: *Exercise psychology*. M.H. Anshel.

Thomson, E. (Director) (2021). *Bear's mission with . . . Jonny Wilkinson* (ITV, Series). www.itv.com/watch/bear's-mission-with.../2a5494/2a5494a0001 [Accessed 26 August 2024].

Thorne, F. C. (1963). The clinical use of nadir experience reports. *Journal of Clinical Psychology, 19*, 248–250.

Thornton, F., Privette, G., & Bundrick, C. M. (1999). Peak performance of business leaders: An experience parallel to self-actualization theory. *Journal of Business and Psychology, 14*, 253–264.

Wilson, C. (2009). *Super consciousness: The quest for the peak experience*. London: Watkins Publishing.

Young, J. A., & Pain, M. D. (1999). The zone: Evidence of universal phenomenon for athletes across sports. *Athletic Insight: The Online Journal of Sports Psychology, 1*(3), 21–30.

8 Peak Experience in Therapy

Introduction

This chapter focuses on the possibility that therapists and their clients may have peak or self-transcendent experiences during the course of their practice together.

People seek help from therapists when something goes wrong or feels wrong in their body or mind. They look for support and help when something needs "fixing" or to propel them into a more helpful state of well-being – what philosophers like Aristotle identified as "eudaimonia." Translated from the Greek, eudaimonia is interpreted as *welfare, flourishing*, or as *well-being* (Kraut, 2018), and, as noted by Evans, the philosophy resonates with Maslow's work: "the essential aspect of eudaimonia is similar to self-actualization: the expression of deeds that advance the highest potential of the individual" (Evans, 2016, p. 19).

Palmer and Whybrow (2007) further recount how the exponents of the humanistic psychology tradition were "typically adamant about the over-medicalisation of psychological phenomena, with theorists including Carl Rogers providing alternative conceptualisations for how we understand the nature of ill-being and well-being" (Palmer & Whybrow, 2007, p. 45). More recently, Taylor (2018) has forged the connection between the schools of humanistic psychology and positive psychology. Both schools advocate the imbalance in psychology, which tends to focus on investigating mental illness rather than "what makes life worth living and what can make human beings flourish" (2018, p. 42).

Maslow (1959) proposed that peak experiences may be therapeutic for people suffering from psychological issues and also in more general ways. He claimed that peak experiences may change a person's point of view in a healthy direction, change their view of other people and their relationship with them, and change, perhaps permanently, their view of the world or parts of it. In addition, Maslow argued that a person is "more apt to feel that life in general is worthwhile, even if it is usually drab, pedestrian, painful or ungratifying, since beauty, excitement, honesty, play, goodness, truth and meaningfulness have been demonstrated to him to exist" (1962, p. 95).

The chapter continues with an overview of the research relating to peak experiences in different types of therapy, especially those that emphasise the humanistic or whole-person approach. We examine the research literature to try and identify

DOI: 10.4324/9781003509219-9

the conditions which can give rise to and enable a peak experience in these contexts. Following this positioning, we then include descriptions of peak experiences from a number of practising therapists.

Review of Peak Experiences in the Therapy Literature

An in-depth review of the literature revealed established areas of research in Gestalt as a particular approach and also in a variety of other therapy contexts. As in other chapters, we make note of concepts related to peak experience. In the therapy context, it was found that epiphany and transcendence are frequently referred to in the literature.

The concept of *epiphany* is often used interchangeably with peak experience in the therapy literature. Liang (2006, p. 3), for example, equates the two explaining how "the transformation resulting from either a peak experience or an epiphany would be as valuable as changes that occur as a result of therapy and that they may even occur in therapy." Bien (2006) also suggested that therapists can observe small changes but that it is rare to observe an epiphany in therapy sessions. In Fletcher's research, an epiphany is described as moments when therapists and clients are "engaged in shared emotional voyages and finely attuned" (2008, p. 31).

Fletcher also refers to a range of terms that have come into use over the past decades in therapy, terms such as "significant moments" (Elliot, 1983) or "helpful events" (Grafanaki & McLeod, 1999). Fletcher cites Jauregui's description of the epiphany as conveying "something of the mystery":

> A revelation usually brought on by some simple, homely, or commonplace experience. . . . Something big is occasioned by something little, something easily missed. And it unfolds from there – sometimes as a flash, sometimes in exquisite slow motion – out of conventional time and space and language. . . . The universe is bigger than it was a minute ago and so are you.
> (Jauregui, 2003, p. 3)

From the foregoing, we acknowledge that the epiphany in therapy is a change or revelation of some kind acquired through therapy. Such transformational processes are also explored by Whitehead and Bates (2016), who researched the transformational processing of two poles of peak experiences, one of which they termed TPpeak and the other, the nadir experience, they termed TPnadir. These two concepts are related to eudaimonia (psychological well-being) and hedonism (subjective well-being). The results of the study revealed that participants who demonstrated transformational processing of nadir experiences had higher levels of both eudaimonic and hedonic well-being. Whitehead and Bates (2016, p. 1592) moreover suggest that well-being can be improved through

> active exploration, connection with, and willingness to be changed by peak experiences, even after there have been positive psychological outcomes (growth) from the experience.

The exploratory narrative processing of peak experiences, they suggest, might enable people to reconnect with the experience and help them to develop meaning from it. Maslow (2010) had also identified such meaning making as likely to achieve subjective well-being.

The second related concept is *transcendence*. Armor (1969) advises that since the term "peak experience" was first used by Maslow, contemporary psychology has recognised the transpersonal nature of human consciousness, leading to an increased understanding of peak experience. Armor suggests that "the peak experience is now thought of as a transcendence of the usual form of consciousness common to all mankind" (1969, p. 48).

Furthermore, Levin and Steele (2005) report that two types of transcendent experiences have been identified. The first is what they call the "green" type, which involves "a profound experience of pleasure, in response to an event or specific physical or spiritual practise" (2005, p. 89). These authors suggest Maslow's peak experience and many experiences described as mystical would fit this category. Levin and Steele then share alternative names for transcendent experiences, including the flow experience, arguing that "Csikszentmihalyi's flow exemplifies what has been termed the green transcendent experience" (2005, p. 90).

They term the second related concept "mature," which is usually characterised as "long lasting . . . a more enduring serenity and equanimity . . . a self-transformational shift in one's consciousness or spiritual perception" (2005, pp. 89–90). This concept is less about transient mystical feelings or phenomena and more about entering into a new state of awareness, similar to Maslow's (1962) concept of a plateau experience. Common to both the "green" and "mature" transcendent experiences is an ineffable quality.

The following subsections examine literature relating to peak experiences in six specific therapy environments: Gestalt, music therapy, psychotherapy and counselling, yoga therapy, hypnotherapy, and meditation therapy.

Gestalt Therapy

Gestalt therapy helps people become aware of significant sensations within themselves and their environment so that they can respond more realistically to situations. It is a needs-based approach (Bluckert, 2023) used for addressing a wide range of issues such as anxiety, tension, and depression. Its goal is to help people become aware of their current environment and the bodily sensations that accompany that awareness so that they can respond differently in difficult situations. Thus, it improves self-awareness and can improve body image (Hender, 2001) through the use of exercises such as the "Empty Chair" dialogue.

Green and Simon (2019, p. 229) describe how the Empty Chair is "one of the lodestar techniques of Gestalt Therapy, whereby a client is invited to imagine the difficult emotion sitting in a separate chair, and then having a back-and-forth conversation with the emotion, to better understand what it is doing, and what its purpose is." Green and Simon confirm that research into this technique, since it directly engages with and challenges emotions, often causes a significant reduction in the intensity of emotions thus bringing about a new awareness.

Maher et al.'s (2011) study was aimed at investigating participants' phenomenological descriptions of how they organised and responded to peak moments of awareness in their Gestalt therapy training groups. Awareness is seen as an aspect of the self that can lead to a peak experience. In the study, all participants described experiencing a peak moment of awareness through engaging with significant personal issues with the group, experiences which often left them feeling exposed and shameful in talking openly to strangers. For example, one of the participants admitted "this peak moment helped me to understand and name my own experience of shame and to identify what I need to support myself and what support I can get from others" (2011, p. 48).

The starting point of investigative interest for Maher et al.'s phenomenological study emerged out of experience at an experiential Gestalt therapy group training in the 1990s. One of the authors recalled an experience of intense awareness when he told the therapist, "I was stuck, and I didn't know what to say or do" (2011, p. 37). Gradually, however, he began to make eye contact with each person and slowly spoke whilst simultaneously maintaining eye contact with each participant. His feeling of reluctance was a common emotion reported by all the individuals and one of three stages of the group therapy experience – isolation, contact, and engagement. Most participants in the study explored a peak moment of awareness as occurring across all three stages. Another participant revealed a feeling of connection to the people around, losing that sense of isolation:

> The most important thing I next felt was the sense of acceptance I had for myself in the end of my work. . . . I remember then giving myself permission to just sit and take in this new awareness . . . physically, I felt my body starting to relax.
>
> (Maher et al., 2011, p. 47)

Gestalt therapy training groups typically aim to provide an environment that explores the here-and-now needs of individuals and communities through reflective practice. Maher et al. (2011) counsel that it is not only experience that is important but also the ability to process and reflect on such experience. Each participant in the group organises their experience differently. One individual experienced incredible growth, self-awareness, and change during their reflection, whilst another reported in detail how she felt from feedback, which then made her respond and reflect:

> I felt very sad and alone. I then received feedback from my trainer "to sit in the mess." When I heard this, I was aware that I initially felt very angry with brief thoughts of "how could she say that?" My breathing fastened and I had to take several deep breaths. I stared at my trainer with a feeling of disbelief. I then felt a wave-like flow of physical and emotional release. My physical body loosened, and I sank back into the bean bag. My facial bones softened though I was still aware of them. The heat left my face and my

throat loosened. My breathing was still deep for some time as my mind and body began to feel the impact of this feedback. I was aware that I felt a sort of integration happening within myself. As I breathed in, it felt as if I was taking in a piece of myself that felt warm, as if I knew it had a place to stay within me. It felt to me as if I had been given a sort of permission that felt very right at that moment. I just sat with this feeling for what felt some length of time. I was aware that I started to take in the presence of the other students.

(2011, p. 46)

Music Therapy

There are synergies between music and Gestalt therapies. Both reflect a meaningful experience for the client and therapist, creating a deeper connection and engagement with both the self and the external world.

Nicholson (2015) explored the potential influence of music-elicited peak experiences on clinical practice, which he defined as "music-related activities that serve as a catalyst for an experience that is deeper, more intense, and otherwise qualitatively different from usual, everyday musical experiences" (2015, p. 59). In this study, the concepts of peak and related experiences are reviewed from the vantage point of transpersonal psychology. The primary goals are defined as

> self-actualization, being truly oneself and in control of one's self and life while also respecting the rights and needs of others, and self-realization, knowing one's true spiritual nature.
>
> (2015, p. 54)

Nicholson makes an interesting point about the relevance of music therapy. He suggests it can help in the treatment of chemical dependency, encouraging clients to recover from drug and alcohol abuse by providing them with "enduring access to healthy, meaningful, drug free peak experiences" (2015, p. 57), fostered through closeness and sharing between group members.

Five overlapping categories emerged from Nicholson's (2015, p. 62) study in his analysis of music therapists' peak music-elicited experiences. We summarise these here:

1) Meaningful Experience: all participants talked about music-elicited peak experiences as being meaningful professionally or personally or both.
2) Connection: all participants identified a heightened sense of connection with their clients as being a significant aspect of their peak music experiences.
3) Change Within: therapists also talked about their sense of connection extending beyond the client and reflected on music and connection both within and outside the therapeutic relationship.
4) Letting Go/Openness: all interviewees identified letting go as a significant aspect of their peak experiences, taking the form of entering a state of increased relaxation, a feeling of effortlessness, letting go of conscious concern with the

physical actions required in playing an instrument, a decrease of conscious thought, and decreased preoccupation with controlling the music experience.
5) Strong Positive Feelings/Significant Physiological Reactions: interviewees experienced strong positive feelings and significant physiological reactions during their peak experiences. They spoke of feelings of joy, comfort, gratitude, satisfaction, surprise, euphoria, beauty, warmth, chills, racing heart, and changes in breathing as part of their peak experiences.

Nicholson moreover reveals his personal reasons for undertaking the study. He describes a peak experience during a group music improvisation in a music therapy class at university. The group consisted of 12–15 students singing and playing a variety of instruments. At some point during the 10-minute improvisation, he observed a shift in consciousness in which he experienced a disappearance of conscious thought and personal individuality. He no longer felt a distinction between himself, the music, and the other musicians. There was an intense sensation of connection, pleasure, and transcendence during and immediately following this experience. After the improvisation ended, the peak experience refused to let him go. All he could think about was wanting more of that intense euphoria and connection, feeling like an addict in need of a fix yet not knowing where to turn to get it. He eventually went to sleep and woke up feeling more or less himself again.

That experience left him wanting to know more about what had happened to him, what allowed the experience to occur, and whether there was a way to foster similar experiences. As a music therapy student, he wondered how similar experiences might occur in clinical settings, and "what meaning therapists and clients ascribe to such experiences, and how they might affect the therapeutic process" (2015, pp. 60–61).

Nicholson had experienced the "disappearance of conscious thought and personal individuality," which is similar to how Maslow described peak experience, and he was hungry for the sensation to return, echoing Maslow's words (1959, p. 65): "he remembers the experience as a very important and desirable happening and seeks to repeat it."

Amir (2001) maintains her goal as a music therapist is to help her clients find meaning in their lives. She contends that the music therapy process can be seen as a whole system that includes the therapist, the client, and the music. Within this system, Amir names five different relationships which develop in both active (doing) and receptive (listening) music participation: (i) music and sounds, (ii) therapist and client, (iii) thoughts and feelings, (iv) the external environment and the internal world, and (v) music and words. She demonstrates the third and fourth of these relationships by preparing herself before therapy sessions:

> I always try to prepare the environment, to have the right conditions that will allow such experiences to happen. For example, before I come into any session, I take a moment and I am centering myself. I do that always before a client comes. I close my eyes, take a few deep breaths, and try to detach

myself from everything that happened before the session. . . . I try to empty myself from "me" and focus on the client who will be coming soon.

(Amir, 2001, p. 211)

She also shows her admiration for Maslow's way of looking at peak experiences:

It is nothing that you plan for, it is nothing that you are going for, it comes usually without you expecting it, but when it comes it is very powerful and can bring a transformation in life. . . . When it is being experienced, there is no differentiation between the variables I mentioned above; the physiological, the psychological, imagination and the spiritual. It is like I cannot really classify it. It is all one, and I am in a different mode of consciousness.

(Amir, 2001, p. 211)

Amir believes that music therapy has the potential to bring clients to peak experience and has witnessed client's transformation by the music they improvised. She sometimes observes clients going into an altered state of consciousness, allowing the music to take them wherever it needs to take them. Amir (2001, p. 210) considers that music "radiates," "resonates," or "vibrates" in specific ways for each person: "There is kind of a physiological sensation, a bodily feeling that can provoke a thought, an association, a memory or bring an image to mind."

Psychotherapy and Counselling

Despite a growth in the theoretical and empirical research on peak experiences and/or self-transcendence since Maslow first began his explorations, the nature of self-transcendent experiences for psychotherapists or counsellors has hardly been investigated.

Some research has examined the spiritual connection. Agnew (2020), for instance, explored the relationship between client spiritual awakening and the consciousness of the therapist within transpersonal psychotherapy. Findings suggested that a willingness to be open to the presence and essence of another, on both sides of the therapeutic dyad, had the potential to contribute to "intense, powerful and profound experiences arising in the therapist" (2020, p. 62). These experiences then led to a deepening of the healing potential within the therapy "whilst simultaneously providing developmental propulsion for each practitioner" (2020, p. 62). Agnew then considered whether the experiences of client and therapist would qualify as peak experiences, bearing in mind Maslow's (1976) description:

[I]n the peak experience there is a very characteristic disorientation in time and space. Or even a lack of consciousness of time and space. Phrased positively, this is like experiencing universality and eternity. Certainly, we have here, in a very operational sense, a real and scientific meaning of "under the aspect of eternity."

(Maslow, 1976, p. 63)

Agnew (2020) concluded that each participant did have a peak experience according to Maslow's description given earlier. However, he acknowledged the interpretation of the peak experience was "filtered through the lens of each participant's personality and individual cosmology" and that participants reporting experiences in a positive light were "already comfortable with an expansion in consciousness gained through natural causes unaided by external substances" (2020, p. 73).

James and Bray (2022) have explored how counsellors and psychotherapists in New Zealand made sense of their self-transcendent experiences and how these then impacted their therapeutic work. The authors define a "self-transcendent experience" as "a short-lived peak event that achieves a perceived connection beyond one's sense of self, which can be difficult to describe in words" (James & Bray, 2022, p. 1). The results of this interpretative phenomenological analysis suggest that contextual factors such as setting play an important part. Indeed, the participants were asked to make sense of their experiences "by couching them in narratives that focused on context and relational circumstances" (2022, p. 27). They were thus able to share stories of personal loss or struggle, insecurity, and vulnerability, as well as positive aspects of love, connection, and transformation. Some participants described how they sensed deep connections with their clients and used open and non-judgemental approaches in the therapy to help clients to make sense of their emergent self-transcendent phenomena.

Yoga Therapy

Posadzki (2010, p. 112) asserts that yoga therapy can promote "self-discovery and enhanced well-being in which individuals develop more flexibility and adaptability in their thoughts, emotions and behaviors." The aim of his study was to explore practitioners' experiences and investigate any cognitive patterns such as thought processes, relaxation, concentration, physical stimuli, experiences of pain, peak performance, body awareness and exploration of their own self and social processes and interpersonal relationships, emotional reactions and feelings, and health benefits associated with yoga practice. Posadzki advises that "yoga exercises are beneficial to personal well-being" (2010, p. 116).

Bhat (2015) is similarly convinced that yoga practice has the potential to be therapeutic:

> [A]s yoga continues to grow, . . . knowing yoga is going to enhance a somatic psychotherapist's ability to help individuals move away from suffering and toward transformation.
>
> (2015, p. 99)

Earlier, Deikman (1980, p. 203) argued that in yoga "conscious concentration" is the first step towards a transcendent or mystic state, where "multiplicity disappears and a sense of union with the One or with All occurs."

Bhat herself encountered a peak experience during her yoga practice and describes yoga as "transforming, transcending and indescribable" (2015, p. 96).

Bhat writes that her peak experience was both traumatic and liberating, shifting her perspective and understanding of a situation. She cites a study by Roth (2014), which elicited four components of yoga that produced a psychological benefit: breath, mindfulness, meditation, and the relationship with the self and connection with the body. Additionally, as a mental health benefit, those suffering from anxiety, trauma, substance, and mood disorders were highlighted, although there is little known about integrating yoga into mental healthcare.

In their study of intense personal experiences, Wilson and Spencer (1990) claim that the experiences they collected from their ashram respondents were most closely aligned to what they call Maslow's "perfect peak syndrome." They were "highly positive, involved an altered state of consciousness, were perceived as having a lasting impact, and were interpreted in mystical and religious terms" (1990, p. 571). These authors qualify their findings by saying that in Maslow's view, a mystical/religious interpretation is non-essential to peak experience. Their findings for non-ashram respondents suggest "some people may experience selected elements of the true peak, very few people come close to approximating the idea-type described by Maslow" (Wilson & Spencer, 1990, p. 571). Interestingly, they found that intense negative experiences can also be meaningful and potentially self-actualising.

Hypnotherapy

Norton (1964) maintains that hypnosis is a stand-alone phenomenon that is completely removed from any other kind of mental state. Subjects undergoing hypnosis enter into a trance-like state "totally like any other and that when they 'wake up' at the end, they have no recollection of what has occurred" (1964, n.p.). This state, Norton argues, is a peak experience: "one which results in an effect or consequence, and particularly for those undergoing hypnotherapy" (1964, n.p.).

Norton reports a popular image of hypnosis perpetuated in part by stage hypnotists and B-movies: "both of which have been largely responsible for the public misunderstanding of hypnosis" (1964, n.p.). There appears to be a dichotomy in Norton's argument, however. He claims that in stage hypnosis participants are unable to remember anything; yet in hypnotherapy clients remember every part of the relaxation process, the induction of hypnosis, and any meaningful suggestions (Norton, 1964).

A study by Kastubi et al. (2017) analysed the hypnotherapy effect on stress reduction in the elderly. Their results ascertained that hypnotherapy, as a non-pharmacological method, worked "at the level of human consciousness, especially at the level of the conscious and the subconscious which can cause a sensation in human beings to be happy" (2017, p. 1). They maintained that hypnotherapy is the "art of communication to influence someone to change the level of awareness by lowering the brain waves and artistic exploration of the unconscious" (p. 2). A very deep meditative state is called the theta state, which is sought by people who practise meditation for its "stillness, tranquillity, depth and the peak of happiness felt within theta. Theta is the 'peak' in 'peak experiences'" (2017, p. 8).

Meditation as Therapy

Farias et al. (2020) suggest that there is a wide range of meditation techniques available originally developed across religious traditions but now focusing on "two techniques derived from Hindu and Buddhist traditions: transcendental meditation and mindfulness" (2020, p. 376). Mindfulness meditation can be defined in behavioural terms such as "relaxation, concentration, altered state of awareness, suspension of logical thought processes and maintenance of self-observing attitude" (Perez-De-Albeniz & Holmes, 2000, p. 50).

According to Garcia-Campayo et al. (2022), there has been little research into the potential for mindfulness meditation techniques to foster well-being in ways other than those involving reduction of stress and anxiety-related disorders. They suggest that peak experiences, as an example of transcendent experience, can be a source of general well-being that can be enhanced through practising meditation.

In mindfulness meditation, breathing exercises, sounds, mantras, or visualisations are used to gain focus and stay in the here and now. Cognitive analysis is avoided as the meditation suspends "habitual logical-verbal construing, and so frees the individual of his/her usual defensive constructions, allowing consciousness to move in new directions" (Perez-De-Albeniz & Holmes, 2000, p. 51).

A number of claims are made for meditation including promoting happiness and relaxation, positive thinking, increased self-confidence, enhanced acceptance, compassion, and tolerance towards others (Perez-De-Albeniz & Holmes, 2000). For example, an intervention study with 96 adults conducted by Hadash et al. (2023, p. 4) suggested peak experiences that resulted from meditation retreats were "primarily pleasant and had a large salutary impact post-retreat."

Peak Experience in Context – Participant Accounts

In this section, we share the reflections of nine participants who discuss their peak experiences in different therapy contexts.

Hannah Ashman works as a music therapist and trained with the Nordoff-Robbins school, embracing Maslow's theory in its approach to music therapy (Nordoff & Robbins, 1998). She works in special education settings: a hospital ward for young people with cancer, a hospice for adults, an autism centre, and a facility supporting families who have experienced domestic abuse.

Peak experience is a concept that threads through her work, often not named as such, but the word "magical" comes up a lot, often remarked upon by staff or family members witnessing her sessions with clients. Comments include "this is the most engaged I've seen her," or "I felt he was really with us, just then." Hannah maintains that music can enable people to reach peak experiences, but there can be desire and pressure to reach these kinds of experiences, which can sometimes hinder her work, preventing her from being truly present and in the moment with clients.

When experiencing a peak experience in music therapy, Hannah is convinced the phenomenon is triggered through the connection between her, the music, and her clients – the shared music experiences built on trust. Hannah considers trust to be multi-layered, and her perception of trust is representative of Amir's (2001) observations:

- both the therapist's and client's trust in therapy itself
- the trust the therapist has in themselves and their skillset
- the client's trust in committing to the therapeutic process
- the trust the client has in the therapist
- the trust in music as a catalyst to trigger a peak experience

Whenever possible, Hannah prepares herself to manage her state before sessions. She practises deep breathing to clear distractions and become present with the person for the duration of the session. She is mindful of boundaries and regularly undertakes supervision to ensure she is working within the confines of her profession. In supervision, she is encouraged to notice judgements about herself and her clients. One peak experience gave Hannah such a strong sense of joy that she discussed the experience with her supervisor to see if such feelings were within the boundaries of her work. Hannah had felt totally at one when making music for a 9-year-old, emotionally challenged boy:

> He was so creative, spontaneous in his rapping and he created a chorus that I latched onto quite quickly and we made our way through the music that felt very in tune. We were both coordinated, and he was totally attuned to what was going on. That is clear in my mind as a peak experience.

Hannah believes that music therapy gives people the opportunity to discover musicality within themselves. She maintains we all have an innate capacity, and for people unable to communicate verbally, music therapy is the ideal medium to enable them to connect without the need for words. As Hannah says, "we might not know what's going on in their mind, but we can share the musical experience."

***

Sarah Potter is a hypnotherapist and shared with us a different name for her peak experience. "Spark" is the word she used, which she sometimes experiences at the end of a session with a client.

In her therapy work, Sarah has a progressive list of behaviours to enable her clients to have the best outcome from the session. It starts with fact-finding about her prospective client by sending a questionnaire for completion. The questions include health issues, ideal outcomes, learning style, and finding out "what they're trying to move away from and where they want to be." Then, before any session, Sarah will focus on what she calls her grounding practice, a meditation ritual to "clear the decks" and focus on her energy to take care of her clients. When they arrive, they chat to see how things have changed since they made the booking. This gives clients a chance to be seen and heard and start to trust her.

Peak Experience in Therapy 189

Each hypnotherapy session has its own pace and rhythm but basically follows the same structure; meeting with the client, establishing trust, witnessing, facilitating, and having a dialogue with the client until they get to the healing place, the release, and sometimes a peak experience. Intuition also plays a key role in Sarah's work. She finds that the root of the problem is very rarely what they think it is. So she listens to their story and finds whatever resources she needs to support them in their journey:

> When I'm in the session the words just come; I couldn't plan that extra layer if I tried. It just happens. If I think about it too much, I just chase the words away. There's a stillness that comes over me when that happens and an absolute trust, just knowing that this is exactly the journey that this client needs to go on. These are exactly the words they need to hear in exactly the way they need to hear them.

We suggested that her process is not dissimilar to the core conditions set by Csikszentmihalyi (1997) to get into flow. She agreed and said she remains in a state of flow during the entire session, confirming: "For me it's about a state where I'm not focussing on anything else and completely in that moment. I'm not even thinking, just doing and completely being in the experience."

Sarah told us her peak experiences don't happen all the time and not with every client:

> I'll feel it in my body and connect in a different way and I'll feel just super happy. And once I get to that point . . . OMG . . . it's actually really energising in that everything else is flowing. I can't explain but sometimes I feel it in my body as a deep sense of calm. Once it's happened, I get a high. Oh My Gosh! The joy that I feel. And then there's just the peak experience and when it comes into conscious awareness that when it's the spark for me.

Sarah went on to describe the "spark" and how long it lasts:

> It's such an affirming thing for me and it's why I do the work – because it's been helpful and positive. It's a recharge for me, especially after a longer session. It's really beautiful.

We asked Sarah if she has experienced the "spark" in any other context, and she immediately recalled the memory of a journey she once took from Milton Keynes to Asia. She was on a train in Kanchanaburi (north Thailand) and recreated an image of herself on the train with her feet hanging out of the door:

> I was just so connected to that moment feeling the wind on my feet. It's such a simple moment, sitting on that train and I don't think it would have made sense to anyone else had they been sitting next to me but it was overwhelming and beautiful and really life-affirming. I couldn't recreate it – a series of

moments, the sense of freedom. I just knew I was on the right path and had made all the right decisions. I felt such a connection to myself. Empowering doesn't even cover it. Whatever it is that's pulling me will always lead me to where I need to be. . . . I can feel it in my chest now. It's like a warmth and I cried tears of joy at the time.

***

Stan Rechcigl has been working for 16 years as a sports massage therapist and soft tissue therapist. He sees his job as helping clients to get better, both physically and mentally, when sorting out injuries and niggling complaints. He provides a space where they can relax – a non-judgemental, trusting environment between therapist and client.

The very act of lying down on the treatment bed is, he says, like an "expunge of air, releasing tension in clients, enabling them to settle into the treatment." Essential for the treatment to work is the need for clients to completely switch off. There is a fine balance between applying pressure on the soft tissue to enable the treatment to be effective while simultaneously helping the client to relax. This is the client's hour. Stan aims for them to leave feeling mentally and physically healed: "if the client isn't in the right place, the body fights back and the treatment fails to work."

When he talked about peak experience, Stan recalled an incident when he was faced with a client who was suffering from extreme sciatica and in excruciating pain to the extent that it took at least ten minutes before the client could lie down on the bed. It was one of the worst cases Stan had come across. He felt desperate and started to panic, trying to pull himself together, quickly recalling previous treatments for sciatica, going through everything he could "because you have to do it – you have the client in front of you – you can't say 'can I get back to you in a fortnight,' can you? You've got to do something in the here and now."

Stan said he went into a kind of intuitive euphoria – a light, empty-headed feeling, where his internal dialogue was saying "let it be, I'm blind, let's just go with it. A sixth sense." That feeling of euphoria is a rarity for Stan. He admitted that he was now more aware of this sixth sense. The whole experience was a labyrinth – the frustration, panic, and doubt about what to do and finally treating the client, relying on his sixth sense to just let his hands do the work needed.

But Stan was still plagued with self-doubt and had a feeling that the client would telephone with bad news. The phone rang at 3:00 p.m. the following afternoon. The client said the treatment was amazing, and he was 90 percent better. Stan was speechless and probably the most euphoric he had ever felt, admitting that it was a bizarre experience, triggered by his self-doubt.

Despite feeling nervous when he saw his client's name on the phone, Stan was half-expecting the call and was elated with the message which validated his treatment and gave him reason to question his self-doubt. Stan had reflected deeply on his ability to treat the patient, resorting to checking textbooks and articles the evening of the treatment to see if he had missed something, questioning what else he could have done, and seeking reassurance that his treatment was exemplary. But he maintains that "it's that self-doubt that makes you improve" and was reassured that what he did was textbook.

Our discussion of peak experience alerted Stan to the possibility of extraordinary experiences happening for him: "Now I'm aware of peak experiences. Maybe people go through life experiencing them but not knowing – now I know I'll be searching for them."

***

In the early days of learning about yoga, **Katy Moses-Hamilton**, who we met in Chapter 3, remembers "lying down and then coming to almost an hour later." She says she felt like a different person without knowing what she'd done:

> And that was it, the bliss I feel from it – not always, but sometimes I walk out in absolute bliss. The way I'd describe it is the happiest it is possible to be in one moment. I get a kind of fizzy nose feeling. I roll up my mat and walk out feeling that I've just had bliss.

She has now practised yoga for ten years, five times a week and for an hour at a time and has unintentionally set up conditions without necessarily aiming for a peak experience. The environment of the yoga studio or personal space, plus laying down the mat and donning the yoga kit, all contribute to anchoring the moment and become part of creating the conditions. She recalls one particular peak experience:

> I couldn't tell you what pose I was in but I know it was with Sam, the Yogi I do a class with every Thursday, but I couldn't tell you exactly what he was saying. I couldn't tell you who was stood at the side of me, or sat at the side or behind me, nor what I was wearing as the experience took over. It just comes on.

She is consciously aware of a "weird feeling of teetering on the edge" when this feeling comes over her. She describes it like "being on the edge of an orgasm."

Katy said that the experience was hard to explain:

> At the time it feels normal; how yoga and meditation should feel essentially. It's afterwards that I appreciate it how lucky I am to feel like that. I'm in the zone at the time it happens but it's more of a memory of how it feels when recreating that feeling and talking about it. I didn't have a name for it until I spoke with you but I think subconsciously you do set yourself up for that experience because you know that's going to make you happy. I'm thinking about one particular yoga session that I had and as I'm thinking about it, I'm starting to get those feelings but to a much lesser extent – like my body is reminded of it but doesn't quite want to take me there.

For Katy, the peak experience in yoga is a sensation of being fully present without any other distractions, almost like being in a vortex and connecting with a part of the self that is there waiting for it to happen. Katy finds it interesting that at the moment of peak experience she is thinking of nothing else:

> [P]articularly someone like me who is always looking for the next thing. I finish my sandwich for lunch and immediately think what am I going to have for dinner. If I'm in the gym at midday I'm thinking about my yoga session at 6 o'clock. I'm always looking for the next thing and always busy. I'm wondering if it's more prevalent in people like me who have a busy brain, doing 12 things at once? Is peak experience heightened because of that? I'm so rarely in the moment. If you saw my desktop with hundreds of things open – I'll write three words then go and hang out the washing out or look at Twitter. I have a concentration span of 45 minutes and make all my meetings 45 minutes. But when that peak experience happens, I don't want to be doing anything else.

We leave Katy with a question she herself posed: "Is the peak experience so blissful because it's the only time I'm in the present space?"

***

Sarah Taylor, a tarot-reader and former psychotherapist, had a peak experience not dissimilar to Waldron's (1998) participants in a case study of the long-term impact of timeless experiences. Waldron's participants described the after-effects of experiences lasting for days and even weeks with one participant reporting it took "about a year to stabilize the immense impact of knowing that came through the experience" (1998, p. 113).

Like Waldron's participants, the feeling from Sarah's peak experience stayed with her for about 18 months. She thinks she was making contact with an archetypal experience that led her to working with tarot. She admitted to having a very strong tap into her intuition and believes her experience hard-wired her into something. "Most of the magic has now gone," she said, but a connection remains that she cannot fully understand.

Sarah explained that there are moments when working with clients when she knows that she is connecting with them in a way that is meaningful; all she has to do is give that connection back to her clients in words, to give something significant whilst remaining true to the non-verbal connection. Sarah has no idea where this sensation of connection comes from, and the challenge is to find the right words. She refers to Jung's collective unconscious. Each Self is unique but also taps into everything else. Sarah believes that explanation of the Self is why she sometimes knows what is going on and sometimes not. Something happens when attuning to the client, but it is unreliable. Sarah experiences this sensation as catalytic and a co-creative experience. Waldron's participants found their experiences not only life-enriching but also life-changing, which Sarah also acknowledged, "I don't know what life would have been like without it so yes, it has been life-altering. It certainly changed my idea of what death is and what life is."

***

Jenny Holcombe became a kinesiologist because traditional medicine had been unable to diagnose her condition. A kinesiologist treated and cured it. Her recovery was so impactful that her instant thought was "this is what I need to do. I need to help people get better. It was really exciting and a real lightbulb moment for me."

Jenny believes healing is not about doctors, medicine, and pharmaceuticals. She maintains that herbs and their natural effect on the body, and the processing of the body and emotions all have a major effect on our recovery from ailments. Jensen et al. (2016) described how kinesiology, also termed manual muscle testing, is a non-invasive assessment tool used to evaluate muscular strength and neuromusculoskeletal integrity. Jenny explains that kinesiology is about getting to the root cause of client's presenting problems: backache, migraines, and even constipation. Some people arrive saying Jenny is their last resort. She says they literally sit with their arms folded, glaring at her. Often, they have nowhere else to go and are quite reluctant to tell her their issues, as if to say "well, you should know." Despite hostility, when Jenny finds the cause and explains her diagnosis, she can see the reaction in clients' faces as though they experience their own light bulb moment when they suddenly realise her explanation makes perfect sense:

> They're often overwhelmed, and many will cry because they realise they're not mad, they're not making it up, they're not hypochondriacs. These things are actually happening to them. I'll just leave people for five minutes because they need to process. Then they go away, follow the protocol, come back and they're actually a lot better.

Also, Jenny is a practitioner of Bowen therapy, a holistic remedial body technique that works gently on top of the skin through the fascia, the connective tissue where all the nerve endings live, allowing the body to realign itself. Jenny explains:

> The fascia is what causes pain in the body and if your gut's not happy and your body is really stressed, then the body's last line of defence is the skin. So, when you're developing problems skin-wise such as eczema or psoriasis, that's basically your body screaming I'm not happy nor have I been for some time – and this is my last call to tell you I'm struggling.

The therapist works structurally through the fascia with the autonomic nervous system, a component of the peripheral nervous system that regulates involuntary physiologic processes. It contains three anatomically distinct divisions: sympathetic, parasympathetic, and enteric. In common parlance this is the fight, flight, or freeze state. Jenny maintains that people get stuck in this state, a throwback: "people freeze when seeing a big grizzly bear that's going to eat me. And that's when they develop eczema. If you're in fight or flight, you'll get eczema. It works on the stress levels."

The peak experience Jenny encountered through using Bowen therapy astounded her. She explained she never really thought the treatment would have such a big emotional shift on a 10-year-old boy. His problem was eczema, which covered his entire body; his skin was weeping, and he was bandaged every night. His mother brought photos for Jenny to see the severity of the case, as Jenny could barely touch him. But, on the fourth treatment, his mother came into the room sobbing and said, "Look at him. It's gone. It's all gone."

Jenny recalls that all she had asked him to do was take some probiotics and had given him four treatments, working on every level – the physical, emotional, and psychological. And the whole lot had gone. He was a completely different child from being really sad, and losing his confidence, to playing football. Jenny kept looking at the photos and then at him and thinking "this is good but it's just not possible to do this with hands-on therapy":

> It was mind-blowing and didn't seem real. It did really spook me for a long while in a good way. It's basically just touching the body and that's what can happen. That was my first big peak experience, I think. That was a sense of wonder, a sense of awe, kind of dumbfounded.

Jenny admitted to a combination of her own intuition and intuitive voices in her head that informed her of root problems. Such voices are explained by Arnd-Caddigan (2021) in a discussion of mind-centred depth therapy – a therapy that holds the therapist's and the client's intuitions at the heart of the treatment. Jenny can differentiate these voices and make the comparison between the softer, more gentle treatment that Bowen therapy offers which corresponds with a female voice. Kinesiology, a more hands-on, physical treatment has a stronger, male voice.

Jenny was unsure whether she had a peak experience as described by Maslow; the ineffable, transcendent encounter that seems timeless. She was, however, confident that she felt rapture and joy because of the undeniable success of the treatment for eczema. She experienced an impactful and indescribable feeling of being of service to the 10-year-old, an affirmation and validation of her intuition and her skillset.

***

Nikki Howlett is a Reiki practitioner and beautician. Her peak experiences are connected with the supernatural – exploring crystals, readings, and visualisation through what she calls the "third eye" – her intuition and spirituality. Nikki believes everyone has a spirit guide: "it's a little voice, that sixth sense, the unconscious mind." The voices trigger coincidences and attract goodness and positive energy and lead to "the universal energy and channelling for the Reiki." When asked if we act as a magnet to attract that energy, she replied that we can tune into it rather like a battery, connecting "the positive which is up there and the negative down here, and it recharges as you connect into it."

Nikki also recalled a peak experience during one reiki treatment that involved her seeing angels singing in the room. After the treatment, Nikki confessed to her client, "I had a really strange experience" and simultaneously, her client said that she too had visualised something that gave her a message: "that's what I need to do going forward." Her client seemed to have achieved an altered state of consciousness, which gave her the answer she needed to enrich her life, and she was motivated to write a book. It is questionable whether each triggered something in the other, but the experience was impactful and long-lasting. Nikki's client did write the book and credited her with the inspiration.

There is a delightful spontaneity in Nikki's experiences. She has learnt a lot of new things that have put meaning into her life and enable her to help others. She believes some people may not be ready for their journey but that everyone is looking for something to help them understand why they are here.

***

Our next participant is **Clare Josa**. Clare, who trained as a meditation teacher and Reiki healer and is now an educator and trainer, also shares her workplace experiences in Chapter 11.

When we asked Clare what peak experience means for her, without hesitation, she shared how the biggest peak experience she's had was during meditation training:

> We were doing processes to get to a very advanced state, called Anandamaya, the bliss state in the layers of being. I got there by accident. It lasted a couple of hours and it blew me away – absolutely blissed out, but with this most incredible sense of oneness.

Clare's blissful state wasn't accidental but, she maintains, was a build-up over two years of hour-long meditations twice every single day. She believes the result was "an awful lot of clearing out of inner stuff, baggage, ego and work issues." Clare understands why people chase that feeling:

> So that for me was the extreme peak experience, and in some ways, looking back it was surreal and hard to understand cognitively. As I went into it, my consciousness went into shock, kind of "my goodness what's happening." I started to cry. And I think what I experienced on that day was really an altered state of consciousness at a much higher level than what we would traditionally call peak experience. It grew over the space of about half an hour and it stayed for hours and hours.

She moreover explained that whilst on a walk with the cohort from the training, she experienced a heightened level of sensory acuity:

> I could feel the energy from strangers walking towards me. It opened up a whole different way of being consciously aware of the world that no one could put into words for me. And I suspect the experience is different for each of us. I've never come quite to that point again, but having had it even once has made me realise what is available to us from the point of view of experiencing life.

Clare explained that in the yoga world people talk about Vijnanamaya Kosha, which is a self-transcendent state of equilibrium that comes from the knowledge emanating from a combination of intellect and the senses (BanditaKar et al., 2022). She believes she was so plugged into that knowing, she feels if someone had asked her something about anything in the world, then that wisdom would have been there:

> What I experience as peak experience now is a very toned-down version of that, but it has some elements that are common. It was what I call my extreme peak experience. I'd love to be able to turn it on like a tap and ancient masters probably can. That was definitely the bliss-type peak experience.

***

Our final participant is **Charlie Efford,** a management consultant and Gestalt therapist. When we asked him what a peak experience meant for him, he immediately brought spirituality and meditation into the conversation:

> I'd describe it as spiritual, and happens whenever I've been in complete harmony with the people around me. It's like meditating, there's a process to get into a groove where you can let go of things. There's an element of surrender.

Charlie has been meditating for a good while, and his meditating process enables him to drop himself into a slightly altered state:

> I think people who meditate regularly can put themselves into a space where things can happen, and there's a discipline to doing that. I have a counting method and I count down from 10 to 1. There's something about setting the scene and I know that works. I go into a fairly relaxed space, and after that it's following a pathway that my mind has learnt.

Also, he revealed that at one stage he started to see a face in his mind's eye, in the back of his eyelids: "If I focussed on it and tried to see what was going on it disappeared, so I had to be relaxed and aware for it to be there – noticing it and not focusing on it."

In setting the scene, Charlie is creating the space to allow things to happen. He didn't articulate this as a peak experience but clearly identified it as something important for him. He is almost creating the conditions for something to happen by being consistent in his approach to meditation, having a countdown ritual, being relaxed and aware, noticing without trying to force anything to happen, being in the moment and surrendering to the process: "by choosing a focus I think it allows your energy and attention to be in one place so that everything else surging through the mind gets put aside for a while."

In that "higher" state of meditation, Charlie explained how he experiences something in his head and somewhere in his chest. This gives him a sense of being in tune:

> It doesn't feel like the gut to me, it's more the heart, and the head isn't so much about thinking, it's more about being aware. My awareness recognises that something is happening. It's like driving a car, something happens

automatically. You haven't got to think about it. It's a case of forgetting about internal dialogue, conscious thinking, and going with that flow of the feeling you're having at that moment.

The Significance of Peak Experience in This Context

Both the literature and our participants' accounts indicate there are significant aspects of therapy that might lead to a peak experience – aspects which we could define as the core conditions required for a peak experience to occur in this context. These aspects are trust and connection between therapist and client, state management for both therapist and client, and the role that intuition can play.

Trust and Connection

The first significant core condition is that trust needs to be built. Such trust may start with a personal recommendation from an already trusted friend or colleague of the client's to see a particular therapist. From the client's perspective, trust in the therapist's guidance then builds through being heard, as many of our participants have pointed out. Trust begins to be established in the first few seconds when talking to a client and establishing the tone and approach to be taken during the therapy. This initial trust becomes deeper as the relationship builds. In addition, as Amir (2001) pointed out, therapists need to have trust not only in themselves but also in their skillset. These two facets can be integrated through self-awareness. If therapists are congruent and aware of their strengths and weaknesses, client expectations can be better managed.

The therapist needs the client's support just as much as the client needs the therapist's support. This is a two-way process as participants have noted. Without the patient supporting the therapeutic process, and being receptive to the treatment, the healing is not as effective. The support of client feedback is essential, giving the therapist assurance about the quality of their work. In addition, trust and mutual support between therapist and client can potentially lead to a peak experience.

State Management and Preparation

A number of participants mentioned the value of "state management" to facilitate ridding themselves of daily hassles, irritations, and judgements and prepare for a therapy session. The literature refers to this as "centering" (Amir, 2001) and involves detaching from the self, everyday tensions, and internal dialogue. This centering resonates with findings in other research on peak experience in coaching (Weijers, 2021).

Similar to coaches, therapists enter a state whereby they almost free themselves from personal distractions so that they can focus fully on their clients through self-awareness. One participant centred himself by focusing and using a countdown process to get into an altered state. Others use meditative strategies. In Gestalt therapy, three of the core principles are to help clients become more aware of themselves, stay present, and process things in the here and now. Our therapists were all aware of the need to create the space for something to happen in a similar way. For example, both the literature and our participants referred to breathing as a means of becoming fully present and centred. One participant called it her "ritual." Others find centering happens the instant they put on their uniform or set out their equipment; they become focused and fully present, anchoring themselves into their state for treating clients. All the therapists also concurred that they bring their experience, skills, and knowledge into the therapy room, leaving their own issues behind.

Intuition

Intuition is linked with the therapeutic treatment. Therapists agreed that at the beginning of their careers there was an urgency to "do everything by the book" and follow taught procedure, whereas after a few years, instinct takes over, simply allowing their hands to do the work through experience and repeated practice. Two participants admitted to being guided intuitively through spiritual guides and voices that steered their instincts. Others have no real idea of where the sensation comes from but somehow tune into their intuition and subconscious to enable the right words to surface for clients.

Peak experiences in this context seemed to happen for some therapists when their internal dialogue faded, enabling them to be focused, and fully present in the moment, and allowing their intuition to take over. Amir (2001, p. 211) believes that when her intuition guides her, she perceives things differently "so, my intuition is much more there. The receiving, the listening, is very different. It is purer than listening in my everyday life." Other therapists refer to their intuition as the third eye, spirituality, a little voice, or a sixth sense.

The peak experiences shared by our therapists seemed not to be transcendental or brief, but they were certainly spontaneous and life-changing. Our participants used words such as "out there," "spark," "dumbfounding," "awe," "rapture," "blissed-out," "joy," and "magical." The *Oxford English Dictionary* (1987) states that one of the descriptions of "peak" is the highest point of intensity; and Hanfling (1992, p. 159) reminds us that the term "experience" can be used in a very broad sense to cover almost every aspect of conscious living but can also be used in a narrower sense to refer to "a particular and perhaps very brief incident or episode." This appears to reflect our participants' descriptions of their peak experiences. It is not for us to say that these interpretations are any less meaningful and life-altering when compared to Maslow's peak experience; they are simply different and worthy of distinction because they add a perspective on life that is totally rewarding and fulfilling.

References

Agnew, C. (2020). Psychotherapists' altered states of consciousness: A study of counsellors' and psychotherapists' experiences of altered states of consciousness whilst conducting therapy. *Consciousness, Spirituality & Transpersonal Psychology, 1*, 62–76.

Amir, D. (2001). Layers of meaning. *Nordic Journal of Music Therapy, 10*(2), 209–220.
Armor, T. (1969). A note on the peak experience and a transpersonal psychology. *The Journal of Transpersonal Psychology, 1*(1) (Spring), 47.
Arnd-Caddigan, M. (2021). *Intuition in therapeutic practice: A mind-centered depth approach for healing.* Routledge.
BanditaKar, B., Mohapatra, C. K., Panda, S. K., Behera, P. K., Raj, K., & Patra, S. K. (2022). Vignanamaya Kosha – From the view point of ancient and modern science. *NeuroQuantology, 20*(8), 2472.
Bhat, D. (2015). Bridging yoga psychology and somatic psychotherapy. *Somatic Psychotherapy Today, 5*(2), 96–99.
Bien, T. (2006). *Mindful therapy: A guide for therapists and helping professionals.* New York: Simon and Schuster.
Bluckert, P. (2023). Gestalt coaching. In E. Cox, T. Bachkirova, & D. Clutterbuck (Eds.), *The complete handbook of coaching*, 4th edition. London: Sage.
Csikszentmihalyi, M. (1997). *Flow and the psychology of discovery and invention.* New York, NY: Harper Perennial.
Deikman, A. J. (1980). De-automatization and the mystic experience. In J. R. Tisdale (Ed.), *Growing edges in the psychology of religion.* Chicago: Nelson Hall.
Elliot, R. (1983). "That in your hands": A comprehensive process analysis of a significant event in psychotherapy. *Psychiatry, 46*(2), 113–129.
Evans, P. G. (2016). *Peak experience in educational encounters: A phenomenological-hermeneutic study.* PhD Thesis, California Institute of Integral Studies, USA, ProQuest.
Farias, M., Maraldi, E., Wallenkampf, K. C., & Lucchetti, G. (2020). Adverse events in meditation practices and meditation-based therapies: A systematic review. *Acta Psychiatrica Scandinavica.* https://doi.org/10.1111/acps.13225
Fletcher, J. (2008). Epiphany storytelling as a means of reinforcing and embedding transformational therapeutic change. *European Journal for Qualitative Research in Psychotherapy*, (3), 30–37.
Garcia-Campayo, J., Hijar-Aguinaga, R., Barceló-Soler, A., Fernández-Martínez, S., & Aristegui, R. (2022). Examining the relation between practicing meditation and having peak experiences and lucid dreams: A cross-sectional study. *Frontiers in Psychology, 13*, 858745.
Grafanaki, S., & McLeod, J. (1999). Narrative process in the construction of helpful and hindering events in experiential psychotherapy. *Psychotherapy Research, 9*, 289–303.
Green, J. A., & Simon, R. A. (2019). Self-mastery: The pathway to peak performance and well-being in the law. *Southwestern: Law Review, 48*, 207.
Hadash, Y., Veksler, T., Dar, O., Oren-Schwartz, R., & Bernstein, A. (2023). Peak experiences during mindfulness meditation retreats and their salutary and adverse impact: A prospective matched-controlled intervention study. *Journal of Consulting and Clinical Psychology, 92*(4), 213–225. https://doi.org/10.1037/ccp0000875
Hanfling, O. (1992). *Philosophical aesthetics: An introduction.* Milton Keynes: The Open University.
Hender, K. (2001). *Is Gestalt therapy more effective than other therapeutic approaches? Southern Health/Centre for Clinical Effectiveness.* Monash Institute of Health Services Research, Melbourne.
James, P., & Bray, P. (2022). Therapists' experiences of self-transcendence: An interpretative phenomenological analysis. *Journal of Humanistic Psychology, 0*(0). https://doi.org/10.1177/00221678221099339
Jauregui, A. (2003). *Epiphanies; A psychotherapist's tales of spontaneous emotional healing.* New York: Prima Publishing.
Jensen, A. M., Stevens, R. J., & Burls, A. J. (2016). Estimating the accuracy of muscle response testing: Two randomised-order blinded studies. *BMC Complementary and Alternative Medicine, 16*, 492.

Kastubi, K., Minarti, M., & Saudah, N. (2017). Hypnotherapy decreases stress in elderly hypertension. *International Journal of Nursing and Midwifery Science*, *1*(1), 1–10.

Kraut, R. (2018). Aristotle's ethics. In E. N. Zalta (Ed.), *The Stanford encyclopedia of philosophy*. Summer edition. [Online] https://plato.stanford.edu/archives/sum2018/entries/aristotle-ethics/

Levin, J., & Steele, L. (2005). The transcendent experience: Conceptual, theoretical and epidemiologic perspectives. *Explore*, *1*(2), 89–101.

Liang, Y. S. (2006). *Peak experience, epiphany, and psychological well-being*. Dissertation, The University of Oklahoma.

Maher, A., Robertson, A. R., & Howie, L. (2011). The experience and development of awareness in Gestalt therapy training groups: A phenomenological study. *Gestalt Journal of Australia and New Zealand*, *8*(1), 36–56.

Maslow, A. H. (1959). Cognition of being in the peak experiences. *The Journal of Genetic Psychology*, *94*, 43–66.

Maslow, A. H. (1962). *Toward a psychology of being*. Princeton, NJ: D Van Nostrand.

Maslow, A. H. (1976). *Religions, values, and peak experiences*. Penguin Compass.

Maslow, A. H. (2010). *The peak experience (recorded interview), the B-language workshop – part 3*. Esalen Institute, CA, USA. www.youtube.com/watch?v=TkqQX896WiA [Accessed 1 September 2013].

Nicholson, B. (2015). Music-elicited peak experiences of music therapists. *Qualitative Inquiries in Music Therapy*, *10*, 53.

Nordoff, P., & Robbins, C. (1998). Edward. *Nordic Journal of Music Therapy*, *7*(1), 57–64.

Norton, A. (1964). Hypnotherapy. *Natural Medicine Magazine*, S. Africa.

Oxford English Dictionary (1987) by J. A. Simpson, E. S. C. Weiner et al. Oxford University Press.

Palmer, S., & Whybrow, A. (2007). *Handbook of coaching psychology. A guide for practitioners*. East Sussex: Routledge.

Perez-De-Albeniz, A., & Holmes, J. (2000). Meditation: Concepts, effects and uses in therapy. *International Journal of Psychotherapy*, *5*(1), 49–59.

Posadzki, P. (2010, September 23–24). Closer to the essence of yoga experience: *Yoga – the light of microuniverse*, 112–118. Proceedings of the International Interdisciplinary Scientific Conference – Yoga in Science – Future and Perspectives, Belgrade.

Roth, A. L. (2014). *Yoga as a psychological intervention: conceptualizations and practice integration of professional psychologist-yoga teachers*. Doctoral Dissertation, University of Minnesota.

Taylor, S. M. (2018). An awakening. *The Psychologist*, *31*, 42–47.

Waldron, J. L. (1998). The life impact of transcendent experiences with a pronounced quality of noesis. *The Journal of Transpersonal Psychology*, *30*(2), 103–134.

Weijers, K. (2021). *Peak moments: The experience of coaches*. Doctoral Thesis, Oxford Brookes University.

Whitehead, R., & Bates, G. (2016). The transformational processing of peak and nadir experiences and their relationship to eudaimonic and hedonic well-being. *Journal of Happiness Studies*, *17*, 1577–1598.

Wilson, S. R., & Spencer, R. C. (1990). Intense personal experiences: Subjective effects, interpretations, and after-effects. *Journal of Clinical Psychology*, *46*(5), 565–573.

9 Peak Experiences in Executive and Life Coaching

Introduction

Coaching has been described as "a human development process that involves structured, focused interaction and the use of appropriate strategies, tools and techniques to promote desirable and sustainable change for the benefit of the coachee and potentially for other stakeholders" (Bachkirova et al., 2024, p. 1). Across all its genres and domains, whether focusing on personal life-coaching, existential coaching, business, or executive coaching, it is regarded as providing a safe space, offering confidentiality and impartiality to add value to people's lives. Further, as Whitmore (2002, p. 4) explained, it is "a way creating a vision of the future or an ideal to aspire toward, as opposed to struggling to survive by avoiding problems." By helping coachees use the processes of transformational learning and critical reflection to evaluate their actions, the coach helps develop new understandings.

Maslow's influence on coaching can be discerned through his focus on the human drive towards optimal functioning and ultimately self-actualisation. He identified that people have strong directional tendencies and described the nature of self-actualisation, even though he did not articulate clearly how this goal was to be achieved (Spence, 2007, p. 256). In addition, as discussed in the Introduction, Maslow originally linked self-actualisation and the ability to have peak experiences. However, his subsequent thinking was that, although highly developed people had a greater tendency towards such transcendence, anyone could have peak experiences. He explained that such experiences may include

> the parental experience, the mystic or oceanic, or nature experience, the aesthetic perception, the creative moment, the therapeutic or intellectual insight, the orgasmic experience, certain forms of athletic fulfillment.
> (Maslow, 1959, pp. 44–45)

Thus, Maslow also implied that peak experience is not limited to a particular type of person or activity. Consequently, there is every reason to assume that coaches also have peak experiences since they occur in practically everybody although often without being recognised or accepted for what they are (Maslow, 1962). Indeed, our own peak experiences whilst coaching have led us to wonder if other

DOI: 10.4324/9781003509219-10

coaches also have intense feelings of connectedness and oneness with the coachee and contributed to our motivation for writing this chapter.

Our search of the coaching literature confirms there is little empirical research on peak experiences during coaching. There is some literature on related experiences for the coachee during the coaching interaction, but the lack of research points to a gap in awareness and understanding of how coaches experience the peak phenomenon. This lack of research could be due to three reasons: (i) the coaching profession is fairly young, and research is lagging behind practice; (ii) the phenomenon is being discussed but using different terminology; and (iii) coaches are already experiencing the phenomenon but, as in other contexts, they find it hard or embarrassing to articulate or discuss (van Deurzen-Smith, 2014).

To address these shortcomings, we begin by examining the range of terms used in the coaching literature that refer to personal transformations such as peak experience. The review is followed by actual accounts from our coach participants who report on their personal encounters of peak experiences while coaching. We then pull together common threads and the core conditions that enable a peak experience in coaching. It should be noted that in the coaching field the terms coachee and client are often used interchangeably and that practice is reflected in this chapter.

Review of Terms Used in the Coaching Literature

In our search of the literature, we uncovered a variety of terms used to describe the kinds of personal transformations that take place during coaching. For example, some authors (e.g., Longhurst, 2010) have focused on aha moments, others have looked at intuition or insight (Murray, 2004; Stern, 2017), pivots (Clancy & Binkert, 2017), tipping points (Kets de Vries, 2013), critical moments (De Haan, 2008a), or shifts in the room (Moons, 2016). More recently, Weijers (2022) examined the trifold concept of peak *moments* during coaching. Peak moments is the term used by McInman and Grove (1991) to embrace peak experience, peak performance, and flow.

A range of concepts used in the more general personal transformation literature was also identified by Stern (2017, p. 73) and included the following terms: "a defining moment, mind-expanding, life-changing, turning point, watershed moment, wake-up call, awakening, and worldview shift." From her exploration, Stern then proposed a classification comprising five types of experience that she called peak, plateau, nadir, epiphany, and liminal state and further conceptualised these types along different continuums; a temporal continuum, an intensity continuum, and on a spectrum "anywhere from an abysmal nadir to an awe-inducing peak experience" (2017, p. 73). She describes peak experience as involving feelings such as "well-being, serenity, joy, trust, transcendence, and love" (p. 73).

In view of this plethora of analogous terminology, we have organised our review of the coaching literature under the following five headings to try and capture the full range of coaching-related exploration: Intuition, Shifts in the Room, Critical Moments, Aha Moments, and Flow. This overview should allow us to assess the status of the research on coaches' peak experiences.

Intuition

Much of the research we found focuses on intuition as a starting point for personal transformations, but as Sheldon (2018) notes there is very little research evidence to support using intuition in coaching practice. We found some coaching literature that reports on breakthroughs for the coachee, particularly when the coach is open to acknowledging their intuition. For example, Murray (2004), de Haan (2008b), Moons (2016), and Sheldon (2018) all endorsed the importance of the coach's intuition to facilitate a creative environment.

It has been reasoned that intuition is rooted in the tacit dimension, the sense of knowing something before it can be articulated (Polanyi, 1966). Thus, an intuition is seen as a non-conscious, rapid, automatic, and preverbal reaction that seems like a peak experience. The act of letting go to discover what emerges, ignoring one's willpower and trusting the gut feel, is a noticeable link between intuition and peak experience. Indeed, Maslow (1962) saw willpower as an intrusion for the emergence of peak experience, implying that coaches would benefit from listening to their intuition to facilitate peak experiences to emerge (Weijers, 2022). However, intuition's apparent reliance on tacit knowledge also points to the idea that the quality of our intuitions develops in line with our level of expertise (Mavor et al., 2010).

Mavor et al. (2010) also reported a consensus among their participant coaches that intuition can be developed, but that it is native and natural to all of us. This seems to be a contradiction until we realise that the quality of intuitions must vary according to experience and understanding. Nash and Collins (2006, p. 486) noted that when coaches operate instinctively, sometimes called using their "gut feel," they are in fact taking advantage of their tacit knowledge "which can be abstract and unarticulated."

Murray (2004) had similarly urged coaches to acknowledge and embrace intuition, which she saw as an opportunity to connect soul-to-soul with coachees. Ignoring our intuition, she advised, risks a tick-box, evidence-based approach to coaching, thus losing the rich connections that intuition brings. Murray (2004) refers to this phenomenon as that part of her that rationality does not fully understand. She uses the word "magic" when talking of a coaching experience and referring to her intuition.

More recently, Sheldon (2018) examined how experienced coaches were actually working with intuition in their coaching practice. Her model of "Working at the Boundary" captures how coaches may notice and respond to their intuitions and suggests ways of working with intuition in coaching relationships.

An indication that coaches are using their intuition is also uncovered by Weijers (2022). However, she found that coaches are often unable to articulate why, for example, they ask a particular question of a coachee. Frequently, important questions seem to come from nowhere. Thus, it could be argued that peak experiences cannot be decreed or commanded but instead emanate from something spontaneous and intuitive. This is the kind of knowing that guides the brush of the painter or informs the coach when listening to their internal dialogue rather than their conscious thoughts (Weijers, 2022).

Shifts in the Room

Smith and Hawkins (2023, p. 232) proposed transformational coaching as a way of helping people to change and achieve a "shift in the room" – a process by which "the coach helps the client to experience an integrated transformation of perspective," accompanied by a change in demeanour and outlook that is discernible in the coaching room – hence the shift.

Inspired by Hawkins and Smith's theory, Moons (2016) explored these transformational shifts with coaches and clients in a grounded theory study. She found that such a shift either happens in one session or evolves over a longer period of time by "planting a seed in the first couple of sessions, which grows into an insight in a later session" (2016, p. 51). Moons also reported that clients experienced a somatic arousal prompted when the unconscious "drops the solution in the conscious mind, the moment in which clients become aware of their insight." (2016, p. 54). This moment is also known as illumination, which Moons's participants described variously as "answers bubbling up" or "insights appearing suddenly."

In her research, Moons found that to make transformational shifts happen for clients, coaches do not consciously apply any particular technique or approach to help them come to their insights but simply use their intuition, which she called a sixth sense or third eye: "developing and acting upon hunches, holding the silence . . . all seem to be critical coaching interventions" (2016, p. 55).

Both Hawkins and Smith's and Moons's descriptions of shifts for the client appear different from peak experiences, and yet there is a parallel. Moons states that such insights appear suddenly. So do peak experiences, as noted by Wilson (2009, p. 51) "sometimes they seem to happen of their own accord, out of the blue, as it were." Another similarity with peak experience is reported by Henderson (2016, p. 4), who shares the use of the term shift in a description by one of her participants: "a shift in the individual's consciousness to a wider, more inclusive and spiritual orientation . . . it holds the potential to make consciousness bigger."

Critical Moments

Laws (2020) describes critical moments as playing a practical role in interactions between people. In our review of coaching literature, we identified studies of critical moments occurring during the coaching process (De Haan, 2008a, 2008b; De Haan et al., 2010, 2020) and looked for similarities with our definition of peak experience.

De Haan's original research question is qualified by a focus on rationalising the experience:

> Describe briefly one critical moment (an exciting, tense or significant moment) with one of your coachees. Think about what was critical in the coaching journey or a moment when you did not quite know what to do.
>
> (De Haan, 2008b, p. 92)

Initially, there appears to be a parallel here with Maslow's description of peak experience, especially when De Haan speaks of exciting, tense, or significant moments. However, the allusion to doubt in the instruction to think about what was critical suggests critical moments lack a sense of spontaneity, lightness, joy, and delight in the coaching experience, and the feelings attached to critical moments seem quite distinct from the hope, energy, joy, passion, and inspiration which encapsulate Maslow's peak experience.

De Haan et al. (2010, p. 113) proposed that critical moments are applicable to both coach and coachees and suggested that critical moments are "a reflection of change through executive coaching as it happens in conversation." Their research questions explored the nature of key moments that coaches and coachees report immediately after a coaching session, and their analysis detailed the ways in which their reports differed and how the results compared with findings from earlier studies. They found no contradictory or idiosyncratic interpretations and reported that coach and coachee were in "substantial agreement about the specific moments that were critical in the sessions and why" (2010, p. 109).

In a more recent study, De Haan et al. (2020) compared the critical moments experienced during coaching by executive coaches and their clients. Descriptions of critical-moments were collected straight after coaching conversations took place, and findings suggested there was substantial agreement about the specific moments that were critical in the sessions. This study augments the findings of the authors' earlier work and sheds light on how descriptions from clients and coaches coming out of coaching sessions can be similar or, as in the earlier study, different, especially where there may be tensions in the relationship.

Aha Moments

Another author who identifies coachees' cognitive peak moments in the coaching process is Kets de Vries (2013, 2021). He talks of "aha" or "eureka" moments for the client, describing such moments as problem-solving solutions for clients when, out of the blue, "a light bulb goes on in our head" (2013, p. 155). Aha moments stem from the Greek term meaning "alethia," to step out of lethargy and into truth. Such moments are related to insight and awareness for the coachee, eliciting positive feelings of happiness similar to Maslow's descriptions of peak experience, "moments of highest happiness and fulfilment" (1962, p. 69). Kets de Vries (2013) also referred to these moments as "tipping points" – significant aha events that contribute to meaningful life changes for the coachee. One of the participants in Longhurst's (2006, p. 69) doctoral research also referred to the aha moment as a turning point, describing it as "the point of inner clarity when I suddenly know how to proceed and why. They are the moments when the doing and being come together."

Longhurst (2006, 2010) considers aha moments fundamental to personal transformation. She defines them as the prime device by which clients in life coaching achieve transformational (rather than incremental or merely behavioural) change. Her results show that the aha moment can be experienced at varying levels of intensity, and unlike other ways of knowing, respondents almost invariably report feeling the moment in their bodies as well as, or instead of, in their minds (2006). So, she argues, the difference between an aha moment and just knowing something new is that the aha is felt in the body. Her findings revealed that the moment can be experienced not only cognitively but also somatically and emotionally

> striking many chords across a spectrum of consciousness from body to mind, to soul, to spirit. The more chords the "aha" moment strikes, the greater the resonance and potential for cognitive and behavioural change.
> (Longhurst, 2010, p. 2)

Flow

Much of the coaching literature focuses on flow as a type of peak experience that commonly occurs during coaching. For example, Moore et al. (2005, p. 3) developed a theoretical coaching model that builds on Csikszentmihalyi's notion of shared flow by emphasising the relational genesis of flow. Moore et al. call their model the intuitive dance, describing the state between coach and the client as "relational flow" (2005, p. 2). They maintain that developing relational flow will help with understanding and promoting mastery in the profession, emphasising the importance of the coaching relationship to promote flow states, growth, and change.

More recently, LaRue et al. (2024, online) examined how entrepreneur coaches often experience flow, which the authors describe as "an immersive, enjoyable state of intense focus that positively affects well-being." In their study of self-employed career, executive, health, leadership, and life coaches, they found that periods of recuperation were vital for entering the flow state. Coaches consequently scheduled regular breaks to support their recovery. The study highlights the benefits of experiencing flow to the performance, motivation, and well-being of coaches.

As noted earlier in this book, most authors perceive flow and peak experience to be closely related concepts. According to McBride (2013), Csikszentmihalyi (1990) was strongly influenced by Maslow's concept of peak experience. McBride's doctoral research explored the coach's experience of flow, following Privette's (1983) idea that flow embraces the value of peak experience and the behaviour of peak performance. McBride talks of an experience for coaches when all sense of time becomes distorted and time flies past, unnoticed. A similar phenomenon is explained by Maslow (1959, p. 50): "in all common peak experiences . . . there is a very characteristic disorientation of time and space." However, the distortion of time where individuals fail to notice how long they have been coaching is when they are in flow and is due to their total engagement in the coaching rather than an altered, transcendent state of consciousness. Transcendence, according to Maslow (1971, p. 279), refers to the "very highest and most inclusive or holistic levels of human consciousness."

Honsova and Jarasova (2018, p. 3) also conducted a study to examine which moments are experienced as peak by coaches or are the strongest positive moments that they identify (2018, p. 1). Coachees were asked to talk about peak experiences and describe a scene, episode, or moment from their coaching that stood out as an "especially positive – peak experience" (2018, p. 5).

According to Flaherty (2022), the intimacy of coaching is dependent upon the coach's experience. He suggests the coach's awareness of their competencies could additionally include an awareness of peak experience. Flaherty recognised the flow and spontaneity of coaching and designed a five-step linear process, an overview of coaching which he named the "flow of coaching." The process begins with establishing the relationship with the coachee, recognising openings, observing, and assessing to enrol the coachee, which leads to coaching conversations. Flaherty (2022) recognised that this process may be too structured for some coaches, inhibiting their natural spontaneity and slowing the flow of their natural intuitive responses. However, he added that knowledge of this structure gradually fades, enabling the coach to freely respond intuitively and in the moment. Our interpretation of Flaherty's model is that if flow involves spontaneity and intuition, then potentially a peak experience could happen when coach and coachee are in flow.

Peak Experience in Context

In this section, we reveal the peak moments of five experienced coaches, noting their intimate thoughts and reactions from their work. Even though peak experiences are scarcely mentioned in the coaching literature, our participants were quite vocal in their defence. For example, one participant reported: "I've heard coaching conversations where coaches become frustrated if peak experiences do not happen in the coaching session."

Our first coach is **Jane Darvill-Evans**, who specialises in intercultural coaching. Jane lived in Japan for seven years, speaks the language fluently, and coaches Japanese and Eastern leaders in English. Her interest in peak experiences stems from a passion for understanding how culture drives unique experiences, saying, "I'm aware that I have those peak experiences more when I'm coaching inter-culturally."

Jane's most memorable peak experience happened when coaching a senior Japanese woman, Mayumi (not her real name). Jane coached her for only two sessions, and coaching felt very stilted. She was unable to get a sense of how Mayumi was responding and whether she was finding it difficult. Mayumi answered her questions but gave no indication of whether they were helpful or not. Although worried that she might offend, Jane decided to take a risk and reveal her feelings to Mayumi. Towards the end of the second session, Jane enquired: "I notice that I'm not getting a sense of how you are receiving my questions and observations, whether you find it useful or not because your answers are OK, yes, fine but no real acknowledgement." Jane was absolutely stunned by Mayumi's response. She smiled broadly, eyes twinkling for the first time. Jane felt a rush of euphoria in that moment of connection. She sensed increased energy in her stomach, rising up through her chest: "I said 'wow' when she smiled and I felt a much greater intimacy with her when she showed her emotion . . . , which is when I made that connection with her."

Jane thinks that peak experience lasted only a couple of minutes, but she felt a kind of glow for the rest of the session, which stayed with her for the rest of the day. Jane is also a musician and compared that amazing feeling to giving a great musical performance. She felt that she had learnt something and gained greater courage because of the risk she had taken. She thinks her bravery meant that she could do it again and go to that zone because the risk was worth the return.

In that moment of mutual acknowledgement of each other, the peak experience was a timeless, transcendent, out-of-this world encounter. Both were feeling it in that moment, an intense flash of eye contact, that sense of connection when they were both there together, "we were both completely as it were, as one." They both experienced an "in the moment, instant feeling of joy and happiness." That feeling has stayed with Jane, and she can re-visualise and recapture that moment, eager to discover it again, saying:

> This is the first time I'd really felt this, and it propelled me to seek out more opportunities to work in that way with more Japanese and East Asian clients. It does feel like something beyond that moment, something I feel comfortable with, and it's encouraged me to live more on the edge in my coaching. I want to repeat that and go further. I want to do more and it's kind of in the relational field working intuitively, soul to soul, and beyond.

Jane explained that the intensity of the experience was enhanced by the fact that Mayumi told her she had never received such feedback before. Jane said it was this "nothingness" that was hard to work with up until that moment. For Jane, the experience felt profound: the connection between them transformed their relationship and allowed them to work at a much deeper level.

Jane's experience reveals two conditions that enabled her peak experience. The first is risk. The contract with Mayumi's organisation was big and at an early stage, which meant that there was quite a lot at stake for Jane. Her internal dialogue just before asking that question was, "Is this going to be offensive? Is she going to shut down?" Although it was only towards the end of the second session and their relationship was not yet strong to take a risk, Jane maintains, "I don't think I could have done this at the beginning of my coaching career. I don't think I would have been ready to take that risk."

The second condition is feedback. Western coaching culture sanctions feedback to feed-forward with clients and sponsors. This is, however, virgin territory in coaching with Japanese and East Asians, adding to the risk involved by such disclosure.

A rewarding outcome from this scenario is the growth factor for both Jane and Mayumi. Jane says it was quite an early experience for her in coaching Japanese leaders in English, yet encouraged her to use herself fully when working interculturally:

> It taught me the real value of being brave when working with different cultures. I think taking more risks in coaching helps to build your confidence

and as an inter-cultural coach that fed into other experiences that I had. It made me bolder in other situations as I'd had this positive experience.

The aim of their coaching sessions was to develop how Mayumi could build better relationships with her non-Japanese stakeholders. Jane maintains that their new connection and the way she was now interacting with Mayumi could be similar to the way Mayumi could interface with these other stakeholders. The connection brought about by the peak experience improved their coaching but, more importantly, may have a broader impact on Mayumi's stakeholders.

Not only did Jane encounter a peak experience, but the feeling which followed suggests she was in flow (Csikszentmihalyi, 1990). It empowered her knowing, confidence, and growth:

> I find myself looking forward to those sessions even more than others and I'm less aware of time. When I feel in flow, I have added confidence somehow that I know what to do. So having a peak experience led to flow for me . . . It's been a revelation for me how much richness we were able to get out of that one experience.

***

Our next participant is **Carmelina Lawton-Smith**, a coach and coaching supervisor. Carmelina believes that the coaching space requires peak performance from both coach and coachee and that a peak experience happens in a co-created space when both parties are functioning at their best through mutual peak performance. She says:

> It's a bit like a dance, when both are instep, the coach feels very much in the space, very present, very in the moment and the coachee too is in that slightly detached, reflective, intuitive, comfortable space. I think it only happens with the two together. when you're working with someone, and you just feel a connection that something is happening.

Carmelina firmly believes that peak performance involves using her skills, knowledge, presence, and expertise to become a really good coach. Conversely, when not performing well as a coach, she feels a lack of connection with the coachee and doubts that any of her questions have a positive effect:

> I'm at my peak when I create that energy in the room that enables them, in some shape or form to achieve a peak experience. Generating peaks requires them to reflect and manage new ways of being and thinking. You can see the person physically grow and expand. They become more animated moving into the space, verifying the credence of the connection that's been created in that communication bubble. I just come out thinking "I've no idea what I did but something happened."

That moment of awareness arises often from a question, even a closed question, which can bring a sense of reality to the context. Carmelina agrees that energy grows and tingles, becoming more evident when an "out of the blue" or "killer question" (Weijers, 2021) is posed. She explains one coachee's reaction:

> When it landed, she looked at me and said, "that's a succinct way of nailing it." It seemed to clarify something in her mind. I think at that point something happened in me to try and elaborate and clarify this for her and she said, "I'm amazed that I got to where I got because I wasn't expecting to get where I did." Part of it was intuitive and part of it was her getting into it. We were both in a groove. I wasn't thinking about having to do a particular technique, I was just following the breadcrumbs. That's the only way I can explain it.

Carmelina makes a direct comparison to Schön's (1987) work on reflection in action and reflection on action. She suggests that an awareness of peak experience is possibly reflective:

> You're actually not really aware that it's happening and only see it when you look back. I think your awareness transcends but I'm not sure you know it at the time. You just feel present and in the moment. It links to flow – time is passing but you're so engaged that you're not actually thinking anything beyond what's happening in the moment.

Connection, according to Carmelina, embraces instinct and intuition. It enables the coachee to think more freely. She notices they slow down, their awareness increases, they are very considered and curious: "it raises reflection, seeing things in a different way and they're not, at that moment, thinking about action points or what they're cooking for dinner – they're absolutely in the moment."

In her experience, Carmelina thinks the coachee's engagement is vital to the co-creation of a peak experience. She used the analogy "you can see the wheels turning" when the coachee is committed and connected. This commitment to the coaching process makes the coach feel more involved and keen to give more of herself: "because you can see it's landing, and being appreciated and valued which encourages that space to emerge." Both coach and coachee feed off one another.

Not only is the coachee's engagement crucial to enabling a peak experience to happen, but Carmelina says she too needs to be fully engaged. She questions whether such a connection and engagement with a coachee is possible in a simply transactional space when she may not feel at the edge of her capability. Like Jane, she sees a contrast between being fully connected and engaged and not being connected:

> When you're working with someone and you haven't got that connection the coaching is just hard work and you seem to be drawing teeth – you ask yourself whether you are asking the right questions. Am I getting to what they want? Are they really getting anything out of this? That questioning of

self is not present when there is a peak experience happening. When you hit a peak experience somehow you've engaged the cogs in exactly the right place at the right time.

Carmelina identifies a possible core condition of attaining a peak experience:

> I hardly ever go into a coaching session and think I'm going to use this tool or this methodology. I have to absolutely leave everything out and just "be" – like an investigative journalist – really curious. That's the point of being at the edge, you don't know where you're going.

For Carmelina then, peak experience is about reaching the zone, the flow state that allows her to be unbridled by process. This is connected with peak performance and the enacting of skills, knowledge, and expertise. Also, she maintains that the core conditions of openness and trust between coach and coachee, the acknowledgement of her intuition, and bringing her whole self into the coaching room are crucial to enabling a peak experience to emerge:

> If you trust the process in coaching, somehow you get somewhere, particularly when you're not thinking about it and you're just with them. There's something about awareness and attention in the moment. I don't experience a sudden sort of aha or fireworks going off. The aha moment is sometimes just an acceptance, an appreciation of what's being discussed. I think it's more about their attention being fully engaged because sometimes the aha moment can come much later. The attention becomes more and more progressively internal, rather than external.

***

Christine Champion, also an experienced coach and coaching supervisor, invites us to look at peak experience from the supervisory perspective.

Christine recalls an experience when one of the male coaches in a group supervisory session asked her a question which triggered her energy. Recalling the incident made the hairs on the back of her neck stand as she re-experienced a moment of connection that seemed to inspire and be felt by the entire group in the room. She recalls that the coach's question raised the bar in how she worked on the issue with the coach, in total connection and oneness together. The coach later wrote to Christine saying, "my coaching has changed so much, I'm so conscious of what I learned, thank you so much for being willing to work through it with me."

Christine's experience again demonstrates how working in the moment, being fully present as either coach or coaching supervisor, produces the space to enable a peak experience to emerge. Like Carmelina's experiences, Christine also says that "it wasn't until afterwards that I appreciated the depth of the learning, the peak of that learning and the peak that performance had created." The peak experience had been created by working in the moment, with Christine showing her very best self as coaching supervisor for the coach. There are two similarities to Carmelina's experiences: peak performance by the coach or coaching supervisor and gaining a second insight of the experience through reflection after the experience.

A second experience for Christine happened during one of the Covid-19 pandemic lockdowns. She believes that relationships in coaching became closer and more meaningful as individuals faced time alone, often prepared to offer a deeper level of disclosure about themselves:

> Certainly, with COVID-19 there's been more openness from leaders to bring their whole selves and vulnerability to coaching. Coaching taking place at home in a more private environment has had an influence. People I've been coaching pre and post COVID-19 bring more vulnerability even for the most resilient – opening themselves up to the coach and being prepared to take more risks.

One coach Christine was supervising was open about sharing his experiences on a ventilator and the different experiences he had – transcendental, almost out of this world, out-of-body encounters. They already had a strong connection from previous supervision sessions, but now, post-Covid-19, their conversations were deeper and more meaningful. They picked up their connection and held real, existential discussions about what was meaningful for him, what he was going to do with his life, and how he was building himself physically, emotionally, and intellectually. Christine said, "you don't reach it with everybody, and they are unique moments that give you that sense of purpose." Her peak experience was due to his level of disclosure:

> It was like I was seeing into his soul through the work he was doing and his appreciation of life. Our conversations were never about what tools should I use, it was never transactional.

For Christine, the experience was very much about the connection and the co-created relationship which led to both being able to be in that space through trust and being able to acknowledge the joy that interconnectivity between two people brings. Christine calls the experience a "communion," not in the religious sense but the ability to see into the soul from both sides as equal partners. She moreover believes that both supervisor and coach need to be equally vulnerable to enable a peak experience.

Christine considers that there are conditions which need to be present for a peak experience to happen. These include a non-processual approach, working in the moment to develop connection and deepening trust resulting in a co-created activity, and also taking the risk of asking killer or out-of-the blue questions. She explains:

> There are times when I get this huge oxytocin rush or even in the moment – this flow and pleasurable feeling. It's just like a quiet rush of energy – something magic has happened here for that person to have opened up. They might

be talking about some really significant moment in their past that's had an impact and so they're living that emotional experience.

Christine firmly believes that there is something about this co-created, different world that represents the greatest service the coach can offer; to just be there, fully present, and open to the experience, following wherever the individual wants to go. She describes how it's not about the next question but about sharing feelings. In a session she might say: "Oh! my goodness, I don't know what's happening to you but I'm feeling this in my gut and I've got this real visceral feeling that's coming up in me. What are you feeling?"

[A]nd then they say, "how can you feel that?" And I say I don't know; I'm just sensing it and I feel all my antenna are out. And so, it can often lead to mutual exploration, but it takes the relationship to a totally different place.

**

Our next participant is **Angela Quereshi,** a coach and trainer. Her coaching revolves around working with the whole person. She explains that

[w]hat's a common feature of my peak experiences in coaching is the presence of the whole person, not just the person confined to their working self, it's that person as a whole and their recognition that there isn't a separation.

Angela approaches this way of coaching by noticing, reflecting-back, and offering what she might be seeing with direct questions or statements that acknowledge the whole self. She feels that it is the way we work as coaches that makes the difference and rewards us with peak moments in coaching.

I go into coaching with an awareness of the person and they just happen to have a circumstance or work issue they're working through. The whole person is going to come out is when they let the barriers down so that is when we can do the real work. That's how I approach things and that's what I hope for. It's what I'm excited about in coaching because that's where I feel the real work happens.

Angela's approach to coaching is crucial to her engagement with coachees. She believes the recognition and acknowledgement of the whole self is "such fundamental coaching stuff. It's what we do as a coach isn't it? See the whole person."

There are several strands in her approach, starting with the Rogerian approach to coaching (Rogers, 1961), showing unconditional positive regard and empathy towards coaches, and congruence in herself. She says the connection in the relationship enables coachees to trust, and out of trust comes the sense of safety for the coachee. Feeling safe, they are then prepared to let down their barriers, which often makes them feel emotional and vulnerable yet prepared to take a risk in disclosing their thoughts and feelings. Angela continues:

> Knowing ourselves, and what can trigger us – it's that kind of conversation that supports people to be vulnerable. Because then that vulnerability isn't going to be seen as a weakness but as something we're going to work with. So, it's getting behind what creates that safe space, the trust between you.

When thinking about coaching experiences that really stay with her, Angela says each of them involved the coachees experiencing a lot of emotion in that moment. The experience really mattered and affected them to the point that they were unable to see their way through it. They were overwhelmed. Angela explains that these are the peak moments for her.

Additionally, an awareness of something hitherto unknown for coachees often produces a depth of emotion that generates peak moments for Angela as she recalls:

> [It] felt to me like something was revealed. We've got somewhere that had a lot more depth to it. The revealing of something deep and momentous that then can be worked on, something really important! I think the additional thing is that it was powerful and we could have a lot of exploration in that realisation, which we did. It wasn't just she's feeling it and I'm feeling it. My bit in the revelation added to my own peak moment rather than just sharing hers.

It seems to be Angela's ability to tune into the coachee, which set up an opening for the coachee to be receptive through self-awareness. It was the connection in the relationship, the ensuing trust, safety, and resultant vulnerability that empowered the coachee to take a risk and disclose their inner feelings. Angela's words echo these conditions:

> When whoever I'm working with, voluntarily or involuntarily connects with the emotion of what's going on, the emotion that they are experiencing in the room in that moment, is going to lead to vulnerability. And somehow, I feel wrapped in that myself. It makes me feel wow, we've got to something really important here – there's so much depth that we can work with and I realise the sense of the power that could come out of this moment. This is partly what goes on for me at these peak moments. We've got this shared feeling and it's a peak of a blend of excitement and of having something here to work on that's going to matter.

Angela recalls a training session with a small group of frontline staff working in the arts; young, energetic, thoughtful people who were new to thinking about themselves. The significance of this group, Angela believes, was that they already came with a trust for one other. These factors came together to create the space for her to come in and allow their receptivity to emerge. They were curious of everything she brought, as she encouraged them to really pause and reflect at each significant moment. Angela then helped by reflecting to them what she was hearing and offering different things for them to consider.

Angela felt there were lots of little peak moments through the course of the afternoon, as each individual gained an insight and realisation about themselves. The last half hour or so was when it was time to sit back and make sense of the whole session. Angela recalls how in the room it felt like nothing else mattered; everyone was fully present, listening to everyone else, and then sharing what felt really honest:

> It felt like a real connection, an enhanced connection, so energetic there was this sort of wonderful hush in the room. Everyone in the room was able to connect and look into themselves and share that with an optimism. I got goosebumps when I heard them sharing – it mattered so much. Goosebumps down the back of my neck, particularly, and a very slight almost breathlessness, holding my breath.

Angela shared that this last half an hour together was the most peak she felt. Although she looked still, her heart was beating faster: "It wasn't just that they were feeling it, I was feeling it. My bit in it added to my own peak moment rather than just sharing theirs."

Angela disclosed three initial questions to invite self-awareness and insights from coachees. These could be seen as classic coaching questions, but within her approach she is not simply looking for a statement of insight but inviting coachees to take something forward and to think in a really reflective way. When working with groups, for example, she might ask people to take a moment and share:

1) What really stayed with you most from our time together this afternoon?
2) What is an insight that you would like to share with the group?
3) What would you like to do going forward?

The trust that existed within the group made it seem as though they were speaking with one voice. They were in harmony and found the space to feel safe and vulnerable enough to take a risk and to share. Encouraged by Angela's noticing and feedback enabled them to move forward with their insights: to really pause and reflect each time at each significant moment through the training; sharing the room with Angela; helping them to see the connections; and really noticing what each other was saying:

> So maybe what I experienced were mini peak moments and then a big peak moment. They were pausing, there was a lot they hadn't thought about before, all of them. So that kind of built and built so they were ready in that final moment, to reflect. They were able to flex that muscle that they hadn't really used much before. They were ready to receive my questions. It felt like a peak moment after the culmination of the mini-peaks on the way: a wow feeling of where we are now, as well as a sense of privilege of being there with them.

Throughout our interview, Angela referred to "peak moments" in coaching. These seemed to be little peaks that grew throughout her sessions and culminated in an ephemeral sense of being fully present, with the final peak at the end. We have already mentioned the concept of peak moments, and how McInman and Grove (1991, p. 334) proposed the term be regarded as "a global entity," encompassing the states of peak experience (Maslow, 1964), peak performance, (Privette, 1983) and flow (Csikszentmihalyi, 1990). The big peak moment for Angela was the culmination of mini peaks along the way:

> I felt absorbed in a good way by them and I felt lost in it all in a positive sense, so absorbed in what they were saying and experiencing and just responding without thought, almost. It's like an out of body experience in a way. I'm totally and fully there, nowhere else but fully there. Nothing else is distracting me but there's a contrast in the same moment of being not there at all as myself. They're there, but I'm not conscious of me being there.

Angela is sure that those peak moments really do remain in a truly positive way because of the emotion that is created at the time

> [w]hen you've felt something happen. It's like after a performance in sport or music – it takes a while to calm down afterwards. You want to hold onto those feelings afterwards as you know it's been great.

Angela's experience is reminiscent of Maslow's (1962) assertion that some of the effects or after-effects of a peak experience may be permanent but the high moment itself is not. For Angela, the euphoric feeling lasts as an after-effect:

> I get a feeling of riding away – the feeling lasts, I'm riding this wave effortlessly and I'm feeling good and nourished and fulfilled which means I can just ride this wave and say – isn't this beautiful – so it's easy to be mindful and to notice.

When considering Angela's experiences and her approach to coaching, process-driven coaching is evidently off-limits. She conveys that some people come to her for coaching to improve their performance, which demands action points, often an organisational requirement. In such situations Angela feels restricted as though wearing a straitjacket since her approach is very much about working with the whole person: "it's so fundamental and where the work happens." She thinks of these situations as heart-sink moments, when some coachees stay at the transactional level. In such situations, coachees are reluctant to let down the barriers to share at the deeper level:

> I don't feel peak experiences without that depth. I feel movement, coachees get their actions so performance is improved. But that to me is more like process

coaching and it's all performance based. I think I get glimpses of the possibility of peak moments, but I don't get a peak moment without the depth.

***

Our penultimate participant, **Sorrel Pinder**, is a coach and retired osteopath. She is very familiar with peak experiences but shared how, when she is coaching, she is not aware of her peak experience in that moment: "because if you were, you'd drop out of it." She explains that her peak experiences are felt as

> [a] sort of heart sensation, an expansion of the heart field. It makes me feel delighted, joyful. I don't think I would use the word joyous, but joyful. And it happens in the moment. And it is a "whoosh" feeling, a kind of a glow, a kind of a warmth and a sort of "oof" like when you get goose pimples. It's only momentary, you couldn't make that happen, it's not transactional, rather it involves connectivity. It's that trust you have with your client – in osteopathy and in coaching. And the trust is created through the rapport you've had in the connection.

Sorrel's description of a joyful experience corresponds with Maslow (1971, p. 176) when he describes the peak experience: "the great joy, the ecstasy, the visions of another world, or another level of living."

Sorrel recalls working with a client on Zoom during the Covid-9 pandemic and the feelings she experienced after the call. Her recollection is that she found herself leaning closer to the screen to focus on her client

> and feeling that deep sense of connection and the rapport you need to get that breakthrough with your client. I suppose it's about connection and when I think about that aspect of coaching it takes on a spiritual dimension. It's like a funnel and I focus entirely on my client. I don't have to worry about stuff being in my head because it just isn't. Then I felt as though the back of my head was completely open to the Universe. All the energy and all the insights were coming from that funnel through to me.

Sorrel believes that the right questions just allow clients to see things in a different way and come from the "funnel."

Another word used by Sorrel is channelling. She explains how, in a discussion, even though it might have been rehearsed, other words appear as though from nowhere:

> You just say something completely different, and you think where did that come from? And then you realise that it came from that huge universal wisdom and you hadn't made it up in your head. It's got something to do with channelling and involves all the feelings and non-verbal communication.

When Sorrel describes her thoughts and feelings as channelling or coming from the funnel, she is referring to cosmic consciousness. Similarly, Longhurst

(2006) argued that feelings of connection with others and the universe are "soul" experiences, an explanation that chimes with Maslow's description of a cosmic consciousness experience: "This is a special phenomenological state in which the person somehow perceives the whole cosmos or at least the unity and integration of it and of everything in it, including his Self" (1971, p. 277).

Sorrel maintains that a feeling of flow happened most of the time when she was working as an osteopath. She was not thinking about what she was doing but working unconsciously. She described this skill as "listening with the hands and responding with the treatment." Sorrel explained how she might be talking with her clients, and her hands just knew what to do.

Sorrel also described a peak experience when her three-year-old daughter fell down a spiral staircase and subsequently complained about a headache. She felt the top of her daughter's neck and the bone at the top had shifted a little bit to the left. Her internal dialogue immediately kicked into action: "Just do what you think you need to do," and Sorrel guided the bone further to the left: "It was a real whooshing sensation. The bone re-adjusted itself." Sorrel was absolutely bowled over by the shift and admitted she didn't know if that could be called a peak experience, but it was quite amazing. It was something extraordinary that happened 25 years ago, yet Sorrel remembers it vividly due to the impact it made on her. During this experience, she explained that she was "fully present, connected, fully focussed – and in flow."

We close our participant revelations with an account of a peak experience from Kay, one of the authors. An extraordinary experience happened during a coaching session when working in a triad with two other experienced coaches. They were on a programme to study coaching with neurolinguistic programming. Kay was acting as the coach and asked a question but cannot recall what the question was, nor where it came from. She does, however, remember that it was not premeditated but seemed to emerge in the moment. The person acting as coachee paused, reflected, and a stillness of an intense magnitude was created while she appeared to consider the question. She answered after what seemed like an eternity but, in reality, was probably only seconds. The phenomenon was experienced by all three, including the person acting as the observer:

> We looked at one another in disbelief and amazement. "How did you do that?", the coachee asked. I remember her words distinctly, as it struck me as odd that she asked me how I had created the moment, rather than what had happened there. Perhaps it was the first time she had experienced the phenomenon and therefore she attributed it to me, but it seemed to happen in the moment, when we three were able to "go with the flow." Something occurred that gave a sense of timelessness, silence and stillness, similar to my experiences as a musician.

The Significance of Core Conditions and Peak Experience in This Context

A review of the literature suggested there is very little research on peak experiences in coaching, either for coaches or for their clients. This made our review challenging, and as a result, we examined similar or analogous terms where some research was available. These terms included intuition, critical moments, aha moments, and flow.

Flow, as already discussed, is different from peak experience. However, some authors suggest that a peak experience can happen as a result of being in flow (Weijers, 2021). Similarly, Allen et al. (2008, p. 711) referred to "extraordinary experiences" that comprise "absorbing, flow, *and* peak experiences" (our emphasis), illustrating how flow is often linked to peak experience. This seems to have been the case for Jane and for Sorrel: when truly engaged and connected, something happens in the relationship, there is a moment of connectivity and unity that could be felt as a peak experience.

The experiences of all our participants suggest that for peaks to occur there needs to be a deep, perhaps fundamental, connection in the relationship between coach and client. Jane even talked of coaching "soul to soul," and Christine said her peak experience with one of her supervisees was like "seeing into his soul." Angela also stressed the need to work with the whole person in coaching, to acknowledge emotions and build trust. This depth of understanding is important when seeking peak experience.

As part of the need for connection and depth, all participants advocated being fully present for the client. Sorrel and Christine, for example, suggested that being present and focusing on the client enabled them to funnel or channel themselves and so improve connection. They felt this focus was important and may promote peak experiences. Conversely, they suggested that transactional or process-driven coaching would not be as powerful.

As well as the coach being present for the client, Carmelina also mentioned the need for engagement by the coachee, something that would demonstrate their connection and potentially lead to a peak experience for both coach and coachee. Connectedness involves sensing, and coaches develop heightened sensory acuity that enables them to pick up information to guide the coaching process. As a result of a profound connectedness with the client, a strong relationship is assured, and this makes peak experiences more likely to occur.

A number of core conditions were noted for encouraging peak experiences. These included taking risks in questioning and how feedback is provided; working to ensure presence, openness, and trust in the relationship; and working with the whole person and their emotions and vulnerabilities, as depth and intensity appear important to peak experience.

References

Allen, J., Massiah, C., Cascio, R., & Johnson, Z. (2008). Triggers of extraordinary experiences within a sub-cultural consumption event. *Advances in Consumer Research*, 35, 711–713.
Bachkirova, T., Cox, E., & Clutterbuck, D. (2024). Introduction. In E. Cox, T. Bachkirova, & D. Clutterbuck (Eds.), *The complete handbook of coaching*, 4th edition. London: Sage.
Clancy, A. L., & Binkert, J. (2017). *Pivoting: A coach's guide to igniting substantial change*. New York: Palgrave Macmillan.
Csikszentmihalyi, M. (1990). *Flow: The psychology of optimal experience*. New York, NY: Harper & Row.

De Haan, E. (2008a). "I doubt therefore I coach" – Critical moments in coaching practice. *Consulting Psychology Journal: Practice and Research, 60*(1), 91–105.

De Haan, E. (2008b). "I struggle and emerge" – Critical moments of experienced coaches. *Consulting Psychology Journal: Practice and Research, 60*(1), 106–131.

De Haan, E., Bertie, C., Day, A., & Sills, C. (2010). Critical moments of clients and coaches: A direct comparison study. *International Coaching Psychology Review, 5*(2), 109–128.

De Haan, E., Bertie, C., Day, A., & Sills, C. (2020). Critical moments of clients and coaches: A direct-comparison study. *Coaching Researched: A Coaching Psychology Reader*, 183–204.

Flaherty, J. (2022). *Coaching: Evoking excellence in others*, 3rd edition. Oxford: Elsevier.

Henderson, E. (2016). *Peak experience as an access to inner direction*, Unpublished Masters Dissertation, Process Work Institute, Portland, Oregon.

Honsova, P., & Jarasova, E. (2018). Peak coaching experiences. *Coaching: An International Journal of Theory, Research and Practice, 12*(1), 3–14.

Kets de Vries, M. F. R. (2013). Coaching's "good hour": Creating tipping points. *Coaching: An International Journal of Theory, Research and Practice, 6*(2), 152–175.

Kets de Vries, M. F. R. (2021). Creating "Aha!" Experiences. *The CEO Whisperer: Meditations on Leadership, Life, and Change*, 91–100.

LaRue, L., Mäkikangas, A., & de Bloom, J. (2024). Entrepreneur coaches' flow and wellbeing: The role of recovery. *Coaching: An International Journal of Theory, Research and Practice*, 1–18.

Laws, D. (2020). What use is a critical moment? *Negotiation Journal, 36*(2), 107–126.

Longhurst, L. A. (2006). The "aha" moment in co-active coaching and its effects on belief and behavioural changes. *International Journal of Evidence Based Coaching and Mentoring, 4*(2), 61–73.

Longhurst, L. A. (2010). *The transformational potential of "Aha" moments in life coaching and beyond*. PhD Thesis, Oxford Brookes University.

Maslow, A. H. (1959). Cognition of being in the peak experiences. *The Journal of Genetic Psychology, 94*, 43–66.

Maslow, A. H. (1962). Lessons from the peak-experiences. *Journal of Humanistic Psychology, 2*(9), 9–18.

Maslow, A. H. (1964). *Religions, values and peak experiences*. USA: Stellar Classics.

Maslow, A. H. (1971). *The farthest reaches of human nature*. New York, NY: Penguin.

Mavor, P., Sadler-Smith, E., & Gray, D. E. (2010). Teaching and learning intuition: Some implications for HRD and coaching practice. *Journal of European Industrial Training, 34*(8/9), 822–838.

McBride, B. W. (2013). *Coaching, clients, and competences: How coaches experience the flow state*. PhD Thesis, Fielding Graduate University, USA. Proquest.

McInman, A. D., & Grove, R. G. (1991). Peak moments in sport: A literature review, *Quest, 43*, 333–351.

Moons, J. (2016). A shift in the room – myth or magic? How do coaches create transformational shifts in a short period of time? *International Journal of Evidence Based Coaching and Mentoring*, Special Issue 10, 45–58.

Moore, M., Drake, D., Tschannen-Moran, B., Campone, F., & Kauffman, C. (2005). Relational flow: A theoretical model for the intuitive dance. *Published by the International Coach Federation in the 2005 Coaching Research Symposium Proceedings*.

Murray, E. (2004). Intuitive coaching – summary. *Industrial and Commercial Training, 36*(5), 203–206.

Nash, C., & Collins, D. (2006). Tacit knowledge in expert coaching: Science or art? *Quest, 58*, 465–477.

Polanyi, M. (1966). *The tacit dimension*. Garden City, NY: Doubleday.

Privette, G. (1983). Peak experience, peak performance, and flow: A comparative analysis of positive human experiences. *Journal of Personality and Social Psychology, 45*, 1361–1368.

Rogers, C. (1961). *On becoming a person*. London: Constable & Robinson Limited.
Schön, D. (1987). *Educating the reflective practitioner*. San Francisco: Jossey-Bass.
Sheldon, C. (2018). Trust your gut, listen to reason: How experienced coaches work with intuition in their practice. *International Coaching Psychology Review*, *13*(1), 6–20.
Smith, N., & Hawkins, P. (2023). Transformational coaching. In E. Cox, T. Bachkirova, & D. Clutterbuck (Eds.), *The complete handbook of coaching*, 4th edition. London: Sage.
Spence, G. B. (2007). Further development of evidence-based coaching: Lessons from the rise and fall of the human potential movement. *Australian Psychologist*, *42*(4), 255–265.
Stern, A. (2017). *Sense of place, sense of self*. PhD Dissertation, Saybrook University, Oakland, CA.
van Deurzen-Smith, S. (2014). Creative inspiration and existential coaching. *Existential Analysis: Journal of the Society for Existential Analysis*, *25*(1).
Weijers, K. (2021). *Peak moments: The experience of coaches*. Doctoral Thesis, Oxford Brookes University.
Weijers, K. (2022). Peak moments: The experience of coaches. *International Journal of Evidence Based Coaching and Mentoring*, Special Issue 16, 159–172.
Whitmore, J. (2002). *Coaching for performance: GROWing people, performance and purpose*, 3rd edition. London: Nicholas Brealey.
Wilson, C. (2009). *Super consciousness: The quest for the peak experience*. London: Watkins Publishing.

10 Peak Experience in Extreme Sport and High-Risk Leisure

Introduction

Peak experiences in sporting and wilderness challenges have been discussed in earlier chapters, but here we are concerned with the link between peak experience and the drives for risk-taking in similar but more extreme settings. Lester (2004), who undertook psychological research with mountaineers, identified a variety of distinguishing features of extreme sport, such as its non-competitive ethic, periods of isolation leading potentially to contemplation, varying degrees of discomfort, plus its thrill seeking and risk-taking elements. Our focus is also prompted by Kohl's (2014) study of high-risk and extreme-risk athletes who have reported more transcendent experiences than lower-risk athletes.

The term "extreme sport" appears to be almost as ambiguous as the term peak experience, with Brymer (2009, p. 6) explaining how the term has become "a descriptor for a multitude of non-traditional, independent and organised alternative sports." Unsurprisingly, this broad definition encompasses an array of seemingly dissimilar high-risk undertakings that include activities requiring high levels of training, personal skills, and commitment, such as "BASE jumping, rope free climbing and waterfall kayaking" (Brymer, 2009, p. 6), as well as activities that, arguably, require less participant skill or previous knowledge, such as canoeing or rafting, trekking, or bungee jumping.

Linking Maslow's idea of peak experience to risk-related activity, Brymer and Oades (2009, p. 115) posit that "certain events that bring us nearer to the reality of our deaths are positive life-changing experiences." Brymer (2009, p. 7) also explains how a peak experience does not necessarily involve peak performance. He says, "peak experiences are joyful events *without superior behaviour* which are characterised by altered perceptions of time and space, floating and flying, calm and stillness and self-validation amongst other experiences."

Senecal (2021) includes contact sports in the extreme sport range, contending that although contact sports like football, boxing, hockey, or wrestling are not typically defined under the heading of extreme sports, this could be seen as an arbitrary divide attributable to the "team nature versus individual nature of these sports" (2021, p. 297). Kunwar (2021) similarly observes that the term *extreme* sport seems to be used interchangeably with *high-risk* sport in much of the literature.

DOI: 10.4324/9781003509219-11

Both high-risk and extreme sport are defined as any sport where there is potential for death or severe injury as an inherent part of the activity.

The terminology used to describe peak experiences in extreme sport and other risk-taking activities varies too. Boudreau et al. (2022), for example, recognised that the study of optimal psychological states, such as peak experience, has been complicated by researchers using terms interchangeably. Buckley (2012) reported that there are at least 50 previous studies of participant motivations in the context of adventure tourism and recreation and identified at least 14 different categories of motivation, including thrill with its attendant excitement and adrenaline rush, fear and the challenge of overcoming it, and control, which enables the physical and mental domination of one's body.

Buckley (2012, p. 963) explained rush as one "particular kind of excitement associated with the physical performance of a specific adventure activity." Using an autoethnographic research approach, he differentiated "rush" from flow and peak experience and concluded that rush is a variety of thrill that, although involving flow, is quite distinct (2012). He explained how the concept of rush refers to the "simultaneous experience of thrill and flow associated with the successful performance of an adventure activity at a high level of skill" (2012, p. 963). One of the distinctions Buckley makes between peak experiences and rush is connected to temporality: peak experience is rarer and recognised only retrospectively, whereas rush is recognised and referred to by participants as a "very concrete physiological and psychological sensation which they can and do look forward to" (2012, p. 964).

Another concept related to rush or thrill in this context is "edgework," which can be defined as the boundary between safety and the constant threat to physical or mental well-being brought about by extreme activities. The edge in "edgework" is symbolic of "life versus death, consciousness versus unconsciousness, sanity versus insanity, an ordered sense of self and environment versus a disordered self and environment" (Lyng, 1990, p. 857). For Buckley (2012, p. 964), the concept of edgework involves people who "like to see how close they can get to death but still escape."

In the extreme contexts identified for discussion in this chapter, as well as peak experience or flow, we find transcendence, challenge, and other context-related vocabulary in evidence. For example, the term "being stoked" is frequently used to describe the high achieved in surfing (Stranger, 1999). We begin the chapter by reviewing previous research undertaken in a variety of environments. Following this, we present accounts of peak and similar experiences from participants who have been engaged in risky pursuits. Finally, we draw together some observations of our own in our concluding section.

Review of Previous Research

Our review of literature has suggested three elemental modalities where extreme sport and risk-taking mainly occur: (1) earth-bound pursuits such as rock and mountain climbing, mountain biking, and polar exploration; (2) air-inspired activities such as skydiving and space travel; and (3) water-driven quests like white-water rafting or surfing. It should be noted that, in each of these contexts, references to peak experience are few and that, the main focus has been on the feelings associated with other optimal experiences such as flow, transcendence, or peak performance.

Mountaineering, Rock Climbing, Mountain Biking, Polar Exploration

In his unpublished journals, John Muir (in Wolfe, 1938) described how mountaineers frequently recount peak experience as arousal. In climbing, he explains, there is danger and whilst natural beauty may be all around "all attention has to be given [to] the ground step by step." This focus on the activity itself may preclude peak experience, but, as Muir argues, such focused care and attention is not without advantages:

> Compared with the alertness of the senses and corresponding precision and power of the muscles on such occasions, one may be said to sleep all the rest of the year. The mind and body remain awake for some time after the dangerous ground is past, so that arriving on the summit with the grand outlook all the world spread below one is able to see it better, and brings to the feast a far keener vision, and reaps richer harvests than would have been possible ere the presence of danger summoned him to life.
>
> (1938, p. 36)

Boudreau et al. (2022) researched optimal psychological states in advanced climbers and found outdoor climbing was the preferred context for experiencing such states. Similar to Muir, they noted that the "diverse possibilities for action in nature . . . create conditions in which participants may be more absorbed, immersed in the moment, and attentive to what they are doing" (2022, p. 10).

Similarly, in their research, Reid and Kampman (2020, p. 8) found that expeditionary adventures, including extreme long-distance running, walking, cycling, or sailing, allowed participants to "truly become their whole selves and self-actualise." The experiences provided "stimulus for adaptation and peak life challenges that enhance resilience" helping participants to develop adaptive systems and coping behaviours. Reid and Kampman further argued that during extreme adventures, learning and growth are intensified and that such adventures serve as "significant peak experiences that enable post-adventure growth: accelerating development towards realising one's own full potential in self-actualisation" (2020, p. 8).

In his mixed methods study, Stranger (1999) explained that at the most challenging levels, people report experiencing a *transcendence* of self where they felt at one with the mountain, the clouds, the rays of the sun. Citing Csikszentmihalyi (1988, pp. 33–34), he repeats the idea that "the mountaineer does not climb in order to reach the top of the mountain, but tries to reach the summit in order to climb." The goal is really just an excuse to make the elevated, transcendent experience possible.

Vogler (2012) conducted semi-structured interviews with 13 participants who had a history of outdoor recreation in activities such as rock climbing, white-water rafting, and mountaineering and found a positive correlation between peak experiences in outdoor recreation and self-actualisation. He found that both rock-climbers and white-water kayakers described risk as a significant factor in their peak experiences because it forced them to be more focused. Findings suggested there were several precursors or triggers to peak experience, including "some form of discomfort, challenge, risk, physical exertion, flow, and natural beauty in a social group" (2012, p. ii). In addition, through the boost of confidence generated by their peak experience, participants revealed a shift in their understanding of self-actualisation.

Taylor and Carr's (2021, p. 11) research indicated that whilst flow experiences were not of primary importance for mountain bikers, they were a welcome by-product of the activity that confirmed to them they had "achieved levels of mastery through commitment to their sport." They explained how participants frequently commented on the buzz or thrill of mountain bike riding. However, very few described how such moments were accompanied by the unconscious control over their actions that is so essential to the flow experience. In some cases, in fact, the converse was true. One participant even suggested that "the thrill in downhill biking comes from fast flowing, being in control." So, while thrill and rush are commonplace while riding, "flow may remain an elusive phenomenon" (2021, p. 9).

Dodson (1996) also researched peak experiences among mountain bikers describing how it promotes a sense of freedom as well as being an absorbing, intense, and physically challenging activity where riders are "constantly faced with opportunities for self-discovery through the testing of mental and physical limits" (1996, p. 317). For riders to achieve such states of riding-freedom, she explained, riders endure gruelling rides and push their bodies beyond normal limits.

Additionally, Dodson highlighted how mountain biking, like other extreme leisure activities (e.g., river rafting or skydiving) provides opportunities for people to achieve peak experiences. Citing Privette (1983), Dodson explains how a peak experience is characterised as "a transformational experience and one that surpasses the usual level of intensity, meaningfulness, and richness," leading to feelings of "joy and self-fulfillment (e.g., the transcendent sense of awe and achievement upon reaching the summit of a ride)" (1996, p. 317). Such an experience, Dodson confirmed leaves a lasting impression requiring riders to

> display clear focus, complete absorption, loss of self-awareness, personal integration with the world or object, personal control and mastery, awareness of personal power, heightened emotion, spontaneity, freedom from everyday cares, and a sense of achievement.
>
> (1996, p. 317)

Dodson (1996, p. 317) draws on a range of literature that further suggests a defining characteristic of peak experience is an intensification of self that is can be characterised by

> increased self-confidence, discovery of internal strength, personal growth in attitudes and feelings, a general sensation of learning more about yourself,

increased ability to believe in yourself, and an overall feeling of rejuvenation and exhilaration (even when physically exhausted).

Dodson also found an interesting connection between the manifestation of a peak experience and the incorporation of the bike, and the activity of biking, into what might be called "the extended self" (1996, p. 317). This intensification of self, Dodson argued, is evident in many leisure activities, particularly where equipment is necessary. Besides mountain bikes, other examples are "rafting equipment, parachutes, motorcycles, or off-road vehicles" (p. 317). In such settings, it seems the equipment becomes intimately involved in the experience and connected with the emotions attached to any peak experience achieved. Objects, like the bike, subsequently become associated with the peak experience and may also become "valued for their potential to lead to subsequent peak experiences" (p. 317).

Finally, in this section, we note that Smith et al.'s (2017) research focused mainly on land-based extreme environments such as polar expeditions. They used four groups of participants: mountaineers, military personnel, Antarctic over-winterers, and Mars simulation participants. Participants in each of the groups identified self-direction, stimulation, and universalism, which they defined as "having an understanding and appreciation for the welfare of people and nature" (2017, p. 141), as important to them, and these aspects were subsequently considered useful for functioning in challenging environments. Smith et al. explained how the extent to which personal value motives, such as universalism, might be generalised across extreme environments since "these settings share similarities with the conditions experienced during space missions, including confinement, isolation and limited possibilities for evacuation" (2017, p. 137).

Space Exploration, Skydiving

Suedfeld et al. (2010) reviewed 125 astronaut autobiographies, interviews, and oral histories to analyse their references to values. They found that value references showed a high degree of concern with individualism, achievement, and enjoyment, but self-direction was ranked the highest. After returning to earth, the astronauts also showed increased concern with transcendence (a combination of universalism and spirituality), and there appeared to be a "broadened set of references to values oriented toward the collective good" (2010, p. 1411). In particular, it was noted that, more than male participants, the females in the study saw spaceflight as "a peak experience that would not be equalled afterward" (p. 1422).

In their study of a long-term simulation of a manned flight to Mars, Šolcová et al. (2016) examined how crew members described their experiences during simulation. Two weeks after the end of isolation, interviews were used to understand the important experiences of crew members during their period of living and working in isolation. They were asked to describe the "peak experience, nadir experience, turning points, important scenes and challenges and other narrative moments that create a story of a simulated flight to Mars" (2016, p. 178). Thematic analysis then showed the times participants felt most uplifted and what they would call a peak experience: celebrations, video messages from significant others, and the simulated Mars landing itself. It seems the turning points were particularly connected to the Mars episode: "The peak experience was Mars, because there was a lot of attention and we had to put in some really good work" (2016, p. 182).

Lipscombe (1999) explored the experiences of skydivers, comparing them with combinations of Maslow's peak experience characterisations. Using a qualitative methodology, he determined the relevance of peak experiences for influencing continued involvement in skydiving. Qualitative data was collected and analysed to understand more about veterans' skydiving experiences. The findings indicated the frequency and significance of peak experiences to the skydivers and the importance of the experience for ongoing participation. Data also showed a similarity across all respondents, suggesting that peak experiences are a frequent experience among skydivers: "So rewarding was the peak that it represented the most important factor explaining why veteran skydivers continued to jump" (1999, p. 267).

Lipscombe (1999, p. 268) also shared how the "exhilaration of the free-fall, the relaxation, the peace and tranquillity, the silence of the parachute ride, and the physical beauty of the landscapes" create indescribable feelings that skydivers consider unique to the activity of skydiving. According to Lipscombe (1999, p. 281), the skydiving experience goes beyond the usual everyday experience of the recreationist:

> The experience, while producing frequent moments that are often indescribable, provided lasting periods of intense emotional uplift referred to by respondents as a buzz, a body rush, a high, an adrenalin charge, moments of wonder, of bliss, and something very special to the skydiver, that produces a desire to repeat the experience.

Lipscombe described the skydiving experience as a form of high-risk recreation that encapsulates numerous peak experience qualities. There is an acceptance that, during the jump, the attendant fear and anxiety sets the stage for peak experiences to happen:

> The risk may play a substantial role, not only in the continued desire to participate in the activity, but may also contribute to the peak experience feeling, characterizations which are reported as part of every jump.
> (Lipscombe, 1999, pp. 281–282)

Despite Maslow's assertion that peak experiences are momentary and rare, once-in-a-lifetime experiences, Lipscombe (1999, p. 283) found that skydiving "provided veteran skydivers with frequent peak experiences, and therefore, an expectation that the experience would repeat itself with each jump."

Participants in Lipscombe's study further reported that peak experiences had qualities that lasted beyond the time of the jump. He therefore concluded that in terms of understanding the nature of the peak experience as a concept, it may be that in challenging and extremely stimulating activities, such as skydiving, there are degrees of peak intensity which may "potentially elevate emotional and physical functioning over a longer period of time" (1999, p. 283).

Kayaking and Rafting, Sailing and Surfing

When discussing transcendence as liberation, Fletcher (2007, pp. 143–144) described in graphic detail one of his own peak experiences whilst kayaking a particularly dangerous stretch of river involving many tricky waterfalls and drops. This key kayaking event prompted him to examine the experience from a philosophical perspective. Transcendence, as he discusses throughout, could be viewed as an example of what Foucault called a limit-experience – one where "the subject reaches decomposition, leaves itself, at the limit of its own possibility" (Foucault, 1991, p. 48).

Fletcher continued to explain transcendence as inaccessible to conscious knowledge and only conceptualised in retrospect – and even then, "can only approximate the ineffable, visceral nature of the experience itself" (2007, p. 144). Recognising the difficulty of definition, he decided to examine what transcendence is not, rather than what it is, concluding that transcendence appears to defy all "standard social theory models for describing human behavior" (2007, p. 156) and that we might describe it simply as the end of constraint:

> In a state of transcendence, the subject is liberated, if only temporarily, from power and resistance, from discourse and rationality, from both social structures and self-conscious individuality as well.
>
> (2007, p. 156)

From experiences such as skydiving, Fletcher (2007) infers that risk plays a key role in the transcendent feelings accompanying peak experiences. He explains how athletes frequently claim experiences of transcendence "make them feel truly 'alive' in a way they do not in the course of everyday existence." One extreme kayaker, for instance, shared that when running whitewater, "It's the only time I really feel alive" (Fletcher, 2007, p. 146).

Earlier, Arnould et al. (1999) also reported the transformative aspects of whitewater river rafting. As well as participant observations, 15 in-depth interviews were conducted with experienced river guides in the United States. Arnould et al. then discuss the conditions that make a magical rafting experience possible and how such river magic is connected to the relationship between humans and the world: "It serves to restructure and integrate the minds and emotions of the actors" (1999, p. 33). The term river magic was seen as capturing the enduring experience of rafting, helping to convey

> the reverence and mystery sometimes associated with rafting experiences and the considerable emotional content that makes them easy to recall, long lasting in effects, but difficult to describe. We called the experience transformative.
>
> (1999, p. 34)

These authors also found that changes in emotional orientation to the river prepared people to experience transcendence and transformation and so "initiate the transformation process." In an interview with one river guide, this double effect is evident as he recounts how they come to see it as a real spirit:

> The tuning down to a slower mode, a "being free from time" . . . signals a readiness to experience transcendence and indicates that clients have entered a liminal state where they are ready to experience significant change.
>
> (1999, p. 41)

Arnould et al. (1999, p. 41) noted that references to "slow time" or "river time" are used by participants to refer to an "an altered consciousness and appreciation of the river environment."

The sense of awe, evoked by the experience of river rafting, is captured in a number of quotes from Arnould et al.'s participants: they said that the river was "vital in putting me back in touch with my priorities"; "wild, continuous, alive"; "high, fast, exciting and beautiful" (1999, p. 44).

More recently, Tavel et al. (2022) explored how Maslow's concept of peak experience can be used to elicit a deeper understanding of heightened states of lived experience. Their extreme research context was the risky crossing of the Indian Ocean for a crew on board a historic sailing ship. They used semi-structured, "Sail Story Interviews" (2022, p. 99) to understand various types of peak experience that emerged, as participants reacted to the external or internal challenges experienced during the voyage. Fifteen crew members took part in the study and shared positive emotions of "joy, excitement, great happiness, or even deep inner peace" (2022, p. 99).

In Tavel et al.'s study, peak experiences are presented in the context of similar concepts, such as plateau experience, flow, and peak performance, with the authors suggesting that these varieties of peak experience "do not depend on the challenges themselves, but on the *responses* to them" (2022, p. 101). For example, they describe one participant's peak experience as a feeling of unity, a feeling often present in explanations of peak experience:

> I guess the peak experience was climbing the mast, going out to the back, I stayed up there for about three-quarters of an hour and about an hour alone in the bow. I liked that, I felt at one with the universe. Just peace, an amazing experience.
>
> (Anne, in Tavel et al., 2022, p. 103)

They call attention to the difference between Anne's experience and the accounts of other crew members, recognising sophistication and reflexivity in her narrative. In the other accounts, Tavel et al. found what they call "excited marvelling and a feeling of happiness," whereas Anne's experience is seen as characterised by reflection and detachment "expressed by the rather abstract term 'unity with the universe'" (2022, p. 104).

Watson and Parker (2015, p. 270) point out that in other extreme sports such as surfing, participants talk about their "communion with nature," describing feelings of "oneness with the environment" and "loss of self in the activity." They explain that the Holy Grail of surfing is when a surfer is "barrelled" inside a cylindrical shaped wave. The authors then give the example of one "soul surfer" who explained barrelling as a time when man and board are "as a centaur riding the waves" and that for a short spell all three (surfer, board, and wave) "unite with a sense of oneness and identification . . . a complete integration of man's natural body and spirit with the violent forces of nature in the most total and satisfying way possible" (Watson & Parker, 2015, p. 270).

Interestingly, Stranger (1999) explained that what Elias and Dunning (1986) called the catharsis of "collective effervescence" achieved at sporting events is missing in the high-risk context, since "risk-taking leisure is typically an individualistic pursuit and spectators are not a necessary component" (1999, p. 265). He further argues that the fundamental individualism, and the orientation towards danger in high-risk leisure, "does not fit the model of modern, rational sport" (1999, p. 266). This suggests to us that the triggers for peak experience will differ too, with "rational" or competitive sport relying more on the emotional energy and stimulation provided by the audience and the competition with others.

Stranger planned his research to explore the importance of the thrill and fear that surfers experience. Using his 30-year experience as a surfer and a mixed methods research design, he collected data during a 10-month field trip of surfing locations in Australia. His findings suggested that inherent in the thrill involved in surfing is the experience of self-transcendence; indeed, 81 percent of Stranger's respondents indicated that thrill was their "impetus for surfing" (1999, p. 267) and is what motivated them to continue:

> Some of the most experienced surfers reported that, although they could still find satisfaction in smaller waves, the thrill achieved was not as intense. The desire to replicate these intense thrills results in the search for larger, more challenging waves.
>
> (Stranger, 1999, p. 267)

Stranger argued that inherent in the orientation of risk in surfing is the chase for the thrill of self-transcendence: "Risk is simply a very effective catalyst for reaching these transcendent states" (1999, p. 273). Further, he argued, the peak experience for the surfer is ecstatic and intrinsically rewarding. He described accounts of the nature of the thrill in risk-taking, emphasising the ecstatic feelings of "oneness with the environment, the loss of self in the activity, and an intense awareness of the moment" (1999, p. 268).

Chapter 4 of Stranger's (2017) book *Surfing Life* also discusses the nature and significance of the embodied experience in surfing. Risk-taking is examined in detail, and the thrill of surfing is depicted as producing a transcendence similar to Maslow's (1969) descriptions:

The result of an intensity of focus upon the wave and the bodily interaction with it (which is itself a response to the subjective perception of the risk/difficulty involved) [is] such that surfers lose any sense of distinction between their selves and their immediate environment in an ecstatic transcendence of self.

(Stranger, 2017, pp. 13–14)

Interestingly, Stranger also found that accomplished surfers experience self-transcendence in less challenging surf. For these surfers, he says, "the sensual experience of surfing appears to trigger the communion learnt in higher risk encounters, and so appreciation of the sublime in nature need not involve images of awesome power or fear" (2017, p. 14). Thus, inherent in surfers' interactions with the ocean, there is a fusion between fear and desire that stimulates ecstatic transcendent experiences. Watson and Parker speak of how mountaineers and surfers experience what might be called "signals of transcendence . . . within the human condition," which can be seen as a "primal longing for something infinitely greater than self, a yearning, however, that is oft buried deep in the caverns of the mind" (2015, pp. 276–277).

Peak Experience in Context

The first of our four participants is an experienced skydiver, **Mary-lou Barratt**, who is the Chair of the Council for British Skydiving. She has completed over 500 BASE jumps and over ten years of competitive skydiving.

Mary-lou recalled for us one of her first peak experiences in about 1992 at 3,500 feet above the Kent countryside. She explained how a day of intense training and a good deal of nervous anticipation led up to that peak experience: "the moment of leaving the aircraft in flight, that surreal threshold moment of projecting my body out of the open door and into the void." She had followed her instructor's directions and had put on all the equipment, boarded the aircraft with all its seats removed and was sitting by the door, nervous and excited, but not really sure she'd be able to do it. Then she described how when they got to the right altitude the aircraft stopped climbing, flew level, and the instructor opened the sliding door on the side of the aircraft: "and then motioned for me to shuffle into the space where the door had been. The instructor shouted 'GO' and I committed to the moment and went." She described the experience in more detail, confirming it as

> intense, overwhelming, sublime, ludicrous fragment of a moment – an absolute commitment made by leaving all that was solid and pushing my body into a space where it was in contact with nothing but the flow of air. It was a breath-taking shift in reality, a stretching of time and a simultaneous compression and expansion of my being, an awakening. My existence as a mere speck and as connected with the whole beautiful universe were both so clear. I felt so very insignificant but at the same time powerful, unstoppable, incredible and vibrant.

Mary-lou moreover admitted that she still finds it really difficult to put the experience and the feelings it evokes into words: "when I do it just seems to sound so unbelievably corny and pretentious." So she usually avoids describing it to anyone who doesn't also have these experiences.

She also observed the transient and unpredictable nature of peak experience:

> It seems quite significant that I can't anticipate these feelings or engineer situations in which they happen. I can't hold onto them in their entirety. They just seem to occasionally appear of their own accord. I just stay open to the possibility of these life-enriching experiences through activities such as extreme sports and meditation and occasionally, randomly they happen.

When asked what were the physical sensations that accompanied the peak experience, Mary-lou described it as

> a stillness, a quietness that merged physical and mental sensations. Perhaps as a peacefulness enhanced by the fact that I had an intense sensory awareness – of ears searching for sounds, my heart beating, my blood pumping and my skin sweating in the face of peril and beauty. In the experience itself all my senses were sharpened, bringing a freshness and clarity. I think that sharpening is comparable to the physical sensations the moments after a huge downpour of rain has stopped and the colours and smells are so vibrant and the world just seems incredible and you just stand still and breathe the whole environment in and out again – just a much more intense version.

We then asked Mary-lou how the peak experience has changed her and made her feel different about herself:

> I believe the experience has had a significant impact on the shape my life has taken. It opened my eyes to the possibilities available to me and made me feel full of power and excitement to take on more challenges, a kind of realisation that anything is possible if you want it enough but also an enduring sense of joy in the moment and in small sensations.

Also, Mary-lou explained how further peak experiences have generated the same feelings. She says that in essence they are always the same, but she finds quite hard to put it into words:

> [S]omething along the lines of a powerful vibrant moment of enlivening in which time becomes malleable and smallness and greatness flow and merge in an incredible swirl. For those moments, nothing else matters, there is only the moment and the flow of feelings. Sometimes this has made me momentarily shake, or become immobile or voiceless, but not always. Sometimes the vibrations fade very quickly, sometimes traces of them reverberate for

days after an experience. I can even vividly recall traces of some of them many years later.

She also explained how peak experiences have led her not to take the mundane or the obvious as all there is but to seek more significant challenges and be confident that she has the emotional and physical resources to deal with them. When she has encountered such challenges, the experiences have given her something to fall back on. Over time they have helped her become resilient and keep things in perspective: "I become someone who is joyful, not held back by obstacles, someone who actively embraces challenges, tests my own boundaries and always seeks the edge."

We asked whether her peak experiences have resulted in changes in motivation or helped solve problems, and she described how problem-solving is a key part of her life these days and how her very high level of drive and enthusiasm enables her to accomplish things that initially seem out of reach. She believes this all comes from having had these experiences and that these experiences give her additional resources, particularly in terms of energy, focus, equanimity, and resilience.

Mary-lou has also had peak experiences in other settings such as during BASE jumping or when mountaineering alone, and sometimes during Vipassana meditation. But she shared how skydiving brings an interesting overlapping of nature and sport – an intersection in which she has had several such experiences. For example, she recalled an experience while flying inside a cloud and in essence becoming entirely invisible,

> quite literally disappearing from the world and dissipating into atoms while knowing I'm being gifted something unique and exceptional, and another while flying above an incredible cumulus cloud and seeing my shadow in the centre of a Brocken Spectre, and several while flying my parachute above mountains and also while absorbing the colours of a setting sun or a moody skyscape.

Mary-lou's peak experiences in other contexts seemed to generate similar kinds of feelings, but she says, "they all involve a particular sense of breathing, a shift in the nature of time, a simultaneous sense of greatness and insignificance, an overwhelming peacefulness." She recalled a pivotal experience that she sees as the starting point for an adult life that embraces risk and challenge:

> I was 13 and on a visit to a castle. My family and I were making our way around walkways that hugged the very tall walls, the floors inside had fallen away. . . . At the highest level of the walkway, I just stopped and was held captive by the idea of leaving the edge, the imagining of it brought incredible feelings of power and peace. This wasn't about harming myself; it was very much about experiencing the space, the letting go and trusting the space. It was something that I found very hard to have words for, it was pretty much impossible to articulate the experience and I didn't know what to make of it so I just held it inside.

Mary-lou explained to us how this experience sparked her curiosity about the sensations and feelings that, at the time, she had experienced but couldn't name. She believes it is this that led her to skydiving, and then BASE jumping and mountaineering, and also to meditation.

Mary-lou has always loved being outdoors in "rugged conditions," among trees, mountains, and even storms, and finds types of extreme risk-management extremely compelling and rewarding, as they make her feel capable and connected. Pursuing extreme sport activities enables her to achieve things that seem entirely beyond her reach, the stuff of dreams. They enable her to push herself and test what she is capable of, to face extreme challenges, and deal with high-level fear and failure. Through extreme sport activities, she says, she is able to "go beyond the everyday, to see the world in different ways, to feel and see the extraordinary."

***

Our next participant, **Sean**, is a rock climber in his leisure time. He began by describing his first peak experience which occurred when he was 20. On returning from the French Alps, he remembered how the alpine meadows were so perfect and beautiful, but how he was so busy climbing when he was there that he hadn't fully appreciated it:

> But when I was walking down my street after getting back, after all the planes, trains, buses and everything about getting home. . . . I just remember I felt unbelievably happy, fulfilled and satisfied. I'd never felt it that intensely before.

Sean described how he had climbed quite hard when he was there and had performed physically. He thought the peak experience came because of the emotions surrounding this endeavour and because he had just turned 20 as well. He was aware of becoming more of a man and remembered that he felt so happy. However, the experience was tinged with sadness:

> I remember the pure joy of just feeling amazingly, unbelievably fulfilled, satisfied, and happy in life because I'd just had that experience walking down the street and then it was followed immediately by "it's only down from here." You know you can't feel like this forever, so you're gonna fall and that kind of tainted it.

When we asked Sean how he feels when reaching the top of a climb, he explained:

> [W]hen you've worked for months or years . . . and you've really focused all your time and energy into getting in shape to do the climb and learning the climb. Then you get to the top and you've finished it and there's the feeling of satisfaction that you've managed to master it. But at the same time you almost immediately think that the second you step off the wall, you'll think "so what now?"

Peak Experience in Extreme Sport and High-Risk Leisure 235

Also, Sean considers that his peak experiences in this context involve the "challenge of seeing if I can overcome myself." He explains how the engagement with the climb enables this:

> [S]ometimes it can just be the experience of the movement on the rock. It can be really poetic. I don't how to explain it. It's when you're really in touch with nature, when you're kind of flowing with it or moving through the rock. It's almost like you've got this bond with nature and with the wall and everything.

He explained how a peak experience happens when he has overcome his fears of how dangerous the challenge might be and shared how some climbs are a mental challenge whereas other climbs are just purely physical: "and then it's the challenge of seeing if I'm good enough or if I can make myself good enough to do that bit of rock." He explained the physical feelings accompanying those experiences and how when doing a climb, he almost does not notice it because he has trained so hard:

> You're just kind of in flow at the point you're doing it and so you're not conscious of thinking . . . you've stopped trying to think about it and you're just doing it.

Sean then recounted a time when he'd been in flow during a climb and dropped out of it at the worst point. He was at the top of a quite hard and quite dangerous grade climb, with no ropes

> and I got to a move where you can't back down. I had reached up to the very last hold. And to actually get your fingers on the top, you have to fall backwards a bit to get the extension of your arm. But there's no coming back from it. Your arm should extend enough that you can get your fingers over the top, but if you missed it, you're going backwards and you've got no ropes.

He got to the move that he'd practised and rehearsed, but still he knew there was a margin of error:

> The conditions were right, the temperature was right. And I got up and I got into the move and I was relaxed. I was just flowing through it. And then I'm just about to do the last move and just stopped. If I'd done it, if I'd moved, I'm pretty ninety-nine percent sure I would've got it and I would've done the climb, but I stopped just as I was in flow and I just dropped out. And I started to think, and as soon as I did that, my body sagged. And then I knew I couldn't do the move because my body wasn't in the right position. So then I was stuck in the move. I was stuck right at the top of a climb with no ropes on a move that I couldn't get down from.
>
> And I just remember thinking, "oh, crap." And quickly got my hand down onto a bit of an edge. But I couldn't get down, I couldn't back up – I just

remember that both my feet slipped at that point. And then I think I just shut my eyes because I thought, "this is it." But then the next thing within a split second, I was hanging, I had one hand on top of the other, holding it down, and I'd obviously just slipped and just grabbed it. And then I got my feet back on the wall in this new position. I'd used so much energy doing that, and I can't believe I held it. It's like, because otherwise there's a big boulder at the bottom of the climb, which I would've landed on, on my back.

Fortuitously, Sean had a friend at the bottom who offered to run up and drop a rope down. But he told him, "I can't hang on" and asked him to just to put the rope up to the grass verge over to one side, and then he jumped sideways where the ground was slightly higher and the fall would be less: "And when I did it, I remember thinking, I'm absolutely one hundred percent going to break both legs doing this, but it's better than breaking my back. So, I did it, I did the jump."

Luckily, despite wet grass there was enough ground, and Sean hadn't broken anything. He remembered that the whole thing was so intense and never did a dangerous climb after that.

> I couldn't because I'd thought that was my last chance. You get a chance, I think, to learn where your limits are and you think that's the time to stop doing dangerous climbs. I don't know if that is a peak experience, but it's one that I've never forgotten. Never will forget. Yes. I suppose it kind of is, it's up there with peak experiences, but it's a different type of experience.

For Sean, this negative or "nadir" experience was important. Maslow (1964, 1968) acknowledged that nadir experiences could be equally as psychologically important as peak experiences. He argued that suffering can have beneficial effects and that more attention should be given to nadir effects since they have a close and possibly symbiotic relationship with peak experience. Taylor (2013) also noted that psychological turmoil can trigger, what he terms, awakening experiences.

After his climbing friends moved to Sheffield, Sean found himself climbing on his own, spending days on his own at the crags and limestone overhangs, training hard, but in the woods, surrounded by nature. Later, after he had children he did not get to go climbing, yet when his stress levels were high in his mind, he would go back to being alone climbing at the crags. He explained how, out there, he was totally present because he had nothing to distract him. He was just climbing and thinking about how to process a move. He shared how reflecting on those moments and thinking about what he had achieved sometimes gives him a retrospective peak experience.

Maslow (1968, p. 103) claimed that when people have a peak experience they are "most their identities, closest to their real selves, most idiosyncratic." He thus aligned peak experiences with acute identity experiences, arguing this is where people feel more at peace, more integrated and synergistic, and have less internal friction. Certainly, Sean emphasised how climbing is at his core: he confirmed that it was the first thing that had given him peak experiences and was the reason why he gravitates towards it. Certainly, when asked how he would describe himself, Sean admitted he would not define himself by his job:

> I'd say a rock climber. Even if I've not climbed for 10 years, I'd still say I'm a rock climber because it's such a part of my identity – when I go to the Lakes, for example, as soon as I can see mountains . . . it reminds me of who I am.

***

Our next participant **Mike Hopkins** is a Welsh mountaineer, rock climber, and expert mountain guide. He fell in love with the outdoors as a young man walking over Exmoor, the Brecon Beacons, and playing rugby. Mountaineering took off for him after injuries prevented him from playing rugby, filling the void for outdoor action. Then he "got the bug." He qualified as a leadership climbing instructor working with groups, corporate teams, youth offenders, and expeditions for the Duke of Edinburgh awards. After 35 years of climbing, he decided to stretch himself and tackle Kilimanjaro, Mount Elbrus in the Caucuses, and Aconcagua in South America. Mike confessed that

> I fell in love with the physical challenge, and the feeling I got when I reached a summit. My mind became very clear, and I felt an enormous peace. I don't know if that is a peak experience, but it was an unforgettable feeling of elation and being at one with myself and the mountain.

Risk is experienced differently for mountaineers and those indulging in other high-risk activities. Mike relishes how he feels at the top of the mountain, enjoying the risk and valuing it as part of the whole experience: "it's like an addiction. Once the buzz is felt, you want to experience that again."

We asked Mike if the fight, flight, or freeze paradigm came into play, the primal urge that produces cortisol and adrenaline in the bloodstream. Mike said this applied more to rock climbing and explained:

> Rock-climbs are graded and if you attempted a climb above your grade you got a huge rush; often it felt very scary but when it came off there was such an adrenaline rush.

He then talked about peak experience and his recollection of sensing something extraordinary while in a risky situation. He said he had many experiences to share, the first being during a trip to Nepal with a special needs team, individuals with disabilities and some with Down's syndrome. One particular participant, Andrew, was allocated to Mike. They made it up to base camp which was truly special. Mike felt a tremendous sense of pride in helping Andrew achieve his goal and said the sense of happiness that spread over Andrew's face was memorable and something he will never forget.

Mike spoke about what, if any, core conditions made a compatible climbing partnership. Was there connectivity, creativity, trust, or simply the love of being in nature and out on the mountains? Could it be the preparation undertaken beforehand? "Yes," he responded, "it's in the preparation and managing the risk. When we climbed in the Alps you'd use the three textures of snow, ice and rock – it was about finding *something* that I felt, as a team, we could do successfully."

We asked him about the "*something*" and he explained:

> In the mountains you're graded . . . but it's your own interpretation of the guidebooks. There is no test involved, just a description of the condition of the route you may be taking. For example, there could be layers of snow prone to avalanche with ice layers in between; crevices and land slips, the clothing you wear, your reading of the conditions and even how you're feeling, getting up at the crack of dawn, climbing at night with only head torches. These are all the "something" elements. These "somethings" are all intrinsic to the success of the climb, avoiding risk in the preparation towards achieving success.

As far as his climbing career is concerned, Mike thought standing on the summit of Mont Blanc for the first time was extra special too:

> We were only three climbers, but we put up the Welsh flag and took a photograph. The feeling of achievement, pride and joy was immense, not only on the summit but on returning home and feeling pride in our achievement which gave us credibility within our community. This gave us a huge buzz.

Expanding on the sensation of buzz, Mike shared how the views from the summit were unbelievable: "I felt a complete joy and a physical sensation of warmth with chemicals whirling around my body." But these feelings of joy were not just for himself but a shared experience with co-climbers and even the experience of taking care of Andrew up to the first camp: "The peaks are not an isolated experience but a shared togetherness with others, the support and help given in getting others to achieve their goals and dreams."

Mike also shared how Denali, a mountain in Alaska, is a tough climb:

> The plane drops you off on a glacier and there are 19 days of lugging your pack under icy conditions. At each camp you have to unpack and build an ice wall to keep warm before thinking of food or drink. When we got to the top two of the three main guides became sick and I was privileged to be asked to take over as the main guide. That was a special peak for me too. There were three of us at the summit and I remember a sight-seeing plane flew overhead and we were furiously waving the Welsh flag, feeling so elated, on top of the world. When I came down, I was just swinging. I could have just flown with pride and excitement.

Denali, Mike said, was a harder climb than Everest, and he had to dig really deep to find the resources to succeed. The guide, who had fallen sick, had clearly seen something in Mike that was reliable, responsible, strong, sound, and skilled to undertake such a challenge as the main guide. He was no longer a paying client but seen as worthy of leading the group to the summit. This gave him authority and kudos and enabled him to experience something extraordinary resembling a peak experience: "I felt really empowered to be asked to lead the group."

Emotions experienced in the mountains are also visible, as Mike recollected:

> [T]ears can stream involuntarily down your face when you're at the top. And the emotions are all part of the extraordinary experience and risk you've taken in getting there. The emotions build up as you've achieved this goal that you knew was going to be really hard and maybe might not come off. And you certainly have a few moments on the way back down, and in your own world when it does come off.

When talking to Mike, it occurred to us that risk for risk-takers is not risk at all but fun and exciting. They take the risk for the sheer joy of it and not for acclaim and glory. For example, Mike delighted in sharing that one of his moments of joy was at the base of Mont Blanc before the climb. He and fellow climbers wanted to keep their pack light so simply dug a hole in the ice, put down a sleeping bag, and slept in the freezing cold. To non-risk-takers that might seem ridiculous, inviting the elements to freeze our body, but to risk-takers it is part of their adventure.

***

Our final participant, **Dan Walmsley**, describes himself as an ultra-runner, caveman, and "dadventurer." His first recollection of any kind of peak experience was as a child, riding on a blue and white bike, coming down a hill, feet off the pedals, and screaming, "Woohoo!" He said he felt so heroic, "and that was probably the first sort of rush I'd ever had in life." Taylor and Carr (2021) noted that the rush feeling was common among mountain bikers, and certainly rush is the word Dan used throughout his interview when describing a peak experience.

Dan explains how, when he gets that first hit, the "whoosh" or rush that dopamine provides, other chemicals fly through his body resulting in a peak experience which he then describes as developing into flow:

> It's always the peak experience then the flow, where first your body is in tune with everything around you and then, when you've been doing it for a time, it's definitely more of a flow state. You're not thinking about anything and just going into that zone.

A second peak experience for Dan came whilst mountain biking. He recalls the addiction to the dopamine hit when he is right at the edge of his comfort zone, the moment of looking over a really steep hill and of getting down to the bottom. He experiences a kind of quiver in his body: "that was bloody awesome, I need to go and do that again."

Dan also admits to chasing that "rush" feeling through drugs when a teenager, which gave him the boost but with a negative effect. He compares the sensation to mountain biking, which gives a positive effect that lasts longer without harming his body – "unless I fall off" he joked. He made the following comparison to the short-term fix from drugs:

> Whereas I know what I get from mountain biking, or running and stuff and I get better at it the more I do, with drugs you just get worse at it the more you do. And it costs lots of money!

Dan admits to having a bit of an addiction for the rush state where he is unable to focus on anything else around him, noticing only the handlebars of the bike. His recall of mountain biking echoes his earlier explanation of being in the zone: "all I can remember is the beginning and the end . . . unless I've crashed. The bits in between aren't there." So nothing else matters around him apart from where he is and a sense of slowing down of time to allow him to focus. Dan thinks this state is fun to play with and is convinced that it is spontaneous but happens only with years of proficiency. This mention of play is suggestive of Csikszentmihalyi's description of flow, but it is not only a feature of flow, it can also suggest peak experience. Maslow (1968, p. 91) suggested that playfulness is "fairly often reported in the peak-experiences."

When asked what other words Dan would use, apart from rush, he replied:

> I don't even know if I have a language for it. It's more a feeling than anything else, a deep feeling. It's a warm feeling, it's everything it's connectedness.

Dan is most at home in the wilderness where he feels truly alive and where he has encountered peak experiences. He shared how in Canada he came across a pack of sea wolves – a euphoric encounter causing a rush of dopamine, the reward chemical. Dan can still visualise the rare sight of the wolves and can still feel goosebumps. He remembers the smell of the day and the sea and time slowing down. Seeing the wolves was a heart-stopping moment for Dan:

> I can see it and smell it, watching these beasts; how rare it was at the time to see them. It's as though I'm in Canada right now and I remember going across the lake, getting out of the boat. It's the memory which then triggers off everything else.

Visualisation plays an important part in preparation, as Dan revealed in his memories of seeing wolves and his mountain biking experiences. He uses visualisation to improve his performance too, recounting how he deliberately imagines the finish line of a massive run he is planning – 450 kilometres over eight days. He tells himself, "you know you can do this," and feels a rush which generates strong emotions in his gut:

> I get this euphoric wave over my chest and heart, then really visceral emotions like tears. My wife said, "are you OK, Dan?" I replied: "I've just completed my run" and she said, "but you're sitting in front of the computer"!

It seems that Dan's peak experiences depend upon the rush of energy and anticipated danger. He says:

> You could easily trip over and fall off the edge of a 500 foot cliff – game over. At the time you don't think about it as it would make you'd hesitate. Running up a mountain people might not see as that risky or powerful, but you know the consequences of what could happen, serious consequences.

A third peak experience happened for Dan when filming a documentary for Channel 4, *Surviving the Stone Age*. He lived completely primitively with eight others as cave people, where all they had to think about was finding food, hunting, pulling out a bow and arrow, seeing a squirrel. He admitted that the peak experiences he felt when catching food and being able to eat was more the thrill of anticipation compared to mountain biking and running. He says those moments were fantastic and caused what he calls a "neuro-chemical shove" in his body, a tiny micro hit:

> It's the simplicity of knowing what I'm doing could potentially give me food. Those peak experiences come when you haven't eaten for days, that dopamine state, knowing that whenever you get into that boat and pull out your bow and arrow there's a chance of eating, which is like the basic human instinct is to survive. And that would happen daily because we needed to go hunting and find water. If you haven't drunk for hours, and you're in the blazing sun and you drink water, that's the best thing ever. You get that peak and then go back to being in the moment.

Dan also talked about runner's high, which he considers different to any other sort of peak experience as it lasts longer. For him it's a feeling of euphoria, a state of "just being when thought simply floats in and out" while running through the mountains or on trails. Dan's experience resonates with Stoll's description of runner's high:

> Mental awareness, physical excellence, ability to suppress pain or discomfort, euphoria, laughing and crying at the same time, feeling free and natural in the surroundings or being at peace in the world.
>
> (Stoll, 2019, p. 1)

Similarly, peak experiences for Dan are life-affirming and make him feel as though he is living. They justify his lust for life:

> Knowing that if I keel over tomorrow, I've had that experience. Follow your dreams and live your life. We put limits on ourselves. I won't do that. I try to do as much as I can which puts me in the here and now and makes me feel alive. If I crash today (hopefully not) I want people to say, "Dan lived his life."

Significance of Peak Experience in This Context

In their review study, Gstaettner et al. (2018) acknowledged risk as a complex concept, with about two-thirds of papers identified as listing risk as a potential negative consequence of participating in recreational outdoor activities. However, a third of papers concluded risk can be a meaningful component of the outdoor experience.

According to Whitehead and Bates (2016), negative experiences, such as that experienced by Sean when he could almost have died, are the low points in a person's life, characterised by strong negative emotions such as disillusionment or despair. But, in line with Maslow (1964), Wilson and Spencer found that intense negative experiences can be "as meaningful and potentially self-actualizing as intense positive experiences" (1990, p. 572). They found that both peak and nadir experiences had the potential to promote personal growth.

However, participants in this chapter mentioned more positive effects of high-risk leisure activities. Mary-lou explained her feelings of oneness from skydiving, and both she and Dan spoke about feeling powerful, unstoppable, or vibrant. Sean, for example, seemed to confirm Lester's (1993, p. 79) findings that while mountain climbing one feels "whole, pulled together, undivided, undistracted." Sean's emphasis on the power of mountain climbing to eradicate his worries and stress also echoed Krakauer's feelings that the "accumulated clutter of day-to-day existence . . . is temporarily forgotten, crowded from your thoughts by an overpowering clarity of purpose and by the seriousness of the task at hand" (1996, p. 143).

In the chapter, we also saw how Dan's visualisation technique produces potential peak experiences. He feels a real rush of adrenaline and other body chemicals when picturing completion of a future challenging run. This is in contrast to the retrospective peaks that Sean achieves by reliving his past peak experiences. However, our skydiver, Mary-lou confirmed she cannot engineer peak experiences, unlike the surfers in Stranger's (1999) research, who looked forward to peak experiences each time they hit the water. This divergence is interesting and suggests that even within the discussion of one specific context (in this case extreme sport and high-risk leisure), participants may not be talking exclusively about the same phenomena. Peak experience is not the same as rush or flow or peak performance as indicated here and in other chapters.

Also significant in this chapter is the emphasis on reflection and recollection. Both Sean and Mary-lou explained that although the peak experience vibrations fade quickly, sometimes traces of them remain and can be recalled some years later. Sean confirmed that reflecting back on a peak experience was possibly the most fulfilling aspect. When he was thinking about what he had achieved he relived the peak experience.

In the literature, reflection is frequently seen as a way of enhancing personal growth and learning (Tavel et al., 2022) and can contribute to self-actualisation (Maslow, 1968). We noted how our participants for this chapter often mentioned aspects of self-discovery and revealed shifts in their understanding of themselves. Mary-lou, for example, believes her experiences have had a real impact on her life, revealing possibilities and giving her confidence to take on challenges.

Finally, and perhaps most evident, was the indication that high-risk leisure activity is not undertaken for glory or recognition. Rather, skydiving for Mary-lou, reaching tops of mountains for Sean and Mike, or undertaking a range of challenges for Dan are all opportunities to make transcendent experiences possible and achieve the special feeling of a peak experience.

References

Arnould, E. J., Price, L. L., & Otnes, C. (1999). Making consumption magic: A study of white-water rafting. *Journal of Contemporary Ethnography*, 28(1), 33–68.

Boudreau, P., Mackenzie, S. H., & Hodge, K. (2022). Optimal psychological states in advanced climbers: Antecedents, characteristics, and consequences of flow and clutch states. *Psychology of Sport and Exercise*, 60, 102155.

Brymer, E. (2009, March 6–7). *The extreme sports experience: A research report*. IFPRA World. https://eprints.qut.edu.au/26118/

Brymer, E., & Oades, L. G. (2009). Extreme sports: A positive transformation in courage and humility. *Journal of Humanistic Psychology*, 49(1), 114–126.

Buckley, R. (2012). Rush as a key motivation in skilled adventure tourism: Resolving the risk recreation paradox. *Tourism Management*, 33(4), 961–970.

Csikszentmihalyi, M. (1988). The flow experience and its significance for human psychology. *Optimal Experience: Psychological Studies of Flow in Consciousness*, 2, 15–35.

Dodson, K. J. (1996). Peak experiences and mountain biking: Incorporating the bike into the extended self. *ACR North American Advances*. www.acrwebsite.org/volumes/7974/volumes/v23/NA-23

Elias, N., & Dunning, E. (Eds.) (1986). *Quest for excitement: Sport and leisure in the civilizing process*. Oxford: Blackwell.

Fletcher, R. (2007). Free play: Transcendence as liberation. In R. Fletcher, *Beyond resistance: The future of freedom* (pp. 143–162). Nova Science Publishers.

Foucault, M. (1991). *Remarks on Marx: Conversations with Duccio Trombadori*. New York: Semiotext(e).

Gstaettner, A. M., Lee, D., & Rodger, K. (2018). The concept of risk in nature-based tourism and recreation – A systematic literature review. *Current Issues in Tourism*, 21(15), 1784–1809.

Kohls, M. A. (2014). *The unintended quest: An examination of transcendence and personal change in high-risk non-traditional athletes*. California Institute of Integral Studies.

Krakauer, K. (1996). *Into the wild*. New York: Anchor.

Kunwar, R. R. (2021). Extreme sport: Understanding the concept, recognizing the value. *Journal of Tourism & Adventure*, 4(1), 89–123.

Lester, J. (1993). The way of climbing. In P. Gillman (Ed.), *Everest*. Boston: Little Brown and Co.

Lester, J. (2004). Spirit, identity, and self in mountaineering. *Journal of Humanistic Psychology*, 44(1), 86–100.

Lipscombe, N. (1999). The relevance of the peak experience to continued skydiving participation: A qualitative approach to assessing motivations. *Leisure Studies*, 18(4), 267–288.

Lyng, S. (1990). Edgework: A social psychological analysis of voluntary risk taking. *American Journal of Sociology*, 95(4), 851–886.

Maslow, A. H. (1964). *Religions, values, and peak-experiences*. Columbus, OH: Ohio State University Press.

Maslow, A. H. (1968). *Toward the psychology of being*, 2nd edition. New York: D. Van Nostrand.

Maslow, A. H. (1969). The farther reaches of human nature. *The Journal of Transpersonal Psychology*, 1(1), 1–9.

Privette, G. (1983). Peak experience, peak performance, and flow: A comparative analysis of positive human experiences. *Journal of Personality and Social Psychology, 45*(6), 1361.

Reid, P., & Kampman, H. (2020). Exploring the psychology of extended-period expeditionary adventurers: Going knowingly into the unknown. *Psychology of Sport and Exercise, 46*, 101608.

Senecal, G. (2021). The aftermath of peak experiences: Difficult transitions for contact sport athletes. *The Humanistic Psychologist, 49*(2), 295.

Smith, N., Sandal, G. M., Leon, G. R., & Kjærgaard, A. (2017). Examining personal values in extreme environment contexts: Revisiting the question of generalizability. *Acta Astronautica, 137*, 138–144.

Šolcová, I. P., Šolcová, I., Stuchlíková, I., & Mazehóová, Y. (2016). The story of 520 days on a simulated flight to Mars. *Acta Astronautica, 126*, 178–189.

Stoll, O. (2019). Peak performance, the runner's high and flow. In *APA handbook of sport and exercise psychology*. Volume 2: *Exercise psychology*. M.H. Anshel.

Stranger, M. (1999). The aesthetics of risk: A study of surfing. *International Review for the Sociology of Sport, 34*(3), 265–276.

Stranger, M. (2017). *Surfing life: Surface, substructure and the commodification of the sublime*. London: Routledge.

Suedfeld, P., Legkaia, K., & Brcic, J. (2010). Changes in the hierarchy of value references associated with flying in space. *Journal of Personality, 78*(5), 1411–1436.

Tavel, P., Chrz, V., Šolcová, I. P., Dubovská, E., & Kalman, M. (2022). Peak experience and its varieties: Response to challenge as a valuable perspective of peak experience and its varieties. *Československá psychologie, 66*(2), 95–110.

Taylor, S. (2013). The peak at the nadir: Psychological turmoil as the trigger for awakening experiences. *International Journal of Transpersonal Studies, 32*(2), 3.

Taylor, S., & Carr, A. (2021). "Living in the moment": Mountain bikers' search for flow. *Annals of Leisure Research*, 1–15.

Vogler, J. W. (2012). *Self-actualization and peak experiences in outdoor recreation*. Master's Thesis, Clemson University.

Watson, N., & Parker, A. (2015). The mystical and sublime in extreme sports: Experiences of psychological well-being or Christian revelation. *Studies in World Christianity, 21*(3), 260–281.

Whitehead, R., & Bates, G. (2016). The transformational processing of peak and nadir experiences and their relationship to eudaimonic and hedonic well-being. *Journal of Happiness Studies, 17*, 1577–1598.

Wilson, S. R., & Spencer, R. C. (1990). Intense personal experiences: Subjective effects, interpretations, and after-effects. *Journal of Clinical Psychology, 46*(5), 565–573.

Wolfe, L. M. (1938). *John of the mountains: The unpublished journals of John Muir*. University of Wisconsin Press.

11 Peak Experiences in the Workplace

Introduction

This chapter discusses the possibility of peak experiences occurring in the workplace. However, despite their potential for adding value to the employee experience and to workplace effectiveness, peak experiences as such are hardly discussed in this context. Fu and Ma (2022) have lamented that we know little about employee peak experiences, how they happen, and what their impact might be. They confirm that peak experience, "as a highly positive experience, has been studied and applied in the field of human resource management only to a very limited extent" (2022, p. 1).

Notwithstanding the lack of prior research into peak experience in this context, there has been some exploration into related concepts such as flow and peak performance. Glick-Smith (2018, p. 171), for example, explained how "flow-based leadership exists when leaders commit to maximizing their own peak performance ('flow') and to facilitating the flow states of others." This, they say, results in team and organisational flow. They also cite how a 10-year McKinsey study has shown that when working in flow, "employee productivity increases by five-fold and has the effect of elevating individual, as well as organizational, well-being" (2018, p. 171).

Similarly, Fu and Ma (2022) have also reminded us that peak experience is linked to *eudaimonic* and *hedonic* well-being and has an impact on people's attitudes to life. These two components of well-being were defined by Ryan and Deci (2000), who explain that *eudaimonia* relates to the consequences of self-growth and self-actualisation, and *hedonia* relates to immediate sensory pleasure, happiness, and enjoyment. As discussed in Chapter 8, both *hedonia* and *eudaimonia* are inherent in Maslow's concept of peak experience.

Also contributing to well-being and meaningfulness in the workplace, and indeed underwriting the likelihood of peak experiences, is the individual's potential for self-transcendence. In the context of meaningful work, self-transcendence appears to be a more commonly studied concept than peak experience. Madden and Bailey (2019, pp. 148–149) clarify, however, that self-transcendence is a complex concept "sometimes explained as a 'way in' to discover our inner spirituality, as a 'way out' to escape the meaninglessness of the world, or as the destination of

DOI: 10.4324/9781003509219-12

our transcendent journey." In any event, as Koltko-Rivera (2006) has noted, self-transcendent people seek to further causes beyond the self, devoting themselves to selfless service to link with something greater than themselves.

In this chapter we begin by reviewing the relevant literature on peak experience in business or workplace contexts, taking into account any relevant research on self-transcendence and other related concepts, such as flow and peak performance. Then, as in other chapters, we present our participants' experiences. Participants were selected to provide insights into a variety of workplaces and afford a range of experiences.

Review of the Research

As mentioned, the literature on peak experiences in the workplace is sparse. However, we managed to find some research that focused on related concepts. This sheds light on peak experiences in this context, and we present an overview of these in chronological order to trace the potential development of ideas.

The majority of the earlier literature in the business or workplace context focused on peak performance rather than peak experience, although there is some overlap in discussions. In 1987, for example, Garfield analysed the characteristics of peak performers in business using interviews with peak performers. He found that Maslow's idea of self-actualising moments, especially in a business context, could be characterised as involving

> greater efficiency, making operations neater, more compact, simpler, faster, less expensive, turning out a better product, doing with less parts, a smaller number of operations, less clumsiness, less effort, more fool proof, safer, more "elegant," less laborious.
>
> (1987, p. 154)

Also, he noticed that peak performing executives were motivated by an internal drive to use their capacities to the fullest and thought that what he called "peak performers" were different from non-peak performers, suggesting:

> [p]eak performers are self-managers with a strong internal drive toward meaningful achievement. That is, they think about improving and competing against a standard of excellence that they set for themselves.
>
> (Garfield, 1987, p. 55)

Garfield further observed that peak performers consistently achieve impressive results and are willing to grow and to learn from work as well as merely to complete it. In his 1986 paper, he reported how some peak performers speak of single powerful occasions or "sweet spots in time" that offer them a glimpse of themselves as capable of "a great deal more than I previously thought possible" (Garfield, 1986, p. 18).

Another early exploration of peak performance in the workplace was undertaken by Thornton et al. (1999) in their study comparing business leaders and university employees. The aim of their research was to examine psychological processes of peak performance in relation to business activity drawing on the peak performances reported by 40 business leaders and comparing these with 42 university men. Participants described their experiences both in interviews and via Privette's Experience Questionnaire (Privette & Bundrick, 1987). The peak performance dyad, involving full focus and clear sense of self and aspects of the peak experience dyad, comprising significance and fulfilment, was endorsed by both samples in the study. Business leaders endorsed sociability and personal discipline and denied playfulness more than the university men, who endorsed fluidity.

Thornton et al. (1999) also found that in assessing their peak performance, business leaders recognised the processes that optimal performance shares with peak experience, that is, significance and fulfilment. Participants described experiences that had profound personal meaning and confirmed the lasting after-effects of their experiences. Business leaders also described their strong or personal best performances as fulfilling and enjoyable, suggesting that, in this feeling dimension at least, their peak performances approached peak experiences. However, the university employees in their study endorsed more strongly the fluidity often associated with peak experiences: "a feeling of wholeness, freedom from outer restraints, spontaneity, intrinsic reward, brevity, lost orientation, a sense of unity, nonmotivation, and playfulness" (1999, p. 261). Thornton et al. (1999) concluded that peak performance has consistent psychological processes that were found to be stable among dissimilar samples and diverse activities.

Just before his death, Maslow was beginning to research his supposition that there are peaking and non-peaking self-actualising people. He viewed self-actualisation as a developmental process involving maturity and transcendence and differentiated between "non-peakers" – the self-actualisers who were healthy but had few or no experiences of transcending, and "peakers" – those for whom transcending experiencing was important and even central (Maslow, 1971). Peakers, he found, are likely to be involved in aesthetics and religion, while non-peakers tended to be influential social workers and "world betterers." Thus, he argued, peakers tended to live at the level of being or becoming, of intrinsic values, and have peak experiences with insights or cognitions that had changed their view of the world and themselves (1971).

Thornton et al. (1999) claimed that their business leaders fitted Maslow's maturity criterion and endorsed peak experience factors. However, they admit they were less supportive of ethereal attributes than the university sample. As a group they did not fit a "peaker" profile. They thus concluded that further research is needed:

> If self-actualization can be operationally defined as the frequent occurrence of peak performance and peak experience, further avenues are opened for application of self-actualization theory in business.
>
> (1999, p. 262)

Thornton et al. (1999, p. 262) further argued that their research supports "the relevance of self-awareness and empowerment to behavioral superiority and productivity of non-peakers as well as peakers." They suggest the link between optimal performance and joy has been found consistently in other studies and is too important to ignore:

> For business this connection means that productivity, in the long run, is bound with the full human experience, including feelings such as joy, fulfillment, and meaning.
>
> (1999, p. 262)

In 2006, Schindehutte, Morris, and Allen examined the cognitive and emotional experiences of entrepreneurs as they performed tasks associated with venture creation. These authors characterise the entrepreneurial context as involving peaks and valleys: "periods of relatively high pressure, stress, uncertainty, and ambiguity and periods of relative stability and predictability" (2006, p. 349). They took the three interrelated psychological variables of peak performance, peak experience, and flow and, via in-depth structured interviews with two samples of entrepreneurs, identified their relevance. The results of the study suggest all three variables are significant aspects of the entrepreneurial context:

> The process of achieving success in an environment characterized by stress, a multiplicity of obstacles and demands, and uncertainty regarding outcomes can produce a type of peak performance. Further, the entrepreneur can find such performance to be rewarding or self-actualizing, resulting in a peak experience.
>
> (2006, p. 364)

Schindehutte et al. (2006) also explained how multiple motives are potential drivers for entrepreneurs during the process of success and that these might change or evolve over the course of time:

> Specifically, where the entrepreneur achieves peak performance, has a peak experience, or encounters flow, the corresponding sense of meaningfulness, fulfilment, self-validation, richness, or joy may become an end in itself. To the extent that this is the case, the entrepreneur becomes further engaged in the venture, producing further growth, or is keen to start additional ventures. To some degree, then, entrepreneurship becomes its own reward.
>
> (2006, p. 365)

The results of Schindehutte et al.'s research further suggested that peak performance, peak experience, and flow are highly interrelated variables in the entrepreneurial context. They describe how a diverse mix of examples was provided by the entrepreneurs, "sometimes with the same event used to describe all three variables" (2006, p. 365).

Venter (2012, 2024) explained that Maslow's identification of higher-order needs has played a major role in the development of organisational leadership and that his sixth level of need, self-transcendence, goes beyond individual needs. Venter further examines the enriching implications that self-transcendence can have on organisational culture and leadership:

> At this level, people view the world and their purpose in it on a more global scale. Self-transcendent leaders are characterized by a common purpose, a global perspective, and joint responsibility for the fate of the whole organization, identifying with a cause greater than themselves.
> (Venter, 2012, p. 64)

Morrison (2018) later pointed out that motivational self-transcendence is valuable for individuals and their organisations, being key to finding meaningfulness in the workplace and contributing to corporate social responsibility and sustainable business practices.

Morrison provides three useful definitions of motivational self-transcendence:

1) Connecting your identity to making a positive impact on the world or the lives of others;
2) Framing your actions in a broader, more meaningful context;
3) A basic human value characterised by benevolence and universalism (2018, p. 16).

Ninio's (2015) qualitative study involved interviews with 18 school principals (ten men and eight women) each of whom had at least five years' experience in post. Findings suggested that a peak experience has three stages:

1) The actual experience which Ninio described as quick, unexpected, moving, and intense;
2) A "turning point" – an event that changes the person's (professional) trajectory and a break in the expected chain of events; and
3) Personal growth, change, or development that comes as a result of the peak experience in the educational or vocational areas.

Ninio (2015) reported how interviews revealed that most principals had experienced a "peak experience" at some time in their careers and that this affected their administrative philosophy and focus. This suggests that the educational and personal process of becoming a school principal may be deepened when it includes a peak experience. Klein and Ninio's (2019) findings further revealed that all respondents implemented "significant changes in their work after undergoing key experiences," (Klein & Ninio, 2019, p. 903) and that those who experienced turning points frequently chose "professional directions not previously considered, leading to significant changes or modifications in their work" (2019, p. 904).

In 2017, Keller and Meaney reported on the way 5,000 executives thought about their peak experiences as team members. They were invited to record the word or words that best described the team environment. Findings suggested three key dimensions of good teamwork:

1) Alignment regarding direction – a shared belief about what the company is striving towards and the role of the team in getting there.
2) High-quality interaction, characterised by trust, open communication, and a willingness to embrace conflict.
3) A strong sense of renewal – an environment in which team members are energised because they feel they can take risks, innovate, learn from outside ideas, and achieve something that matters – often against the odds (2017, p. 81).

This study showed that team composition is important initially to try and build the team dynamic. It is in the dynamic that the character of the team as a whole is revealed, and their ability to work together can be observed.

Bakker and Van Woerkom (2017, p. 47) studied flow in the workplace and defined it as "a short-term peak experience that is characterized by absorption, work enjoyment, and intrinsic work motivation." They report how flow is positively related to indicators of job performance, and workers can proactively create their own optimal experiences. These authors use self-determination theory (Ryan & Deci, 2000), proposing that workers might use specific strategies to satisfy their basic needs, facilitate their flow experiences, and also increase their job performance. The four self-determination strategies proposed are self-leadership, job crafting, designing work to be playful, and the use of strengths. Bakker and Van Woerkom also suggest that "factors within the organizational context – such as human resource practices and leadership, as well as personal resources – such as self-efficacy and optimism, moderate the effectiveness of these strategies" (2017, p. 47).

One of the most recent studies in the area of peak experiences in the workplace is by Fu and Ma (2022). Their research is based on the affective events theory and the two-factor theory. They looked in depth at employees' peak experience via three quantitative studies culminating in an examination of the relationship between employee peak experiences and their triggers and impacts.

These authors define an employee peak experience as a highly positive feeling: "the moment of the highest a happiness and fulfilment in employees' work experiences" (Fu & Ma, 2022, p. 3). Their findings demonstrated factors such as:

1) Elevation – moments that transcend the normal course of events;
2) Insight – moments that rewire employees' understandings of themselves or the world;
3) Pride – moments where employees are at their best, and they realise the significance of their work;
4) Connection – moments of bonding with others through either concern for their welfare or working together towards the same goal.

These four factors can trigger peak experiences, and employees are more likely to display proactive behaviour and word-of-mouth referrals after such peak experience.

Peak Experience in Context: Participant Accounts

In this section, we present seven accounts of peak experiences shared with us by managers, leaders, and others who have experienced peaks in the workplace.

Kevin Harris, who we also met in Chapter 7, has had a business career spanning management in aerospace and a variety of senior executive-level positions. He is currently self-employed with two chief executive roles in multiple sectors. His experience in a workplace setting warrants inclusion here because, as Kevin says, "this is a story about a peak experience at work that completely changed my life."

Kevin's story begins when he was about to break down stones as hardcore for a patio base and was stopped in his tracks when his wife suddenly shouted "Stop, they're original limestone coping stones and worth something." He reluctantly took them to a salvage yard.

At that time in his life Kevin was a burly 18-stone plus rugby player and hurled the stones into a pile from his truck at a salvage yard as though they were polo mints. His strength did not go unnoticed by the owner who approached Kevin and said, "You're a strong fellow, I could use someone like you." They chatted about an opportunity, and the scene was set.

That conversation "hung heavy" in Kevin's mind, and he returned the next day and accepted a job offer which was way below his status and earnings in his former engineering career. But the lure of viewing the world from the outside rather than from inside a factory was irresistible. He was in his mid-forties at the time, the children had left home, and the timing was perfect for him to think about himself and what he wanted from the rest of his life, despite friends and colleagues thinking he had gone mad.

Kevin explained how the job offer made him feel:

Something grabbed me at all levels, emotionally, physically and mentally and I had a hunch that something was going to happen in my life, something I couldn't identify but something significant. I was just drawn to it. And that feeling has stayed with me. I still get goose bumps thinking about it. This was my peak experience – the excitement of something new, listening to my intuition and taking a risk that turned out to be the best thing I ever did in my life.

When challenged about whether this was truly a peak experience or simply a happy memory, Kevin was quite adamant that it was a peak experience. He had the feelings of joy and sensed the visceral excitement of working in what turned out to be a highly respected architectural salvage centre as operations director: "It took me all over the country dismantling wonderful Victorian and Edwardian buildings and re-erecting them elsewhere."

Kevin proudly admitted that they turned that business into one of the most successful architectural salvage yards in the country, stripping out renaissance sections of, for example, the Victoria and Albert Museum and the original 50-metre balustrade off Westminster Bridge: "it was the most wonderful experience and I met extraordinary people that changed my life – royals, designers, and such interesting individuals."

We challenged Kevin to think about whether his peak experience was evident only on reflection. He said not, as so many elements were aligned – from simply building a patio to going to the salvage yard to meeting the owner – all arbitrary events that he could have ignored. But he followed his intuition and experienced something magical. He had a split-second window to either smash the stones for the patio base or heed his wife:

> When I look back, I felt I was being steered. I literally felt that I was being controlled, as though someone had got hold of me to do that, go there, listen to that, do that, get out of there and take it there. An uber powerful force. A change of job wasn't on my radar – not even a dream but something happened. My intuition was so, so strong that something was going to happen, something that had been with me for a while – it went on for months and months then suddenly, Bang!

We asked him what was "peak" about it, and he explained:

> I still get emotional about it. It makes me tearful but I'm not sad. They're not tears of sadness but really powerful vibes I suppose – even thinking about it now. I'm still feeling it to this day. I still talk about it with absolute passion because it was such a brilliant moment in my life.

Kevin expressed his belief that everyone stays in roles far too long, often unhappily but often through necessity:

> [S]tepping away from a successful career and taking control allowed me to experience such an immense peak that stays with me forever. It was a massive learning and growth experience and made me the person I am today. Sometimes you have to be brave and do whatever you want to do. People say I went backwards from earning very good money with prestige to less. But the currency of my life values went exponentially the other way. When I think about the people I met, and the projects I was involved in all over the country, wow!

As far as peak experience and business are concerned, Kevin's advice would be to listen to your intuition and be prepared to make a change. When asked how much risk played a part, he replied: "I didn't see it as a risk. Others did as they looked at it from a financial point of view. I didn't. I just wanted to change my working day into something completely different." So this was a values-based decision for

Kevin. He started looking out to a wider world which takes courage. The timing was perfect; his kids had grown up, and he no longer had family responsibilities: "when I look back now, I think it absolutely was a peak experience. It's in my core. I draw on it even now when I need to make decisions."

***

Philippa Lowe, who we met in Chapter 3, is a business manager whose peak experiences as an amateur musician have also had a significant impact on her working life leading diverse teams across multiple locations.

Philippa described how she is part of a leadership development programme at work, which focuses on "me being at my best" and the profound impact role-modelling can have on teams and organisational effectiveness:

> Through the programme we are encouraged to talk about our feelings and apply what is unique and special about each person to make work more meaningful and fulfilling. This is a new approach for work but is familiar ground for me as now I am able to bring what is best about being a musician into my work.

Philippa then explained how extraordinary and emotional musical experiences have acted as catalysts for a remarkable growth in her leadership and influencing skills at work. She likens these experiences to a therapy session: "It feels like I am working through unresolved issues and concerns to a point of resolution. The notable difference is not saying anything, as the dialogue is purely through the expression of the improvisation."

We asked Philippa if there were any ways in which her experiences have impacted her approach in the workplace:

> I am also gaining a growing awareness of the value of music and the way musicians interact and connect in a business setting. I am using my musical experimentations with improvisation to be more effective at work. It enables me to be at my best and in balance, drawing on my rational and emotional sides. My music is my creative reset button which re-charges my batteries every weekend. I am able to anchor these peak experiences and the associated sense of wellbeing to create a healthier mindset, which enables me to be more resourceful and resilient in the work environment.

Philippa believes her improvisation experience is an uncensored, true expression of her feelings; raw, honest, and authentic:

> In improvisation musical rules and "wrong notes" don't exist. All you need to do is let go, be in the moment and accept your vulnerability. What I love about the music improvisation is what it reveals. It gives me an ability to think about who I am, what I'm doing and feeling. It's a post reflective experience but in the moment you're fully present.

Links have been made in the literature between improvisation and peak experience. Romanelli et al. (2019, p. 285) explained how peak experiences are moments that encompass "an unusually high affective and cognitive experiencing of intensity, meaningfulness, richness, spontaneity, expressiveness, and thoughtlessness." They are also more "creative, playful, flexible, and improvisational" (Romanelli et al., 2019, p. 285).

Additionally, Ratten and Hodge (2016, p. 14) found that in business, when a person is improvising they are under time pressure to create something new. This is increasingly the case in today's fast-paced business environment where time-pressured improvisation can be seen as producing creative and adaptive innovations. Maslow (1961) argued that at such times, people are functioning at their best and are closest to their real selves.

***

Nikki Forward is an experienced human resources director. She was interested to explore whether peak experiences had happened in her working life, as she recognised that peak experiences are more readily associated with music and the creative arts.

Work has always been very important to Nikki, and she derives personal satisfaction from providing affordable homes for local people in a rural area: "It brings me great joy to think anything I'm doing, or we're doing, in the business is helping to solve a housing crisis in our local area."

Nikki started to think about whether peak experience or peak performance could benefit the business and individuals, particularly new starters:

> Do they have a set of qualities around things like curiosity or authenticity, ownership or responsibility? Could you have the sort of people in your business who are focussed on moving towards self-actualisation and peak experience? Is there some sort of common denominator you could look for in recruitment, so that you're going to put more people through your business who share a self-fulfilment and self-development sort of mindset?

Her next thought was whether she had herself encountered a peak experience from work. This immediately took her back to an event in 2022, when the executive group had a business challenge to solve and co-created a solution as part of their overarching corporate strategic vision. They had worked intensely together over a few months bringing their strengths, expertise, and skillsets to different aspects of the project:

> This is where I know we all experienced peak experience on that day – it was that moment when we had done so much preparation, rehearsed and practiced, in fact a collective effort. We came out of that event having convinced the board that this was the right solution and got their approval, doing a high five with each other, jumping up and down because in that moment it was a shared experience.

Nikki makes an analogy to music, suggesting they all played to their strengths, demonstrating the power of teamwork:

> We were physically in the room together like you bring an orchestra together. We got the end result; the Board approved it, and we could go forward with it. What I understand of peak experience and flow I definitely experienced, so did the rest of us. That is a part now of our shared language as an executive group. To do something so well, we all refer back to how we felt on December 8th. It's become one of those kinds of anchored moments that we all share, and we can all remember exactly that moment and how we all felt.

Nikki also identified how the peak experience felt by the group involved a sense of surrender to the moment of execution and resulted in a stronger sense of togetherness and identity. There was also a lack of personal ego, something identified by Maslow (1968) as key to a peak experience. Nikki explains: "We had all let go of our own personal egos or wanting to shine. We had become completely in it as a team."

A second example of a peak experience for Nikki happened at an induction training. She approached the session really lacking energy:

> I really wasn't in the frame of mind to deliver a great session, but I set my attitude and frame of mind and started delivering the training. As the day went on, I was completely getting in flow. My energy and that of my co-facilitator brought the participants along, and together with their energy and engagement we suddenly produced another high five at the end. The new starters were completely engaged and picked up on the energy in the room.

This contagion of energy to produce the flow state, resulting in Nikki's description of a peak experience and the "high five," is recognised by Bakker, who said that the reaction between teacher and student results in "the crossover of peak experiences" (2005, p. 26). For this to happen, three elements have to be present, namely absorption, enjoyment, and intrinsic motivation. These are the elements Nikki demonstrated, but she suggested there may also be a fourth element:

> I like the term "mastery" and it's not often I blow my own trumpet but there's certain things that I do when I know I bring mastery to it. I know my stuff inside out, I know I deliver it with passion, intuition and authenticity and I do believe that energy is given in return. I read body language, I understand the mood and energy in the room, I can observe people individually and as a group. I have all of that intuitive skillset which I don't often recognise enough.

Nikki then explained her business challenges and the fact that she is always looking for a magic bullet that will solve all her leadership problems and enable her to train people to consistently deliver at a reliable level. This led Nikki to explore what peak experience can deliver:

> I think there's something about creating space and time with a shared purpose that allows for creativity and letting go of the ego; everyone being in agreement, comfortable and happy to let that go for the greater good of the new team. I also think physical presence has a lot to do with it as well. There's something in my head that's saying if we could identify some of the key pillars of peaks experience.

Nikki concluded that attitudinal behaviours and curiosity were integral in recruitment to encourage the flow state and create the space for a peak experience to happen:

> There's got to be people who go on their instinct, their authenticity and lack of ego . . . people who are willing to take ownership or responsibility – some elements like that. Because if you don't have an inquisitive mind or you don't have any instinctive reactions to things, I think you're less likely to experience peaks.

It seems that when discussing peak experience with our participants, their awareness of peak experience becomes infinitely more acute as demonstrated here by Nikki. They seem to be able to quickly identify their experiences, reflect on them, and be aware of the possibility of peak experiences happening again.

***

Andy Sayers, who we also met in Chapter 6, is an entrepreneurial business consultant. His peak experience recall goes back to a time when he was recruited into a tech business owned by General Electric and was challenged with turning the business around. The business was in poor shape, but Andy reduced the team and focused on employing higher-calibre people. There were occasions where everything they touched turned to gold. Similar to other participants, he recalls how his peak experience happened through teamwork:

> We ended up with this cohesive team of eight players in the UK and four in the Netherlands. As the naysayers were taken out, the others just blossomed. The whole team was incredibly positive and it's one of those things that will stick with me forever. There was probably a period of about 6 months that were just electric. The whole thing was just so incredibly unique and positive. It's kind of a skin tingling feeling in my head – I'd describe it as joyful. It was a play hard, work hard, becoming a cohesive family type environment. Everyone had each other's back. It was quite magical.

Andy believes there was an element of sustained peak performance attached to the peak experience:

But the "aha" was when you suddenly realised that you were living what you'd tried to create, which was everybody in that groove, rowing very, very hard in the same direction. Everyone working together like this creates a very harmonious and actually quite a fluid environment as well. It just seems to flow. If I look back, it's as if the team had achieved a group state of flow. Everyone was growing, earning well, doing what they needed to do and more – and having a really, really good time. It was a very tight knit unit.

Interestingly, as ascertained in our earlier research (Weijers, 2021), a peak experience can sometimes happen when coming out of flow or even at the pinnacle of a peak performance. This, Andy agreed, was evident in his team. They were all in harmony, pulling together and working hard. We asked Andy if the team's united harmony, getting into flow, and performing at a peak were precursors to having a peak experience. And he replied, "I'd say that's probably about right." Weijers's (2021) research also suggests that there are core conditions to trigger a peak experience, and Andy confirmed: "I would say it wouldn't have happened without those conditions. It wouldn't have become the machine that it became." In Andy's case, the core conditions could be identified as:

- weeding out the naysayers
- recruiting people who you believed in
- giving them an opportunity to shine within the business context
- having the challenge of creating your own goals
- surpassing your goals

Not only were these core conditions essential to trigger a peak experience in this context, but Andy pointed out that, in business, having a growth mindset and the vision are vital to put those conditions in place:

I think growth, positivity and a really strong "why" factor are in there as well. Outside of any personal goals there was a willingness to win because of where our start point was. For me, doing the things you've said you're going to do is really important: showing up with integrity, leading from the front, being prepared to do the things you're asking other people to do. And that role was probably the first time I'd been able to bring those values to the table and really execute in that way.

***

Ruth has more than 25 years' senior commercial experience in corporate and consultancy environments in the UK and Europe. Her talent lies in her ability to read people and the energy in a room. She says, "it's a curious dynamic." Ruth joined the workforce in the 1990s, when this skill, now highly prized, was still considered to be strange and a bit "touchy feely." Ruth thinks her awareness enables her to hear and also interpret what people are actually trying to express. She believes these interpretations contribute to her peak experiences when enabling people to find meaning:

> If you have a different way of looking at something other than the functional, the value you bring is huge. Looking at that body language in that meeting, what did you think he was trying to say? How did it make you feel? Coaching people to increase their comfort level because their work is incredibly stressful and technical, is high stakes and it's pressured.

We asked Ruth what she thought facilitated an open discussion about peak experience, and she came up with several factors that affect peak experiences in the work context. These are discussed here.

Emotional Factors

Ruth believes that some people are reluctant to discuss their experiences, and the reason is heavily rooted in an emotional response. In business, she believes, the focus is on delivery and driving people to do more; yet to achieve maximum productivity people need to be in their best shape emotionally and physically. As authors, we also encountered resistance to openness while researching this book. Not only did some people not want to discuss their experiences but also asked to not be sent any further information on peak experience. Ruth thinks: "the recognition that there is a handshake between the two is still missing, and that people are much more fearful in life about identifying with something that could feel emotional in business."

Gender Dynamic

Ruth maintains that a lot of resistance is rooted in the gender dynamic. The current view of business is still heavily weighted, particularly at levels of seniority, towards the male demographic. Furthermore, men in those jobs are now at the most senior tiers, men who will be 60+ which means they joined the workplace in the 1970s. She believes that change will happen further only down the line with a different set of cultural and social influences, when the gender balance will be different with a far great proportion of women. And therefore, a dilution effect will begin to happen, "but right now it is a difficult conversation to have because it's an alien conversation."

Although fewer in number, Ruth also includes many senior women in her argument. She says she sees this suppression of emotion all the time: "It's such a compounding, accumulating effect, but to be the best of either gender, you have to connect the two, the emotional and the physical."

Collective Experience

Ruth believes everything in life is influenced by generational patterns and the "behaviours of the state of mind." Also, she thinks the pandemic in 2020 had an impact on people's states of mind:

> I think the whole thing about peak is being shaken up and changed because no one is working in a really healthy dynamic right now. How on earth can you possibly work closely with someone and really engage and exchange ideas when you're sitting and constantly looking at them through a screen?

Ruth then makes an interesting point about the future of peaks. She suggests it has taken generations of humans to get to the stage where there's comfort in large groups.

> If you go to a football match or a concert to do something collectively, it is a joyful human experience – the workplace is like that. It connects you to everything else. If we keep saying working at home in isolation is OK, the number of things we will lose by carrying on saying it's OK are incalculable. We get experience from being together in the workplace. If we continue to pretend that collective in-person experience is somehow outdated and just pre-pandemic corporate nonsense, then peak experience will be something that will become rare because people won't be able to identify what peak is. They're not practising it enough, and they have to practise it with other people – in a collective environment, as humans – that's the point. It's an individual experience, but it happens because something has triggered it.

Connectivity and Relationships

Ruth maintains that her life's work experience has given her an appreciation of business relationships and learning how important connection is to create a peak experience. She fears that younger people will miss out on the social interconnectivity office life offers and by not connecting to others, they will miss out on peaks.

> Young people are unsuited, emotionally and socially, when entering a competitive world. I think that is disenfranchising. That's not to say all office and work culture is a full and wholesome thing, but at least there is an element of participation and an element of the relationship between the personal and the professional, the private and the public. If you're not experiencing anything that you would have experienced from day-to-day input with other people, because you are working at home, how can you possibly engage with someone over time? What is a peak actually going to mean?

We asked Ruth for her own experience of peaks, and she replied:

> When I've experienced peaks at work it's generally because of connectivity and relationship with another person. I can see that the benefit of me working with them improving the ease with which they're able to undertake their work. The work I'm doing with them just enables them to open their mind a little bit and bring themselves away from task and function. It's not about what you're doing but how you feel about what you're doing. So, I feel peak when I see that happening in other people – a feeling that knowing something is absolutely right. Part of peak for me is also the practice of honesty, and respect for honesty.

Ruth's experience appears to focus on peak performance at work. She achieves her peaks because of the way she performs in the workplace using her ability to empathise and to understand people. She values the collective working environment because the human connection it enables allows relationships to flourish.

***

Clare Josa is a keynote speaker, educator, and trainer specialising in imposter syndrome. As an engineer and marketing director, Clare incorporates all her knowledge, experience, and processes into her current work, having also worked as a meditation teacher and Reiki healer. The combination of engineering and business acumen that primarily uses the cognitive side of the brain, creatively combined with her awareness of intuition and sensory acuity, enables her students to access profound insights and develop sensory skills.

Clare admitted that she can quickly get into what she calls a "flow-type peak experience," a different state of consciousness, but there are conditions which affect her:

> I find there's a direct link between my environment; things I'm doing, and the stress I might be experiencing. Also, what I've been eating and drinking, and also how much sleep I've had. by. I'm going through menopause and if I'm feeling sleep deprived, then it's much harder to get into that flow/peak experience state compared to a couple of days when I've actually slept through.

While we were talking, a second condition also emerged:

> So, the first thing is, I get out of my head and consciously move my awareness to my heart centre, not the physical pumping thing. And when I do that, it immediately shifts and I can get out of my thinking head.

By bringing her awareness to her heart centre, Clare is also focusing her attention on the present moment, a third condition, "and being in the presence of others who are doing the same thing means we kind of combine our energies that can make that kind of thing easier."

In her current work, Clare is often invited to make keynote talks and frequently gets into a flow state: "and that's very much about getting into the heart." Each of these conditions seemed to reveal another as her thoughts evolved. She says posture is important and finds that standing rather than sitting is the answer, "I don't tend to get into flow when I'm sitting down. There's something about the energy moving around." Nor does she wear high heels but prefers to feel the connection with the earth with her feet flat on the floor, bringing energy into her heart and out of her thinking head, which shifts her focus and makes it about the other person and not her. She described the process:

> [A]nd it's that sense of excitement, of knowing that I know my stuff so well, and I'm about to co-create with my audience something that's better than

anything we could do on our own. And knowing that there are lives it's going to touch. Just one person in the audience out of a thousand who makes a different decision as a result of that talk – that is the person I'm doing this for, and I feel such excitement for them.

Intuition is another core condition, but Clare interprets this as:

> Not actually my intuition. It's that wisdom, that knowledge body, that connectedness and that sense of oneness, taking out the ego, and coming from a collective wisdom. My thinking mind solves problems, but I have to be able to be a conduit for that energy, that intention, whatever it is. And I think that's why standing up, feet flat on the floor or flat in my slippers I need that grounded-ness to allow the energy to flow through. I think that's one of the absolute keys.

Clare is committed in her belief that one of the reasons her extreme peak experience occurred during meditation, as recounted in Chapter 8, was that she wasn't trying to hold onto her energy but just allowed it to course through her:

> I never felt such expansiveness in my whole life. I think that's key that the energy has to flow through. If I try to do flow and peak experience, trying to generate that energy from inside, it doesn't last very long, and I have a migraine next day. So, I think it's that grounded-ness allowing the energy to flow through, and allowing that essence, whatever it is, to come from outside of me, rather than generating it myself, getting my ego and my thinking head out of the way. I also think when I get in flow another key bit for me is my mastery zone. I know my stuff so well. It's 20 years since I've been teaching. I don't have to think about the "how." So, any wisdom that comes through isn't hindered by me having to use my cognitive brain. Clients will say "how on earth did you know?" And I just say, "I don't know."

We asked Clare if the fact that she's so experienced in meditation and yoga has enabled her to open up a conduit to experience flow and peak experience in her teaching work, and she immediately agreed:

> I think that's definitely contributed and allowed me to start working with energies in the work that I'm doing and not just the cognitive side. I do a lot of energy work and I'm very aware of where my energy or vibration is. I'm also very aware of the impact food and drink can have on energy so I think it's a combination of that.

Another example of a peak experience for Clare was an immediate recollection of a previous emotional exchange. She plunged straight into the memory, explaining: "I'm not having to think about things, I'm going back to the emotion, and finding an emotion in the memory banks is actually a lot quicker than remembering an event."

***

Our next participant, **Carl Grose,** is an experienced senior telecoms leader and currently chief operating officer for a growing, alternative network full fibre provider. His peak experiences started when he was in his early twenties competing with the British bobsleigh squad in European championships. These experiences have been crucial in his development as an individual, team member, and leader: "the rush of adrenalin and cortisol is breath-taking but equally, there is a sense of relief as you've put your team members at risk going down a track at 80mph."

We asked Carl about how he has used his experiences in business and as a leader – the experience of performing at his best, being in flow, and ultimately getting a peak experience. He admitted that it has been a critical foundation to his business:

> I've used my experience in sport and tried to translate that by talking about it and also behaving and organising around it. What's the purpose and vision of the team? Are they motivated and all pushing in the same direction? How do you deal with challenge and conflict?

In his current role, Carl has a young team, and together they work through uncertainty and massive change to perform at their peak and engage with flow so everyone in the team is of one mind and purpose. And they're succeeding, turning around a company from low to high engagement. The response he observes from his team is rewarding:

> I see it in their faces. Some who are normally short of words suddenly become enthusiastic to express their sheer delight at being singled out for their performance which, in turn, motivates and engages the whole team.

Carl believes it all comes down to energy and flow. Energy is contagious and so is flow. Furthermore, he believes the role of the leader in today's crazy world is to bring flow and energy through interventions and setting an example. Seeing his team members grow and glow gives Carl a sense of cohesion between individual members and the team itself, which ultimately benefits the organisation:

> And from a cultural perspective it endorses values held by the company. It does energise us and I associate energy with flow. Getting people's energy up is such a big thing. I have to get myself into play at 5.00 am to be able to energise the team.

We asked Carl how he is able to motivate himself to drive the team to perform and experience flow and peak experience:

Whether training for sport or leading an organisation, it's rituals and routine that regulate the results to evoke flow or peak experience. Without them, things go off the rails. With them you can feel a buzz in the organisation, see people getting excited, and showing pride in delivering – putting in the extra mile to get that result.

Carl's results with his team reinforce Keller and Meaney's (2017) findings that team members become more energised when they feel trusted and able to learn, innovate, and take risks.

The Significance of Peak Experience in This Context

As noted in the summary of research earlier in this chapter, in the context of the workplace, self-transcendence seems to be more often studied than peak experience itself. For example, Morrison (2018) identified self-transcendence as valuable for helping to find meaningfulness in the workplace, and contributing to important ideals such as corporate social responsibility and sustainable business practices. This finding supports Koltko-Rivera's (2006) view that transcendence can influence world views and help promote a greater sense of purpose that extends beyond personal needs. Venter (2012, 2024) similarly argues that self-transcendence can lead to identifying a greater cause than the self. This creates a shift to a wider perspective for individuals involved in leadership and organisational management, and as Maslow (1971) indicated, changes their view of the world and themselves.

We would argue, however, that self-transcendence is not exactly the same as peak experience. Although self-transcendence is essential to peak experience, conversely, a peak experience is not necessary for self-transcendence to occur. As Koltko-Rivera (2006) argued, the ability to be self-transcendent involves fostering causes beyond the self and devoting ourselves to selfless service. Frankl (1985) also made a useful link between self-transcendence and self-actualisation, arguing:

> The more one forgets himself – by giving himself to a cause to serve or another person to love – the more human he is and the more he actualizes himself. . . . self-actualization is possible only as a side-effect of self-transcendence.
> (Frankl, 1985, p. 133)

Correspondingly, self-transcendence appears to be an important element in team building and cohesion. Participants in this context invariably identified experiencing self-transcendent peaks in a team setting, particularly when there was trust being built and collective effort involved. Nikki explained how it is essential to her that she is doing something to benefit individuals and the business and recalled an experience of what we might call "team togetherness" that created a peak for her. This team togetherness involved shared purpose within the team and a loss of ego. Andy's peak experiences were also linked with team cohesion and purpose, and everyone "rowing very, very hard in the same direction."

Echoing Thornton et al.'s (1999) finding that business leaders had peak experiences that achieved lasting after-effects, we note that Kevin and Nikki shared similar experiences. Kevin spoke of how his decision to take control and step away from a successful career enabled him to experience a peak that stays with him. Nikki reported how a team peak experience became part of the shared language for the group, what she subsequently called an "anchored moment."

The connectivity and relationship with others is discussed by several participants as an important part of peak experiences. For Ruth, a peak experience is when she sees others "open their mind a little bit and bring themselves away from task and function." She gets a feeling that something is absolutely right.

Carl used his experience in sport to promote the purpose and vision of his team and ensure they were motivated and pulling in the same direction. He speaks about the rituals and routines of preparation being important. Carl's young team have worked through uncertainty and change to perform at their peak and ensure everyone is of one mind and purpose. As identified by Fu and Ma (2022, p. 3), these "moments of bonding with others" are vital.

Similarly, Philippa shows how her connections with music have led her to being able to connect new sensations with the leadership development programme at work, a programme interestingly about achieving your best. Philippa says she is able to connect and "anchor these peak experiences and the associated sense of wellbeing to create a healthier mindset." This enables her to be more resourceful and resilient in the work environment.

Several participants talked about experiencing flow in conjunction with, or as a precursor to, peak experience. Ruth linked the use of her personal skills to the flow experience. In the literature, Schindehutte et al. (2006) explained how peak performance, peak experience, and flow are highly interrelated variables which embrace significant aspects of entrepreneurs. This entanglement of the variables is illustrated by our contributors, Clare, Andy, and Kevin, who all agreed that uncertainty concerning outcomes can produce peak performance, which is rewarding and self-actualising and may in turn result in a peak experience. Such a peak experience is felt as meaningful and self-validating – a kind of richness and joy. Participants admitted that they often then became further engaged in the project, producing more flow experiences, growth, and a keenness to start another venture.

References

Bakker, A. B. (2005). Flow among music teachers and their students: The crossover of peak experiences. *Journal of Vocational Behavior, 66*, 26–44.

Bakker, A. B., & Van Woerkom, M. (2017). Flow at work: A self-determination perspective. *Occupational Health Science, 1*, 47–65.

Frankl, V. E. (1985). *Man's search for meaning*. Simon and Schuster.

Fu, X., & Ma, J. (2022). Employees' peak experience at work: Understanding the triggers and impacts. *Frontiers in Psychology*, 6692.

Garfield, C. A. (1986). *Peak performers: The new heroes of American business*. New York: William Morrow.

Garfield, C. A. (1987). Peak performance in business. *Training & Development Journal, 41*(4), 54–59.

Glick-Smith, J. L. (2018). Flow-based leadership through emergent design. In *Exceptional leadership by design: How design in great organizations produces great leadership* (pp. 171–192). Emerald Publishing Limited.

Keller, S., & Meaney, M. (2017). High-performing teams: A timeless leadership topic. *McKinsey Quarterly*, *3*(July), 81–87.

Klein, J., & Ninio, R. (2019). School principals' key experiences and changing management patterns. *International Journal of Educational Management*, *33*(5), 903–918.

Koltko-Rivera, M. E. (2006). Rediscovering the later version of Maslow's hierarchy of needs: Self-transcendence and opportunities for theory, research, and unification. *Review of General Psychology*, *10*(4), 302–317.

Madden, A., & Bailey, C. (2019). Self-transcendence and meaningful work. In R. Yeoman, C. Bailey, A. Madden, & M. Thompson (Eds.), *The Oxford handbook of meaningful work* (pp. 148–164). Oxford University Press.

Maslow, A. H. (1961). Peak experiences as acute identity experiences. *The American Journal of Psychoanalysis*, *21*, 254–262.

Maslow, A. H. (1968). *Toward a psychology of being*. Princeton, NJ: D. Van Nostrand.

Maslow, A. H. (1971). *The farther reaches of human nature*. New York: The Viking Press.

Morrison, M. A. (2018). Increasing the meaningfulness of work with motivational self-transcendence. *International Journal of Existential Psychology and Psychotherapy.* Special Issue: Proceedings of the 2016 Meaning Conference, pp. 1–16.

Ninio, R. (2015). *Peak experiences in principals' career as designing and changing management patterns*. Unpublished Masters Dissertation, School of Education, Bar-Ilan University Ramat Gan, Israel.

Privette, G., & Bundrick, C. M. (1987). Measurement of experience: Construct and content validity of the experience questionnaire. *Perceptual and Motor Skills*, *65*(1), 315–332.

Ratten, V., & Hodge, J. (2016). So much theory, so little practice: A literature review of workplace improvisation training. *Industrial and Commercial Training*, *48*(3), 149–155. https://doi.org/10.1108/ICT-08-2015-0053

Romanelli, A., Moran, G. S., & Tishby, O. (2019). I'mprovisation – Therapists' subjective experience during improvisational moments in the clinical encounter. *Psychoanalytic Dialogues*, *29*(3), 284–305.

Ryan, R. M., & Deci, E. L. (2000). Self-determination theory and the facilitation of intrinsic motivation, social development, and well-being. *American Psychologist*, *55*(1), 68–78.

Schindehutte, M., Morris, M., & Allen, J. (2006). Beyond achievement: Entrepreneurship as extreme experience. *Small Business Economics*, *27*, 349–368.

Thornton, F., Privette, G., & Bundrick, C. M. (1999). Peak performance of business leaders: An experience parallel to self-actualization theory. *Journal of Business and Psychology*, *14*, 253–264.

Venter, H. J. (2012). Maslow's self-transcendence: How it can enrich organization culture and leadership. *International Journal of Business, Humanities and Technology*, *2*(7), 64–71.

Venter, H. J. (2024). Maslow's concept of self-transcendence, the underutilized factor in human capital. *International Social Science and Humanities Studies*, *4*(1).

Weijers, K. A. M. (2021). Peak moments: The experience of coaches. *Submitted in Partial Fulfilment of the Requirements of the Award of Doctor of Coaching and Mentoring*. Business School, Oxford Brookes University.

12 Peak Experiences in Relationships, Love, and Sex

Introduction

In humanistic psychology, love is regarded as the key to realising human potential. Indeed, belongingness and love are seen as necessary underpinnings in the quest towards self-actualisation, as the pinnacle of that potential. Physical love has also been identified as important for the attainment of peak experiences, and Maslow (1971) actually considered that one of the easiest ways of getting peak experiences is through sex. In this chapter, we are concerned with peak experience in different types of love relationships, including familial and romantic as well as the more physical.

The humanistic conception of love has its origins in the platonic idea of love as the foundation of virtue. However, the ancient Greeks identified six kinds of love (Konstan, 2018):

1) *Storge*, which is the familial love like parents have for children;
2) *Philia*, (or Philos) involving a dispassionate regard for a friend or an equal;
3) *Eros* or romantic and intimate love;
4) *Philautia* or self-love;
5) *Xenia*, the Greek word for guest-love or hospitality, and
6) *Agape*, which is divine or unconditional love.

In his 1957 sermon, Martin Luther King, Jr. pinpointed *eros, philia*, and *agape* in his quest to realise the injunction to love one's enemy. He defined *eros* as a "yearning of the soul" that, like desire, is unidirectional; *philia* as "intimate affection" or "reciprocal love"; and *agape* as "the understanding, creative, redemptive goodwill for all men . . . that seeks nothing in return" (King, 1957).

One of the most complete theories of love, however, is provided by Fromm (2000), who described love as an "attitude" or "orientation of character which determines the relatedness of a person to the world as a whole, not toward one 'object' of love" (2000, p. 42). Dropping the Greek terminology, Fromm presented a typology that encompassed motherly love (altruistic love for a child), erotic love (romantic love with the craving for complete union with another person), brotherly love (the love for all beings), self-love, and love of God.

Of her ten love-types, Beddoes-Jones (2017) correlates seven with the Greek and identifies three others Material Love, Love 2.0 (a concept introduced by Meadows-Klue, 2008), and the Love of Nature. These three she proposes may have evolved from the extended ways in which we now think about love and the things we feel passionate about.

In C. S. Lewis's (1975) work on types of love, he explored four categories: Affection, which he equates to the Greek *storge*; Friendship, which is *philia* in the Greek; Eros, which, like the Greek *eros*, is the state of being in love; and Charity, which is linked with *agape*. Lewis distinguished between these four loves but also recognised how each may merge into another. He points out, for instance, that friendship develops out of companionship and suggested that when friendship exists between man and woman, it sometimes changes into romantic love or *eros*. Lewis (1975) also explained how, as soon as humans are fully conscious, they encounter loneliness and need others physically, emotionally, and intellectually. Lumbreras (2020, p. 187) also highlights the importance of love, pointing out that life experiences activate particular biological mechanisms in our bodies and that oxytocin (one of our regulating hormones) has been linked to feelings of love and connectedness.

As with other chapters in the book, we continue our discussion with what the literature reveals about peak experience in different love contexts. We also highlight any alternative terminologies used for peak experiences in these contexts. We then present our participant accounts and their encounters with peak experience in love contexts.

Review of the Research

Maslow (1954) identified love as a central phenomenon in people's lives. However, during the 1950s and 1960s, humanistic and positive psychology were in their infancy and little research had been undertaken, especially in relation to peak experience and love. We have therefore taken the decision to divide our review of the literature into parts that correspond to the types of love identified by the Greeks, who were prolific in their exploration of this topic. We did not find a connection between peak experience and *xenia*, and so we have focused on peak experiences in relation to *storge, eros, philautia, philia*, and *agape* contexts.

Storge: *Familial or Parental Love*

Familial love is the love we feel for close family members and includes maternal, paternal, sisterly, and brotherly love. It even extends to other family members like aunts, uncles, and grandparents. It may be "passionate but not romantic, physically intimate but not sexually intimate" (Beddoes-Jones, 2017, p. 58). The Greek word *storge* means to cover or protect and according to Beddoes-Jones is the basis for the phrase "blood is thicker than water."

Lewis (1975) makes it clear that parental or familial love is a form of love that is "rich and complex," and Fromm (2000) emphasised the unique and profound features of parental love, where a child is loved unconditionally. As a child "there is nothing I have to do in order to be loved – mother's love is unconditional. All I have to do is to be – to be her child" (Fromm, 2000, p. 36).

Our review revealed research into peak experiences connected to both maternal and paternal love, so in the following two subsections we examine this in more detail.

Maternal Love and Peak Experiences

While discussing maternal love, Maslow observed that a mother can experience something similar to a peak experience when marvelling at her child:

> [L]et's say, a mother sitting quietly looking, by the hour, at her baby playing and marvelling, wondering, philosophizing, not quite believing. She can experience this as a very pleasant, continuing, contemplative experience rather than as something akin to a climactic explosion which then ends.
>
> (Maslow, 1970, p. 88)

In her research, Thompson (2010) has drawn comparisons between Maslow's explanations of peak experiences and positive birth experiences. She noted how some of the women she interviewed voiced surprise that birth could be an enjoyable event, with women explaining they were able to enjoy, love, and even relish childbirth. Thompson (2010, pp. 201–202) found the majority of women had euphoric reactions to their positive birth experiences, even using metaphors such as "conquering" and "on top of the world" to express their feelings. Surprisingly, one participant in the study also described her planned Caesarean section in terms of a peak experience: "you couldn't get that feeling with anything [else] on earth, drugs, alcohol, anything, I just wanted to bottle it and keep it forever that feeling, and I still get it."

Thompson records that fulfilling, positive birth experiences left women feeling "strong," "powerful," and "capable of anything" (2010, p. 202). Like peak experiences, they appeared to involve an overflow of energy (Maslow, 1970). Similarly, the disorientation of time and space that Maslow associated with peak experiences was also in evidence.

Lumbreras (2020, p. 194) similarly notes that motherhood provides one of the most intense physical experiences of love: "the hormone cocktail rushing through a new mother's veins supports the feeling of immense and life-changing love." Oxytocin, which is produced by the hypothalamus and released by the pituitary gland, has a fundamental role in "social bonding, sexuality and childbirth" and is labelled the "love hormone" (Lumbreras, 2020, p. 192).

Lumbreras also identified that motherhood presents an avenue for transcendence which is deep-seated in our biology: breastfeeding is purported to instil perfect happiness in new mothers, "mediating the milk ejection reflex, which often elicits feelings of immense, calm love" (2020, p. 194). Maslow (1968a) similarly noted that breastfeeding fosters peak experience.

Inviting us to imagine, feel, and appreciate the depth and vastness of meaning, often overflowing, when a new baby is born, Crowther (2017), a senior lecturer in midwifery, believes that childbirth is a transformative and self-actualising experience, saying that

> birth can provide meaning, fulfilment of purpose and be personally transformative for all whether as a peak moment in time of overwhelming joyful experience or a gradual process of being self-actualised.
>
> (2017, p. 91)

In his description of awe, Paquette also gives the example of the birth of a child as being a time when people have felt "overwhelmed by beauty or encountered something so mind-blowing that it shook [them] to the core" (2020, pp. 6–7). Paquette details how such moments impact us and affect our physiology:

> Awe affects us deeply in a physical level and can lead to a specific changes in our brains and bodies that help explain its powerful impact . . . creating changes to our nervous system, our inflammatory response, our heart rate and even our brains.
>
> (2020, p. 47)

Paternal Love and Peak Experiences

In a study conducted by Moyers (1977), first-time fathers were asked how they perceived their psychological status immediately following the birth of their first child and to what extent peak experiences occurred. That the study was possible at all is interesting, since Maslow struggled and fought with the authorities to attend his own children's births:

> [W]hile women talked about peak experiences from having children, men didn't. Now we have a way to teach men also to have peak experiences from childbirth. This means, . . . being changed, seeing things differently, living in a different world, having different cognitions, in a certain sense some move toward living happily ever after.
>
> (Maslow, 1968a, p. 168)

The results from Moyers's (1977, p. v) study revealed:

- Peak experience occurred more frequently in fathers who attended childbirth classes and availed themselves of other sources of preparation.
- Fathers who viewed themselves as active members of the childbirth team more frequently reported peak experiences.
- Peak experience was dependent upon how fathers felt about assistance received from nursing and medical personnel.
- Fathers reporting peak experience also gave a more positive description of the mother.

In Chapter 1, we met Colin when he shared peak experiences in a religious context. He also shared his paternal feelings of joy, awe, and deep gratitude at the weddings of his daughters:

> Both were extraordinarily wonderful celebrations of the love of our daughters and their fiancés, and then their husbands – and there was a real sense of the love that was being shared.

Colin also has two young granddaughters and explained the surprise he felt at the strength of love he has experienced as Grandpa:

> I just didn't see it coming. I hoped it would be great and wanted to love them and be with them, but just the strength of it! It is qualitatively different from any love I've ever experienced.

Maslow experienced a similar peak experience when his first child was born, and interestingly it confirmed for him that the stimulus-response, prediction-control model of behaviourism was too constraining:

> [W]hen my baby was born that was the thunderclap, that settled things. I looked at this tiny, mysterious thing and felt so stupid. I was stunned by the mystery and by the sense of not really being in control. I felt small and weak and feeble before all this. I'd say anyone who had a baby couldn't be a behaviorist.
>
> (Maslow, 1968b, p. 37)

Eros: *Romantic and Physical Love*

Protasi (2008) expressed a preference for using Greek terms to explain the types of love context, suggesting *eros* is a better term than erotic, romantic, or sexual love. She points out that sexual love risks "being conflated with sexual desire, and puts too much emphasis on the role of sexual attraction in eros" (Protasi, 2008, p. 70). She suggests we should think of *eros* in terms of "the passionate attachment we feel for one special individual, who is seen as beautiful, desirable and valuable." This is especially important since romantic love may put too much emphasis on sentimentality and embodies historical and cultural mores.

Indeed, according to de Rougement (1956), there is no Greek word for romantic love because it is a medieval construction.

Both Fromm (2000) and Lewis (1975) pointed out that *eros* is erotic love but is much more than sexuality. Sexual experience can occur without being "in love" and "Eros includes other things besides sexual activity" (Lewis, 1975, p. 85). In their conceptual paper, Dörfler et al. (2010, p. 23) summarised how *eros* can be seen as involving complete fusion with another person and focuses on exclusivity, reporting that "as we are not capable of total fusion with all other people, the erotic love is exclusive; a union with a single other person."

Maslow himself often made reference to love experiences. He noted "it is possible in the aesthetic experience or the love experiences to become so absorbed and 'poured into' the object that the self, in a very real sense, disappears" (1968b, p. 79). He also described the sexual experiences of self-actualised people as mystical and the pleasures as overpowering and ecstatic (Maslow, 1954).

Our review of peak experiences in the context of *eros* revealed several papers exploring models and methods for measuring sexual ecstasy. For example, Mosher (1980, p. 1) proposed that the depth of involvement in physical love is a complex of psychological processes "in which there is an interaction of fundamental emotions (interest excitement and enjoyment-joy) with cognitions and actions." Mosher argued that involvement in sexual role enactment deepens as participation shifts from (i) disinterested to (ii) casual to (iii) routine to (iv) engrossed to (v) entranced to (vi) ecstatic depths (1980, p. 8). He noted, however, that reaching the "ecstatic depths" is unusual and may be characteristic only of "fully developed trance states, transpersonal experiences, and archaic or mystical unions" (1980, p. 8). Here, he explains, the self is lost, and oceanic feelings, such as those thought to accompany peak experience, are common: union with the partner is complete, and the experience is described as a peak.

Mosher (1980) makes a link back to Maslow (1971), who described the physical act as transcendence to meta-values that are realised in the union. Mosher explains how it transcends the partners as particular people, explaining that individuals become "universal man and woman, and the human act of loving becomes a spiritual sharing of a universal union that is the source of life"(1980, p. 21).

> In the engagement with the partner the synergy of their loving passes over into a spiritual, mystic, or archetypal plane in which the boundaries between self and alter, between now and then, between here and there are transcended. . . . The person transcends all consciousness of self in the absorption of being thrown into union.
>
> (Mosher, 1980, pp. 21–22)

Lashua (2018) examined whether spiritualisation of sexuality predicted increases in sexual satisfaction and couple satisfaction. Exploring the relationship between transcendence, sacredness, and sexuality, she identified four subscales: sacred, transcendence, peak experience, and spiritual importance. She found deep, transcendent connections between a couple can lead to transcendent qualities of sex and the feeling of loss of self often reported during peak experiences.

Beddoes-Jones (2017) similarly considers that *eros* or romantic love enables more peak experiences. She simplifies *eros* or romantic love into two stages: Stage 1: I'm in love with you – the honeymoon fantasy period, obsessive, lusty, and sexual; and Stage 2: I love you – the mature love and reality, the partnership and companionship. She argues that peak experiences within Stage 2 may be blissful, meaningful events that are both memorable and enjoyable, but they are not the sizzling, passionate peak experiences encountered in Stage 1.

Elfers and Offringa (2019, p. 3) described a measure to explore the cluster of features that emerge during peak states of awareness triggered by sexual arousal. They used the term "peak sexual experience" to encompass various terms for the altered states of consciousness that result. They observed, most notably, "altered sensory perceptions, intense emotional connection, feelings of bliss and ecstasy, and a powerful connection with a transcendent divinity" (2019, p. 3). They concluded that the ecstatic nature of sexuality is more than an exceptional orgasm and more than an emotional connection with a partner.

Woodward et al. (2009, p. 429), in their study of peak experiences and their relevance to the functioning of relationships, found participants identifying as having peak experiences were "on average significantly older, more passionate, more sexually responsive." They confirmed that participants' perceptions of their peak experiences were associated with positive relationships and deeper bonds. They found meaning in such experiences and a sense that their relationship was "fated and meant to be" (p. 438).

As noted earlier, Maslow connected self-actualisation with peak experiences, suggesting peaks could be a catalyst for further human development. Aron and Aron (2014, p. 50) have asked how much a marriage can contribute to this development arguing that "sexual ecstasy and other moments of passion can certainly be peak experiences that couples may experience together." However, Aron and Aron also note the value of individual inner practices, such as meditation and their link to enhancing "self-actualisation-type qualities" (2014, p. 51). Even watching a sunset, they say, may be best done alone otherwise we may be "worrying about whether the other is enjoying it or perhaps wants to go to dinner now" (2014, p. 51). This privacy aspect of self-actualisation, Aron and Aron predicted, might become stronger as individuals come closer to the peak, they may become "more dissatisfied with a marriage of pure togetherness" (2014, p. 51). Indeed, Maslow's (1950) semi-experimental study of self-actualising people showed that two of the characteristics they possessed were the capacity for detachment and a need for privacy and autonomy. For Maslow, then, solitude is seen as an important factor at the peak.

Philautia: *Self-Love*

According to Fromm (2000), self-love (*Philautia* in the Greek) develops from emotional maturity or, as Maslow would argue, from self-actualisation. We cannot love others fully without loving ourselves first.

Fromm's analysis (2000) of mature love (as differentiated from symbiotic love) is based on the Delphic motto, "know thyself." He sees the components of mature love as caring, respect, responsibility, and knowledge, and so a key part of this maturity is self-love. He also clarifies that "selfishness and self-love, far from being identical are actually opposites. The selfish person does not love himself too much but too little" (2000, p. 55).

Pope (1991, p. 386) similarly expressed his frustration at the muddled portrayal of self-love when he wrote:

> The excessive narrow construal of self-love as the pursuit of isolated self-interest or the gratification of arbitrary and idiosyncratic desires constitutes a substantial impoverishment of the concept.

As Fromm (2000) pointed out, Freud erroneously treated self-love as inseparable from the concept of narcissism. Fromm (2000) thus argued against using narcissism and selfishness interchangeably with self-love, considering that both terms are not indicators of the excess of self-love but are quite different concepts, being caused by the very lack of self-love.

Maharaj and April (2013) also explained how self-love has been the subject of much misunderstanding that seems to be fuelled by opinions that view self-love as being "selfish, sinful and prohibitive of one's ability to love another" (2013, p. 122). They identify various studies that imply negative and positive correlations between love styles and self-esteem levels, suggesting that "people with lower self-esteem are unable to truly give love to others in relationships" (2013, p. 122). Self-love, according to Ferris (1988, p. 50), involves respect for our own physical, emotional, mental, and spiritual health: inherent in the concept are attributes such as self-knowledge, spirituality, clarity of intention, self-acceptance, and interconnectedness.

Maharaj and April (2013) further describe how Maslow identified the ability to love as an important trait, and although he does not overtly discuss self-love, it is implied in his description of self-actualised individuals. Maslow (1968b) suggested self-actualised people possess "a healthy selfishness, a great self-respect." He even argues that the contrasting dynamics of love for the Being (B-Love) of another person implies "unneeding love, unselfish love," whereas deficiency love (D-love which is part of the hierarchy of needs) involves "love need, selfish love." Maslow considered love as a need that had to be fulfilled before self-actualisation could be achieved and that once fulfilled, individuals are able to give love in return as part of their self-actualised being. Maslow (1954, p. 257) further noted that the love relationship in self-actualisation is "a fusion of (1) the ability to love and (2) respect for oneself and other." It is this fusion that prepares the ground for peak experiences in the love context.

Similarly, drawing on the thinking of St. Thomas Aquinas, Pope (1991, p. 399) has argued that not only is "neighbor" love (discussed in our next section) made possible by true self-love, but "true self-love requires and gives rise to self-giving neighbor love" in a kind of "mirroring" interaction.

> The selfish person does not fail properly to love the other because of his or her selfishness – rather, failure of love for the other is of a piece with failure to love the self properly and fully.
>
> (Pope, 1991, p. 399)

Thus, we see how self-love, rather than being a hindrance, actually enables the ability to genuinely love others: "Self-love enables neighbor love which then leads to the sense of connectedness that is essential to the innate social spirit in man" (Maharaj & April, 2013, p. 124).

Philia: *Brotherly, Friendship, Neighbourly Love*

Like Protasi (2008), we consider the use of Greek terms for love, such as *philia*, helps us avoid some ambiguities and are aesthetically pleasing and conceptually stimulating. However, Protasi points out that our modern conception of friendship may be very different from the Greek idea of it. She acknowledges, for instance, that C.S. Lewis's discussion of the topic was influenced by the classic and arguably narrower conception of a male relationship as "an almost sacral bond between educated and noble souls" (Protasi, 2008). Conversely, Protasi argues, *philia* was a wider concept; it could refer to feelings for "people in the same family or mere acquaintances, fellow citizens, and sexual partners, and . . . spouses" (2008).

Fromm (2000) described this kind of brotherly love as "the most fundamental kind of love, which underlies all types" (2000, p. 42). He suggested it is a love between equals, and it does not involve exclusiveness:

> Brotherly love is love for all human beings; it is characterized by its very lack of exclusiveness. If I have developed the capacity for love, then I cannot help loving my brothers.
>
> (2000, p. 43)

According to Herrmann (2019), brotherly love is the continuation of God's love through our relations with others and is ultimately a precondition for the perfect love of God through *agape*. Referring to the Gospel of St John, Herrmann explains, "the only way to understand brotherly love is to see it as stemming from the Father's love for us expressed through His Son." God's *agape* is thus seen as "the source and a model for any other kind of love" (2019, p. 213) and as such is a precursor to peak experiences through those other kinds of love.

Agape: *Divine, Universal, Altruistic Love*

Post (2002) reminds us that *agape* is a Greek word adopted by the writers of the New Testament to present a form of unlimited altruistic love. The Greeks also seemed to include various kinds of affection as *agape*, including caring for children and love between spouses and so the definition could additionally be translated as contentment or appreciation, as well as love. Post explains *agape* is essentially "altruistic love universalized to all humanity as informed by theistic commitments" (2002, p. 56). This definition makes it distinct from *philia*, which involves affection, and *eros*, which is passionate love (Finn, 2013).

Going further, Protasi (2008) has summarised the role of *agape* as referring to at least three loving attitudes: "that of God toward us, that of us toward God, and that of us toward humanity." According to Protasi, in Christian and other Western spiritual traditions, the word *agape* refers to "human beings manifesting God's pure love, or an intentional and unconditional love for others, including enemies."

The synergy between *agape* as the demonstration of God's love and the manifestation of our own altruistic love is taken up by Dörfler et al. (2010, p. 23), who explained that "if love governs us towards unity with other people, then *agape* . . . governs us to embrace the whole of nature, the whole universe." They argue that *agape* is all-consuming and in its purest form "can be observed in saints who go among people to help them and hermits who leave the world of people to be united with the general force of life" (2010, p. 23). Beddoes-Jones also adds that this kind of "agapistic," universal love, "is a wholly selfless love. . . . It is the unconditional regard for all people irrespective of age, creed colour, disability and despite their behaviour towards us or anyone else" (2017, p. 46). Equally, Post (2002, p. 58) argued that *agape* must "be contrasted with romantic love (*Eros*) without denying it." He describes romantic love as focusing attention on a single other "and tending to blot out the remainder of the universe." Agape, by contrast, is based on an appreciation of the distinctive value of the other "against a backdrop of equal regard and attentiveness."

The embracing of *agape*, almost as a constituent within other types of love, was also recognised by Maslow (1959, p. 44). He considered that self-actualising people, who were "by definition gratified in their basic needs, including the love need," were also more loving as well. Maslow linked this kind of love – what he called "love for the essence of or the Being of the other person" – with the Greek formulation of *agap*e and the theological concept of godly love: "it is love for another person because he is what he is, rather than because he is a need-gratifier" (Maslow, 1959, p. 44).

Peak Experience in Context: Participant Accounts

The first of our seven participants is **Francesco**, whose understanding of peak experience in this context is specifically oriented towards *eros*, towards physical contact and desire. He is now in his mid-sixties and is someone who has led a colourful life as both a heterosexual and a gay man.

Until the age of 40, his relationships had been driven by his need and pursuit of casual, sometimes one-off yet intense meetings with people, initiated often by an intense look of lustful desire which resulted in a passionate affair. He thought the whole period of his life between the ages 20 and 40 had been punctuated by what he called peak experiences, as the initial meetings were blindingly intense. Yet he was unable to recall why each encounter had failed to continue, nor why each had ended.

Francesco's peak experiences were linked to a powerful frisson between himself and individuals who were also looking for excitement and, as he called it, "the chase." We asked him what he was experiencing when this frisson happened, and he was able to express it as a rush of excitement and a feeling of not being able to get one particular person out of his everyday thinking until the next meeting. Francesco recalls how he felt at that time:

> Adrenaline running around the body . . . excitement and everything. . . . I couldn't get him out of my mind. I couldn't wait to get back up to Glasgow, it completely took over my life. I eventually returned to Glasgow, and we started upon this passionate relationship.

Francesco's feelings illustrate Beddoes-Jones's (2017) observation that peak experience is a response to stimuli or triggers; the brain, heart, and each cell of the body vibrate and sizzle when a peak experience happens.

Francesco talked of embarking on these encounters as "passionate relationships," yet he remained aloof about reciprocal feelings. Francesco recalls how they were in a music club one evening, and "he was telling me how much in love with me he was, and this was totally new to me." All Francesco was interested in was finding out what the band was playing and remembers that occasion through the music and not the person.

Another peak experience, he recalls, came from depression. He found himself walking the streets of Glasgow, feeling low but unable to remember the cause. Suddenly, a car drew up, stopped, and the driver asked Francesco if he was all right. Another encounter and the start of another "passionate affair."

Interestingly, Francesco thinks that these passionate affairs were made all the more intense due to the secrecy of homosexuality in the late 1970s and early 1980s. He said he was unable to share his experiences and had to keep them to himself so the intensity of the experience increased. It was "just me, so I had the whole of the experience to myself; I couldn't un-burden it onto someone else." He maintains that in the sharing with another, one loses something to someone else, an interesting perspective, "part of it leaves you when sharing with someone else."

He agreed that in all of these encounters he reacted in the same way – a rush of cortisol and adrenaline, a feeling of utter excitement, the frisson, and the thrill of the chase. Francesco described it as something he almost regrets and seemed to rue that this part of his life was over whilst still accepting that life was safe and secure with his partner:

> It's the most fantastic thing that I miss now. Not that I would do it anyway, but I miss the chase. That initial meeting and seeing if you are reading the right signals, messages and language? It's the chase. That is so, so exciting and exhilarating and there were many occasions with many men, and women as well.

It is curious that, although these affairs were "part of the chase," he could remember vividly the names of at least three encounters of longer-term relationships that started as passionate encounters. He admitted they were memorable, chiming with Maslow's concept of peak experience. Yet when he considered whether peak experiences served a purpose for human beings to differentiate them from the animal kingdom, he explained:

> But we're all animals. We've got animal instincts. I think it's just pure sexual lust, an animal reaction. Because looking back at those relationships, sex was key. When told how much in love people were with me, when compliments poured, it meant nothing to me. I didn't feel it back. It was all sexual lust and physical contact and I and went after people for that reason. The mind and the heart never came into it. It was physical. And I absolutely craved it.

Francesco did, however, agree that his peak experience was a *mutual* physical lust – the look, the eye contact, and the ensuing chase that both parties felt. It wasn't one-sided but a physical connection between two people. He went on to consider how his peak experiences changed with age. He has now been in a permanent relationship with one man for almost 30 years:

> It wasn't the physical contact as it was weeks and weeks, even a year, before that happened. I had peak experiences just seeing him walking before me in the corridor at work or seeing him walk past my door. Just seeing him. It was as good as having sex. I thought I was being the careful one, but it was only later that he told me he was stalking me. My peak experiences had changed.

When asking Francesco where in his body he was experiencing his peak, he said it was the heart and tummy and was a different feeling from the early years of chase and frisson:

> In my view of it, however naïve this may seem, a peak experience is exactly what it says, an experience that is remembered, a pinnacle in your life. But my experience has definitely changed. When my now partner and I got together it became very physical.

We asked him if he felt differently because it was a relationship involving love. He replied immediately, asking:

> What is love? Being infatuated with someone? Not being able to live without them? You might ask if I'm in love with him now . . . no, I'm not. But do I love him? Yes. Being "in love" and "love" are two different things. And I think you could ask the same question to many others who would agree.

We enquired when and if a change happened to the peaks in this relationship, and Francesco said he didn't know, "it's between two people and the chemistry between them." He did, however, admit that emotions started to play a part in his feelings towards his partner, feelings which grew, resulting in the longevity of their relationship:

> Even sitting here now is a peak because I can say that I have been faithfully married for 30 years – unheard of in the gay scene. It is satisfying and makes me feel safe and proud that I'm gay and have been able to rise above prejudice in my work and career. I am a proud Yorkshireman, the son of a copper. Even as a gay man, has been able to successfully infiltrate the higher echelons of education and religion and hold my own with respect and acclaim from others.

These achievements are another peak for Francesco. People now know of his relationship and feel comfortable and safe in his company.

On a final note, Francesco was brought up in a devout Roman Catholic house and remains religious. His concept of pinnacles and peaks could be said to reflect his religious beliefs. He said that his entire pinnacle of sexual peak experiences lasted a while, but he has settled down.

God said that sex and lust has got nothing to do with God. It has to do with the devil. Pure lust. Because according to Catholic teaching and God, what is the reason for sex? Procreation. Lust is a sin. Fornication is a sin – Sodom and Gomorrah. The procreation of life is the one reason for sex. And the other is lust. But unfortunately, we are all sinners, and we all fall into this trap. Is there an element of love in there? Yes, but it's still very much an element of lust.

We discussed how peak experience is linked with connectivity and that as human beings we seek and need connection through lust and sex. There is something integral to that need that leads to a peak experience. Francesco agreed but said all people are different, and all relationships between others are different.

Francesco's peak experiences now are still triggered by anticipation but more measured. He realises that the frisson and the chase that were once prominent have been relegated to his youth:

It's almost as though we've reached the speed we're going to go at and have put on cruise control. We've had a hell of a lot of fun getting there but now we're getting older and settled down to that old cliché of being a couple with our baby, our adorable dog. I've learnt to accept things and you know what, I'm happy in my life now. So, I'm just going to put myself in overdrive and just enjoy my life with my husband. The thought of returning to my wayward youth is out of my mind.

***

Our next participant, **Fiona Beddoes-Jones**, is a chartered psychologist and author. Her recollection of a peak experience in this context was a moment when time seemed to stand still, and yet the experience was over in a flash. She attributes this peak experience to romantic love, the sort of love where one subjugates oneself to another for the pleasure of giving. She said she has thought a lot about it over the years because she both loved her partner and was in love with him at the same time. She also found him powerfully attractive, making love-making very easy. There were no barriers.

During the peak experience, Fiona felt completely happy, relaxed, and safe. She recalls feeling so connected to him and the universe that she couldn't actually tell where his body finished and hers began: there was no conversation, and she could hardly speak or form a sentence. It was a very spiritual experience, which she says made her feel connected with the universe, with the connection being made through him, as though he were the catalyst.

Fiona's feelings of transcendence and connection with the universe resonate with Maslow's (1962, 1999) position on peak experience – that some of the effects or after-effects may be permanent but the high moment itself is not. The feeling of unity, togetherness, and oneness associated with a peak experience makes such experiences memorable, easily recalled, and leave a deep impression:

> [F]or example, lovers come closer to forming a unit rather than two people, the I-Thou monism becomes more possible, the creator becomes one with his work being created, the mother feels one with her child.
>
> (Maslow, 1999, p. 117)

Fiona also made a connection between peak experience and the Caesarean birth of her daughter. She said she has the same feelings about childbirth as those she had in her earlier peak experience – a feeling of safety and oneness with the universe – a feeling she associates closely with maternal love:

> If I were to die now, that would be OK because I'm as happy as I could be. It's a completeness, there's nothing missing. It's not that the future doesn't exist: the future doesn't matter. Had anything gone wrong, had it be a choice between me living or her living I would have chosen her in a heartbeat and quite happily died.

As already noted, Maslow also made a connection between peak experience and childbirth. His studies suggested peak experiences could come from "the great moments of love and sex . . . from women giving natural birth to babies – or just from loving them" (1962, p. 10).

Fiona also recalls what she calls "universal love" or *agape*, the theme of loving all mankind, triggered perhaps by prayer, song, or a community environment such as a gospel choir. She shared a peak experience from the theology course she was doing when she experienced this kind of universal love:

> Before the course started the students would go into the Chapel in the Bishop's Palace for a service. On this occasion the service was led by a vicar, a former jazz saxophonist, before entering the Ministry. He accompanied the hymns, playing jazz sax and it was an amazing, unforgettable experience. It was *the* moment on the course when I felt *the* happiest. I felt totally connected with God, the universe and the other students in the room.

Her understanding is that peak experiences are "memorable, things you don't forget and encounters that are easily recounted." She calls them "extraordinary encounters." The sound of the saxophone and a particular hymn, *Here I am Lord*, immediately take her back to that occasion, and the experience can be replayed in her mind.

We asked Fiona if she could share any peak experiences within familial or *storge* love. She is a twin and recalled an emotionally charged memory with her twin brother when he lay on his deathbed. However, such an unbelievably tense and sad circumstance was too emotional an experience for her to detail. She said she had a video of the time but shared how "it was the last conversation I had with him and find it too painful to watch."

Another experience happened when she was about 18, feeling depressed and miserable. She remembers waking up suddenly and feeling scared. Her grandmother, who she felt particularly connected to, had died some years earlier but she felt her presence. Her grandmother then told her that "everything is going to be OK. There is no need for you to be scared." Fiona firmly believes this was a peak experience and could be described as transcendental. She said:

> That connection to the universe, that spiritual connection is where we are taken out of ourselves. I think there is a particular area of the brain that is triggered when that happens.

Maslow (1970) has a description that fits Fiona's experience when she felt taken out of herself. He calls it a "unitive consciousness" experience – a special phenomenological state in which the person somehow perceives the unity and integration of the cosmos.

Finally, we asked Fiona if the state of being totally engaged in an activity is related to self-love or *philautia*. She said she thinks that self-love is

> [w]hen you are doing something entirely for yourself. And there is healthy self-love or there is too much self-love when you go into narcissism. It has to be that healthy aspect. My memory of self-love goes back to when I was 18 and read Jonathan Livingston's *The Seagull*. That was a peak experience because I was really, really able to connect with myself but beyond myself. Because I found it fundamentally moving. The Seagull is a metaphor for living and personal development. It's very powerful.

***

The following two vignettes could be illustrations of *eros* or romantic love, or they might be examples of *Ludus*, another Greek term for playful and non-committal love, involving flirting, seduction, and casual sex (Hendrick & Hendrick, 1986). Beddoes-Jones similarly believes peaks can come from a brief encounter, since there are different forms of peak experience for each type of love. This thinking reflects the moments of connection discussed in Fredrickson's book, *Love 2.0* (2013) and is the sort of love that can happen between two strangers.

The first vignette is shared by **Kay** (one of this book's co-authors), and this is her story:

> I met him three years ago on a dating site – an illicit dating site. We exchanged emails and messages and there was a frisson even before we met, which was only twice in three years; two lunches, each a year apart. We drifted apart, but we caught up, always by email, never by text and only once spoke on the phone. It was always he who contacted me: "where's my friend?" . . . "I'm here."
>
> Our exchanges were playful, flirty, sometimes serious, often about work, his and mine and he vowed that we would always be friends. We had never kissed. We'd never had physical contact but there was a promise, a rumbling of something more, that may or not be fulfilled.

And then it was. Fulfilled. We met. We made love for two and a half hours . . . sheer bliss, sheer eroticism, sheer indulgence.

We met for a second time. The ecstasy was intensified, to the point that we felt out of control yet somehow safe – something mutual and dangerous and exciting. Two bodies becoming one, time standing still, no jerks, no nudges, no embarrassment just sheer ecstasy and flow.

We met a third time. The same. Passion fused with lust and a tacit understanding of each other's bodies. Already. And then silence. It was as though he felt shame at the intensity of our encounters or simply forgot about my existence. It was hurtful, incomprehensible. And the pattern continues to this day . . . the fear of being without is unthinkable.

As Beddoes-Jones (2017) reveals, stage 1 of romantic love is also the honeymoon period when love is blind. We accept because we cannot bear the thought of being without the other, as Kay says.

The impact of this love affair is also apparent in a dream that Kay experienced. She describes how, in the dream, she had the most serene yet utterly rewarding moment with her lover. They were in a room, a familiar room which resembled her kitchen:

There were people milling around in the surrounding space, but they seemed to be out of focus as though in a badly taken photograph. Nobody was recognisable. He was standing behind me. Time seemed to stand still but he slowly turned me around, faced me, looked deeply into my eyes, and simply said "You know I love you, don't you?" That's it! A moment I shall always remember and re-live as it felt so real. There was no tension, no feeling of emergency, just simplicity.

When Kay awoke and remembered what had happened, she wondered if her unconscious mind was playing tricks and creating a desired state. "Who knows?" she says, "It doesn't matter. I felt something unique, ephemeral and ethereal which can only be described as a peak experience in slumber."

Kontula (2021, pp. 22–23) established that there are a number of memorable types of sexual experiences, including first times or surprises, exceeding the allotted time or having limited time, and idyllic situations or ideal partners. He found such memorable experiences typically were related to "the initial experiences with a new partner, experimenting with new ways of having sex, or making love in a new type of environment." These potentially peak experiences are characterised by the attraction to something new.

***

Our next vignette is from **Ben,** who found it much more difficult than he had imagined trying to put his experience into words. The peak experience itself went so far beyond the confines of language. He felt that using words to try to capture it imposed limits and restrictions.

> Exploring language in all its variety and subtlety is a great joy for me – I love using it, playing with it. For certain things, however, it seems inadequate – sensations and emotions don't include words.

Ben explained how he was quite late to sexual activity, but at the age of 21 he became involved with a fellow student. He explains how the sex was "very low key," but, as it was his first experience, this was how he assumed it was: "I had nothing with which to compare it. It became more and more frustrating, as I realised her view of sex was that it was something a man does to a woman – she wasn't an active participant."

Ben then described how, after about five years, he had an involvement with an older woman, and a world opened up which he could never have imagined.

> She was an active and enthusiastic partner and though she had more experience than I, she was also astonished by the intensity of the passion. Our bodies reacted so instantly to each other. And we would make love for hours at a time – I would be erect for three hours or more. Prior to this, if anyone had tried to describe such a thing to me, I wouldn't have believed it.

The intense physicality arising from previously unknown and unimagined capabilities was all-consuming for Ben, involving a kind of "self-abandonment to that mutual physicality which created previously unknown states of consciousness – our entire beings transformed, transported to another place." Ben described how it was

> the most complete fusion of two beings in total harmony – entirely in tune with one another. There was never talk along the lines of "what shall we do next?" It flowed naturally, seamlessly, instinctively. It was the most enriching and fulfilling life experience.

Rokach and Patel (2021) studied how peak experiences occur in relation to people's sexual lives, finding that people, much like Ben, described positive sexual experiences using attributes similar to those identified by Maslow. These descriptions included features such as a sense of peace, bliss, growth enhancing and healing, and a feeling of timelessness (Rokach & Patel, 2021, p. 339).

***

Stokke (2021, p. 142) describes how spiritual love relations are distinct from romantic love: soul mate meetings lead to "immediate, mutual bonding, and secure attachment." In this section we present three short accounts where participants talk about their first encounters with a partner – events that were potentially love at first sight.

Andrew Barton (known as Barty) is the award-winning hairdresser we met in the Creative Arts context. He described to us how he first met his partner and describes it as a peak experience. He and Phil had been speaking for almost five months but had never met in person. Barty recalls the laughter in their communication before actually meeting but how he felt nervous when that moment arose. The morning of that day was memorable; deciding what to wear, was the weather going to change – and yet his nervousness was short-lived. He got off the train onto the platform and remembers seeing Phil standing on the concourse smiling. Barty says he just took one look and knew that he was going to spend the rest of his life with him:

> I don't know how I explain that feeling and interestingly that's never changed as we've got to know each other better over the last three years. We've had arguments and clashes at times yet I still sense that it's not changed for me at all.

Barty admits that he's not sure how to describe such feelings:

> There's a sense of assurance and a feeling of confidence. It just feels right, even when he is a challenge at times. There's a lot of giddy excitement and that happens most days when I'm just giddy – just seeing him or hearing his voice – giddy as a kipper. It's the excitement of wanting to spend time with him, I guess, after that initial thought of "I'm gonna spend the rest of my life with you." And all the time we got to know each other I became very respectful towards his needs as well. It feels part of the giddy, dizziness for me because I care very much about him.

***

The next extract in this triad is from **Fiona Haygreen,** who we met previously in the Creative Arts context. She shared a peak experience from the time when she first met her husband, Ian.

> We'd both had a period of depression, and were in a very low place. When we met each other, it was like a breath of fresh air. And thrilling. And we had an experience together which I would describe as almost spiritual. We just connected on a really personal level, just holding onto each other. It was like the rest of the world completely disappeared and I felt like we were melding into one in a way. It was so difficult now to remember as I've never come close to that feeling again. It's in my memory, the thrill of that connection between us.

Fiona shares how the experience was mutual: they both felt an immediate togetherness, to the point that Ian was going to ask her to marry him a week after they met.

The peak experience happened a few weeks into their relationship, an emotional and spiritual connection which they both felt and talked about afterwards. It wasn't sexual but simply emotional. They were both swept away. It was one of those moments where they felt totally connected:

> We were in an embrace, and I just remember holding onto him. We were just close to each other. I felt there was this big bubble around us; we were one person. We just had this moment of connection and we bonded together. When that feeling had gone, I felt like a different person, that I'd changed. It gave me this ongoing confidence that I need never worry about this relationship and his commitment to me. In that moment we became one. It probably only lasted a couple of minutes because time seemed to stand still. We could have been there an hour for all I know – it was as though time didn't count. It was just in that moment.

Fiona explained that when she first met Ian she had been on a spiritual journey to discover more about herself. The trance state, a transcendent, altered state of consciousness, was familiar to her as she had experienced it before. She described it as "a sort of slightly out of body feeling." Fiona recalls that during that more spiritual part of her life she had deliberately tried to put herself into trance yet, in subsequent years, had lost her spiritual direction. Her journey to address this imbalance was inspired by a chance meeting with a tarot card reader when travelling. The influence and connection Fiona felt in this chance encounter resulted in her learning to read tarot cards herself, seeking to regain her spiritual self. Spirituality was thus omnipresent when she and Ian got together. She thinks they were both quite stunned by a feeling that something unusual and special had occurred.

***

Elaine, one of this book's co-authors, shared her peak experience of what Stokke (2021) would call a soulmate experience. She was attending a children's Christmas party organised by a single-parent organisation together with her 10-year-old son. They entered the hall where the party was being held and found seats next to a recent acquaintance. As they sat down, Elaine was suddenly struck by the sight of a man on the other side of the room. Incredibly, at the very same time, an intangible, ethereal voice told her: "He's the one."

When recalling this peak experience, Elaine held up both her hands in a questioning gesture: "Where had that voice come from?" she asked, "was this a transpersonal or spiritual experience?" She thinks it was. The voice definitely came from outside herself and irrefutably impacted on her: she sensed a presence other than herself that felt deeply meaningful and in union with all things. She described her attraction to the man as different from what she would have expected:

> I felt a calm assurance and confidence, rather than the sense of urgency or panic that might normally happen with a sudden attraction. There was a definite inevitability about it.

Laubach (2004, p. 239) described spiritual experiences that are perceived by the actor as not originating within the "self" as "intrusions in the stream of consciousness that have the same facticity as empirical experience." He further confirms that such intrusions, because of the perceived origin of the information they convey, get built into beliefs that are ultimately "accepted as supernaturally validated" (Laubach, 2004, p. 252). Such transformational effects then cause people to "move beyond former frames of reference and risk change" (Myers & Williard, 2003, p. 149). This certainly happened in Elaine's case.

In a very short while, the man came over to ask if the chair next to her was vacant, and as they began talking, it emerged that Chris (which coincidentally was also her grandfather's name) lived some 25 miles away in the small village where she had grown up as a child. She had moved away with her parents when she was 13 and never returned but had always held very fond memories of her childhood village and longed to revisit it. Chris also said he lived at number 27, the same number as her current home. These seemingly small coincidences provided Elaine with evidence of synergy.

Stokke (2021, p. 134) talks of a number of transpersonal phenomena that can occur in spiritual love relations, including instant recognition, past life connections, and other synchronicities. Elaine who was also very interested in astrology at the time, asked Chris for his date of birth so that she could later check the alignment of their planets. In line with Stokke's (2021) observations, there was a merging of masculine and feminine archetypes: she found both her sun and Chris's moon were on the same degree in the sign of Cancer – another strong synergy.

As they spent more time together over the coming weeks, Elaine recalls how she was very emotional and frequently cried with the depth of passion she felt, especially when they lay together playing Chris's music: she felt it moving her in new ways, touching her "dark night of the soul," and lightening her darkness. Certainly, she felt she was on a roller coaster of ecstasy and pain as their relationship began to heal past traumas and at the same time awaken karmic patterns. Elaine knew almost from the start of their relationship that they would marry and that this could be the beginning of growth and healing for them both.

***

The Significance of Peak Experience in This Context

In this chapter we began by highlighting the origins of theories of love in the ancient Greek and acknowledge particularly the later contributions of Erich Fromm and C.S. Lewis. Having noted also that Maslow (1971) frequently identified loving relationships as being the most promising contexts for peak experience, our aim was to explore the nature and occurrence of peak experiences in a variety of love relationships. Maslow (1971, p. 101) had observed that peak experiences came from "profound aesthetic experiences such as creative ecstasies, moments of mature love, perfect sexual experiences, parental love, experiences of natural childbirth, and many others."

Our literature review began with a review of research related to *storge* and particularly parental love. Maslow had been particularly affected by the birth of his two daughters and saw childbirth and parenthood as key contexts for peak experience.

Our discussion of *philautia* led us to conclude that the development of self-love is vital for the subsequent ability to give and receive love. In 1970, Maslow had been concerned that his ideas were leading to extreme or dangerous, one-sided practices. He felt too many hopefuls, in their quest for peak experiences, were trying to bypass the maturation and hard work necessary for self-actualisation and the self-realisation and self-love that accompanies that. Relatedly, Mouton and Montijo (2017) discussed how their participants most often described love, passion, and peak experiences involving other people as a possible mechanism for integration, learning, and growing. This emphasis on personal growth is important in relation to the development of self-love and particularly the mature capacity to give love.

Seven participants shared their peak experiences in relation to their love relationships.

The flurry of excitement and rush of adrenaline and cortisol in Francesco's early relationships and Kay's experience are definitely erotic. They correspond with Beddoes-Jones's Romantic Love Stage 1 (2017, p. 79), which she describes as a kind of love "biochemically induced, obsessional [and] almost addictive." Francesco's description of his relationship after the age of 40, as settled and happy with a husband, is very much indicative of Stage 2 of romantic love; an enduring, thoughtful, and caring love with acceptance of each other's faults and habits and an awareness of mutual physical and emotional well-being. Perhaps, the first stage of romantic love can promote or affirm self-actualisation, leading ultimately to a more mature love in the second stage. Fiona Beddoes-Jones described a number of relationship peaks, not only sharing experiences in a romantic setting but also detailing *agape* or universal love, familial love, and self-love events.

Whilst Kay and Ben described essentially physical relationships, where blindness and obsession led to them accepting imperfections in their relationships, our final three participants, Barty, Fiona and Elaine, explained more spiritual love encounters. These involved feelings of confidence, spirituality, and connection, which in turn were seen as indicators of a permanent love relationship. Elaine's and Fiona Haygreen's accounts, for example, are of a more transpersonal nature that involved recognition of a soulmate. Stokke (2021, p. 130) uses the term spiritual love to describe the variety of transpersonal experiences that can occur when soulmates meet. The term soulmate, he explains, is commonly used as a "metaphor for intense romantic love, but in New Age contexts it connotes a spiritual and karmic past life connection." This type of relationship does not seem to have an equivalent in the Greek typology used in this chapter, but could be subsumed under *eros* or *agape* – or possibly a combination of both.

References

Aron, A., & Aron, E. N. (2014). Climbing Diotima's mountain: Marriage and achieving our highest goals. *Psychological Inquiry*, *25*(1), 47–52.

Beddoes-Jones, F. (2017). *Love is the answer*. London: Blue Ocean Publishing.

Crowther, S. (2017). Childbirth as sacred celebration. In S. Crowther & J. Hall (Eds.), *Spirituality and childbirth: Meaning and care at the start of life*. London: Routledge [online], Chapter 2. www.taylorfrancis.com/books/e/9781315389639

de Rougement, D. (1956). *Love in the western world*. New York: Pantheon.
Dörfler, V., Baracskai, Z., & Velencei, J. (2010). Understanding creativity. *Transactions on Advanced Research, 6*(2), 18–26.
Elfers, J., & Offringa, R. (2019). Sexual ecstasy scale: Conceptualizations and measurement. *International Journal of Transpersonal Studies, 38*(1), 6.
Ferris, R. (1988). How organisational love can improve leadership. *Organisational Dynamics, 16*(4), 41–51.
Finn, T. M. (2013). Agape. In *The encyclopedia of ancient history*. Wiley Online Library.
Fredrickson, B. L. (2013). *Love 2.0: Creating happiness and health in moments of connection*. Penguin.
Fromm, E. (2000). *The art of loving: An enquiry into the nature of love*. London: Bloomsbury Academic.
Hendrick, C., & Hendrick, S. (1986). A theory and method of love. *Journal of Personality and Social Psychology, 50*(2), 392.
Herrmann, T. (2019). Brotherly love as condition for perfect love of god (1J 4: 12). *Studia Theologica Varsaviensia*, 211–219.
King, M. (1957, November 17). Loving your enemies. *Sermon at Dexter Avenue Baptist Church*. http://mlk-kpp01.stanford.edu/index.php/kingpapers/index
Konstan, D. (2018). *In the orbit of love: Affection in ancient Greece and Rome*. Oxford University Press.
Kontula, O. (2021). The sexual mind. In *Exploring the origins of arousal*. Helsinki: Väestöliitto ry.
Lashua, B. U. (2018). *The development and validation of a measure of beliefs about sex and spirituality*. A Dissertation Presented in Partial Fulfillment of the Requirements for the Degree Doctor of Philosophy Liberty University.
Laubach, M. (2004). The social effects of psychism: Spiritual experience and the construction of privatized religion. *Sociology of Religion, 65*(3), 239–263.
Lewis, C. S. (1975). *The four loves*. New York: Harvest Book/Harcourt Brace Jovanovich.
Lumbreras, S. (2020). The transcendent within: How our own biology leads to spirituality. In M. Fuller, D. Evers, A. Runehov, K. W. Sæther, & B. Michollet (Eds.), *Issues in science and theology: Nature – and beyond*. Issues in Science and Religion: Publications of the European Society for the Study of Science and Theology (Vol. 5). Cham: Springer. https://doi.org/10.1007/978-3-030-31182-7_15
Maharaj, N., & April, K. A. (2013). The power of self-love in the evolution of leadership and employee engagement. *Problems and Perspectives in Management, 11*(4), 120–132.
Maslow, A. H. (1950). Self-actualizing people: A study of psychological health. *Personality, Symposium, 1*, 11–34.
Maslow, A. H. (1954). *Motivation and personality*. New York: Harper & Row.
Maslow, A. H. (1959). Cognition of being in the peak experiences. *The Journal of Genetic Psychology, 94*(1), 43–66.
Maslow, A. H. (1962). Lessons from the peak experiences. *Journal of Humanistic Psychology, 2*(1), 9–18.
Maslow, A. H. (1968a). Some educational implications of the humanistic psychologies. *Harvard Educational Review, 38*(4), 685–696.
Maslow. A. H. (1968b). A conversation with Abraham H. Maslow. *Psychology Today, 1968*(4), 37.
Maslow, A. H. (1970). New introduction: Religions, values, and peak-experiences. *Journal of Transpersonal Psychology, 2*(2), 83–90.
Maslow, A. H. (1971). *The farther reaches of human nature*. New York, NY: Penguin.
Maslow, A. H. (1999). Peak-experiences as acute identity experiences. In A. H. Maslow, *Toward a psychology of being* (3rd ed., pp. 113–125). New York, NY: Wiley.
Meadows-Klue, D. (2008). Opinion piece: Falling in Love 2.0: Relationship marketing for the Facebook generation. *Journal of Direct, Data and Digital Marketing Practice, 9*, 245–250.

Mosher, D. L. (1980). Three dimensions of depth of involvement in human sexual response. *The Journal of Sex Research, 16*, 1–42.

Mouton, A. R., &. Montijo, M. N. (2017). Love, passion, and peak experience: A qualitative study on six continents. *The Journal of Positive Psychology, 12*(3), 263–280.

Moyers, M. M. (1977). *The occurrence of peak experience at childbirth: Fathers' perceptions*. A Thesis Submitted to the Faculty of the University of Utah in Partial Fulfillment of the Requirements for the Degree of Master of Science, College of Nursing, University of Utah.

Myers, J. E., & Williard, K. (2003). Integrating spirituality into counselor preparation: A developmental, wellness approach. *Counseling and Values, 47*(2), 142–155.

Paquette, J. (2020). *Awestruck*. CO, USA: Shambhala Publications Inc.

Pope, S. (1991). Expressive individualism and true self-love: A thomistic perspective. *The Journal of Religion, 71*(3), 384–399.

Post, S. G. (2002). *The tradition of agape*. Oxford University Press.

Protasi, S. (2008). A necessary conflict: Eros and Philia in a love relationship. *Icelandic E-Journal of Nordic and Mediterranean Studies, 3*(1), 68–97.

Rokach, A., & Patel, K. (2021). Sex therapy. Chapter 12. In *Human sexuality: Function, dysfunction, paraphilias, and relationships* (pp. 339–377). Elsevier. https://doi.org/10.1016/B978-0-12-819174-3.00008-5

Stokke, C. (2021). Exploring the transpersonal phenomena of spiritual love relations: A naturalistic observation study of soulmate experiences shared in a new age Facebook group. *Journal for the Study of Spirituality, 11*(2), 130–144.

Thompson, G. (2010). Psychology and labour experience: Birth as a peak experience. In D. Walsh & S. Downe (Eds.), *Essential midwifery practice: Intrapartum care* (pp. 191–211). Oxford: Blackwell Publishing.

Woodward, A. J., Findlay, B. M., & Moore, S. M. (2009). Peak and mystical experiences in intimate relationships. *Journal of Social and Personal Relationships, 26*(4), 429–442.

Conclusion and Insights

At the start of this book, we set out our aim to build on Maslow's concept of peak experience through an appraisal of how people have encountered peak experiences in different everyday settings. Our hope was that through exploring the extant research on peak experiences, and then examining participants' accounts, the value of peak experiences in our lives could be better comprehended and encouraged. We believed there could be commonalities or differences between people's experiences in different contexts that may challenge existing conceptualisations of peak experience. So, whereas Maslow appeared concerned with common characteristics, our enterprise in this book has been to examine ways in which people's peak experiences differ in different contexts.

Drawing on Maslow's work, Armor (1969) suggested two models of peak experience. The first proposes that individual "peakness" follows a continuum ranging from low or "foothill" experiences to higher, more self-transcendent dimensions. This model holds that everyone has a "threshold of perceiving and experience which is uniquely his own" (1969, p. 47); a threshold level which is determined by variables that are part of the individual's own psychological history and life space. This model appears to follow William James's (1902–1928) idea of cosmic consciousness, where he concludes that some people tend to have a very wide field of consciousness while others have a narrower field.

Armor's second model (1969, p. 49) embraces the idea that peak experiences are not merely extensions of *individual* levels of perceiving and experiencing, rather they are "excursions into a realm of consciousness that is considered extant and universal though contacted only rarely by most" (1969, p. 48). In this formulation, individuals attribute the significance of the transcendent experience to having, as Armor puts it, "ventured into a qualitatively new and different form of consciousness, a form quite distinct from the 'ordinary' consciousness of the entire species" (1969, p. 49). Citing James (1902–1928, p. 388), Armor clarifies these excursions: "We may go through life without suspecting their existence; but apply the requisite stimulus, and at a touch they are there in all their completeness."

We begin this chapter with a discussion of the varieties of peak experience. Here we summarise the different conceptualisations that emerged from participants' descriptions of their peak experiences in the different contexts. It was found that although the transcendent peak experiences described by Maslow did occur in most

DOI: 10.4324/9781003509219-14

contexts, participants reported a variety of what we might call individual "peak-like" experiences that could be aligned with Armor's first model. The section ends with a summary of transcendent peak experience which links with Armor's second model of peak experience.

In the second section, we synthesise the themes that emerged from participant accounts: these include connectedness; physiological reactions; memory and recall; growth; and core conditions. We conclude this section by suggesting that rather than being the preserve solely of the self-actualised state, feelings of "peakness" might occur when Maslow's basic or physiological needs (i.e., sex, sleep, rest) or deficiency needs (i.e., safety, belonginess, love, and respect) are being met.

In the third section, we discuss the benefits of peak experiences in relation to the positive emotions identified by participants and close the chapter in the fourth section by identifying emerging research topics.

Varieties of Peak Experience

In this section, we focus on how peak-like experiences are defined in variety of ways. Ward (2011) submitted that terms such as epiphany, ecstasy, mystical experience, or cosmic consciousness are just different names for the *same* peak experience phenomenon, albeit experienced in varying degrees of intensity. We dispute this suggestion. We found that although the kind of transcendent peak experiences described by Maslow did occur in most contexts, many participants reported what we call "peak-like" experiences that appeared to be non-transcendent experiences. These could be more accurately grouped under other familiar headings such as peak performance, flow, or awe rather than peak experience.

As Maslow indicated, using language to describe an intensely subjective experience is potentially problematic and can lead to confusion in the analysis of the phenomenon.

He pointed out that attempts to define peak experiences by mere words could be considered to lead to altered or inaccurate representations (Maslow, 1968). Part of the problem, we suggest, is that our synonyms for "peak" are too vague and provide no clues as to the nature of the transcendent experience Maslow was trying to explain. Dictionaries explain the meaning of "peak" as the highest or most important point or level. So the word tends to suggest different things to different people and is why a peak performance may be viewed by some as a peak experience.

In many of our chapters, we have highlighted the difficulty some participants had in talking about peak experience. Dan, in the high-risk leisure context, for example, said he did not have the language for it: "There's not enough language in the English language to describe it." Mary-lou had a similar difficulty and shared how she found it quite hard to put the feeling into words. Correspondingly, in the religious context, Colin says, "It's very hard to find the words." In the music context too, David explained the difficulty he had, saying that to try and describe what is inside and bound up with feelings diminishes it. In the introduction we even mention that some people said it would be too difficult or painful for them to share their experiences and so did not want to participate.

Fabb (2021, p. 17) referred to this impasse as "structural ineffability," where any attempt at description is going to be "too fine-grained for verbalization." Not having a familiar vocabulary for their peak experiences, our participants sometimes used their own made-up words to describe the feelings generated by a peak experience. For example, one therapist used the word "spark" to describe a beautiful, calm yet rejuvenating experience. Another therapist talked about the "bliss" she feels following a yoga session.

In what follows we draw on our findings in different contexts to reinterpret the discussions of peak experience and related concepts already begun in the Introduction. We ask whether participants' everyday experiences are akin to flow or peak performance or other concepts, or whether they align with Maslow's notion of transcendent peak experience. During the course of this synthesis, we argue that not all peaks are transcendent but that all peaks are beneficial to personal well-being. We begin with a discussion of peak performance.

Peak Performance in Everyday Lives

Privette (1983) defined peak performance as superior functioning that involves a clear focus and provides a sense of self-fulfilment. Similarly, Thornton et al. (1999, pp. 253–254) referred to it as "exceptional accomplishment." Maslow himself called it a state of "pure success" (1962a, p. 47). Moreover, Maslow (1971) also suggested that peak experience can result from peak performance, implying a reciprocal relationship between the two. In their empirical research, Marotto et al. (2007) found that musicians who transcend their normal level of performance felt the joy and rapture associated with the peak experience.

Peak performance is linked with peak experience, not just in music, but in a number of other contexts too, particularly in sport where people are focused on achievement for themselves and their teams. It is interesting to note that in high-risk leisure situations, which are often sporty in nature, the emphasis on peak performance is not so evident as in competitive sport. Rather, as participants in the high-risk context described, risky endeavours made them feel vibrant, whole, or undivided. In their experience of risk, the self was often transcended, whereas in peak performance a clear focus on both the activity and the self are critical. As Brymer (2009) pointed out, peak experiences do not *necessarily* involve clarity, focus, or superior performance but may be more characterised by altered perceptions of space and time.

In the workplace too, as in competitive sport, there is more focus on peak performance than peak experience. This suggests to us that peak performance is influenced by fundamental elements of audience, competition, and especially competition with ourselves, which leads to mastery. These elements are absent in descriptions of peak experience. Both Nikki and Clare, participants in the workplace context, mentioned mastery as a form of self-competitiveness. Mastery is where success is achieved in a particular skill domain and so is closely related to peak performance and flow. It tends to boost people's confidence and promote good feelings, so it can feel like a peak experience. Bandura's (2012) research in the sport context suggested that mastery experiences are the most effective way to build self-efficacy, which in turn affects success.

Insights in Everyday Lives: Epiphanies, Aha, and Wow Moments

Whilst researching the peak phenomenon in different contexts, we encountered some experiences that have a distinctly different and more cognitive aspect. We have grouped these as "insights." Insight experiences commonly occur during problem-solving activities, such as coaching or therapy or in creative pursuits. They occur when an individual sees something clearly for the first time and may also be referred to as epiphanies, aha or wow moments, or sometimes light bulb moments.

Kien (2013, p. 578) defined an epiphany as an identifiable moment of lived experience that can be identified as a turning point. Jarvis (1996, p. 61) similarly described epiphanies as moments of transformation or recognition: profound personal transformations "resulting in the reconfiguration of an individuals' world assumptions." They are classified as a type of "discontinuous psychological change experience (DPCE), similar to insight, religious conversion, and transpersonal experiences" (Liang, 2006, p. 27) but lacking the transcendent aspect of peak experience.

In the music context, Green (2015) suggested that peak music experiences might also be epiphanies since they impact people's lives. However, epiphanies seem to be different from peak experiences since they are more retrospective and reflective. Liang (2006, p. 132) considered that, although epiphanies and peak experiences seem alike, examples of peak experience tend to contain more emotional features than those reported for epiphanies: epiphanies tend to contain "more cognitive loading and an emphasis on change." Indeed, Chappell (2019, p. 95), in her definition of epiphany, contended that epiphanies "need to teach us something." Her conceptualisation of epiphany stresses not only the overwhelming or sudden nature of the phenomenon but also the feeling it gives of "coming from outside," teaching us something new and necessitating a response.

The cognitive aspect and the prominence of change in Liang's (2006) definition leads us to link epiphanies with aha moments. Laukkonen et al. (2021, p. 918) suggest that perceptions involving insights, such as aha moments, are "defined by metacognitive suddenness" and are often perceived as true and valuable despite their "unexpected manifestation." Thus, aha moments involve a similar cognitive extension and, like peak experiences, they involve awareness.

Kets de Vries (2013) called aha moments "tipping points," which signal experiences of great significance that can contribute to meaningful life changes. Discussing the coaching context, Kets de Vries, explains how coaches expect incremental changes in their clients but they can also be privy to aha moments, which, when they happen, are "very different from the small successes that characterise the 'normal' coaching experience" (2013, p. 153). Also, he points out that aha moments grow out of "hours of thought, reflection, and preparation." This suggests a considerable cognitive aspect as the aha is the result of many, often small, preparatory interventions: "While 'Aha!' moments cannot be engineered, coaches create an ambiance that becomes conducive to such transformations" (2013, p. 153).

In the Creative Arts context, Tanya linked her moments of realisation with peak experiences calling some of her experiences aha moments. Other participants referred to their aha moments as light bulb moments. For example, in the therapy context, Jenny referred several times to light bulb moments when she or her clients got a sudden realisation.

In the coaching context, our participant, Angela, explained her peak moments as coming after the culmination of mini-peaks, which she called wow feelings. Also, in the music context, Anthony identified how he felt elated when wow moments happened and how they were unexpected and made him smile. In our view, wow doesn't have the cognitive loading of epiphany or aha – it doesn't involve the clarity and new awareness – it's just wow, an acknowledgement that something unusual and interesting happened.

Flow in Everyday Lives

In the Introduction, we distinguished flow from peak experience by highlighting Csikszentmihalyi's (1990, p. 54) assertion that flow occurs during activities requiring skill, concentration, mental activity, or physical exercise: it does not happen "without the application of skilled performance." Csikszentmihalyi also argued that the true self is manifest in the experience of flow, resulting in a tendency for the self to try and reproduce the experience: "to keep on experiencing flow becomes one of the central goals of the self" (1988, p. 24).

Throughout our chapters, however, we have noted that, for many people, being in flow is viewed as an example of, or is a different way of thinking about, peak experience. This is because flow and peak experience share some features, for example, timelessness. Creative artists, in particular, shared how they become so immersed in their work that they lose all sense of time, and in the music context similarities between features of flow and peak experience have resulted in a conflation of the two terms. As Groarke and Hogan (2020) suggest, features of peak experiences during music listening align the listener with flow-like states of consciousness.

Since being in flow is an enjoyable experience that necessarily involves experiencing a sense of timelessness and a loss of self-consciousness (Seligman, 2002), it is easy to see how the misperception occurs. However, even though flow experiences are not necessarily transcendental or fleeting as in Maslow's definition of transcendent peak experience, they can still be spontaneous and life-changing (Csikszentmihalyi, 1988). In fact, many flow experiences may be no less meaningful and life-altering than peak experiences; they are simply different. They even, according to Ford et al. (2020), impact emotional connectedness and interpersonal relationships. The state of flow is, therefore, linked to not only improved performance and concentration but also increased happiness.

Mosing (2024) reports on research looking at how flow may be associated with positive outcomes including better mental and physical health. The results of

Mosing's study indicate that people who were more prone to flow had a lower risk of depression, anxiety, schizophrenia, or bipolar disorder. They had less worry and stress-related disorders and less cardiovascular disease. This is because when in flow people spend less time worrying and thinking about problems and more time engrossed in a rewarding activity.

In the context of the workplace, Andy talked about everyone in his team working together to create a harmonious and fluid environment and achieve a group state of flow. More often, however, flow is experienced individually, as reported by Ali during his marathon running.

In the coaching context, Jane connected what she identified as a peak experience with the flow experience that followed. This suggests that the peak experience she had may have been more accurately termed an insight or an epiphany. In the high-risk leisure context, we similarly noted that participants may not always be talking about the phenomenon of peak experience; often it is another concept, such as awe, which we examine in the next section.

Awe in Everyday Lives

Paquette (2020, p. 6) has explained how awe is the feeling that comes "when we are in the presence of something so vast or profound that it transcends our understanding of the world." Earlier, Keltner and Haidt (2003) suggested a wide variety of awe-inducing stimuli can give rise to what they called different "flavours" of awe. These various stimuli may include beauty, ability, or virtues, although some awe experiences involve fear of danger or the supernatural. Awe may, therefore, result in positive and/or negative feelings depending on how the trigger and the awe experience itself are interpreted. In this aspect, awe is different from, say, flow or peak experience, which, as we have seen, are invariably viewed as positive.

Awe has further been described by Keltner and Haidt (2003) as involving two key features, the perception of vastness (relative to self) and the psychological act of accommodation. Vastness has been explained as involving imposing physical size, like a mountain vista or panoramic landscape, or forceful or powerful attributes such as a thunderstorm. Keltner (2023, p. 7) argues that because awe is the feeling of "being in the presence of something vast that transcends your current understanding of the world," it involves an emotional response and some kind of cognitive accommodation. Awe thus challenges our interpretation of the world, impacting our mental schemata causing their reconfiguration during the accommodation process.

Keltner and Haidt (2003, p. 297) have argued that awe is central to the experience of religion as well as to the appreciation of nature and art and that "fleeting and rare experiences of awe can change the course of a life in profound and permanent ways." In the context of religion, they give the example of Saint Paul's awe-filled conversion on the road to Damascus, where he saw a flash of light from heaven and heard the voice of Jesus. When his confusion lifts he is "transformed and embraces new values, commands and missions" (2003, p. 299),

In sports contexts, participants often reported feelings of awe, particularly when mountain biking, trekking, or sledding. For example, Ali recalled his team stopping for a second to look at a memorable sunset during the Snowdon challenge and remaining silent in wonder and awe. This resonates with Liu et al.'s research in the sporting context indicating that the "perceived vastness of the natural environment and perceived professionalism represent a necessary condition for awe" (2022, p. 278).

In research by Chirico and Gaggioli (2021, p. 1), it is suggested that awe is a "complex and transformative emotion that can restructure individuals' mental frames so deeply that it could be considered a therapeutic asset for major mental health major issues, including depression."

Researchers have also found that awe, as a self-transcendent emotion, can be correlated with prosocial behaviours such as altruism and creativity (Piff et al., 2015), and experiences of awe have been found to increase ethical decision-making, generosity, and other helping behaviours. In fact, Dai and Jiang (2023, p. 3) report how awe, which is theorised as being a self-transcendent emotion, can lead individuals to "transcend their daily mundanities." It could be that transcending everyday problems in this way is what makes experiences like awe or flow beneficial to health (Worth & Smith, 2021; Wong, 2023).

Self-Transcendent and Peak Experiences in Everyday Lives

Both self-transcendent and peak experiences involve a dissolution of the sense of an egoic or separate self (Gordon, 2023, p. 2), where "boundaries of an isolated and skin-encapsulated 'separate self' seem to fall away, and feelings of greater connection and oneness with something larger tend to occur." Thus, self-transcendent experiences, sometimes called transpersonal experiences, or peak experiences in Maslow's scheme, are defined as transient mental states characterised by "reduced self-salience and intensified connectedness with the surrounding context" (Dai & Jiang, 2023, p. 3).

Self-transcendent experiences have been similarly defined as those in which "the sense of identity or self extends beyond (trans.) the individual or personal to encompass wider aspects of humankind, life, psyche or cosmos" (Walsh & Vaughan, 1993, p. 203). Accordingly, transcendence involves going beyond the self; it emphasises connection to others, as well as the more transcendental aspects of going beyond space and time. In the extreme sport/high-risk leisure context, we reported Stranger's (1999) research where participants recounted their experiences of self-transcendence and their feelings of being at one with the mountains and clouds. Yaden et al. (2017, p. 1) also explain how self-transcendent experiences work and how the experience of reduced self-salience and the corresponding increase in feelings of connectedness result in the sensation of oneness:

> [U]nder certain circumstances, the subjective sense of one's self as an isolated entity can temporarily fade into an experience of unity with other people or one's surroundings, involving the dissolution of boundaries between the sense of self and "other."

In addition, Maslow (1971) provided 35 meanings of transcendence, including loss of self-consciousness, letting things happen, unselfish love, enjoying the cosmos, surpassing one's limitations, being fully accepting of the self, having intrinsic conscience, being absorbed in what one is doing, and integrating dichotomies. At the end of his list, Maslow gives a condensed statement summarising what he understands by transcendence:

> Transcendence refers to the very highest and most inclusive or holistic levels of human consciousness, behaving and relating, as ends rather than as means, to oneself, to significant others, to human beings in general, to other species, to nature, and to the cosmos.
>
> (1971, p. 269)

More recently, Taylor and Egeto-Szabo (2017, p. 45) have referred to such experiences as an awakening, where "our state of being, our vision of the world and our relationship to it are transformed, bringing a sense of clarity, revelation and well-being." They say we perceive "a sense of harmony and meaning, and transcend our normal sense of separateness from the world, experiencing a sense of connection and even unity" (2017, p. 45). In Chapter 2, one of our participants, Sarah, described her peak experience as hitting "a wave of ecstasy," where the world disappeared, and she merged into everything, and everything merged into her. At that moment she experienced oneness with the universe, with no fear, just total understanding of who she was and why she was here.

Peak experiences, according to Maslow, are also important indicators of self-actualisation. He referred to them as "acute identity experiences" (2013, pp. 97–106). These experiences, he claimed, involve individuals feeling whole and completely their true self, allowing them to understand and see the world in a new way. He said they may even view themselves more positively and see life as more worthwhile and meaningful. However, echoing the difficulty our own participants had relating their peak experiences, Fletcher (2007) has concluded that transcendence defies current models for describing human behaviour. He suggests that transcendence can be conceptualised only retrospectively, and even then it can only approximate its indefinable nature.

For Maslow, the term peak experience is meant to capture feelings of ecstasy or bliss in every context. He was at pains to explain how he decided on his choice of the term despite its inherent ambiguity. He thus describes his use of the term peak experiences as

> a kind of generalized and abstract concept because I discovered that all of these ecstatic experiences had some characteristics in common. Indeed, I found that it was possible to make a generalized, abstract schema or model which could describe their common characteristics. The word enables me to speak of all or any of these experiences in the same moment.
>
> (Maslow, 1971, p. 105)

Recently, Yaden et al. (2017), drawing on Maslow's work, suggested a possible spectrum for peak experiences that included flow and awe as well as mystical and peak experiences. They suggested peaks are experienced

> along a spectrum of intensity that ranges from the routine (e.g., losing yourself in music or a book), to the intense and potentially transformative (e.g., feeling connected to everything and everyone), to states in between, like those experienced by many people while meditating or when feeling awe.
> (Yaden et al., 2017, p. 1)

This spectrum is useful and echoes our own attempt at grouping and synthesis presented in this section.

Themes

The chapters in this book have focused on a range of contexts – some creative, some physically demanding, and some involving cognitive activity. In what follows we discuss six key themes that emerged across the contexts: connectedness; physiological reactions; memory, recall and novelty; growth; meeting basic needs; and core conditions.

Connectedness in Peak Experience

Edwards (2010) noted during her research that peak experiences tended to be emergent and unplanned but with a strong unfolding sense of connectedness and even transcendence. She found that none of the peaks emerging from interpersonal interactions involved careful planning or purposefully crafted strategies or indeed what we might call communication competence. More recently, Gordon (2023, p. 1) has defined peak communication experiences as "times of highest happiness and fulfilment arising from our communication with others."

In our research, connectedness was linked with peak experiences in every context. In the spirituality and religion context (Chapter 1), we saw the connection with God through prayer and a profound spiritual connection between heaven and earth. Peak experiences arose through communication of kindness, through being intentional and focusing attention on community and connection.

In the education and learning context (Chapter 5), one participant, Sue, explained how each of her peak experiences added to her sense of connectedness and being in the world. In the writing and reading context, Liz shared her thoughts on how peak experiences may be connected through our senses to how we survive as a species. She suggested awe and peak experiences could be connected to bonding, as a kind of glue that sticks us to our home and our environment. Liz also described the ability to absorb herself into another world through reading and connecting with ideas and so expanding and enlarging the mind. Similarly, Christine recognised the power of connection with characters in a text; what she called "becoming one with a character." She explained how she abandons herself fully into the consciousness of a fictionalised entity.

In the coaching context (Chapter 9), Jane shared how, in a moment of connection of mutual acknowledgement of each other, the peak experience was experienced as timeless, transcendent, and out of this world. In that moment, both coach and client felt an intense flash of eye contact, a sense of connection when they were both completely "as one." Another coach, Carmelina, saw a contrast between being fully connected with her client, and not being connected. For coaches, connection is seen as paramount; it involves being present for the client, and they see this as important for deepening their relationship and being able to work together more meaningfully.

Both music and art are forms of communication aimed at connecting with an audience. In the music context, Graham admits that the main preoccupation in an orchestra is communicating. He talks of the "sideways concentration" and the need for professionals to play for each other. Two instrumentalists in the chapter also explained how they were reliant on the communication from a conductor or other musicians to create the core conditions for a peak experience to occur. Tanya, in the creative arts context, talked about the sense of connectedness with the people and the environment during her excavation project.

Peak experiences in nature also generated feelings of connectedness and of merging with nature and the universe. For some, there was a distinct sense of connection, feeling at one with everything, which was triggered by being in the natural environment or through encounters with animals. Alongside this, for others, was the transpersonal or transcendent awareness of the vastness of the universe. These experiences generated feelings of humility and timelessness as well as connection. For example, echoing Maslow's (1969) views on cosmic consciousness, Paul shared how he views everything, including his own existence, from the perspective of being connected to the wider universe rather than just existing on the surface of our one planet.

In the relationship chapter we also noted the connectedness people felt in response to peak experiences. For example, Fiona Haygreen shared how depressed she and her new partner were previously but that when they met it was thrilling, like a breath of fresh air. She described how the rest of the world completely disappeared, and they felt they were "melding into one." She remembers the experience: "It's in my memory, the thrill of that connection between us." Similarly, Fiona Beddoes-Jones linked her connection to the universe, with a spiritual connection, which she says is "where we are taken out of ourselves."

In the sporting context, the feeling of connectedness was a common by-product of peak experience. Some participants had what we might call "vicarious peak experiences," which came about from training others or watching them succeed. Others found deep connection with their teams and also with equipment they were using, like a sled or a kayak. For example, Amy shared how her out-of-body peak experiences were quite exceptional. She felt a wonderful connection, a feeling of being at one with the sled and almost sliding without the sled underneath her.

Physiological Reactions to Peak Experience

According to Williams et al. (2023, p. 735), awe involves "aesthetic engagement" and proneness to "aesthetic chill." Such chills can also herald a peak experience or generate feelings similar to those of peak experience, but equally they are significant moments in their own right. Keltner and Haidt (2003) similarly hypothesised chills as a physiological feature.

In the music context we highlighted how peak experiences have engendered quite intense physical responses, including thrills, chills, shivers down the spine, tears, and other physical responses. In research with 2,937 people from a range of backgrounds, Christov-Moore et al. (2023) found in their quantitative study that even controlling for prior state and trait differences, chills were positively associated with self-transcendence. They refer to such aesthetic chills as peak psychophysiological responses that are characterised by "pleasurable, cold sensations, and subjective qualities and outcomes intuitively similar to self-transcendence" (2023, p. 1). In the music context, some of our own participants linked their transcendent experiences with shaking and feeling goose-pimply all over. They used descriptions such as "my spine tingles" or "my head would just zing."

In fact, physical experiences seem to be very prevalent in the music context. Graham explained how the peaks are like electrical impulses – mini peak experiences that produce physical responses, like a buzz in the chest. Similarly, David described the sensation of his peak experience in music as an "uplift" which extended to a hard to describe "gut feeling." Anthony, in the same context, mentions involuntary smiling and grinning in those peak moments.

In Chapter 10 (on extreme sport), Mike also mentions the sensation of buzz that he experienced at the summit of one mountain, describing the feeling as complete joy and "a physical sensation of warmth with chemicals whirling around my body." Similarly, as a trainer, Keith noted how when he was watching his swimmers in a competitive race he was physically shaking and giddy with excitement because they were doing so well. He said his heart seemed to be beating faster, and "I just sort of exploded at the end of the race."

In the creative arts context, Tanya explained how her peak experiences happen through her eyeballs, resulting in an extraordinary and blinding, out-of-body experience. She explained how she had to close her eyes, and there was gold all around her which just exploded inside her chest and behind her eyeballs. These physical manifestations accompanied a feeling of oneness. She felt as if the boundaries in her body no longer existed.

Similar physical responses are also evident in other contexts. In the spirituality and religion context, Colin shared how, when he felt a joy and an awe that he had never experienced before, he also felt dizzy – almost as if he wasn't in his body in the same way. Also in that chapter, Ny described how he felt a warmth in his stomach and chest. Charlie similarly shared how when meditating, he experienced a kind of awareness in his head, and also somewhere in his chest – a happy feeling in his heart. In her therapeutic yoga practice, Katy was conscious of a weird feeling when the peak sensation came over her: "like being on the edge of an orgasm."

Memory, Recall, and Novelty in Peak Experience

Cox (2013, p. 11) reminded us that experience is a "pre-reflective phenomenon," occurring in the sensory world prior to any cognition. She noted Dewey's (1934, p. 24) observation that "thought withdraws us from the world." The fact that we found people generally had difficulty explaining their peak experiences could be because experience can never be captured in its entirety: as soon as we begin to recall and conceptualise our experience we are abstracting away from that experience. It is also why, although writers attempt either to convey their own peak experiences in their work or to evoke the peak experiences of a protagonist, their communication falls short. As we reported in Chapter 2, although readers may appreciate the representation, and even identify with it, they will not directly experience it themselves. Thus, a transcendental peak experience in the writing and reading context is unlikely. We concluded that only when the senses are activated directly is a peak able to be experienced, and consequently, it cannot be experienced vicariously. As our participant Liz suggested, there needs to be the "raw immediacy of experience for a peak to occur – you've got to experience it in that moment for yourself without anything in-between and then it touches the emotions."

Similarly, Clare in the nature and wilderness chapter explained how when a peak experience happens, it is being processed on a physical level and not on a cognitive level. In relation to memory and recall, Clare shared how she can go back to the experience instantly, but it is not as intense as being there. Anytime she wants to recall the experience she can close her eyes and relive the feel of it, she can go back to it, but the experience is still in a "diluted form." In the therapy context, Katy recalled one particular yoga session and how as she was thinking about it, she began to get the same feelings but to a much lesser extent: "like my body is reminded of it but doesn't quite want to take me there." So, as Proust (1913–1927) had also found, a peak experience cannot be experienced retrospectively, even though senses, such as smell or taste, can be re-engaged and seemingly simulate the experience. There is a strong connection between our sense of smell and our brain, which facilitates connections with the memory.

Even though peak experiences cannot be reproduced in their entirety, participants still remembered their peaks as meaningful. Participants in the high-risk leisure chapter shared how, although their peak experience vibrations quickly faded, traces of them still remained, enabling them to be recalled some years later when reflecting. David, in the music context, shared one occasion when he felt so elated and fulfilled that it still enables him to revisit how he felt – even 40 years later. Alison, in the writing and reading context, related how when she revisits the original texts of her own writing, she can be transported back to those moments even though they no longer have the novelty of the peak experience itself: "I can smell the Owl pub, I re-find the riding crop, buried under leaves."

Maslow noticed how, besides an element of surprise, disbelief, and aesthetic shock in the peak experience, there is "more the quality of *having such an experience for the first time*" (1970b, p. 88, our emphasis). This suggests we will not experience a peak unless it has some element of novelty and produces a real-world surprise for us. Additionally, according to Skavronskaya et al. (2020, p. 8), novelty influences the intensity of emotions, enhances "stronger memory and therefore affects the ease of the experience reconstruction (memorability) and reminiscence." Novelty is, therefore, linked with the variety of complex and intense feelings necessary to achieve and remember peak experiences and is closely linked with memory and recall.

The inability to relive peak experiences is not always a failure of memory: rather they are forgotten in us through the changes in perception that have occurred. This is why when we try to recreate our peak experiences or respond to the vicarious peak experiences recounted by authors in literature, it just does not work. Malouf (1989, p. 64) has argued that moving back into the experience to experience that novelty again would demand "an act of un-remembering, a dismantling of the body's experience that would be a kind of dying, a casting off, one by one, of all the tissues of perception."

This emphasis on novelty could enable us to distinguish further between different types of peaks. Some varieties of peak experience are direct, immediate, and are not repeatable because they involve novelty. For example, in love relationships, transcendent peak experiences for our participants were often linked to the attraction to something new and novel. Other peaks, such as peak performance, flow, or awe are not so reliant on novelty, and repetition appears to be possible. One example we reported was Colin's repeated feeling of awe *every time* he sees a kingfisher.

Growth Through Peak Experiences

In the educational context, we reported Schlarb's (2007) study in which adult women related how their childhood peak experiences had been ignored and even suppressed. The women considered this to have had a negative emotional or psychological impact, especially as they got older. In our chapters, participants often shared an earlier or childhood experience that had stayed in their memory but had only later been seen as influencing their later life, often through recalling them during our interviews. Frick (2001, p. 9) refers to this phenomenon as "symbolic latency" where the "powerful images and emotions of youth and childhood . . . remain latent in their meaning until brought to fruition through additional experience and emotional readiness."

In his 2001 paper, Frick focuses on Wordsworth's notion of "spots of time" to elucidate two ways of responding to and processing previous experiences. The first, as Schlarb (2007) also found in his research, involves recall of memories with great emotional intensity, such as peak experiences, that only later achieve meaning or are transformed as they are related to new experiences and emotions. Indeed, Frick argues that growth can come only by tapping into these previous experiences via symbolic growth activities (Frick, 1990, 2001). Barfoot (1999) similarly suggested such experiences tend not to be meaningful at the time but take on meaning when evoked in a new context. In our research, several participants noted this phenomenon. For example, Nicole recorded:

As I wrote the last answer, I realised that these beautiful times as a child are so clearly linked to my experiences as an adult! It's been so interesting and valuable to contemplate what a peak experience is and whether I have had one, or none, or many! Thank you for the opportunity to explore such thoughts and my memories, and how they have contributed to who I am or why I seek what I seek in life.

The second way of responding to experience involves the cognitive processing of what Frick (2001, p. 10) refers to as the "symbolic possibilities within one's immediate experience." Symbolic growth experiences, which he defines as "the translation of immediate experience into symbolic form and meaning," contribute to the process of self-creation and are natural healing and growth-inducing experiences that help develop personality (Frick, 1990). This is very like the growth and learning that comes from the achievement of self-actualisation that Maslow (1962b, para. 43) described:

[W]e must learn, from growth theory and self-actualization theory that the future also now exists in the person in the form of ideals, hopes, duties, tasks, plans, goals, unrealized potentials, mission, fate, destiny, etc.

Core Conditions for Peak Experiences

In this section we consider whether there can be essential or core conditions for the attainment of peak experiences. It has been claimed that many aspects of peak experience can be cultivated through mindfulness practices, meditation, and other contemplative rituals that involve creating the right conditions for them to occur (Tavel et al., 2022). Other examples of creating core conditions could involve going into nature, making time for artistic pursuits, listening to music, or fostering connections with others: essentially creating core conditions would mean making time and space for peak experience.

In our coaching chapter, the core conditions were seen as the need to be present for the client to build trust and encourage openness. This in turn enabled coaches to take risks in their questioning. Another core condition for them was to work with the whole person to ensure depth of engagement with emotions. These contributory factors are similar to the core conditions which enabled peak *moments* to emerge in the coaching context in Weijers's (2021) study; connectedness, co-creation, trust, and rapport. However, Weijers (2021) found transcendent peak experiences were rare, but that flow, as a peak moment or "peak-like" experience, was regularly experienced in that context. Three similar conditions were identified as requisite for a peak experience in the therapy context: trust and connection between the therapist and client; a focus on state management for both therapist and client; and attention to the role that intuition can play.

In different contexts, different core conditions were identified. In the religious context, for example, a culmination of factors led Sebastian to feel what he described as "ineffable joy." These included having a reserved seat in the church for his mother, the respect shown towards his mother by the priest and parishioners, and the serene atmosphere of the church itself. In the writing and reading context, Liz considered a peak experience must be about understanding, seeing, and perceiving differently, and, as already mentioned, she was certain that we must experience it directly through our senses: "It's got to be naked experience without any filters. A raw immediate experience."

For our music chapter, Graham shared how the mental build up to playing *The Rite*, his visualisation of the performance, his use of adrenalin, and the overcoming technical challenges, all contributed to his peak experience. This emphasis on preparation was also recognised by participants in other contexts, particularly competitive sports, where participants like Amy and Anna used preparation techniques such as visualisation to increase their chances of peak performance. Similarly, in the context of the workplace, Nikki's experience of a co-created work solution, which seemed peak to her, relied on preparation for its effectiveness: "we had done so much preparation, rehearsed and practiced, in fact a collective effort."

Many participants prepared themselves in readiness for their work. This, in effect, is preparing for a peak-like experience, as it is a way of either getting into flow or planning for peak performance. Therapists and coaches, for example, prepare themselves to manage their state before sessions. They practise deep breathing to clear distractions and become present with their clients. Despite this emphasis on preparation and having the conditions right, peak experiences cannot be planned. As Maslow argued in a number of places, a peak experience is a sensory and perceptual experience, usually brief and profound (Maslow, 1970a), and "peaks are not planned or brought about by design; they happen" (Maslow (1943, p. 370).

Thrash et al. (2010, p. 488) have likewise reminded us that many of the experiences people find the most fulfilling, such as peak experiences, "cannot be controlled or directly acquired, because they involve the transcendence of one's current desires, values, or expectations." More recently, following Maslow, Levine (2021, n.p.) explained how peak experiences cannot be planned on demand:

> One cannot simply "order up" an afternoon or evening of indulging in a profound peak experience. One can certainly try, for example, by immersing oneself in magical settings or vistas like a mountaintop or lake, or participating in intense group rituals, or by using psychedelic agents. But without the magical (mystical, spiritual, ineffable, noetic) interactions between the specific setting/activity and the personal open mood and sensory status of the individual, no such experience will occur.

Interestingly, however, these observations contrast with something Maslow also observed:

> My experience has been that whenever I have lectured approvingly about peak-experiences, it was as if I had given permission to the peak-experiences of some people, at least, in my audience to come into consciousness.
>
> (Maslow, 1970c, pp. 88–89)

This is an example of the Baader-Meinhof phenomenon (Varkey et al., 2022) in action and was also evident in our research. Several of our participants considered how to create more peak experiences is actually to be aware of them. As already mentioned in Chapter 6 on nature, for Nicole, some peak experiences came into consciousness as a result of our interview. This was also the case for Nikki in the context of the workplace, and for Stan in the therapy context, where our interview alerted him to the possibility of peak experiences happening: "Now I'm aware of peak experiences . . . I'll be searching for them." It seems raising participants' awareness made them better able to identify peak experiences, reflect on them, and so potentially increase the chance of more peak experiences happening.

Peak Experience as a Response to Meeting Basic Needs

Maslow reasoned that peak experiences are unmotivated by basic needs because those needs will have already been met for self-actualisation to have been reached and thus for peak experiences to occur: "As lower needs were met, higher needs emerged, taking the individual on a journey of increased self-actualization" (Maslow, 1987, p. 100). Self-actualisation, as Maslow (1968/2013, pp. 30–31) consistently argued, involves a "progressive gratification of basic needs to the point where they 'disappear'" and only then can people have peak experiences.

In the course of writing this book, we have noted that some of the aspects of peak experiences identified by Maslow (1968/2013) were more prevalent in some contexts than in others: for instance, the feeling of being at the peak of our powers and being fully functioning, feeling more creative, having a sense of connectedness and empathy with others, or freedom from inhibitions, fears, or doubts.

These observations have led us to consider a rather controversial idea, namely whether some reported peak-like experiences arise as a result of one or more of Maslow's lower or basic needs (D-Needs) being met in that moment. In other words, could peak-like feelings (e.g., feelings of awe, elation, happiness, or satisfaction) be synchronous with the arousal of feelings of safety, connection, belonging, love, or esteem? It seems from our research that some participants were getting peak-like feelings when basic needs were being met.

In the sport context, for example, Kevin's peak experiences came via his recollections of the young people he had coached in rugby and their subsequent growth and achievements. His descriptions suggest his peak experiences are linked to the meeting of an esteem need, especially since his peak experiences are prompted by realising the achievements of those he has coached, influenced, and supported. In the same context, Amy recalled a "massive peak" at the Winter Olympics in Vancouver. She explained how she felt it in her chest as she walked in with her teammates, with the Olympic rings and Union Jack flags. She said it was a huge wow moment and one of the top experiences of her life. Again, this could be construed as an esteem need being met.

In the religion, music, creative arts, nature, and extreme sport contexts, the main features of what we distinguish as "transcendent peak experience" were mentioned most often. For example, several of the aspects Maslow highlighted, such as feelings of timelessness or feelings of oneness, were found in the extreme sport context:

> It was a breath-taking shift in reality, a stretching of time and a simultaneous compression and expansion of my being, an awakening.
>
> (Mary-lou)

> I just remember I felt unbelievably happy, fulfilled and satisfied. I'd never felt it that intensely before. but it was an unforgettable feeling of elation and being at one with myself and the mountain.
>
> (Sean)

These feelings can be contrasted with the "peak-like" feelings found in the competitive sport and the workplace contexts, where the emphasis is more on peak performance:

> It's a joyous place I guess, because you're performing at your best and allowing the mind and body to take over really without too much thought.
>
> (Anna)

> I'm using my musical experimentations with improvisation to be more effective at work.
>
> (Philippa)

We noted that Clare, who was interviewed initially for the workplace chapter, stepped away from that context momentarily and drew on her meditation training to share a transcendent, altered state of consciousness experience. In fact, no one in the workplace context reported a *transcendent* peak experience, although some did have *transpersonal* experiences, where their need for connection was met when working closely with others in team settings.

Maslow's insistence that transcendent peak experiences are not motivated by needs suggests to us that the peak experiences some of our participants report do not meet Maslow's criteria for a peak experience but are indeed the other valuable experiences we have discussed: flow, awe, or peak performance. It is clear to us that transcendent peaks, which involve passivity, loss of self, unity or oneness with the universe, and being outside of time and space, were more rarely experienced by participants. More often they spoke about their equally beneficial flow experiences, or of aha moments or peak performances, and sometimes awe.

Benefits of Peak Experiences

According to Maslow, a peak experience can have a permanent effect on our lives, giving meaning to life and changing how we view ourselves and those around us. He explained how "once we have been in it, we can remember it forever, and feed ourselves on this memory, and be sustained in times of stress" (1968, p. 154). He thus considered the peak experience to be beneficial in a number of ways, increasing attributes such as empathy, free will, self-determination, and creativity.

Maslow (1970c) also listed a number of characteristics that describe all varieties of peak experience, whatever the context. He described them as unifying, ego transcending, and infusing people with a sense of purpose and integration. These conceptualisations could easily include descriptions of positive emotions like joy or gratitude that benefit physical and psychological well-being. Thus, significant meaning, depth, and resilience are added to the lives of those who have had a peak experience:

> The peak-experience seems to lift us to greater than normal heights so that we can see and perceive in a higher than usual way. We become larger, greater, stronger, bigger, taller people and tend to perceive accordingly.
>
> (Maslow, 1970c, p. 25)

In every chapter we saw how peak experiences, however individually defined, had the power to impact the lives of participants. We were fascinated to see how peak experiences have a lasting effect, promoting both growth and creativity. In the education context, for example, people said they were transformed by their peak experiences: Sue described the experience as "expansive," and it gave her a sense of joy and generosity. In the writing and reading chapter, Alison shared how peak experiences spark and inspire her creative writing even though the writing itself is completed later.

In the context of nature, there were reports of blissful experiences, and a sense of oneness and connection. For some, the peak experience became an anchor they could return to – something that led to self-discovery and that could not be taken away. Similarly, in the extreme sport context, participants frequently spoke about significant changes in their understanding of themselves. Mary-lou, for example, believes her experiences opened up different possibilities and gave her the confidence to take on new challenges. In the creative arts context, Barty saw his experience of doing the hair of a deceased client as taking him to a different emotional state. He learnt things from it about himself and about his relationships with others.

Several researchers in the music context highlighted how music is associated with well-being. Rana et al. (2009) reminded us that involvement in music is well-known to reduce stress hormones and anxiety. Groarke and Hogan (2020, p. 1) also confirmed the benefits of strong experiences of music, describing them, for example, as life-enhancing and as increasing hope and self-esteem. Similar personal transformation and interpersonal change were evident in Cohen's (2009) research in prison choir contexts. Cohen's participants shared how peaks experienced during choir singing were both inspiring and motivating: they used expressions such as "it changed my life," "it blew my young mind," "it was amazing."

Many benefits of peak experience in music were also identified by our participants. David, for example, shared that a peak experience opened up the possibility for more intense music experiences that not only improved his playing but also raised his awareness of higher levels of performance and passion: he upped his game. He suspected there could also be mental health benefits from peak experiences and suggested they should be nurtured or cultivated to encourage people who have never had them, or who tend to repress them, to discover personal fulfilment and growth (1970a, p. 179).

Emerging Research Topics

In this section, we identify the topics that seemed to be on the periphery of our research but that we feel still need further exploration in relation to everyday lives: nadir experiences, plateau experiences, cultural variations in peak experiences, and the psychobiology of peak experience.

Nadir Experiences

We saw in Chapter 10 how peak experiences may not always be joyous. Sometimes, as our participant Sean found, they can be meaningful and momentous without bringing feelings of happiness. Sometimes they bring the opposite – fear or sadness. Maslow (1970a) was also aware of the link between the suffering and turmoil that nadir experiences bring and the consequent beneficial effects. He even suggested that peak and nadir experiences have a close, symbiotic relationship in that both can promote self-actualisation and "experiences of death, tragedy, and trauma can be important learning experiences bringing permanent change to a person's outlook and character" (Taylor, 2013, p. 2).

Indeed, recent research has shown that post-traumatic growth can result in a more positive self-concept and other long-term positive effects (Taylor, 2013). Taylor's studies demonstrate that almost a quarter of what he terms "temporary awakening experiences" were as a result of intense turmoil and distress. Taylor (2013, p. 1) explains that such "intense psychological turmoil" can result in dramatic transformations and permanent shifts of consciousness and identity. Similarly, in earlier research by Miller and C'de Baca (2001) into what they termed "quantum change," it was found that half of the sudden psychological transformations studied arose as a reaction to intense unhappiness or tragedy. Although not a tragic incident, we saw in Chapter 6 how Paul felt very alone in the darkness of a strange village after a car breakdown. He had a feeling of being quite scared and small, which led to a growing awareness of a cold, dark, and empty universe where we, as human beings, are seemingly insignificant. As a result, he concluded we must "observe the planet and nature and learn to live within the bounds of both."

Cultural Variation

Our research for this book did not specifically target cultural variances, rather we looked at contextual differences. We were, however, aware that cultural aspects might be fruitful to explore in relation to peak experience.

Maslow (1971) supported the idea of the universality of peak experiences, deeming that some aspects were recognisable across time and cultures. To test this premise, Privette et al.'s (1997) quantitative research with 129 Taiwanese and 123 American students looked at the potential cross-cultural generality and cultural sensitivity of peak performance and peak experience. They found that when they described peak experiences as more significant, more fulfilling, and more companionable, generally Americans, more so than Taiwanese, validated Maslow's model of peak experience. However, although there were cultural differences with regard to the American students being more enthusiastic about experiences of highest happiness than the Taiwanese, the study found that peak experiences were generally consistently described by both sets of participants. Privette et al. (1997, p. 1478) explain how the Taiwanese are "educated to control emotional expressiveness and assume humbleness and modesty in facing an event of great happiness." Nonetheless, although they tended to downplay emotional responses, they did support the attributes of receptivity more than the Americans, something Maslow himself thought essential to the experience.

A later study by Ho et al. (2012, pp. 247–260) recruited 115 Hong Kong Chinese and 117 Brazilian students who were asked to recall a childhood peak experience and consider its enduring impact. Both student groups used the words "interpersonal joy" most frequently, but "external achievement" was prevalent for the Hong Kong sample, while "developmental landmark" was important for the Brazilian sample. The analysis suggested the Hong Kong Chinese students were more socially focused than the Brazilians.

Cultural challenges were highlighted by our participant, Jane, who coaches Japanese and Eastern leaders. She pointed out the differences she observes in the control of emotional expressiveness and how, when she approached one particular client directly, she broke into big smile. Jane saw this as a breakthrough in their relationship leading to increased connection between them – something which is vital in coaching.

Neurobiology and Peak Experience

When we experience a profound sense of awe or a peak experience, change is created within our body, impacting our nervous system. This was evident in the responses of our participants in various chapters, and so we identified this as an area of research interest.

At the time Maslow was arguing that peak experiences were more prevalent in music, sex, and childbirth (1968), neurobiology was less developed. However, Kets de Vries (2013) suggests that specific neural activities are associated with transformational experiences in such contexts and that oxytocin has a vital role to play in setting up the conditions to enjoy a peak experience. He points out that neuroscientists have long been intrigued by "tipping points," a phrase used to represent transformational shifts similar to peak experience and "signalling events of great significance that contribute to meaningful life changes" (2013, p. 153). Lumbreras (2020) also explained that our mind, our emotions, and our own biological mechanisms all seem to be linked to feelings of love and connectedness and that the oxytocin released in the first stages of life reinforces "oxytocin cascades," influencing social behaviour and the ability to trust or love: "It is typically involved in the development of prosocial behaviours, such as trust and attachment, and has been labelled the 'love hormone'" (2020, p. 192).

Lumbreras also explained how the vagus nerve is activated during self-transcendent positive emotions (such as awe, compassion, or love) and that people with an increased vagal tone have been shown to have a higher propensity for self-transcendent experiences (2020, p. 192).

Kitson et al. (2020) explained the role of the vagus nerve as a cranial nerve that interfaces with the heart, lungs, and bladder. Its response is associated with a sedative state and increases "when the body is at rest or in a peaceful state, which could be associated with positive emotions such as self-transcendence" (2020, p. 6). Beddoes-Jones (2017) also identified that love engages the vagus nerve, prompting the release of oxytocin and other organic, feel-good chemicals within us. We sense this engagement of the vagus nerve as butterflies in our tummy or a feeling in our solar plexus of complete calm or joy. She further confirms that the emotional highs people experience when they are immersed in nature "all engage the vagus nerve and release oxytocin. This is magnified by feelings of awe and inspiration" (2017, p. 18).

This link between peak experience, awe, and the vagus nerve is still under scientific investigation. In our research, however, we interviewed Gus de la Querra, who specialises in lymphatic work as a Bowen therapist. His work has led him to recognise the importance of the vagus nerve for immune and overall health and well-being. We asked him for his opinion on how peak experience could be linked. He described how there is a connection between the insular cortex and the vagus nerve, which is involved with memory recall and plays a role in diverse functions usually linked to emotions or the regulation of the body. Gus explained that if the vagus nerve is out of kilter (due to an excess of stress) the "vagal tone" level goes down, probably lessening our chances of a peak experience happening:

> When stress levels are high, the vagal tone goes down; serotonin levels also decrease. If serotonin slows down, so does the gut and everything links up to that. I guess serotonin being the happy hormone is part of that peak experience.

Plateau Experiences

We consider what Gordon (2023, p. 1) calls "the under-told story" of Maslow's significant end-of-life conceptualising of plateau experience to be an area of peak experience research that needs additional clarification and understanding. Maslow himself argued that a further model was needed that would include "plateau" and "high plateau" experiences. Of his own transition from "peak" to "plateau" experiences, he commented that

> [t]he result has been a kind of unitive consciousness. . . . I can define this unitive consciousness very simply for me as the simultaneous perception of the sacred and the ordinary, or the miraculous and the ordinary, or the miraculous and the rather constant or easy-without-effort sort of thing.
> (Maslow's conference contribution, cited in Krippner, 1972, p. 113)

Cleary and Shapiro (1995, pp. 5–6) reported how Maslow (1970a), following his near-death experience, came to believe that chasing peak experiences might hinder or impede the manifestation of a more enduring phenomenon. Maslow felt the peak experience provided only a fleeting glimpse of transcendence, rather than a sustained experience, and thought that continuously looking for highly charged and emotionally stimulating peak experiences might result in "neglecting paths that lead to more sustained transcendent experience" (Maslow, 1970b, p. xvi). He saw the plateau experience as less emotionally intense, calmer, and more serene than peak experiences and more available and lasting. This sustained state of heightened awareness is, he suggested, more voluntary and could also be better integrated into the rest of daily life (Gordon, 2023).

In the therapy chapter, we shared how Clare's ability to achieve deep meditative states through continued practice can lead to what she calls her "extreme peak experience" that continued for some hours. Indeed, Kautz and Kautz (1997) conducted an exploratory study to explore what can generate plateau-like experiences. Their respondents described meditation as one trigger among others such as attending Quaker Meetings, engaging in art, or studying Buddhism. They concluded that "the legacy of the plateau experience" may, with further development and understanding, prove to be a significant part of Maslow's uplifting vision of "the farther reaches of human nature" (1997, p. 22).

***

In this book we have attempted to show the importance of peak experiences in our everyday lives. Although, as we have seen, transcendental peak experiences cannot be engineered since they are transitory and ephemeral, other types of peaks can be fostered when the conditions are right. Flow and peak performance, in particular, can be encouraged via preparation and visualisation techniques. All types of peak experiences may also be understood through individually designed "symbolic growth" exercises (Frick, 2001) that help make sense of previous experiences and their associated emotions. So, however we may define them, we conclude that peak experiences are worthy of our attention, as they have the power to impact our spiritual and physical well-being, our work and leisure activities, and our relationships.

References

Armor, T. (1969). A note on the peak experience and a transpersonal psychology. *Journal of Transpersonal Psychology*, *1*(1), 47–50.

Bandura, A. (2012). Cultivate self-efficacy for personal and organizational effectiveness. In E. A. Locke (Ed.), *Handbook of principles of organizational behavior: Indispensable knowledge for evidence-based management* (pp. 179–200). Wiley.

Barfoot, C. C. (1999). Milton silent came down my path: The epiphany of Blake's left foot. In W. Tigges (Ed.), *Moments of moment: Aspects of the literary epiphany*. Atlanta, GA: Rodopi.

Beddoes-Jones, F. (2017). *Love is the answer*. London: Blue Ocean Publishing.

Brymer, E. (2009, March 6–7). *The extreme sports experience: A research report*. IFPRA World. https://eprints.qut.edu.au/26118/

Chappell, S. G. (2019). Introducing epiphanies. *Zeitschrift für Ethik und Moralphilosophie*, *2*(1), 95–121.
Chirico, A., & Gaggioli, A. (2021). The potential role of awe for depression: Reassembling the puzzle. *Frontiers in Psychology*, *12*. https://doi.org/10.3389/fpsyg.2021.617715
Christov-Moore, L., Schoeller, F., Lynch, C., Sacchet, M., & Reggente, N. (2023, October 19). *Self-transcendence accompanies aesthetic chills*. https://doi.org/10.31234/osf.io/tsrve
Cleary, T. S., & Shapiro, S. (1995). The plateau experience and the post-mortem life: Abraham maslow's unfinished theory. *Journal of Transpersonal Psychology*, *27*(1), 1–23.
Cohen, M. L. (2009). Choral singing and prison inmates: Influences of performing in a prison choir. *Journal of Correctional Education*, *60*(1), 52–65.
Cox, E. (2013). *Coaching understood: A pragmatic inquiry into the coaching process*. London: Sage.
Csikszentmihalyi, M. (1988). The flow experience and its significance for human psychology. *Optimal Experience: Psychological Studies of Flow in Consciousness*, *2*, 15–35.
Csikszentmihalyi, M. (1990). *FLOW: The psychology of optimal experience*. New York: Harper and Row.
Dai, Y., & Jiang, T. (2023). Inspired by awe: Awe promotes inspiration via self-transcendence. *The Journal of Positive Psychology*, 1–15.
Dewey, J. (1934). *Art as experience*. New York, NY: Capricorn Books.
Edwards, A. (2010). Toward a generative theory of peak communication experiences. *Paper presented at the 96th Annual Convention of the National Communication Association*, San Francisco, CA.
Fabb, N. (2021). Experiences of ineffable significance. *Beyond Meaning*, *324*, 135.
Fletcher, R. (2007). Free play: Transcendence as liberation. *Beyond resistance: The future of freedom*, 143–162.
Frick, W. B. (1990). The symbolic growth experience: A chronicle of heuristic inquiry and a quest for synthesis. *Journal of Humanistic Psychology*, *30*(1), 64–80.
Frick, W. B. (2001). Symbolic latency: Images of transformation across space and time. *Journal of Humanistic Psychology*, *41*(3), 9–30.
Ford, J. L., Vosloo, J., & Arvinen-Barrow, M. (2020). Pouring everything that you are: Musicians' experiences of optimal performances. *British Journal of Music Education*, *37*(2), 141–153.
Gordon, R. D. (2023). Peak and Plateau Communication Experiences (PCEs): An international call for inquiry. *Kome: An International Journal of Pure Communication Inquiry*, 1–24.
Green, B. (2015). I always remember that moment: Peak music experiences as epiphanies. *Sociology*, *50*(2), 333–348.
Groarke, J. M., & Hogan, M. J. (2020). The eudaimonic functions of music listening scale: An instrument to measure transcendence, flow and peak experience in music. *Frontiers in Psychology*. https://doi.org/10.3389/fpsyg.2-2-.566296
Ho, M. Y., Chen, S. X., & Hoffman, E. (2012). Unpacking cultural variations in peak-experiences: Cross-cultural comparisons of early childhood recollection between Hong Kong and Brazil. *Journal of Happiness Studies*, *13*, 247–260.
James, W. (1902–1928). *The varieties of religious experience: A study in human nature*. Forgotten Books.
Jarvis, A. N. (1996). *Taking a break: Preliminary investigations into the psychology of epiphanies as discontinuous change experiences*. Amherst, MA: University of Massachusetts.
Kautz, W. F., & Kautz, A. (1997). Similar to a plateau experience. *International Journal of Transpersonal Studies*, *16*(1), 5.
Keltner, D. (2023). *Awe: The transformative power of everyday wonder*, Kindle edition. Penguin Books Ltd.
Keltner, D., & Haidt, J. (2003). Approaching awe, a moral, spiritual, and aesthetic emotion. *Cognition and Emotion*, *17*(2), 297–314.

Kets de Vries, M. F. R. (2013). Coaching's "good hour": Creating tipping points. *Coaching: An International Journal of Theory, Research and Practice, 6*(2), 152–175.

Kien, G. (2013). The nature of epiphany. *International Review of Qualitative Research, 6*(4), 578–584.

Kitson, A., Chirico, A., Gaggioli, A., & Riecke, B. E. (2020). A review on research and evaluation methods for investigating self-transcendence. *Frontiers in Psychology, 11*, 547687.

Krippner, S. (1972). The Plateau experience: A. H. Maslow and others. *The Journal of Transpersonal Psychology, 4*(2), 107–120.

Laukkonen, R. E., Ingledew, D. J., Grimmer, H. J., Schooler, J. W., & Tangen, J. M. (2021). Getting a grip on insight: Real-time and embodied Aha experiences predict correct solutions. *Cognition and Emotion, 35*(5), 918–935.

Levine, S. (2021). A sense of awe, and "peak experiences". *Psychology Today*, www.psychologytoday.com/gb/blog/our-emotional-footprint/202105/sense-awe-and-peak-experiences

Liang, Y. S. (2006). *Peak experience, epiphany, and psychological well-being.* The University of Oklahoma.

Liu, Y., Yu, C., & Damberg, S. (2022). Exploring the drivers and consequences of the "awe" emotion in outdoor sports – A study using the latest partial least squares structural equation modeling technique and necessary condition analysis. *International Journal of Sports Marketing and Sponsorship, 23*(2), 278–294.

Lumbreras, S. (2020). The transcendent within: How our own biology leads to spirituality. *Issues in Science and Theology: Nature – and Beyond: Transcendence and Immanence in Science and Theology*, 187–197.

Malouf, D. (1989). *12 edmondstone street.* Victoria: Penguin.

Marotto, M., Roos, J., & Victor, B. (2007). Collective virtuosity in organizations: A study of peak performance in an orchestra. *Journal of Management Studies, 44*, 388–413.

Maslow, A. H. (1943). A theory of human motivation. *Psychological Review, 50*(4), 370–396. https://doi.org/10.1037/h0054346

Maslow, A. H. (1962a). Notes on being-psychology. *Journal of Humanistic Psychology, 2*(2), 47–71.

Maslow, A. H. (1962b). Some basic propositions of a growth and self-actualization psychology. *Perceiving, Behaving, Becoming: A New Focus for Education*, 34–49.

Maslow, A. H. (1968). *Toward a psychology of being*, 2nd edition. New York: Van Nostrand Reinhold.

Maslow, A. H. (1969). Various meanings of transcendence. *Journal of Transpersonal Psychology, 1*, 56–66.

Maslow, A. H. (1970a). *Religions, values, and peak-experiences.* New York: Viking Compass.

Maslow, A. H. (1970b). New introduction: Religions, values, and peak-experiences. *Journal of Transpersonal Psychology, 2*(2), 83–90.

Maslow, A. H. (1970c). *Motivation and personality*, 2nd edition. New York: Harper Row.

Maslow, A. H. (1971). *The farther reaches of human nature.* New York, NY: Penguin.

Maslow, A. H. (1987). *Motivation and personality*, 3rd edition. New York: Harper & Row, Publishers.

Maslow, A. H. (2013). *Toward a psychology of being.* Simon and Shuster.

Miller, W., & C'de Baca, J. (2001). *Quantum change.* New York, NY: Guilford.

Mosing, M. (2024). Flow: People who are easily absorbed in an activity may have better mental and cardiovascular health, *The Conversation.* https://theconversation.com/flow-people-who-are-easily-absorbed-in-an-activity-may-have-better-mental-and-cardiovascular-health-227696

Paquette, J. (2020). *Awestruck: How embracing wonder can make you happier, healthier, and more connected.* CO, USA: Shambhala Publications.

Piff, P. K., Dietze, P., Feinberg, M., Stancato, D. M., & Keltner, D. (2015). Awe, the small self, and prosocial behavior. *Journal of Personality and Social Psychology, 108*(6), 883.

Privette, G. (1983). Peak experience, peak performance, and flow: A comparative analysis of positive human experiences. *Journal of Personality and Social Psychology*, *45*, 1361–1368.

Privette, G., Hwang, K. K., & Bundrick, C. M. (1997). Cross-cultural measurement of experience: Taiwanese and Americans' peak performance, peak experience, misery, failure, sport, and average events. *Perceptual and Motor Skills*, *84*(suppl_3), 1459–1482.

Proust, M. (1913–1927). *Remembrance of things past.* Volume 1: *Swann's Way: Within a Budding Grove.* The definitive French Pleiade edition translation by C. K. S. Moncrieff & T. Kilmartin (pp. 48–51). New York: Vintage.

Rana, S. A., Tanveer, S., & North, S. C. (2009). Peak experiences of music and subjective wellbeing. *Journal of Behavioural Sciences*, *19*(1–2), 41–57.

Schlarb, C. W. (2007, December). The developmental impact of not integrating childhood peak experiences. *International Journal of Children's Spirituality*, *12*(3), 249–262.

Seligman, M. E. P. (2002). *Authentic happiness: Using the new positive psychology to realize your potential for lasting fulfilment.* New York, NY: Free Press.

Skavronskaya, L., Moyle, B., & Scott, N. (2020). The experience of novelty and the novelty of experience. *Frontiers in Psychology*, *11*, 322.

Stranger, M. (1999). The aesthetics of risk: A study of surfing. *International Review for the Sociology of Sport*, *34*(3), 265–276.

Tavel, P., Chrz, V., Šolcová, I. P., Dubovská, E., & Kalman, M. (2022). Peak experience and its varieties: Response to challenge as a valuable perspective of peak experience and its varieties. *Československá psychologie*, *66*(2), 95–110.

Taylor, S. (2013). The peak at the Nadir: Psychological turmoil as the trigger for awakening experiences. *International Journal of Transpersonal Studies*, *32*(2), 1–12. http://dx.doi.org/10.24972/ijts.2013.32.2.1

Taylor, S., & Egeto-Szabo, K. (2017). Exploring awakening experiences: A study of awakening experiences in terms of their triggers, characteristics, duration and after-effects. *Journal of Transpersonal Psychology*, *49*(1), 45–65.

Thornton, F., Privette, G., & Bundrick, C. M. (1999). Peak performance of business leaders: An experience parallel to self-actualization theory. *Journal of Business and Psychology*, *14*(2), 253–284.

Thrash, T. M., Elliot, A. J., Maruskin, L. A., & Cassidy, S. E. (2010). Inspiration and the promotion of well-being: Tests of causality and mediation. *Journal of Personality and Social Psychology*, *98*(3), 488.

Varkey, T. C., Varkey, J. A., Sivakumar, M., & Merhavy, Z. I. (2022). The Mongoose Phenomenon: A new logical heuristic. *Galician medical journal*, *29*(2), E202226.

Walsh, R., & Vaughan, F. (1993). On transpersonal definitions. *Journal of Transpersonal Psychology*, *25*(2), 199–207.

Ward, G. (2011). Super consciousness: The quest for the peak experience (2009). In C. Stanley (Ed.), *Around the outsider: Essays presented to Colin Wilson on the occasion of his 80th birthday* (p. 274). Alresford: John Hunt Publishing.

Weijers, K. (2021). *Peak moments: The experience of coaches.* Doctoral Thesis, Oxford Brookes University.

Williams, P. G., Johnson, K. T., Bride, D. L., Baucom, B. R., & Crowell, S. E. (2023). Individual differences in aesthetic engagement and proneness to aesthetic chill: Associations with awe. *Psychology of Aesthetics, Creativity, and the Arts.* https://psycnet.apa.org/record/2022-24160-001

Wong, P. T. (2023). Pioneer in research in existential positive psychology of suffering and global flourishing. *Applied Research in Quality of Life*, *18*(4), 2153–2157.

Worth, P., & Smith, M. D. (2021). Clearing the pathways to self-transcendence. *Frontiers in Psychology*, *12*, 648381.

Yaden, D. B., Haidt, J., Hood Jr, R. W., Vago, D. R., & Newberg, A. B. (2017). The varieties of self-transcendent experience. *Review of General Psychology*, *21*(2), 143–160.

Glossary and Further Reading

Awe

Keltner and Haidt position awe as a moral, spiritual, and aesthetic emotion in the "upper reaches of pleasure and on the boundary of fear" (2003, p. 297). They identify how vastness and accommodation are its key features. Awe leads to feelings of disorientation and insignificance, which require us to expand our current mental schema to accurately accommodate the new stimuli.

Keltner, D., & Haidt, J. (2003). Approaching awe, a moral, spiritual, and aesthetic emotion. *Cognition and Emotion, 17*, 297–314.

Epiphany

Epiphany, from the Greek *epiphaneia*, has been used in religious contexts and refers to the appearance or manifestation of a deity. In secular contexts, epiphany focuses on moments of recognition or transformation resulting in "the reconfiguration of an individuals' world assumptions" (Jarvis, 1996, p. 61). In both contexts, revelation is a key aspect.

Jarvis, A. N. (1996). *Taking a break: Preliminary investigations into the psychology of epiphanies as discontinuous change experiences.* Amherst: University of Massachusetts.

Flow

Rather than the fleeting feeling of oneness that is descriptive of a peak experience, flow is a sustained and uplifting event involving a sense of mastery and control. It has been explained by Csikszentmihalyi (1990, p. 3) as providing "a deep sense of enjoyment that is long cherished and that becomes a landmark in memory for what life should be like." Immersion in the present leads to detachment from our surroundings and often altered perceptions of time.

Csikszentmihalyi, M. (1990). *Flow: The psychology of optimal experience.* New York: Harper & Row.

Nadir

Stagg (2014) gives examples of nadir experiences as deep emotional traumas such as bereavement, depression, loss, or a crisis of existence. Like peak experiences, nadir experiences are transcendent but in a negative way. They result in a significant shift away from ordinary everyday life and are thus our worst moments, the moments of least hope and least achievement. However, as Maslow also recognised, despite their devastating effect on our quality of life, nadir experiences challenge our core beliefs and offer opportunities for reflection, personal transformation, and psychological growth.

Stagg, R. (2014). The nadir experience: Crisis, transition, and growth. *Journal of Transpersonal Psychology*, *46*(1).

Peak Experience

Maslow defined peak experience as a transitory emotional experience involving moments of extreme happiness and fulfilment. A peak experience provides a sense of personal integration and oneness with the world (Maslow, 1999) and can be described as involving acute intensity of perception, depth of feeling, and significance. Peak experiences often bring strong positive emotions such as joy, peace, and a sense of well-being.

Maslow, A. H. (1999). Peak-experiences as acute identity experiences. In A. H. Maslow (Ed.), *Toward a psychology of being*, 3rd edition. New York, NY: John Wiley and Sons.

Peak Moment

McInman and Grove (1991, p. 334) suggested that the term *peak moments* should be adopted as a "global entity" to unite the terms peak experience, peak performance, and flow, making them each a category of peak moments.

McInman, A. D., & Grove, R. G. (1991). Peak moments in sport: A literature review. *Quest*, *43*, 333–351.

Peak Performance

Privette (1981) defined peak performance as behaviour that exceeds our usual average performance, becoming an event of superior functioning. Defined operationally as behaviour that exceeds one's predictable level of functioning, peak performance represents the superior use of potential in any human endeavour (Privette, 1981).

Privette, G. (1981). Dynamics of peak performance, *Journal of Humanistic Psychology*, *21*, 57–67.

Plateau Experience

According to Maslow, people who are highly self-transcendent may also experience "plateau experiences," whereby they consistently enter and/or maintain a state of serenity and higher perspective. He saw peak experiences as forerunners of this more permanent self-transcendent state, which he also explained occurred more frequently and was longer-lasting than a peak experience.

Maslow, A. H. (1970b). New introduction: Religions, values, and peak-experiences. *Journal of Transpersonal Psychology*, *2*(2), 83–90.

Self-Actualisation

In his early work, Maslow considered self-actualisation to be the pinnacle of human development, encompassing the need for realisation of our full potential and involving a search for autonomy and excellence. In his initial hierarchy of needs, he described several characteristics of self-actualised people, only to realise through later work that he had fused the their characteristics with those of self-transcendent people. In his 1999 work, he clarified how self-actualisation is a step on the path towards transcendence.

Maslow, A. H. (1999). Peak-experiences as acute identity experiences. In A. H. Maslow (Ed.), *Toward a psychology of being*, 3rd edition. New York, NY: John Wiley and Sons.

Self-Transcendence

Self-transcendence involves going beyond the limits of the self, rising above the ego, and having a broader sense of purpose and connection to others. According to Maslow, it is the peak of human experience, where people are "closest to their real selves" (2011, pp. 97–106). They become other-focused and concerned with higher aims rather than self-serving aims. Self-transcendence generates peak experiences in which people transcend their own personal concerns and see the world from a higher perspective.

Maslow, A. H. (2011). *Toward a psychology of being*, CT, USA: Martino Publishing.

Transcendental And Transcendent

Transcendental and transcendent are very similar in meaning. Transcendental is used to signify the conditions and limits of humanly possible experience, while the term transcendent is used to describe something that goes beyond those conditions and limits (Pihlström, 2023). So the term transcendental is used to refer to things that lie beyond the practical experience of ordinary people – things that cannot be discovered or understood by ordinary reasoning – while transcendent is when people, exceptionally, go beyond those limits, for example, when they have a peak experience.

Pihlström, S. (2023). The Transcendental and the Transcendent. In E. Tarasti (Ed.), *Transcending signs: Essays in existential semiotics* (pp. 47–76). Berlin & Boston: De Gruyter Mouton.

Transpersonal

Transpersonal experiences have been defined as those peak experiences in which our sense of identity or our "self" extends beyond (trans) our individual or personal concerns to encompass wider aspects of community or the cosmos. Daniels (2001) explained how the transpersonal is about the expansion and extension of our sense of self. It is about the "transformation of the self beyond its relatively enclosed and impermeable egoic boundary" (2001, p. 9).

Daniels, M. (2001). On transcendence in transpersonal psychology. *Transpersonal Psychology Review*, 5(2), 3–11.

Unitive Consciousness

Maslow (1994, p. 68) described peak experiences as involving "unitive consciousness," which he described as an intense, temporary experience that we necessarily return from to live a normal life. Unitive consciousness has also been explained as a spontaneously occurring state characterised by a sense of unity or oneness that transcends sensory and cognitive understanding (Stace, 1960). Frequently, this is accompanied by an ineffable certainty that the ultimate truth has been perceived and may be accompanied or followed by feelings of joy and bliss.

Maslow, A. (1994). *Religions, values, and peak experiences*. New York, NY: Penguin Books.
Stace, W. T. (1960). *Mysticism and philosophy*. Los Angeles: Jeremy P. Tarcher.

Index

Aaltola, E. 135
absorption 10–11, 70, 95, 111, 156, 159, 161, 250, 255
Adam, M. T. 23
Adams, D. 10, 117
adult learning literature 118–119
aesthetic chills 299
aesthetic experiences: alternative approach to 99; in audience perception 97–100; through creative arts 91, 94–96; defined 97; in nature 136
aesthetic qualities 137, 139
affection 267, 274
agape 266, 274–275, 279
Agnew, C. 184–185
aha-moments 49, 58, 101, 104–105, 116, 129, 205–206, 292–293
air-inspired activities 223–224
Allen, J. 219, 248, 264
Almond, P. C. 29
altered state of consciousness 52, 84, 111, 160, 184, 186, 284, 305
altruistic love 274
Amir, D. 183–184, 188, 197, 198
Anandamaya 195
anchored moment 264
'The Ancient Sage' (Tennyson) 45
animals 141–142
anxiety-reducing effects of music listening 74
April, K. A. 273
"Ardessa" (Cather) 58
Aristotle 178
Armor, T. 180, 289–290
Armstrong, T. 115, 124
Arnd-Caddigan, M. 194
Arnould, E. J. 228–229
Aron, A. 272
Aron, E. N. 272
arousal, feeling of 139

art as revelation 49
Ashley, P. 139
audience perception, peak and aesthetic experiences in 97–100
awakening experiences 296, 307
awe 2, 3, 17, 31, 68, 114, 142, 164, 174, 299; defining 138; and emotions 138; in everyday lives 294–295; feelings of 57, 61; with music 61; and mystery 22; Paquette's description of 75, 269; and peak experiences 61, 62, 309; in relation to wilderness 138; as self-transcendent emotion 295; sense of 39, 40, 59, 60–61, 130, 165, 229, 308; and transcendence 60
awestruck 142–143, 165

Bailey, C. 245
Bakker, A. B. 68, 111, 129, 250, 255
Bandura, A. 291–292
Barfoot, C. C. 46, 48, 53, 301
Barrett, E. 95
Barton, B. 93
BASE jumping 233
basic/deficiency needs 5, 290, 304–305
Bates, G. 179, 242
B-cognition/B-values 6, 39
B-(being) creativity 92
Beauchamp, G. 10, 117
Beddoes-Jones, F. 267, 271, 275, 280, 281, 286, 309
"being away" theme 137, 139
being needs 5, 26
Beja, M. 49, 50, 54
belongingness 16, 147, 266
Bennetts, C. M. 97
Benning, T. B. 39
Benzecry, C. 73
Bethelmy, L. C. 138

Bhat, D. 185–186
Bien, T. 179
Birch, R. 28
Blake, W. 52
"the blazing moment" 43, 49
bliss 49, 57, 70, 93, 195, 291
bodhisattvas 20, 28, 39
Boudreau, P. 223, 224
Bowen therapy 193
Boy's Brigade 31
Bray, P. 185
Breemen, A. 97–98
Breslauer, S. 27
brotherly love 274
Brunner, S. 162
Brymer, E. 222, 291
Buckley, R. 223
Buddhahood, state of 35, 39
Buddhism 28, 35, 36, 37
Bundrick, C. M. 12, 100, 158
Burke, M. 45, 52

Carr, A. 225, 239
Castelo, N. 136, 140
Cather, W. 58
C'de Baca, J. 116, 131–132, 307
change within 182
chanting, in spiritual practices 27–28, 36
Chappell, S. G. 46–47, 48–49, 51, 292
Characteristics of Self-Actualization Scale (CSAS) 9
charity 267
Chenoweth, R. E. 136
childbirth: peak experience and 279, 285; as transformative and self-actualising experience 269
childhood and adolescent literature 115–118, 301
chills 299
Chirico, A. 68, 295
choral music experiences 70
Christov-Moore, L. 299
Clare, J. 55
Cleary, T. S. 310
coaching literature: aha moments 205–206; critical moments 204–205; flow 206–207; intuition 203; shifts in the room 204
co-creation of peak music experiences 87
cognition: of Being 6, 39; bodily experience and 53
cognitive development 98
Cohen, M. L. 70, 306
Collins, D. 203

Collins, M. 69
Collins, R. 73
communication competence 297
communion 24, 34, 95, 101, 212, 230, 231
competitive sport 15, 156–176
connectedness 8, 137, 148, 152, 153, 175, 297–298
connectivity 87
consciousness 4, 54, 159, 289; cosmic 22, 147, 153, 217–218, 289, 298; *see also* altered state of consciousness
consolation and desolation 32
constructivism 26–29
consummation 94–95, 98
contact sports 222
contextualism 29–31
control 175
Cook-Greuter, S. 119
core conditions for peak experiences 302–304
Cornell, J. 139–140
Corraliza, J. A. 138
cosmic consciousness 22, 147, 153, 217–218, 289, 298
counselling/psychotherapy 184–185
Coutts, R. A. 159
Cox, E. 29, 300
Cox, S. 66
creative arts: aesthetic experience through 94–96; participants in context of 100–110; peak experiences in/through 14–15, 91–111; self-transcendence through 93–94
critical moments 204–205
Croucher, B. 161
Crowther, S. 269
Csikszentmihalyi, M. 10, 11, 12, 68, 108, 110, 118, 159, 189, 206, 224, 240
cultural and well-being aspects 73–74
cultural influence 117
cultural variations 307–308
Cumes, D. 138, 146

"Daffodils" (Wordsworth) 48
Dai, Y. 295
Damasio, A. R. 53
d'Aquili, E. G. 39
Davis, J. 3, 13
D-(deficiency) creativity 92
Deakin, R. 56
Deci, E. L. 245
Dedalus, S. 49
deficiency needs 5, 26, 290
de Haan, E. 203–205

Deikman, A. J. 185
De Manzano, Ö. 68
DeMares, R. 141, 152
Dennis, L. J. 4
de Rougement, D. 270
desolation 32
despair 242
Dewey, J. 4, 91, 94–95, 97, 99, 109, 110–111, 300
Diamond, S. 93
Dibben, N. 72
Diebels, K. J. 149
discontinuous psychological change experience (DPCE) 292
disillusionment 242
Dodson, J. 175
Dodson, K. J. 225–226
Dörfler, V. 270, 274
Douglas, K. 74, 78
Dunham, F. 97
Dunning, E. 230
Dutoit, T. 53

earth-bound pursuits 223
ecstasy 12, 24, 26, 49–50, 151, 161, 281, 290, 296
ecstatic transcendent experiences 231
edgework 223
educational settings 15, 114–132
Edwards, A. 297
Egeto-Szabo, K. 296
ego 119
Einstein, A. 22
electronic dance music 72
Elfers, J. 272
Elias, N. 230
Emerson, R. W. 140
emotion and spontaneity 95
employees' peak experience, at work 245, 250–251
"Empty Chair" dialogue 180
engaged listening experiences 72
enlightenment 98
entrepreneurs, cognitive and emotional experiences of 248
epiphany(ies) 44, 46, 116, 119, 292–293; defined 292; environmental 136; ethos of 119; interpretations of 46; Jarvis's description of 292; Jauregui's description of 179; in modern novel 49; as necessary concomitant of realism 50; peak music experiences as 67, 292; as subject-object interaction 50; in therapy literature 179; wild 136; *see also* literary epiphany

eros 266, 267, 270–272, 286
"the essence of things" 43
essentialism/perennialism 23–26
eudaimonia 178, 179, 245
Eudaimonic FML scale 68
euphoria 12, 109, 131, 167, 168, 183, 190, 241
"eureka" moments 205
Evans, J. 116, 130, 150
Evans, P. G. 120–121, 124, 131–132
executive and life coaching 16, 201–219
expeditionary adventures 224
experience: meanings of 1–2, 4, 198; as pre-reflective phenomenon 300
"the extended self" 226
extreme sport 16, 222–243

Fabb, N. 53, 55, 66, 291
familial/parental love 266, 267–268, 269–270
Farias, M. 187
Fatemi, J. 64, 166
felt peak experiences, in sports settings 160–162
Ferris, R. 273
five-stage process model 99
Flaherty, J. 207
Fletcher, J. 179
Fletcher, R. 228, 296
flow 159, 161–162; -based leadership 245; as "being in the zone" 159–160, 171–172; characteristics of 156; during coaching 206–207; Csikszentmihalyi's notion of 161, 240; distinguishing 10–11, 158; in everyday lives 293–294; and peak experience 68–69, 109, 111, 118, 159, 219; Schuler and Brunner's notion of 162; in sport literature 157–160; -type peak experience 260; in workplace 250
Ford, J. L. 68
forest environments, transcendence in 140
Foucault, M. 228
Frankl, V. E. 263
Fredrickson, B. L. 280
Frick, W. B. 48, 50, 175, 301–302
friendship 267, 274
Fromm, E. 266, 267–268, 270, 272–274, 285
fulfilment 2, 7, 8, 9, 21, 67, 161, 205, 247, 250, 297
Fuminori Akiba, F. 98–99
Funch, B. S. 99
Fu, X. 245, 250, 264

Gabrielsson, A. 67, 72
Gaggioli, A. 295
Gakkai, S. 35
Gallwey, T. 79, 158, 175
Garcia-Campayo, J. 187
Garfield, C. A. 246
Gary, K. 119
Gee, C. M. 136, 138
gender dynamic 258
Gestalt therapy 180–182
Giddens, A. 67
Ginsberg, A. 52
Glick-Smith, J. L. 245
Gobster, P. H. 136
God 31–34, 274, 297
Goode, M. R. 140
Gordon, R. D. 297, 309
Green, B. 66, 67, 70–71, 292
Green, J. A. 180
green transcendent experience 180
Groarke, J. M. 68, 72, 306
Grof, S. 9
group-level peak performance 70, 75
Grove, R. G. 156, 159, 160–161, 202, 216
growth through peak experiences 301–302
Gstaettner, A. M. 242

Haberlin, S. 117
Hadash, Y. 187
Haidt, J. 294, 299
Hanfling, O. 1, 96, 198
happiness 2, 9, 12, 35, 67, 158, 168, 205, 250, 297, 307–308
Hardesty, C. L. 93
Hari Narayanan, V. 21
Harney, C. 74
Hart, L. A. 141
Harvey, D. 140
Hawkins, P. 204
Haynes, C. J. 31
hedonia 245
hedonism 179
Heery, B. 161
heightened awareness 98, 137, 310
Henderson, E. 204
Herrmann, T. 274
hierarchy of needs 5, 92, 114, 118, 129
high-risk leisure activities 16, 222–243
Hodge, J. 254
Hoffman, E. 117
Hogan, M. J. 68, 72, 306
Ho, M. Y. 9, 117, 308
Honsova, P. 206
Hood, R. W. 23

Horne, J. R. 27
human-environment transaction 140
humanistic psychology 1, 5, 16, 178, 266
humility 138, 140, 145, 146, 153, 298
Hunt, J. 74
hypnotherapy 186

Ignatian spirituality 31–33
Imbir, K. 98
incongruity/insignificance 54
individual meditation 27
ineffable joy 302
Inner Child model 38
Inner Game 79
The Inner Game of Tennis (Gallwey) 158
insight experiences 292–293
inspiration, as artistic process 95
inspiring energy/awe 138
insular nuclear family 116
integrated hierarchy 5
intense musical experiences, effects of 67–68, 71, 76
intense personal experiences 186
interpersonal joy 308
intrinsic work motivation 111, 255
intuition 189, 194, 198, 203, 252, 261
involuntary memory 48

Jacob, M. J. 95
Jacobs, J. 56
James, P. 185
James, W. 4, 14, 22–25, 43, 289
Jarasova, E. 206
Jarvis, A. N. 292
Jensen, A. M. 193
Jiang, T. 295
Johnson, S. H. 45, 63
Jones, R. H. 23, 27, 28
Jones, R. M. 30
joy 12, 21, 70, 86–88, 110, 116, 161, 168, 194, 225, 248, 291, 308
Joyce, J. 43, 49, 50

Kampman, H. 224
Kapała, M. 1
Kaplan, S. 138
Kapusta, J. 5
Kasapa, S. S. 36
Kastubi, K. 186
Katy B 66
Katz, S. 29
Kaufman, S. B. 9
Kautz, A. 310
Kautz, W. F. 310

kayaking/rafting 228–231
Keller, S. 250, 263
Keltner, D. 294, 299
Kets de Vries, M. F. R. 205, 292, 308
Kien, G. 63, 292
Kilrea, K. A. 159
kinesiology 193
King, Martin Luther, Jr. 266
Kinoshita, D. 35
Kirchner, J. K. 68
Kitson, A. 309
Klein, J. 121, 249
Koenig, H. G. 21
Kohls, M. A. 222
Koltko-Rivera, M. E. 20, 246, 263
Kontula, O. 281
Kruger, M. C. 22
Krycka, K. 141, 152
Kunwar, R. R. 222

Lamont, A. 67, 72–73
Landy, R. L. 100
Langbaum, R. 46, 48, 50, 52, 54, 60
LaRue, L. 206
Lashua, B. U. 271
Laski, M. 46, 135
Latham, K. 4, 97
Laubach, M. 284–285
Laukkonen, R. E. 292
Lavaysse, L. 67, 70
Laws, D. 204
learning 114–132
learning experiences 175
learning state 37
Leary, M. R. 149
Leontiev, D. 1
Lester, J. 222, 242
letting go/openness 182–183
Levine, S. 303
Levin, J. 180
Lewis, C. S. 267, 270, 274
Liang, Y. S. 179, 292
light bulb moments 83, 129, 193, 292
liminality 45
limit-experience 228
Lincoln, A. 22
Lindström, S. 67, 72
Lipscombe, N. 227
listening, music 71–73, 97
literary epiphany 43, 44–50, 53, 62;
    as experiences of recollection
    46–49; as experiences of revelation
    49–50; as experiences of secular
    significance 44–46

Liu, Y. 295
Lockwood, L. 3, 13
Longhurst, L. A. 205–206, 217–218
"the look of the Other" 98
love: belongingness and 266; brotherly/
    friendship/neighbourly 274; divine/
    universal/altruistic 274–275, 279;
    familial/parental 266, 267–268,
    269–270; kinds of 266; maternal
    268–269; oxytocin and 267, 268,
    308–309; participants peak experiences
    in relation to 275–285; physical 266,
    270–272; playful and non-committal
    280; romantic 266, 267, 270–272, 275,
    286; self-love 266, 272–273, 280, 286;
    spiritual 282, 285, 286; types of 267
Love 2.0 (Fredrickson) 266–267, 280
Loveday, K. 109
love hormone 268, 309
Lowis, M. J. 71–72
Lowney, C. 24, 28–30
Luber, M. 115–116, 130
Ludus 280
Lumbreras, S. 267, 268, 308–309
lust and sex 278

MacKnee, C. M. 22–23
Madden, A. 245
Maharaj, N. 273
Maher, A. 181
Ma, J. 245, 250, 264
Malouf, D. 301
Mansfield, K. 49, 51
manual muscle testing 193
Marotto, M. 10, 70, 75, 78, 88, 96–97, 291
Marshall, I. 140–141
Maslow, A. 39–40, 110, 123, 127, 180, 184,
    203, 206, 216, 255, 275, 278–280, 286,
    290–291, 303–307; childbirth and peak
    experience, connection between 115,
    268, 279; concept of peak experiences
    1–2, 7–9, 21, 23, 25, 27, 30, 35, 36,
    43–44, 63, 96, 119, 140, 158, 168, 229,
    236, 266, 268, 296; concept of plateau
    experiences 309–310; constructivist
    description of peak experiences and
    Buddhist thought 28; creativity 91;
    cultural influence on peak experiences
    117; on education 118, 120; on epiphany
    46; hierarchy of needs 5, 92, 114, 118,
    129; influence on coaching 201; love and
    peak experience 266–267, 285; mountain
    climbing symbolism and his hierarchy
    140–141; on music 66, 87, 183–184;

nadir experiences 236; on nature and wilderness 136; paternal love and peak experiences 269–270; perfect peak syndrome 186; perspective on maternal love 268; position of universality of peak experiences 97, 307; on religion 26; religious aspects of peak experience 15, 22; risk-related activity and peak experience, linking 222; on romantic and physical love 271; on self-transcendence 7, 92; theory of motivation 5; theory of self-actualisation 5–7, 91, 119, 120, 125, 246, 247, 272, 273, 302, 304; therapeutic benefits of peak experiences 178; on transcendence 296; view of cosmic consciousness 147, 153, 218, 298
mastery 255, 291–292
maternal love and peak experiences 268–269
mature transcendent experience 180
Mavor, P. 203
May, K. 27, 39
Mayor, F. M. 57
Mayseless, O. 139
McBride, B. W. 206
McDonald, M. G. 137–138, 153
McInman, A. D. 156, 159, 160–161, 202, 216
Meaney, M. 250, 263
meaningful experience 137, 182
meditation 27, 196; therapy 187
memory 300–301
#MeToo movement 102
Miller, W. R. 116, 131–132, 307
mind-centred depth therapy 194
mindfulness meditation 187
"moments of being" 43
Montijo, M. N. 286
Moons, J. 203, 204
Moore, M. 206
Morgan, J. D. 159
Morris, M. 248, 264
Morrison, M. A. 92, 93–94, 106, 249, 263
Mosher, D. L. 271
motivational self-transcendence 249
Motivation and Personality (Maslow) 2
motivation, theory of 5
motor-sensory, with music 69
mountain biking 224–226
mountain climbing symbolism, and Maslow's hierarchy 140–141
mountaineering 224–226
Mouton, A. R. 286
Moyers, M. M. 269

Muir, J. 135, 141, 224
Murphy, M. 157–158
Murray, E. 203
music: awe with 61; benefits of peak experience in 306; cultural and well-being aspects of peak experiences and 73–74; emotions and strong experiences with 67, 72; flow and 68; peak experiences and 14, 66–88; therapy 182–184, 187–188; as tool for anxiety management 74, 306; well-being and 306; yoga and 86
Musical Involvement and Reaction Questionnaire (MIRQ) 72
music listening 28, 71–73
music-making/performing 69–71
mystery 22, 40, 114
mystical experiences/mysticism 23, 24, 27, 29, 30, 39, 116, 135, 161

nadir experiences 179, 236, 242, 307
Naor, L. 139
Nash, C. 203
nature 15, 135–153
needs, hierarchy of 5, 92, 114, 118, 129
negative experiences 236, 242
Neto, M. 118
neurobiology 308–309
Newberg, A. B. 39
Nichols, A. 44–45, 47, 50, 51, 63
Nicholson, B. 182–183
Ninio, R. 121, 249
noetic quality 24, 27
Noltemeyer, A. 9
non-transcendent peak experiences 132
Norton, A. 186
novelty 300–301
Nukarinen, T. 135

Oades, L. G 222
Oasis band 66
O'Brien, K. T. 159
oceanic cognition 52
Offringa, R. 272
olfactory bulb 48
oneness 16, 114, 159, 278; believing in 149; and connectedness 8, 137, 148, 202, 295, 306; feelings of 153, 230, 242, 279, 299, 305; of/with the universe 28, 44, 54, 59; sensation of 295
openness 182–183, 211
optimal functioning 157, 201
optimal psychological states 223, 224

outdoor recreation, and self-actualisation 224–225
outdoor spaces 141
out-of-body experiences 161, 164, 171
overcoming limitations 137
oxytocin 267, 268, 308–309

Pahnke, W. 22
Pain, M. D. 159–160
Pale Blue Dot 146
Palmer, S. 178
Panzarella, R. 69, 97
Paquette, J. 68, 75, 142, 164, 165, 174, 269, 294
parental/familial love 266, 267–268, 269–270
Parker, A. 23, 230, 231
participants' peak experiences: in context of coaching literature 207–218; in context of competitive sport 162–174; in context of different therapy 187–197; in context of education and learning 122–131; in context of high-risk leisure activities 231–241; in context of love 275–285; in context of music 74–86; in context of nature and wilderness 142–152; in context of religious practice and spiritual experience 31–38; in context of variety of creative arts 100–110; in context of workplace 251–263; in context of writing and reading literature 54–62
passionate love 274
Patel, K. 282
Pathak, V. 67–68
Paxman, J. 66
peak moment 62, 122, 156–157, 159, 160, 181, 202, 213–217, 302
peak performance: achieving through preparation processes 109; characteristics of 156; distinguishing 11–12, 158; in everyday lives 291–292; as exceptional accomplishment 291; group-level 70, 75; and self-actualisation 158; in sport literature 157–160; in workplace 247
peak performers in business, characteristics of 246
Pelowski, M. 98–99
perennialism and essentialism 23–26
perfect peak syndrome 186
Perry, G. 27–28, 36
philautia 266, 272–273, 280, 286
philia 266, 267, 274
physical love 266, 270–272

physiological needs 5, 290
physiological reactions 299
piriform cortex 48
plateau experiences 7, 309–310
playful and non-committal love 280
playfulness 240
polar exploration 224–226
polysemy 67
Pope, S. 272–273
A Portrait of the Artist as a Young Man (Joyce) 49
Posadzki, P. 185
positive birth experiences 268
Post, S. G. 274, 275
Powers, J. F. 4
pre-peak experience 115, 130
Privette, G. 10, 11–12, 46, 74, 97, 100, 153, 156, 157, 158, 206, 225, 247, 291, 308
Protasi, S. 270, 274
Proust, M. 43, 46–48, 62–63, 300
psychedelic drugs 143
psychological well-being 139, 179
psychotherapy/counselling 184–185

quantum change 116, 307

Raab, D. 92
Raettig, T. 118
rafting/kayaking 228–231
Rahtz, E. 30
Rames, A. E. 142
Ramyar, R. 141
Rana, S. A. 73–74, 306
Rancière, J. 97–98
rapture 37, 70, 88, 194, 291
Ratten, V. 254
Ravizza, K. 157
reader epiphanies, as individual and personal 52–54
realisation 37
The Rector's Daughter (Mayor) 57
reflexive project of the self 67
Reid, P. 224
relational flow 206
relationships 16–17, 266–286
religion: peak experience in spirituality and 20–40; promoting prosocial behaviour 28; purpose of 21; and spirituality 21
Religions, Values, and Peak Experiences (Maslow) 15
religious contextualism 29
Revelation as Art 49
rhetorical epiphanies 50; as literary device 51–52

Richman, R. 52
Risden, E. L. 45
risk: managing 238; in recreational outdoor activities 242; as significant factor in peak experiences 225, 227; in transcendent feelings 228, 230
risk-taking in earth-bound activities 16, 222–243
Robinson, E. 115
rock climbing 224–226
Rogers, C. 178
Rokach, A. 282
Romanelli, A. 254
romantic and physical love 270–272, 286
Rosenblatt, H. S. 25–26
Rosenblatt, L. M. 51–52
Roth, A. L. 186
rush 223, 225, 239, 275
Ryan, R. M. 245

Sagan, C. 146
sailing 228–231
Sartre, J. P. 98
Satori 28
Schafer, T. 67, 71
Schindehutte, M. 175, 248, 264
Schlarb, C. W. 116, 117, 132, 301
Schön, D. 210
school principals' key experiences 121
Schouten, J. W. 11
Schuler, J. 162
Scott, D. G. 116, 130, 150
self-actualisation 5, 131, 182, 304; and adult cognitive development 119; and being-cognition 39; and coaching 201; in cognitive development literature 131; and creativity 91; as developmental process 247; diffuse nature of 9; and eudaimonia 178; and nature 141; needs 119; in outdoor recreation 224–225; and peak experience 70; and peak performance 158, 272, 296; and self-transcendence 20, 39–40, 92, 263; theory of 5–7, 22, 302; view of 118
self-determination theory 250
self-efficacy 109, 250
self-esteem 138
self-love (*philautia*) 266, 272–273, 280, 286
self-realisation 138, 182
self-transcendence 6, 7, 20, 39–40, 92, 119, 162, 249; anecdotal illustration of 93; and chills 299; through creative arts 93–94; experiences of 230–231, 295; finding meaningfulness in workplace 263; and meaningful work 245; motivational 249; and peak experience 92, 185, 263, 295–297; and self-actualisation 263; in team building and cohesion 263; workplace 16
Seligman, M. E. 2, 69
Senecal, G. 10, 161–162, 222
sensory shock 96
serotonin 309
sex 16–17, 270–272
sexual ecstasy 271
sexual love 270
Shakyamuni Buddha 35
Shapiro, S. 310
Sheldon, C. 203
"shift in the room" 204
Simon, R. A. 180
Simons, H. 70
Sinclair, B. R. 28
Skavronskaya, L. 301
skydiving 226–228
Smith, N. 204, 226
Solberg, R. T. 72
Šolcová, I. P. 226
soulmate experience 284, 286
space exploration 226–228
space, in spiritual and euphoric states 141
Spencer, R. C. 186, 242
spirituality 20–40
spiritual love 282, 285, 286
spiritual transcendence 141
spontaneity 95, 120, 207
sport 15, 156–176; competitive sport 15, 156–176; extreme sport and high-risk leisure 16, 222–243
"spots of time" 43, 54, 301
state management, for therapist and client 197–198
Steele, L. 180
Stern, A. 202
Stoeber, M. 30
Stokke, C. 282, 284, 285, 286
Stoll, O. 159
storge (familial/parental love) 266, 267–268
Storie, M. 136, 153
Stranger, M. 224, 230–231, 242, 295
Straś-Romanowska, M. 1
stress reduction in elderly, hypnotherapy effect on 186
strong positive feelings/significant physiological reactions 183
structural ineffability 66, 291

students' peak experiences 117
subjective isolation 28
subjective well-being: hedonism 179; and music 74; and sport 159
Suedfeld, P. 226
Surfing Life (Stranger) 230
surfing 228–231
Sutherland, I. 70, 87
symbolic growth experiences 175, 302
symbolic latency 48, 301
Szubielska, M. 98

tacit knowledge, in coaching 203
Talbot, J. F. 138
Tanyi, R. A. 21
Tavel, P. 229
Taylor, S. 23–24, 178, 225, 236, 239, 296, 307
teachers 120–121
teaching literature 120–122
team peak experiences 164
team togetherness 263
teamwork, key dimensions of 250
temporary awakening experiences 307
Tennyson, A. 45
therapy 15–16, 178–198; Gestalt therapy 180–182; hypnotherapy 186; meditation 187; music therapy 182–184; psychotherapy and counselling 184–185; yoga therapy 185–186
theta state 186
thin places, and Celtic tradition 145–146
Thompson, G. 268
Thornton, F. 158, 247–248, 264, 291
Thrash, T. M. 303
thrill 223, 225, 230
Tigges, W. 46, 50, 51
timelessness, feelings of 8, 139, 140, 145, 146, 153, 160, 218, 293, 298, 305
time, perception of 158, 163
tipping points 205, 292, 308
Toward A Psychology of Being (Maslow) 8
TPnadir 179
TPpeak 179
transactional reader response theory 51
transcendence 180, 201, 226, 268, 295–296, 303; and connection 278; as emotional sensation 60; feelings of 141; Koltko-Rivera's view on 263; as liberation 228; Maslow on 6, 142, 206; of self 224; signals of 231; spiritual 141; and sublime experience 138; and transformation 229; *see also* self-transcendence

transcendental unity 8
transcendent experiences 30, 131–132, 187, 222, 302, 304–305; in forest environments 140; types of 180
transcendent moments 43, 140
transformational coaching 204
transformational processing, of peak and nadir experiences 179
transformative experiences: within learning contexts 119; in nature 139
transpersonal experiences 2, 9, 161, 271, 286, 295, 305
trust 87, 105, 188, 197, 211

unconsciousness 5
Under My Skin single 66
"unitive consciousness" experience 280
unitive experiences, positive effects of 159
universal love 274–575, 279
University Challenge (Caldwell) 66

vagus nerve 309
value education 118
Van Deurzen-Smith, S. 95–96, 98, 100–101
Van Woerkom, M. 250
The Varieties of Religious Experience (James) 4
vastness, perception of 294
Venter, H. J. 117, 249, 263
verbal archetypes 51
vicarious peak experiences 298
Vijnanamaya Kosha 195–196
Vining, J. 136, 153
Vipassana meditation 233
visualisation 176, 240
Vogler, J. W. 224

Wade, J. 119
Waldron, J. L. 192
Walking Meditations on Literature, Nature and Need (Marshall) 140
Wang, Y. 94
Ward, G. 43–44, 290
Warmoth, A. 27
water-driven quests 224
Waterhouse, P. 121–122
Watson, N. 23, 230, 231
Watts, A. 28
Weger, U. 118
Weijers, K. 46, 202, 203, 302
Weijers, K. A. M. 87, 257
well-being 3–4, 73–74, 120, 153, 178, 179, 245, 306
Whaley, J. 69

Whitehead, R. 179, 242
White, K. 140
White, R. A. 157–158
white-water river rafting, transformative aspects of 228
Whitmore, J. 201
Whybrow, A. 178
Wilber, K. 50, 119
wild-animal triggered peak experiences 141–142
wild epiphanies 136
wilderness: defined 137; peak experience in 137–139
Wilkinson, J. 160
Williams, K. 140
Williams, P. G. 299
Wilson, C. 12, 162, 204
Wilson, S. R. 186, 242
wonder 8, 40, 91, 114, 138, 157, 194, 295
Woods, R. 23

Woodward, A. J. 272
Woolf, V. 43
work enjoyment 111, 255
workplace 16, 245–264
wow-moments 49, 129, 292, 293
Wright, C. 3, 13
writing and reading: peak experiences in 43–64; *see also* literary epiphany

xenia 266

Yacek, D. W. 119
Yaden, D. B. 295, 297
Yalom, I. D. 1
Yeagle, E. H. 97
Yee, Alex 161
yoga: music and 86; therapy 185–186
Young, J. A. 159–160

"the zone" 158, 159–160, 171–172